Psychological Services
for
Law Enforcement

Psychological Services
for
Law Enforcement

THEODORE H. BLAU

A Wiley-Interscience Publication

JOHN WILEY & SONS, INC.

New York • Chichester • Brisbane • Toronto • Singapore

Library of Congress Cataloging in Publication Data

Blau, Theodore H.
    Psychological services for law enforcement /
Theodore H. Blau.
       p.   cm.
    Includes index.
    ISBN 0-471-55950-4 (cloth : acid-free paper)
    1. Police psychology.   2. Police—Mental health services—United
States.   I. Title.
HV7936.P75B53   1994
363.2'01'9—dc20   93-28411

Printed in the United States of America

10 9 8 7 6 5 4 3 2

When felon's not engaged in his employment—
Or maturing his felonious little plans—
His capacity for innocent enjoyment—
Is just as great as any honest man's—
Our feelings we with difficulty smother—
When constabulary duty's to be done—
Ah, take one consideration with another—
A policeman's lot is not a happy one.

> When constabulary duty's to be done,
> The policeman's lot is not a happy one.

Gilbert and Sullivan
The Pirates of Penzance
(First produced at the Opera Comique, April 3, 1880)

Acknowledgments

Writing is a solitary venture. Acknowledgments suggest a contribution. This may be gracious but is usually mythical. Not so in the present case. True and grateful appreciation is due Sheriff Charles Wells for appointing me to the Manatee County, Florida Police Academy, for allowing me to work in almost every department of the Manatee County, Florida, Sheriff's Office, and for supporting the establishment of a full-service Behavioral Science Unit (BSU). He provided most of the creative ideas leading to the research published by the BSU. Most of all, he put up with me and gave me unstinting support and wise counsel for almost 8 years while I learned enough to write this book. Charlie Wells is a peace officer and a man of whom his family, friends, and community can be justly proud.

The cops, psychologists, cop-psychologists, and psychologist-cops who helped me immeasurably in my work include the following:

Len Brady	Mike Mayer	Mike Rey
Mel Gravitz	Dwayne Mobely	Nancy Rogers
E. A. Hambacher	George Mount	Tony Stone
Stan Jacobson	Ken Pearson	Gary Wells
Keith Keogh	Randy Price	Walter Wingfield
Chuck Major	Jim Reese	

Special thanks to John Super, Ph.D., for his help and what I learned from him during his post doctoral Internship and subsequent Fellowship.

With apologies to the men and women I may have unwittingly omitted. This work would not have been completed without the loyal and expert efforts of Ms. Peggy Barnes and Ms. Darlene Hansen. Many thanks.

T. H. B.

Contents

APPENDIXES

Introduction

This is a book about cops and psychologists. In some cases, psychologists are also cops, and in others, cops are also psychologists. In most cases, they are one or the other.

Everyone in today's society needs the services of an effective and efficient law enforcement establishment. There has been a plethora of criticism of what cops have done and what they should do, and a host of problems have been attributed to cops. No one has ever seriously proposed that we shouldn't have cops. The same cannot be said for psychologists, although this is unlikely to happen since psychologists have proven themselves useful in a variety of situations.

Psychologists demonstrated their helpfulness in solving a wide range of human problems and challenges in World War I, when they developed tests to help create a massive and efficient army. In World War II, psychologists again provided invaluable guidance in issues of selection, training, human factors, mental health treatment, psychological warfare, and rehabilitation. Psychologists were also involved in establishing the United States' earliest major espionage organization—the Office of Strategic Services.

At the end of World War II, the American Psychological Association (APA) comprised about 2,500 members. By 1992, over 75,000 psychologists belonged to this organization, and there were an additional 25,000 psychologists in North America unaffiliated with the APA. During the past half century, an occupational need was being filled as the science and profession of psychology achieved credibility and general approval.

Among the major bureaucracies, law enforcement was one of the last to utilize psychologists. Although sociologists had been developing a field of "criminology" for almost a century, law enforcement agencies, as recently as the 1950s, rarely called on psychologists. Prison systems began using psychologists in their classification centers in the 1930s. Law enforcement leaders, however, showed little interest until recently. The police psychology movement, if it can be so labeled, is only beginning.

Forward-thinking police managers have begun to be concerned about the efficiency and effectiveness of policing in the 21st century. This has given rise to the Commission on Accreditation for Law Enforcement Agencies, which in 1989 established the first *Standards for Law Enforcement Agencies*. Included in these first national standards are descriptions of and requirements for psychological services (see Chapter Three for details). Over 300 agencies in the United States are already accredited, indicating that requests for psychological services will continue to accelerate.

The resistance of cops at all levels to serious consideration of psychology as an ally is understandable. The rapid growth of cooperation and comradeship between cops and psychologists is a credit to the interest and persistence of a small number of cop-psychologists, psychologist-cops, psychologist consultants, and bright, relatively young, progressive police managers. This book presents an overview of the services that psychologists can offer to law enforcement.

Chapters One, Two, and Three present a history of policing throughout the world and then, with more detail, the story of American policing. The third chapter focuses on the use of psychologists and behavioral science by law enforcement agencies.

Part Two, comprising Chapters Four through Six, describes psychological assessment methods and procedures used by law enforcement agencies. These applications include recruit selection, fitness-for-duty evaluation, special unit testing, and other assessment applications.

Part Three addresses intervention techniques and applications. Chapters Seven through Nine describe the helping procedures available for critical incident counseling, stress reduction and prevention, family problems, drug and alcohol abuse, and other areas of concern common to police agencies. These chapters consider peer counseling procedures and employee assistance referrals as well as health and wellness programs.

Chapters Eleven through Fifteen consider operational assistance in hostage negotiation, psychological profiling, psychological autopsy, and operational consultation with management and departments.

Training is addressed in Chapter Sixteen. This chapter includes the psychologist at the policy academy, the internship in police clinical psychology, and continuing education.

The concluding chapter considers the current state of police psychology and opportunities to expand general knowledge. The Appendixes provide a variety of practical information and work samples.

The information and experiences presented in this book are not all-inclusive, but represent an extensive and current picture of the application of psychology to the mission and functions of law enforcement agencies and officers. Updated references are provided.

Police officers and law enforcement agencies are ready to seek and use psychological services. It is time for psychologists who teach, train, conduct research, and practice to attend more closely to these critical needs among those serving an increasingly turbulent and uncivil society.

PART ONE

The Nature of Policing

CHAPTER ONE

Historical Development of Policing

EARLY POLICING

Police as an administrative and functional arm of organized society is a product of the 19th century. Previously, all forms of policing had been ancillary roles for the military, private guardian forces, or voluntary citizenry. Citizen police duties were frequently an obligatory avocational activity (Klockars, 1985). Until the end of the 1800s, private citizens performed the majority of policing when called on by the community's leadership to deal with specific crises. The American "posse" of the early West was an example of obligatory avocational policing. A bank would be robbed. The town's only law officer, a sheriff or marshal, would then choose men of the town to pursue the thieves. He would "swear in" or deputize the selected townsmen who would then give chase to the villains.

Reese (1987) suggests that policing existed for over 2000 years since history points out that the Roman Emperor Augustus maintained order by forming the Praetorian Guard.

The earliest recorded form of obligatory citizen policing was known as the "Frank Pledge." Developed in the south of England at the end of the 11th century, the system required every male age 12 and older to form a group, called a "Tything," with nine of his adult male neighbors. Each member was required to apprehend and deliver to the local court any one of the Tything's members who was thought to have committed a crime. The Tything men were also required to hold suspects in custody while they awaited disposition by the court. If any member of the Tything failed in his duty, fines were imposed on all members of that Tything.

This system of policing died out toward the end of the 13th century. The turmoil of unstable and frequently changing central authority in England in that era failed to support local efforts (Bailey, 1989).

The Parish Constable

At the end of the 13th century, the *Statute of Winchester* decreed the establishment of the *parish constable*. The statute established a system requiring that each parish designate one man who would serve as the parish constable for a year. He was not paid by the parish. The job rotated annually among the able-bodied men, who were appointed by the elders of the parish.

The parish constable was required to organize a group of watchmen to guard the gates of the village at night. When a serious disturbance to the tranquillity of the parish occurred, the constable was empowered to order as many men in the parish as necessary to quell the disturbance. When the constable raised what came to be called the "hue and cry," all men of the parish had to respond or face a fine.

The parish constable system lost effectiveness as central government in England consolidated and strengthened. Support for the parish constable deteriorated because the politics of a relatively unstable central government interfered with effective local policing. In 1361, the *Justices of the Peace Act* was passed. This law mandated the establishment of county and city justices who controlled the activities of the parish constables.

From the early 1400s to the 1700s, the office of the Justice of the Peace maintained local control of the policing in most towns, counties, and parishes of England. This unpaid position was usually given to persons of independent wealth and added strength to their already powerful role as economic and political leaders. Because these justices were appointed by the central authority, they conducted policing operations to conform with the wishes of that authority. Justices and constables collected fees for their work resulting in widespread corruption.

It was possible to escape service as a parish constable by illegally buying a "Tyburn Ticket." This certificate was issued to anyone who caught a felon and brought him or her to trial. The ticket exempted the bearer from a year's parish constable duty. These tickets sold for a wide range of sums and allowed the more affluent men of the parish to escape police duty.

At the end of the 17th century, the *Highwayman Act* was passed in England. This act decreed that anyone who captured and delivered a thief to trial resulting in a conviction would receive a fee of 40 pounds sterling. This considerable reward resulted in the growth of a system of "thief takers." In the 19th century, such a system developed in the United States, where the thief-takers became known as "bounty hunters." These independent enforcers—often ex-lawmen or presumably reformed badmen—created many legends in the American West.

The Vigilante Movement

Essentially an American development, almost 500 vigilante groups were formed between 1767 and 1900. The first of these, the "Regulators," originated in colonial South Carolina. Mostly found in major cities and in some cases more populated rural areas, these groups were more or less formally constituted as citizen police. They quelled civil disturbance and apprehended wrongdoers. Membership was considered prestigious and often represented the more affluent and politically powerful citizens of the community (Bailey, 1989).

Vigilante groups ranged in size from units with as few as a dozen members to the San Francisco Vigilance Committee with a membership that fluctuated between 6,000 and 8,000 at the end of the 19th century. Actual group functions ran the gamut from social clubs to organized mobs. Their avowed purpose, however, was to deal with serious problems of crime, civil unrest, and safety that the groups' leaders declared were insufficiently addressed by the legitimate police authority of the community. Many eminent American historical figures have been members of such vigilante groups. Presidents Andrew Jackson and Theodore Roosevelt proudly admitted to such membership.

Even today, vigilante groups exist. The "Maccabees," organized in the 1980s in New York City by the community of Hasidic Jews, maintains a radio car patrol in neighborhoods populated primarily by elderly Jews. Their purpose is to decrease or eliminate attacks on this older ethnic group. Members have no official status but maintain close liaison with local police precincts by acting both as a citizen alert group for the authorities and as a preventive presence.

The best-known modern vigilante group in the United States is the organization known as the "Guardian Angels." Formed in New York City by Curtis Sliwa in 1979, this organization functions in many large urban areas. Wearing distinctive shirts and red hats, the Guardian Angels patrol in high-crime areas. They work in groups, establishing a presence where they believe crimes against persons are likely to take place.

Once a very active vigilante group, the Ku Klux Klan, or the "Knights of the White Magnolia," now claims to be a purely social, ethnic, and political society. In earlier times, this group enforced its members' philosophy and beliefs with considerable violence and intimidation.

Constituted authority has always viewed the vigilante movement as a dangerous threat to civil order and law enforcement. Such movements have developed as a result of citizen dissatisfaction either with the existing statutes or with their implementation (Chapman & Johnston, 1962; Klockars, 1985).

The Texas Rangers

As settlers moved into the western territories of the United States in the early 1800s, concerns about law and order developed. In 1823, Stephen Austin, the then military leader of the American colonists in the Texas territories, employed 10 men to be peace officers for the loosely organized area. They were called "rangers" because of the vast distances they traveled to conduct their duties.

In 1826, the Texas-Americans organized their territories into six military districts. As part of this organizational plan, each district was to appoint 20 to 30 rangers to be in service at all times. This force became a permanent law enforcement body in 1835 at the outbreak of the Texas Revolution, which created the Republic of Texas. Mexico, as well as independent marauders, continued to harass the borders of the new republic. To deal with these threats as well as other disturbances and Indian attacks on settlers, squads of mounted men rode along the republic's borders to repel or destroy raiding parties. Although at first they were designated "mounted riflemen" (and sometimes "gunmen" or "spies"), they soon became universally known as the Texas Rangers.

After Texas became a state, these territorial peace officers continued to patrol the borders, chase criminals, and often administer "frontier justice" at the end of a rope or with their long-barreled Colt pistols.

During the Civil War, the rangers continued to serve as a border patrol. Strong negative feelings by some Texans brought the rangers into disfavor because they had not served in the Confederate military during the war. The rangers were disbanded following Appomattox. A state police force was created by the Texas legislature to replace the rangers. This peace-keeping force was disbanded in 1873 after the chief, James Davidson, absconded to Europe with the organization's funds.

Lawlessness in Texas had grown to alarming proportions. Local peace officers and posse enforcement methods were ineffective in stemming the rising crime wave. In 1874, the governor of Texas, Richard Coke, charged the legislature to create two crime-fighting forces. The first, under Major John B. Jones, was designated the Frontier Battalion. It consisted of six companies of men, each under a captain. Their tasks, as a paramilitary organization, were to patrol the borders, fight Indians who attacked settlers or who stole livestock, and to thwart those who incited riots, developed feuds, committed murders, and robbed trains and stagecoaches.

The second group, under Captain L. H. McNelly, was called the "Special Force." Consisting of about 30 men, their duty was specifically to suppress cattle theft and general brigandage. All these rough and ready, loosely supervised peace officers were called "Texas Rangers."

Today, the Texas Rangers operate as part of the Texas Department of Public Safety. Maintaining the legends of the Old West, they are still considered second to none in the role of free-agent law enforcers (Bailey, 1989).

THE DEVELOPMENT OF MODERN POLICING

Many forms of policing existed before the 19th century. Most of these were military or paramilitary forces to protect the persons or property of the wealthy and the influential. For centuries, military leaders and potentates employed agents who operated clandestinely to provide their employers with information useful in the conduct of commerce, war, and political ambitions. Such agents eventually became the more formalized "secret police" of the 17th century and later times.

Under pressure from the church or the elders of a community, communities and cities initiated many forms of protection, such as providing watchmen, gate guards, and lamplighters to deter lawlessness. Prevention of crime and the pursuit of felons, however, were at best sporadic and haphazard ventures.

As the industrial revolution resulted in greatly increased travel and commerce between hamlets and towns, towns and metropolitan areas, and then countries, governments began to organize and operate under codes and laws. Transgressions became codified with penalties and remedies. Lawlessness became more clearly defined.

In the 19th century, individual citizens began to disarm themselves. The wearing and carrying of swords, daggers, and guns as a usual and customary style began to disappear, especially in the eastern United States and England. On the American frontier, armed life survived longest. The private use of force came to be in disrepute, especially in urban areas. This social change, together with growing urban crime, provided the necessary impetus for the development of community-sponsored law enforcement (Miller, 1958).

The Metropolitan Police Force

The Metropolitan Police Force was established in Great Britain as a result of the escalating numbers of brutal crimes and violence that seemed to emerge in London between the late 18th and early 19th centuries.

For almost 50 years, various commissions had been established to recommend steps to deal with public concerns about crime. The great novelist Henry Fielding was instrumental in moving for police reform in London during the early part of the 18th century. Before he died, Fielding was a judge and magistrate in the city of London. As a magistrate, together with his younger brother, he struggled against corruption in the courts and worked with commissions to establish regular crime detection and apprehension of criminals. The work eventually laid the background for the Metropolitan Police Force, which was formed in 1829. Though he died in 1754, Henry Fielding has a place in the history of modern policing (Thomas, 1991).

There was great resistance to the development of police as an arm of the central government. Many thought that a formal police force would suppress civil liberties. Before the 1800s, policelike groups had been used to suppress riots and public opposition in brutal fashion. These events led to a popular conception of policemen as mindless thugs hired to impress the will of a few on the population at large. This concept exists to this day among many people (Lyman, 1964).

Sir Robert Peel, English Home Secretary, established the first organized urban police force in London in 1829. Municipalities all over the world quickly adopted this model, modifying it in accordance with their own culture, traditions, and political organization (Reith, 1956).

Called the "New Police," or more popularly the "Bow Street Runners" (after their first headquarters' location), these men were not popularly received. Groups fearing repression rioted against the first "bobbies" (after their founder "Bobby" Peel). In their first day of formal duty, one of the constables (their proper title) was killed. At trial, the young rioter who committed the first "cop killing" was exculpated with a finding of "justifiable homicide" by the courts.

To direct the formulation and operation of the "New Police," Peel appointed two forceful and experienced men as police commissioners. Army Colonel Charles Rowen and Irish barrister Richard Mayne brought to the nascent police organization concepts of military organization and strict adherence to the letter of the law.

Three thousand men were recruited for the new force. They were unarmed except for a small truncheon that was to be concealed beneath their coats. They were uniformed in an effort to soften the public's persistent fear of "secret police." Their mission was confined to foot patrol for the prevention of crime. Sir Robert issued the following initial orders for a Constable's conduct to the Metropolitan Police:

> He will be civil and obliging to all people of every rank and class. He must be particularly cautious not to interfere idly nor unnecessarily in order to make a display of his authority; when required to act he will do so with decision and boldness; on all occasions he may expect to receive the fullest support in the proper exercise of his authority.
>
> He must also remember that there is no qualification so indispensable to a police officer as a perfect command of temper, never suffering himself to be moved in the slightest degree by any language or threats that may be used; if he does his duty in a quiet and determined manner, such conduct will probably excite the well-disposed of the bystanders to assist him, if he requires them. (Klockars, 1985: 47–48)

Peel's orders remain binding on all British police officers to this day.

Between 1829 and 1838, the New Police ranks reached 33,000. During that period, there were 3,000 dismissals for cause and 6,000 resignations. In 1842, the first plainclothes detectives were formed into a unit to aid the Metropolitan Police solve particularly intolerable crimes. The early detectives also infiltrated and spied on reactionary groups giving some credence to the public concern about the curtailment of civil liberties.

In 1878, the detective branch of the Metropolitan Police was completely reorganized. The Criminal Investigation Division (CID) was formed to pursue crime solution in a more organized and methodical manner. This branch became known as "Scotland Yard" after the location of its London headquarters.

The Early Policeman's Life

The first "peelers" marched forth in London on September 29, 1829. They had been recruited and selected according to Commissioner Richard Mayne as ". . . not of the rank, habits, or station of gentlemen." Seventeen divisions were formed to serve all of London and its surrounding environments. Each division was commanded by a superintendent, who was aided by four inspectors. Each inspector (whose modern American equivalent would be captain) commanded four sergeants. The patrol officer was called a constable (the vernacular "peeler" labeled the patrol constable as one of Sir Robert Peel's men).

The pay for the constable was poor. He was literate enough to read his orders and to write or log simple reports. One day was much like another in the life of a Victorian policeman—dull, plodding routine, occasionally interrupted by highly dramatic incidents. Each day started with a "parade" (similar to today's morning or shift roll call). The constable would receive orders and a "pep talk" from his sergeant. After this, the constable walked his assigned "beat" from 9:00 A.M. until 6:00 P.M., when he would report to headquarters and be relieved of duty (unless special circumstances required that he stay later to assist in special activities of his division). He talked to people, listened to complaints, looked for anything that seemed "out of the ordinary," and made notes of anything that should later be discussed with or passed on to his sergeant. The ordinary patrol tour would include such events as arrests, fights, fires, deaths, and crimes. Some mornings were spent in court and some afternoons in bed—in preparation for evening or night duties as they might occur.

The constable's role was to provide a presence to prevent crime in his patrol area. If a crime was committed, the constable was to find or help detectives find the culprit. The goals of his work were to protect life and property in his area of jurisdiction and to preserve public tranquility.

The Victorian policeman could enhance his meager wages with tips for special services from townspeople on his beat, rewards for special services to his unit, and assistance to the detective branch. He might also receive extra money by rendering special services to shopkeepers and factory owners, such as awakening watchmen, finding casual labor, or delivering messages. Early policemen earned small sums by acting as wake-up services for gentlemen.

Victorian policemen walked a lot. Their feet always hurt. Their habit was to soak their feet in vinegar at night, believing it strengthened the soles of the feet and prevented foot odor.

By the time Sir Robert Peel died in 1850, his Metropolitan Police Force was well established. A detective branch was in operation and beginning to win the respect and goodwill of the public. The detectives, assisted by constables who knew their areas, conducted "raids" to arrest wanted criminals. The constables went along to guide detectives through the back streets, to identify the known hiding places of criminals, and to provide the muscle to break down doors when this was necessary to apprehend the sought miscreant. Newspaper journalists were often invited along on these raids in an attempt to enhance the public's view of the danger and importance of police work (Garforth, 1974).

The Proliferation of the Metropolitan Police Model

Although the older model of town constables and watchmen persisted in many settings through the mid-19th century, the Metropolitan Police model spread rapidly throughout Great Britain. Liverpool established its police force in 1834. By 1856, there were many police forces in 31 British counties.

In the United States, the reaction to the British model of community policing was favorable. A committee from New York City was sent to London to study the new model. As a result, the New York Bill was passed establishing the New York City Police Department in 1844. This bill required that all police recruits would come from the municipal wards in which they would serve. They were appointed by the mayor of New York, upon nomination by the alderman and two tax assessors of their ward. Thus the political control of community police was established as a custom in the United States (Chapman & Johnston, 1962; Klockars, 1985).

The first New York policemen were very independent. For 12 years, in spite of regulations, they successfully refused to wear uniforms. The conflict was settled temporarily in 1856 when the city fathers mandated that the police of each ward could decide on the color and style of their uniforms.

Following the British system, New York City policemen were forbidden to carry weapons. By the early 1860s, however, New York police officers (as well as the newer Boston police) armed themselves, against orders, in an effort to cope with criminals who were shooting, stabbing, and beating them (Klockars, 1985).

POLICING IN THE TWENTIETH CENTURY

Police as we know them have only existed for 150 years. Modern police departments emerged from the street violence and industrial unrest that swept England and other European counties in the 19th century. The early police forces were military and paramilitary units developed to interfere with civil disorder. As communities formalized police departments, they became the tools of the political machinery of the community. Corruption was fairly common (Sparrow, Moore, & Kennedy, 1990).

In the early 1900s, the police presented an image of ineffectiveness. Many citizens saw the police as enemies of the people and tools of the affluent and the politically powerful. Others saw the police as the last bastion of defense against an increasingly complex and disorganized society. Variability was the rule. In the 1920s, the Berlin Police Department was relatively free of political pressure, represented a high level of education among its members, and tolerated little corruption. At the same time, the police in major American cities were very corrupt, subject to all levels of political pressure and the manipulation of the affluent. Yet, in other perhaps more practical terms, the exemplary Berlin police lost control of the streets to riot and mayhem, whereas the recriminable American police managed to maintain order (Mosse, 1975).

Although police were changing in the early part of the 20th century, the image and reality of police continued, albeit less universally, to be that of brutal, corrupt, slothful thugs, poorly educated and insensitive to their allegiance to the public welfare (Smith, 1960).

Police forces have not been and are unlikely ever to be perfect. Officers can break under stress no matter how carefully selected, trained, or supervised. Police themselves have been victims of prejudice as well as unrealistic expectations. Politically disenfranchised or generally dissatisfied citizens classically turn on the police as the instigators of problems rather than directing their dissatisfaction to the powers that control the police (Mosse, 1975; Smith, 1960).

Early European and American police had certain strengths. They were drawn from their own communities and neighborhoods. They operated in areas that they knew well and where they were well known. They often received a considerable degree of support and approval from their neighbors and local political leaders. They did a great deal of practical good. They helped put out fires, operated as the first ambulance and emergency medical services, ran soup kitchens for the poor, collected garbage, and gave shelter (often at the station house) to the homeless during the worst weather. All these functions developed before social agencies came into common existence (Sparrow et al., 1990).

Following World War I, communities everywhere faced a new industrial revolution—the Age of Technology. Rapid developments in communication, transportation, and weaponry allowed criminals to operate more broadly and to escape apprehension more frequently. From the 1920s until the 1960s, police were far behind the felons. The criminal element had better cars, automated weaponry, and even aircraft to help them break the law and to escape capture.

After 1950, police forces became more organized and received the support necessary to develop new and sophisticated methods of selecting, training, equipping, and supporting police officers. Radio patrol cars became universal. National and international record keeping and information exchange about felons and crime events became increasingly common. Specialized techniques were developed to help officers understand, track, prevent, and apprehend various kinds of lawbreakers. After 1960, cross-training among local, national, and international police groups became common. Reform and professionalization were the hallmarks of late-20th-century policing.

THE TWENTY-FIRST CENTURY: QUO VADIS?

In the final years of the 20th century, policing has started to feel the effects of massive social change. The balance of political power and philosophical imperatives throughout the world have undergone significant and in some cases cataclysmic modification. Police have always represented the more conservative and traditional values of the communities they serve. Selection, training, and performance of police tend to lag behind real-time changes in the community or nation.

Changing racial and ethnic balances in almost all modern countries are a contemporary reality. Police are under rising pressure to become sensitive to the social and political needs of minorities that are becoming majorities. New kinds of training and regulations in respect to citizens of varied cultures and languages have become increasingly necessary.

Police officers of the 21st century are more likely to be college educated, multilingual, trained in psychology and sociology, and more aware of social trends than their 20th-century forebears (McCord & Wicker, 1990; Trojanowicz & Carter, 1990).

Almost all major systems on which society depends are in simultaneous crisis. Massive dislocations are not only predicted but have begun. Social disapproval should be society's first line of defense against criminality and disorder. When this fails, the police are expected to be the second line of defense. Police managers and leaders know this and have begun to plan for the 21st century (Tofler, 1990).

Psychologists and other behavioral scientists can be helpful to police and police departments in meeting the challenges that come with these changes.

CHAPTER TWO

Policing in the United States

To meet the needs of law enforcement organizations and individual police officers, it is of signal importance that the psychologist understand policing. Although an understanding of an individual's work is a given for all psychological service, certain aspects of policing require a deeper and more involved understanding of the job and the people.

Industrial and organizational psychologists attempt to accomplish this important prerequisite to service-delivery through *task analysis* or as some prefer, *front-end analysis.* In these procedures, the job is observed and the workers are interviewed to create an objective picture of the job and the way in which the workers use means or process to achieve an outcome or a product (Kaufman, 1991).

Useful and traditional as these procedures have been, they are insufficient for an understanding of law enforcement jobs and those who work in these settings. There are those activities that appear in job descriptions, organizational charts, and "general orders"; and there are the things that cops really do. Much of what cops are, think, and do is hidden from nonlaw-enforcement people, or "civilians," as cops more politely refer to noncops. Extensive work has been done by psychologists in describing the work of American police officers (Bittner, 1970; Goldstein, 1960; Remington, 1965; Russell & Beigel, 1982; Skolnick, 1967; Wilson, 1963). These studies and projects are useful but not sufficient. Psychologists who intend to be maximally effective working with police need to know more about the inner workings of both law enforcement agencies and police officers.

This chapter provides an inside as well as an objective observational view of police and policing. A thorough and detailed analysis of policing is beyond the scope of this volume. In addition to the material provided herein, the psychologist working in the law enforcement setting will learn from either being a cop (some 50 or more police psychologists in the United States are or have been sworn and serving officers) or being with cops over a period of time in a variety of settings.

Policing is big business in the United States. At this writing, there are more than 600,000 sworn police officers in more than 22,000 departments at state, county, and municipal levels. This excludes the vast federal law enforcement community of the Justice Department (including the Federal Bureau of Investigation); the Treasury Department and its many enforcement components such as the Secret Service and the U.S. Customs Service; the State Department; various intelligence organizations; and other federal agencies with security and enforcement responsibilities (Jamieson & Flanagan, 1989).

HISTORICAL DEVELOPMENT OF POLICING IN THE UNITED STATES

As early as 1691, New York City watchmen began wearing uniforms and were the police of that era (Cramer, 1964).

The Nineteenth Century

Although the British model of policing as developed in Peel's Metropolitan Police of London served as impetus and model for the development of 19th-century policing in most modern countries, policing developed in varying ways around the world and in specific municipalities. In some settings, it was a method of imposing the will of a small but powerful minority on an often fearful and silent majority. In other settings, the police were developed to keep minorities in check. Sometimes, police acted as a corrupt, local power brokerage (Sparrow et al., 1990).

From the beginning, the style of U.S. policing reflected certain uniquely American, regional characteristics. In the major metropolitan areas, selection and promotion were plums distributed by ward bosses and other politicians. In small communities, popularity among the citizenry was the primary basis for selection. An attachment to the neighborhood and a tendency to adhere to the spirit of the region rather than the letter of the law has uniquely defined and to some extent still does define the community peace officer in the United States. Cramer (1964) states that by 1812 the various "watches" in the United States were referred to as "police."

Early American police officers wore no uniforms or selected their garb locally. The badge was the emblem of authority. It might be worn openly or concealed. Police in eastern urban areas at first were prohibited from carrying weapons. Most officers, however, carried a gun; a truncheon or baton; a weighted sack, or "blackjack"; and often a knife. They disobeyed the rules because they learned early on that the people with whom they dealt in their duty to prevent crime and apprehend felons carried such weapons and rarely hesitated to use them, even on or sometimes especially on police.

The First American Crime Wave

Following the Civil War, the first American crime wave developed. Until that time, police had spent their time maintaining the status quo. Little imagination or "detection" was required (Tafoya, 1990). In the 1870s and 1880s, organized gangs, often made up of Confederate or Union war veterans began to pillage and rob in a manner never before known in the United States. Mostly operating in midwestern and western territories, these gangs robbed banks, murdered and robbed wealthy citizens, and held up stagecoaches and trains. Policing on the local level was ineffective unless the brigands were accidentally caught in the act or the town had an effective posse or vigilante capability. The gangs rode off beyond the reach or jurisdiction of the local law. Although the jurisdictional issue was addressed by the development of a corps of U.S. marshals who operated throughout U.S. territories, this group was small and poorly supported. Sometimes, major financial interests such as stockmen or railroad officials hired private police (e.g., the Pinkerton Agency) to detect the criminals, organize armed groups, and track down the gang that offended the particular employer. The task of identifying and apprehending these bandits was made more difficult by the propensity of the national press and individual journalists to ignore the brutality and aggrandize the derring-do of these violent men (and sometimes women).

Police selection in the 19th century was simple and pragmatic. In the urban areas, tough, young, aggressive, politically favored men were sent out on the streets to patrol and maintain some semblance of order. In rural areas, the job was given to those who wanted it, were popular, and had political connections. In the western territories, the town council appointed the local sheriff. Many former badmen were asked to become peace officers in the West on the theory that they were tough and willing to go up against their former partners or colleagues for either money or respectability. Many a legend grew out of this haphazard, uniquely American method of policing.

The U.S. stereotype of the city police officer at the end of the 1800s was a man who was uneducated, brutal, quick to attack, and slow to reason. The term "dumb flatfoot" became a cliché. Theodore Roosevelt was appointed Commissioner of Police of New York City at the end of the 19th century. An apocryphal story has it that Roosevelt, anxious to do a good job, felt he had to win the respect of the cop on the beat. To do so, he went to a low saloon in the Bowery and proceeded to antagonize several patrons. As they prepared to teach this young gentleman a lesson (with several police officers looking on and clearly not intending to interfere), Roosevelt, a practiced boxer, began to thrash several of the local worthies. When the cops started to arrest the pugnacious uptown snob, Roosevelt revealed that he was their new boss, thus getting off to a good start with a group of police officers who apparently had high regard for brutal strength skillfully applied.

Early Twentieth-Century Policing

As the United States entered the 20th century, the format of community policing changed very little. Following the English model again, American police departments, particularly in urban communities, were paramilitary organizations with rigid operational structure and strong political ties, and were not very subject to community control or reform. In smaller communities and rural areas, a variety of peace officers—sheriffs, constables, justices of the peace, and even watchmen served law enforcement roles that were generally quite limited and mostly ineffectual. Serious crimes that were not prevented or immediately solved either received the attention of special units of state police, were addressed by courtesy help from urban departments nearby, or were investigated by private police in the employ of affluent citizens.

Following World War I, a number of influences began to change the diverse nature of American policing. Great advances in communication and transportation coupled with a growing urban population resulted in an increasing public demand for efficient and responsible police organizations. The people no longer were willing to accept fragmented, idiosyncratic police departments that were ineffective in controlling crime. All over the country, political police boards were replaced with commissioners. Departments began to develop extensive and capable staffs. Central departmental headquarters began to expect performance and adherence to standards by line supervisors and patrol officers. At first, police officers and supervisors resisted reform, but as senior police managers began to see this as an opportunity to formalize and professionalize policing, they viewed reform process as uplifting police rather than degrading them. The new model of the police officer was a better educated and better trained person, who could be competent, independent, authoritative, and able to trust his or her own judgment, yet adhere to correct and lawful standards (Sparrow et al., 1990).

With reform came departmentalization and centralization of authority. The patrol officer remained the cornerstone of policing in neighborhoods. In addition, highly specialized officers were selected and trained to deal with homicide, sex crimes, burglary, fraud, arson, and other specialized activities of the criminal community.

The Second American Crime Wave

A second great crime wave hit the United States after World War I. The wave of morality sweeping the country at that time resulted in passage of the Volstead Act forbidding the manufacture and sale of alcoholic beverages. An enormous illicit industry arose to manufacture, import, distribute, and sell such beverages. The public supported these criminal ventures, which generated enormous profits. Gangsterism became rampant in all major urban areas, and the distribution and sale of alcoholic beverages became one of the biggest businesses in the United States.

Those involved in acquiring and distributing alcohol were at war with each other as well as with law enforcement agencies. By utilizing modern communication equipment, semiautomatic and automatic weapons, and fast automobiles (as well as boats and airplanes), these gangsters created an era of murder, extortion, bribery, and mayhem heretofore unknown in this country.

The Federal Bureau of Investigation was created, in part, to deal with this disastrous situation. As in the first American crime wave, the media tended to aggrandize the gangsters. With motion pictures added to the newspapers, the general public received very mixed messages about those who instigated and maintained criminal activities.

Local departments were relatively unhelpful in dealing with the alcohol gangsters. As the crime groups—sometimes regional and sometimes broadly ethnic—became more organized and cooperative, criminal activities involving alcohol led to other antisocial and illegal activities including prostitution, loan sharking, drug distribution, and control of union activities and funds. Chaos in law enforcement became more the rule than the exception, which set in motion another wave of reform, with greater cooperation between federal and local law enforcement agencies.

Depression in the early 1930s enhanced the growth of crime. In a pattern somewhat reminiscent of the crime wave after the Civil War, small groups or bands of brigands robbed banks, jewelry stores, and other affluent institutions, often escaping in powerful automobiles and a hail of bullets. Again, the media tended to glamorize such characters as "Pretty-Boy Floyd," John Dillinger, Bonnie and Clyde, and "Ma" Barker and her "boys." To the present day, legends about these thugs and criminals continue to provide material for the motion picture industry. Americans have had a long romance with the criminal element.

The repeal of the Volstead Act and the entrance of the United States into World War II ended the crime wave. Beginning in 1950, considerable reform in policing methods and philosophy began to emerge (Wilson, 1967). Strong efforts were made to professionalize police and hold them accountable in most major communities. The public still considered police in a negative way. Ethnic minorities, young people, and newspapers automatically tended to take a negative view toward police. Police and community leaders began to anticipate the problems of the second half of the 20th century and sought to develop imaginative, analytic, and prescriptive styles of policing within a more professional framework (Tafoya, 1990).

As the 1950s began, those wishing to reform and professionalize police departments faced increasing barriers. Up to that point, the courts had shown little interest in how police treated defendants for adjudication. After 1950, constitutional constraints began to limit the police in exercising enforcement as they chose. Judges began to insist on the constitutional rights of defendants suspected or arrested.

Appellate court rulings on the admissibility of evidence have directed and influenced police practices at all levels since that time (Barth, 1961; Friendly, 1965).

As with other job categories in the second half of the 20th century, police departments found they were having more and more difficulty retaining officers for an entire career. High employee turnover created a serious problem in cost-effectiveness for police departments. Issues of recruitment, testing, hiring, training, and equipping replacement officers became matters of serious concern in reform and planning (Pape, 1990).

The Federal Bureau of Investigation developed a National Crime Information Center (NCIC) during the late 1960s. This extremely useful central data bank allowed local law enforcement to track and identify criminals in a way that had never been possible in the past. This tended to balance somewhat the court's insistence that police adhere rigidly to the constitutional rights of criminals in conducting investigations or making arrests. Efforts to modernize policing in the United States have been hobbled by the policing habits of the past (Sparrow et al., 1990).

The Third Great American Crime Wave

In the 1960s, a wave of criminal activity began that resembled the situation in the early 1930s except that it focused primarily on the acquisition, importation, and distribution of illicit drugs instead of alcohol. Whereas previous crime waves were of relatively short duration, drug-related crimes continue to this day.

Current criminal patterns are more sophisticated forms of those developed during the first two crime waves. Communication, mobility, the availability of enormous sums of money, and cooperation and organization among gangsters has resulted in worldwide cartels to maintain criminal drug distribution. The gangsters have better equipment, better communication, and in many cases better organization than the police. They are unrestrained. They have private armies and private police forces. There are no human rights or constitutional rights among the drug barons. The profits are enormous and personnel recruitment is no problem whatsoever. In the effort to deal with this third great wave of crime during the past 40 years, federal, state, and local law enforcement agencies have had a closer, more cooperative relationship than ever before in the history of policing.

As the 20th century draws to a close, police managers, the judiciary, elected officials, and the general public have become increasingly interested in police reform. There is a consensus that innovative police chiefs can make the difference between a backward, ineffective department and a modern, professional department by discovering and redefining the potential of their agencies. They are doing this now, within the framework of the democratic challenge that policing should respond thoughtfully and effectively to crime and conflict. Openness and public review are the rule rather than the exception. Although historically, law enforcement has been required to maintain the "status quo," anticipating crimes and dealing with the vast array of unruly public behavior have now become part of the policing responsibility. Crime, fear, drugs, and disorder devastate not only individuals, but neighborhoods and communities.

The Concept of Community Policing

As larger communities became desperate to reverse the physical decay in those areas where drugs had been prevalent, the concept of "community policing" emerged. A President's Commission on Law Enforcement reported just after mid-century that rigid departmental rules lack an appreciation that police officers must develop professional discretionary methods within each community for crime control and peacekeeping (Lohman & Misler, 1966). Those in power assumed that the concept of a police force that fights crime vigorously, answers calls promptly, and investigates cleverly nearly always draws community support. This is not always so; in some communities, patrolling purposely and answering emergency calls promptly as well as investigating crimes systematically has not worked out. These are usually large urban settings in which the conditions of life are so poor that crime is not a matter of great concern to the inhabitants. Vigorous policing doesn't help very much in a community struggling to keep its head above water. In impoverished neighborhoods, burdened with trash, broken windows, street prostitution, and drug dealing as well as incessant family disorders, the community sees little value in traditional policing.

In certain cities, the concept of community policing has been introduced. The police are attempting to establish a new, vital relationship with neighborhoods so that the energy of the community can be combined with the activity of the police to bring greater force to bear against crime and disorder. The police as well as the citizens are beginning to understand that there is power in partnership. In some major cities, they have developed an administrative role for supervisors called "lead officers." These supervisors print newsletters, introduce themselves around the neighborhood, encourage their officers to hand out business cards, go to block meetings, meet with City Council representatives in their areas, and have their own station house and even mobile phone telephone numbers and answering machines so that they can deal more directly with the citizens. Police forces that have attempted this procedure have reported very positive results (Sparrow et al., 1990).

Modern policing methods don't always work out. In 1972 Kansas City tested three areas, which were given different degrees of attention. One received no patrol at all, with officers only answering emergency calls. The second area was patrolled by two or three times the normal number of officers. The third was patrolled in the usual manner with a single officer and a single patrol car. Analysis of hundreds of measures of crime and fear as well as neighborhood surveys resulted in a finding that surprised everyone: There was no noticeable difference in the level of crime and fear in the three areas (Kelling, 1974).

The strategy of community policing holds great promise. Vandalism, unruly public behavior, and other forms of physical and social disorder that increase fear in the neighborhood also increase the likelihood of crime. Where teams of police officers have sponsored athletic events, have organized cleanups, and have referred troubled youths to self-help programs, the communities become much more cooperative and participate with the police in maintaining order. Police who ask neighborhood citizens "What can we do to make things better?" begin the process of community policing and mutual cooperation in the best interests of the people who live in the area.

In some communities, police have been very effective in helping neighborhoods clean themselves up, get funding for repairs, and increase pride and esteem. This leads to a decrease in the unruly behavior and sloth that characterize a high-crime area. Offering to help and asking what needs to be done are the first steps in persuading citizens to participate (Tafoya, 1990). In no way can we say at this point that the important advances of the 20th century have succeeded in dealing with the essential goal of policing—to maintain civil order. There are significant limitations to the reform model of professional law enforcement. In spite of increased support, the new professionalism, better management, and community policing, police are failing in the primary mission of crime control. Crime and the requirement of police intervention have gone well beyond the eight major crimes (murder, rape, robbery, assault, burglary, larceny, arson, and auto theft). Law enforcement must now deal with wife battering, child abuse, sexual abuse, fraud, confidence games, white-collar crimes, protection rackets, loan sharking, drug dealing, prostitution, vandalism, panhandling, public drinking, traffic, parking and litter violations, and so forth. As community policing has demonstrated, the public often cares far more about these matters than about felonies that generally do not touch them.

Law enforcement is not winning. Crime rates remain at historic heights in the United States. Clearance rates for crimes remain relatively low. Less than 30% of robberies and 15% of burglaries are cleared. Many broad, demographic, social, and economic trends account for some of this. Yet, more people are in prison today in the United States, than at any other time in history (U.S. Bureau of the Census, 1990).

In spite of this, community policing seems to be the wave of the future. Police are discovering (or perhaps rediscovering) that ordinary people in the neighborhood are the first line of defense in controlling crime and fear. Police cannot succeed without a successful partnership with the neighborhoods in which they serve. The residents provide eyes and ears to extend police surveillance. People in the neighborhood can call the police, provide descriptions of offenders, give accounts of events, and serve as witnesses. These activities, all of which require a willingness to come forward, are most likely to be enhanced by an increase in the personal contact between officer and citizen that comes with community policing.

BECOMING A POLICE OFFICER

Until the early 1960s, young children frequently said that they wanted to become a police officer. As negative attitudes toward the police became rampant after the early 1960s, fewer and fewer children expressed this wish. Even today, there continues to be a negative attitude toward police officers and the police profession. A recent publication, the *Bulletin of the Council on Inter-Racial Books for Children,* in analyzing the content of new children's books and educational materials, states that children should be leery of books in which "law enforcers are depicted as the people's best friend" (Hymowitz, 1991). Figure 2.1 presents a more traditional, positive view of police as concerned friends of lost children.

In spite of a current general negative cultural attitude about police, the number of those who apply to become police officers far exceeds the availability of appointments. Despite all the criticism and complaints about the police, no one seems to suggest society should get rid of them. The public wants policing, security, and the prevention of crime. By 1990, there were 859,000 private security guards in the United States. At the same time, there were only 643,000 local police. This is probably unfortunate, since the people who hire private security guards are less likely to support the public police (Sparrow et al., 1990). "Real" police refers to private security with derision as the "rent-a-cops." Those who seek esteem and legitimacy apply for positions as commissioned police officers.

Selection

Until the 1950s selection of police officer candidates was largely a political and availability process. During the past four decades, the public and police executives themselves have sought a better class of recruits. At first, requiring a high-school diploma for police recruits was a major step in upgrading educational requirements. Most major departments now require some college education for those applying to become police officers. The educational requirements are moving steadily higher as policing becomes

FIGURE 2.1   This Photograph Illustrates the Traditional View of Police as Helpers

more complex. The state of Minnesota recently announced plans to open a single-degree bachelor's program for peace officer education. This program is likely to be offered at the Metropolitan State University in St. Paul (Clark, 1991).

Some police departments recruit and select police officer candidates through the *civil service commission system*. Advocates of this procedure cite fairness, equal opportunity, and absence of political interference as benefits of this approach. A second major selection system used by local departments is the *personnel department system*. Proponents of this practice advocate the importance of home rule in selecting recruits who will do the best job in the community where they will serve. Those in favor of the personnel department approach also suggest that the complex legal and administrative aspects of policing are better addressed through personnel department recruiting and selection, which is better able than the civil service commission system to respond flexibly to social and technical changes (Bailey, 1989).

Training

In most jurisdictions today, specific training is required to become a state-certified police officer. At one time it was possible to become a cop simply by being selected, put into uniform, and told to report to the station house. Those days are now over. The police establishment has become aware that the untrained or poorly trained police officer is a likely source of chagrin and litigation for the department.

Selection is a two-part process; the recruit first applies for acceptance in a police academy. This usually requires an extensive evaluation of the candidate's academic background, previous employment, reputation in the community, polygraphic examination, and psychological testing. In some cases, mainly in response to statutory mandate, the polygraph and the psychological testing may take place after academy training and before hiring by an agency.

Some academies are full-time academic institutions and may be affiliated with junior colleges. The recruit may be a probationary member of the police department that sends him or her to the academy.

Academies provide between 300 and 700 hours of training. Some academies are as short as 8 weeks of full-time participation. "Night academies" are as long as $5^1/2$ months; usually, the recruit attends 4 hours an evening, 5 days a week. Academy faculty consists of a wide variety of teachers ranging from experienced patrol officers who provide job-oriented training to professors of criminology who give theoretical lectures. Psychologists may lecture on such topics as "Stress," "Recognizing the Mentally Disturbed Person," and "Interviewing the Child Witness." Except in the larger jurisdictions, classes tend to have between 20 and 40 participants. The training is intense and covers a full range of information, laws, and techniques that every police officer is expected to know.

On graduation from an academy, the applicant may or may not be offered a commission. This depends to some extent on the applicant's record in the academy, as well as employment conditions in the community. Often, a significant number of graduating academy class members may not receive job offers because of budget limitations. Some of these graduates may go on to be commissioned in other departments; others may accept work as correctional officers, await openings in the community of their choice, or simply go no further in policing.

Once graduates are commissioned and sworn, they receive initial assignments with a *field training officer*. Although at this point, the novice cops carry a weapon and have powers of arrest and deadly force, they are still considered "rookies." Field training usually consists of formal and informal interactions with specific experienced officers who are skilled in passing on to new recruits the lore of policing. During field training, novice officers learn the intricate details of the demography and sociology of the community in which they will serve. Field training generally takes place at roll call, on patrol with the field training officer, and at special audiovisual sessions on specific topics.

No matter how elaborate an academy education or field training may be, most cops agree that it is about 2 years before new officers graduate from the rookie classification. To become skillful, effective, reliable cops, rookies must gain experience in all aspects of the patrol job. They must arrest suspects, break up fights, help calm troubled neighborhoods, defuse dangerous domestic violence situations, rescue cats, assist in traffic tragedies, and function as school resource officers. This is by no means a total list of the situations that rookies confront during the first 2 years on the job.

When police officers finish training and start their tour with their field training officer, they tend to be frightened, unaware, and confused. When they perceive how the training officer understands the neighborhood and the people in it, they are astonished. Eventually, the rookies learn these techniques, but at first, the training officer's expertise is a great mystery (Fletcher, 1991). After 5 years on the job, there is virtually nothing that police officers don't know about their community, particularly in a big city. They have handled and seen almost everything.

Most states now require that certified police officers acquire a minimum number of credits of continuing education. This "renewal," mandated over a 4-year period, frequently requires 40 or more credits of specialized training.

The Federal Bureau of Investigation operates its own academy: As one of its many services in support of local policing, the Justice Department has established the FBI National Academy at Quantico, Virginia. Here, relatively young, experienced local law enforcement officers may apply for admission to an 11-week resident program. During this time, the officers receive intensive training in the most modern aspects of criminal investigation, police tactics, forensic science, and appropriate utilization of the FBI's considerable resources. Most FBI National Academy graduates return to their own departments, promoted to executive positions.

WHY DO MEN AND WOMEN CHOOSE TO BE COPS?

The general public doesn't really know why men and women choose to become police officers, nor why police officers stay on the job as long as they do. The pay is poor in most instances. The working conditions can be abominable, particularly during the early years of the police career, and in many cases, promotion is extremely slow (U.S. Department of Labor, 1992). About 80% of police officers spend their entire career as line officers, on patrol, or as plainclothes detectives; 15% become supervisors; and only 5% rise to executive rank.

The general public is often heard to say, "It's a power trip." Many people still hold the concept of police as semidisciplined thugs. Although no two individuals have exactly the same motivation to become police officers, recruits at police academies and rookie police officers have some consistent characteristics. A number of applicants choose policing because it's "in the family." Some believe that it is an opportunity for excitement and variety. One of the motivations seems to be the promise of security in a bureaucratic setting that has fairly good benefits and a pension plan at the end of 20 years. Some applicants seek power and mastery. Almost all recruits seek and are reassured by the respect the role carries. This is one of the counterpoints to the negative beliefs that the community holds about police.

Many cops speak of early childhood wishes to become a police officer. In talking about motivation for the policing profession with a large number of officers in many jurisdictions, not as a psychologist, but as "cop to cop," it becomes evident that nearly all career police officers have had someone in their early background—a grandmother, an uncle, a parent—who had strong moral values involving the concept "We are our brother's keepers." This moralistic/religious concept often was expressed in an informal way rather than through strong religious pronouncements or practice. Almost universally, when talking to other cops and reminiscing about their daily life and their beginnings in police work, such a reference will emerge.

Staying on the Job

Policing is a tough and demanding profession. Police officers have to take a lot of abuse and disappointment in addition to the danger, the boredom, and the injustice that they all come to know. A good many officers drop out of the job before they are fully experienced—usually after 2 to 3 years; the problems and difficulties outweigh the benefits for these people.

Those who stay on the job as a career find their job satisfactions inconsistently available. Rewards, such as the thanks of an individual given protection or help, commendations, appreciation for a job well done, promotion, and other direct reinforcements, serve as variable ratio rewards to keep police officers on the job in spite of the pain and pressure of the work.

The motivation to continue includes the following for experienced officers:

- The feeling that they are the protector of their hometown turf.
- The feeling that they are keeping the bad elements of society at bay.

- The security of a job that leads to a pension.
- The safety of being in a job that provides clothing, cleaning, automobile, gas, vacations, and sick leave.
- The camaraderie of other police officers.
- The feeling of being an admired, feared, respected member of the community and a valued part of the community's infrastructure.

Cops don't usually enter the profession to "help people." By the end of 5 years on the job, however, this has become an important reinforcer for continuance "in the job." By this time, the officer has had the experience of being a significant intervenor or participant in many useful or critical circumstances. Such activities then become a motivating factor.

Those who make a lifelong career of policing are also motivated by the specialness of the almost secret society within which they function. Friendships with partners and other cops are deep and long-lasting. A bright 24-year veteran officer who had risen through the ranks to an executive position responded to the question "What keeps cops on the job for 20 years or more?" as follows:

> You start out believing all kinds of things about this job. You want to do "good things," you want respect, you want the pension. Maybe you want the girls to admire you. The main thing you get out of a police career though is a few really good friends for life.

In truth, although frequently denied either directly or with characteristic cop humor, most police officers continue to be motivated on the job by playing the role of "my brother's keeper" and being viewed by the community as part of the thin blue line that separates civilization from the criminal jungle.

WHAT COPS DO

Police serve the community by establishing and maintaining order, preventing criminal acts against persons and property, and apprehending crime perpetrators. Police are enforcers of the law. In small departments, officers are patrol cops or may become "specialists" working on specific crimes or crime-related activities. As problem solvers, police may ask questions, direct citizens, and when necessary, use force. Cops catch criminals, drive officials, administer first aid at accident scenes, evict drunken persons from bars, control crowds, and direct traffic. They care for lost children, separate battling relatives, and do much more. Police officers must often act quickly and intuitively to provide peremptory solutions for complex human problems. Because police officers are defined as those who wage war against crime, they are expected to demonstrate the warrior virtues of strength, valor, obedience, and esprit de corps. In addition, each cop is held personally responsible for the correctness and practicality of his or her every decision or action. The job of policing poses enormous, and in many cases seemingly irresolvable, conflicts. Yet, amazingly, police officers in most situations are able to bring such resolution about (Bittner, 1970).

Police officers expect to face danger. From 1980 to 1989, 801 police officers were feloniously killed. This means that annually, approximately 1 in 4,000 police officers is killed on the job (Major, 1991). The majority of the police officer's time is not spent in dangerous pursuits. Between 50% and 90% of dispatch calls concern traffic, loud neighbors, lost pets, missing people, and other common problems and frictions of life (Sparrow et al., 1990). Police officers often describe their work as long stretches of tedium punctuated with moments of sheer terror (Bouza, 1990).

In many larger communities, the police serve as the shield or the whipping boy to protect the mayor or the city council from responsibility for neglected ghetto problems. Rioting, teenage drug usage, and other social problems are frequently blamed on police underreaction or overreaction (Robinson, 1975). Part of the police officer's job is to tolerate this unfair blaming and make no public response.

Crank and Jackson (1993) studied police officers in eight Illinois municipal police departments. They were able to acquire 205 usable questionnaires in their efforts to evaluate the relationship between police belief systems and attitudes toward police practices. They found that the longer an officer was in a department, the longer he/she was likely to display positive attitudes in support of street justice, and the less likely they were to be antagonistic toward due process concerns. Officers with longer tenures were also less likely to favor subcultural impenetrability (the code of secrecy which protects the police subculture from outside penetration).

In the final analysis, every police officer is expected to face a wide range of situations that require action and to make decisions that turn out to be correct (Remington, 1965).

The Patrol Officer

Patrol officers perform the fundamental job of policing—they are the frontline officers. The concept of the "first responder" describes much of their job. Whether patrol officers are on patrol in a vehicle, on foot, or in the station house, they are the first ones to respond if any occurrence in the community requires the responsibility of law enforcement.

Over 80% of the patrol officer's time is spent answering service calls, primarily involving social regulation. Patrol officers maintain order. The calls may involve family fights, mentally disturbed persons, intoxicated citizens, suicidal attempts, motor vehicle accidents, other accidents, assaults, rape, or any number of neighborhood problems. The patrol officer frequently meets with highly emotional citizens who may respond with aggressiveness, anxiety, depression, or hysteria. Whether their skills are the result of formal training or "on the job" experience, all police officers must develop crisis-intervention expertise (Goldstein, Monti, Sardino, & Green, 1979; International Association of Chiefs of Police, 1977).

Traffic control and crowd control remain the primary jobs of patrol officers. Because traffic rules are defined in the statutes, police officers can easily discern most violations, but there is still room for some judgment. Although most citizens expect police officers to enforce traffic laws, drivers generally resent receiving a citation. Police officers are trained to act with discretion and restraint, knowing that confrontations with citizens frequently lead to complaints.

The patrol officer learns to act definitively and aggressively. In almost all situations in which a patrol officer is called on to intervene, it is the officer's responsibility to "establish control." This requires a certain degree of aggressiveness, awareness of the situation, and knowledge of proper procedures. Early in their careers, patrol officers tend to "go by the book." Later on, most patrol officers modify their aggressiveness and try to promote the best possible outcome for any conflict situation. This particular discretionary element of the job marks the American police officer as unique among law enforcement officers the world around.

Patrol officers have the responsibility of responding to "911" calls. This system is becoming universal throughout the United States. Citizens who have any kind of conflict, or even simple questions, dial "911." This is a useful community service but tends to clog the communication center of the police department. Dispatchers have the responsibility of separating out the most serious from the least serious calls. They are not always correct in their judgments, and many citizens complain that it takes a long time for the police to respond to 911 calls. If a riot is taking place, it is unlikely that a citizen will receive a visit from a patrol officer to help bring a cat down from a tree. Table 2.1 shows some of the things that a patrol officer does during a single day of duty in a medium-size city (Russell & Beigel, 1989). The calls shown represent an average shift. Where the patrol officer can settle the issue (disperse the crowd, counsel the conflicting family members, issue a summons, arrest a perpetrator), he or she will write a detailed report of the occurrence.

In a department where specialists are assigned to specific crimes, the patrol officer will secure the crime scene (as in a burglary, an armed robbery, or a homicide), after first calling dispatch and requesting detectives assigned to that particular crime to report to the scene. Until the specialist arrives, the patrol officer must keep people away from the crime scene, maintain a chain of evidence that may be important later in prosecuting

TABLE 2.1   First Responder Calls of a Patrol
Officer during a Single Eight-Hour Shift

Type of Call	Time Spent (minutes)
Accident (auto)	32
Family disturbance	17
Neighbor problem (noncriminal)	14
Juvenile problem (noncriminal)	7
Burglary	20
Disturbance (noncriminal)	29
Armed robbery	26
Traffic warrant	36
Accident (auto)	8

Note: From *Understanding Human Behavior for Effective Police Work* (2nd ed.), by H. Russell and A. Biegel, 1982, New York: Basic Books, Inc. Copyright 1982 by Basic Books, Inc. Reprinted with permission.

perpetrators, make sure that the crime scene is in no way changed, and maintain general order until relieved.

It may be necessary to detain witnesses, take names and addresses, or even arrest suspected perpetrators. When the detective assigned to that particular crime arrives, the patrol officer reports all these preliminary police actions and observations. After answering the detective's questions, the patrol officer may be sent back on patrol or may be asked to stay and maintain order at the crime scene.

Patrol officers develop a tremendous amount of "lore." It appears in no book or training manual. They learn it from other cops.

> On patrol at 11:00 P.M. Some suspicious characters are seen on the corner. The experienced patrol officer knows that after passing this group, putting on the brake lights will make them run. The experienced officer taps lightly with the emergency brake, which slows the car without signaling with brake lights that the patrol car is stopping. (Fletcher, 1991)

The complexity of patrol work is greater than that of the basic worker in any other profession. Cops are supposed to be nurturing, caretaking, sympathetic, gentle, teaching, commanding, demanding of respect, able to demonstrate courage and control, to withhold hostile impulses, and to meet great physical hazards. The patrol officer must control crowds; prevent riots; apprehend criminals; chase speeding vehicles; and deal with school traffic, illness and injury, delinquency, suicide, and missing persons (Levy, 1966).

The line police officer is "on duty" even when he or she is off duty. About half of all departments in the United States require officers to carry a concealed weapon when off duty and be prepared to intervene whenever they observe someone breaking the law. The remaining 50% of the departments recommend strongly that off-duty officers carry a weapon. In general, police officers off duty will act as police officers within their own jurisdiction (Fyfe, 1980). The unspoken and unwritten rule for a police officer traveling or visiting in another jurisdiction is "be a good witness, assist other officers when necessary, but make no arrests."

The Plainclothes Officer

Most police officers who move up to plainclothes duty are considered to be "detectives." In some cases, this is very formally designated; in small departments, it may be assumed. Most but not all police officers see promotion to plainclothes as a significant career step. This tends to be more so in large departments that in small agencies.

Detectives are part of the American persona of toughness. Lore, primarily from the motion pictures and television, represents detectives as having certain characteristics of gangsters. They are supposed to be tough, unorthodox, but ultimately humane. They cut through rigid rules, take shortcuts, and speak with brief, flat, hard statements. Terse language is their communication medium. These fictional heroes are hard-boiled, lower-middle-class, laconic, streetwise police officers in cheap suits who persistently and relentlessly pursue rich marauders and psychopathic killers (Wilkinson, 1984).

In reality, detective work is plodding, boring, and laborious. Although a prestigious assignment, it is difficult and requires a great deal of persistence and attention. When properly done, it frequently pays off. The plainclothes detective's essential job is to collect information, sort it out, and prepare reports and summaries. A tremendous amount of legwork and interviewing make up the detective's job. Detectives, or members of a criminal investigation division, meet regularly in staff meetings to review cases and to share information.

Most crimes that are going to be solved are solved within several days of the time of occurrence. Retrospective investigation by detectives solves very few crimes. Although this certainly happens—in some cases many years after the crime—it is the exception rather than the rule. Only when the victims or witnesses are able to identify the offender are crimes usually solved and the perpetrators brought to justice. The other crimes are essentially unsolvable because of the absence of useful clues. There is a great mythology of detectives clearing cases through long, arduous, painstaking investigation that covers months or years. Although techniques are available to deal with complex cases and advanced forensic science techniques are extremely helpful in establishing a chain of evidence, most crimes that are going to be solved by detectives are solved relatively early (Sparrow et al., 1990).

Generally, detectives receive a higher rate of pay than patrol officers and, in addition, sometimes have a greater opportunity for overtime work to increase their income. Detectives also have somewhat greater flexibility in the use of their time.

The larger the department, the more likelihood that plainclothes officers will specialize in their duties. Detectives may focus on commercial crime and fraud, vice, undercover operations, homicide, burglary, juvenile crimes, or sex crimes. Some of the largest departments even have detectives who specialize in crimes involving art and jewelry.

Desk Duty

Very few police officers enjoy desk duty. Uniformed officers are assigned duties at desks or at reception centers in police stations to deal with citizens who walk in with complaints or questions, or to process arrestees. In criminal investigation divisions, desk duty consists of answering the telephone, preparing reports, and sifting through information. As in many bureaucracies, the paperwork is enormous, seemingly unnecessary in many cases, and almost never brought up to date. Nevertheless, there are many essential clerical procedures such as developing rosters, assigning personnel to specific tasks, keeping work records, and planning assignments.

Forensic Science

The larger the department, the more likely that there will be forensic crime laboratories within the structure of the organization as well as mobile crime laboratories. In recent years, considerable training has been provided to local police departments in such esoteric techniques as blood-spatter analysis, hair and nail evaluation, fingerprint acquisition, crime scene photography, chemical analysis of materials, and more recently DNA analysis. Detectives are even trained to participate in autopsies to acquire as much information as possible in homicide cases. Small departments request forensic laboratory services from nearby larger departments, from state agencies, or in some cases from federal agencies.

With the growing body of information on crime scene analysis, centralized local, state, regional, and national forensic science laboratories are now available for a wide range of crime scene material analysis.

The primary purpose of forensic science in police work is to enhance the *chain of evidence*. Although it is the job of the police to apprehend the perpetrators of crimes, the American system of justice requires that a suspect be charged and tried before a conviction can be obtained. Police officers know that the chain of evidence is vital if the perpetrator is not to escape justice through some technicality. Forensic science and crime scene data can be vital for this purpose.

Undercover operations represent the most dangerous and most demanding plainclothes assignments. Undercover officers attempt to infiltrate an illegal operation and then to collect the necessary evidence to secure an arrest and conviction. Frequently, the officer must pose as a criminal or an aspiring criminal to gain the confidence of the target individual or group under surveillance. To be successful in undercover operations requires a special kind of commitment and personality. These qualifications will be addressed in some detail in Chapter Six.

Internal Affairs

The role of the internal affairs division in any police department is to investigate and report to the chief or to the commissioner or to the sheriff any wrongdoing by members of the department. Much of the work of the internal affairs division is in response to citizens' complaints.

Members of the internal affairs division are not held in high esteem in most departments. They are sometimes called "shooflies." Whenever a complaint of wrongdoing is received, the internal affairs division conducts an investigation to collect information that results in a complaint being sustained or not sustained, or in a finding of "exonerated" when the officer's action was found to have really occurred but was determined to be "reasonable." In most cities, approximately 5% of complaints against police officers are sustained. In such cases, the penalty is decided through some procedure within the department. It may range from a verbal reprimand to firing or even recommendations of criminal prosecution (Bailey, 1989).

A properly run internal affairs division is made up of some of the most intelligent and dedicated senior officers within a department. Their responsibility is heavy. They report directly to the top executive. It is a very stressful role.

Special Weapons and Tactics (SWAT)

This is a relatively new development in police function, which began around 1964 at the Philadelphia Police Department. The development of special weapons and tactics teams came about as a response to an alarming increase in bank robberies. This function was rapidly integrated into the work of the Los Angeles Police Department.

SWAT teams are a major departure for traditional police agencies and represent a new method of crisis management. Police executives recognize that highly motivated, specially armed, and specially trained officers, under expert leadership, can deal effectively with heavily armed criminals or hostage incidents.

SWAT teams are staffed by regular police officers who are selected after meeting certain stringent criteria. Currently, psychological testing is considered an important part of both selection for and maintenance of status on SWAT teams. Distinctive uniforms, special weapons, and scheduled training and planning exercises enhance such teams' effectiveness.

Most teams average about 12 men, who are usually divided into two groups: the assault group enters and clears structures, and the cover group protects the assault group and the perimeters of the operation.

SWAT teams are on 24-hour call. They frequently work in close cooperation with hostage negotiation teams, both in training and in action. The hostage negotiation team attempts to defuse volatile situations, where hostages have been taken. The SWAT team acts as a last resort, where negotiations fail (Kolman, 1982).

Public Relations

At one time, only the largest departments had a public information officer. Now, even small agencies maintain a public relations function. All cops believe that the media will look for the worst possible scenario in describing police officers and their work. The traditional approach has been to avoid the media, hoping for the best. In recent years, police managers have come to understand that the public is interested in police activities, as well as their outcome, and has the right to know what the police do and why they do it.

To address these concerns, many departments have a specific individual who functions as the public relations officer. This may be an experienced police officer who has an amiable personality and good rapport with the press. More recently, departments have hired professional media specialists who have a strong background in public relations and public information. They make contacts with the local media and reach out to provide realistic and complete information. Many departments have taken a proactive stance, using their public information department to present regular programs on the role and function of the police department within the community.

In no way has the preceding discussion presented the full range or details of what cops do. The *Encyclopedia of Police Science* is a useful resource for those who wish to learn more about the broad range of present-day police activities (Bailey, 1989).

THE POLICE BUREAUCRACY

Law enforcement agencies are enormously complex organizations whose administration involves executing government policies. Professional police administration has changed considerably over the years, particularly since the 1950s. Originally, police work was under strict and rigid central government control. The police were highly responsive to political pressures.

When the reform movement swept through American police departments, police bureaucracies changed. The new concept was to direct police activities by rational decision making. Efforts were made to separate politics from administration and to ensure that trained professionals directed law enforcement agencies. Part of the way this was accomplished was through civil service and merit system selection and promotion. As a result, top executives in various law enforcement agencies gained considerable independence from political processes.

The standard today remains professional police administration. One negative result, in the opinion of some, is that in a strictly professional law enforcement agency, the top executives have lost contact with the community itself. Being more concerned with strategies such as motorized patrol, highly complex communication systems, and increased use of forensic science, police managers have separated themselves from the community.

The latest changes in police administration have been instigated by an unfortunate fact: The professional model failed to achieve crime control in the 1970s and 1980s. It is likely that community-oriented policing will return as a major element of the police style in the 21st century.

The traditional three categories of police activity are (a) *operations tasks* (patrol, criminal investigation, traffic and traffic control, and other direct assistance to the public), (b) *administration tasks* (training, budgeting, personnel functions), and (c) *service tasks* (administration of the jails, detention of other sorts, communication and dispatch centers, and forensic laboratories). Again, it is traditional that administrative and service tasks function in support of operations.

Police administrators must manage the department's function as well as interaction with its environment. The *classical approach* to police administration is still operant in most jurisdictions. It emphasizes the structure of the department, unity of command, chain of command, clear-cut authority, and much detail in planning and controlling.

A more recent development is the *human relations approach*. It is beginning to dominate police administration. No one is quite sure how effective it is going to be in the future. This approach focuses on police productivity as a function of people productivity. Management of people is the prime focus of the police executive in this approach. Emphasis is on morale of personnel, communication, motivation, group dynamics, and leadership skills.

The most recent movement in police administration is the *strategic management approach*, which emphasizes establishing objectives and delineating tasks. Planning and task design are thought to lead to achievement of organizational objectives (Kaufman, 1991).

A number of departments focus on the *institutional approach*. In this method of management, the environment is held to be of greatest importance. Internal management duties are secondary to policy execution. This approach restores the police administrator's interest and involvement with political leaders, city managers, the media, the unions, and members of the community (Cordner, 1989).

Most law enforcement agencies have a fairly rigid chain of command. Although tasks and responsibilities may vary considerably from department to department, they tend to reflect the pattern described in the following paragraphs.

Sergeants and Corporals

Sergeants and corporals are first-line supervisors. Sometimes they are instructors and sometimes they are "the boss." They tend to be the first leader at the scene of the crime, called into play by the first responder. The crime is reported, and the line supervisor goes to the scene to take charge and to direct operations until a higher officer or specialist arrives. The less important the case, the less likely that a higher officer will be on the scene; the corporal or sergeant will probably direct the entire operation.

The Lieutenant

Lieutenants are shift commanders. Sometimes they function as desk officers or unit commanders. They are second in command to many units and will take over when the captain is unavailable. Where sergeants may be responsible for 6 to 12 officers, lieutenants may supervise 30 to 50 personnel. Lieutenants are frequently required to record events in a log or a ledger.

Captains

Captains, who are middle managers in any police agency, have much power. They command a unit that serves either specific functions or geographic locations. They are highly experienced police officers who show some capacity for leadership and organization. They exercise a considerable amount of discretion. They are the "whips" who ensure proper and timely completion of all the paperwork and casework.

Officers advance up the ladder by taking both written and oral promotional examinations. In some cases, an *assessment center* is used for promotional purposes. Assessment center procedures are described in Chapter Six.

If the agency is governed by civil service, the top executives have little or no control about hiring and firing. Where the chief executive officer is an elected official (usually a sheriff), civil service rarely applies and the top executives can have a significant effect on the selection and promotion of middle managers.

The Chief Executive Officer

The top executive in a local law enforcement agency is likely to be a *chief*, a *sheriff*, or a *commissioner*. This officer sets the tone for the department.

Where the chief is open, available, and community oriented, the department will tend to be that way. Should the chief be more traditional, limited, overly aggressive, or manipulative, members of the department will reflect this in their behavior.

The Underbosses

The undersheriff, the chief deputy, the deputy commissioner, and the deputy chief all represent the second level of executive power. They act as the chief's expediters. The larger the agency, the larger the number of underbosses. This level of executive management serves as a conduit passing on the chief's expectations to lower level supervisors, and filtering information from the department back to the chief.

This brief review can only illustrate in general the complexity of the police bureaucracy as well as the diversity from department to department.

THE PERSONALITY OF POLICE OFFICERS

The psychological and sociological research literature offers relatively little information about the personality of police officers. This is not to suggest that social scientists are incapable of delineating characteristics and traits that may be associated with effective versus ineffective policing. It is simply an area that has attracted relatively little interest. Research studies that are available generally focus on the search for pathology.

Early studies of the police personality (Rokeach, Miller, & Snyder, 1971) suggest that police are different from other occupational groupings in their attitudes and beliefs. According to this research, police officers tend to place relatively low value on such things as independence, freedom, equality, and aesthetics. By contrast, they tend to place a relatively high value on self-control, obedience to the organizational structure, a comfortable life now and in the future, and the pursuit of pleasure.

Reiser (1972) stated very simply "There is no police personality."

Alpert and Dunham (1986) asked police officers to evaluate aspects of their own behavior. A factor analysis indicated that police officers believe that the effective cop has judgment, initiative, ability to deal in human relationships, dependability, the ability to get along, and a capacity to use discretion. The "good cop" is yet to be defined (Fyfe, 1988).

Even if research effort were directed more extensively to the study of the police personality, considerable difficulties would arise in conducting such research. Part of the police spirit includes telling no one more than the person has to know. Every police officer has important information that he or she does not share with anyone (Breckenridge, 1949).

Being a cop means being part of a secret society where loyalty, silence, and a kind of isolation are endemic. Most cops tend to learn early in their careers that no one understands them except other cops. This makes it extremely difficult to study police officers as well as to provide them with adequate mental health services.

The behavioral scientist who intends to work with police officers must never lose sight of certain cogent realities. The average cop handles the worst of society. Detectives and investigators handle the most significant, high-profile cases (the criminals who upset society the most). Cops observe the human individual's dark underside. They are called on to control other people's worst instincts and appetites, and as a result, they become profoundly skeptical. Civilians don't and probably can't understand cops (Bouza, 1990).

The Public Persona and the Public View

Much of what people think of police officers reflects their experience with the media rather than personal interactions with police. Many motion pictures, books, and television dramas depict police work since this subject seems to fascinate the general public. The American cop is presented as tough, sentimental, risk-taking; funny, wisecracking, naive; willing to bend the rules in the interest of closing a case; often crooked, devious, manipulative, and brutal; and constantly involved with high risk and evil individuals. Relatively invulnerable to personal injury or death, the public persona of the police officer is one of masculine derring-do.

Officer candidates at the police academy often view police work in this media style. Within 3 or 4 weeks of attendance at the academy, they find out that the job is considerably different than anticipated and requires qualities and traits that they may not have or wish to utilize.

The American public has always held relatively negative attitudes toward police as overzealous enforcers and unfair possessors of power. These attitudes became more prevalent during the turbulent and rebellious period between 1960 and 1980. Police officers were almost singled out as the focal point for the frustrations of a society in turmoil. This was an extremely difficult period for most police officers, who really wished to be seen as "good guys."

The public view of police in the United States is very different from that of many other cultures. American police officers are idealized as persons who should be perfect. They should be helpful, available, brave, honest, dedicated, and possess a host of other altruistic characteristics. In addition, they should always present a cheerful attitude.

At a recent meeting, the head of the German police agencies, in describing the role and mission of German police officers, indicated that German cops are not social workers. They are only interested in the enforcement of the law and the arrest of criminals. He scoffed at the American attitude of providing all sorts of personal services to the citizenry. He suggested that if social work services are that necessary, they should build a social work station next to the police station.

In the United States, the citizens expect police officers to be social workers and more. They must direct people where they want to go, get cats down from trees, administer first aid, help people cross the street, give lectures to children to enhance parental discipline, and perform a variety of other "courtesy" tasks. In reality, the average American police officer spends about 85% of working hours providing such community service. One of the young police officer's most difficult tasks is to learn to accept that the general population includes large numbers of people who resent the presence of a police officer—not only "bad people" but others who have simply developed antipolice attitudes with no substantial basis for this prejudice.

The Private Persona

Very little of the cop's real world ever becomes known to the general public. Police officers tend to be isolated in many ways and resist intrusion into this isolation. They reveal what they have to reveal. The ability to evade, deny, and withhold is an inherent part of the police job and the inner personality of the experienced police officer.

Although cops laugh at what they see on the media, they will generally do nothing to dispel the public's distorted view of their work. Cops are pretty happy to promote the image of heroism, constant terror on the job, danger, and other elements that sell entertainment. This is not only a part of maintaining a somewhat positive image in the eyes of the public, but also a way of enhancing the secretness that is so much a part of police work.

Cops are basically cynical and hardheaded. They will talk with nonpolice officers (civilians) and often agree with the civilian's suggestion that a certain television show is realistic. This cynical agreement with what they know is absolutely false is sometimes referred to, among themselves, as "pissing in their pockets and telling them it's raining."

Generally, the line officer considers the media to be the enemy. Almost every police officer has had his or her words or acts distorted, overblown, or confused by the media. Newspeople always seem to be in a rush to provide news or entertainment. Most cops develop a superficial, pleasant, cooperative attitude in responding to the media, but in reality, they deflect probing questions and explorations.

Cops are generally physically brave and willing to take risks. They tend to have an absolute belief that this is part of their role and they must be prepared to play it at all times. Physical courage is characteristic of most cops, but moral courage can become bent, often as a result of the "us against the world" attitude.

Cops bond together by sharing dangerous experiences, secrets, power, and even special language.

Most cops are good people. Probably less than 1% of police officers ever do anything seriously bad. The opportunity is certainly ever present. It is heartening to realize that few officers actually fall by the wayside. Why would this be so? In all probability, it is some combination of certain factors that are necessary for success in police work. Cops see themselves as protectors of the community. They are fearful of disappointing partners, supervisors, and their department. Cops fear losing the respect of the community, of their family, and of their children. There is great satisfaction from a self-conceptualization as "the good guy" who helps people in distress. When cops go bad (or are "bent"), all of this is lost, including the respect of partners and colleagues (Lohman & Misler, 1966; Skolnick, 1967; Southworth, 1990; Wilson, 1963).

In a study of policemen's view of themselves versus what they considered the "ideal" officer, 99 police officers from three different departments were asked to describe the ideal police officer. There was almost total agreement that the ideal officer should be good at his or her work, decisive, active, strong, fast, right (versus wrong), responsive, masculine, flexible, and considerate. They also felt that such traits as firmness with warmth and not too much distance would be extremely helpful. Most officers felt that they came close but did not meet the ideal (Storms, Penn, & Tenzell, 1988).

WOMEN IN POLICING

Policing has always been considered to be a job for men. Traditionally, the police officer has been characterized as a stolid, tough, courageous, and relatively powerful male figure, intimidating, and willing to take risks. This job-profile is in conflict with the traditional view of the nature and capacities of women.

The advent of affirmative action has established the right of women to apply for and to obtain jobs in policing. Currently, slightly less than 10% of police officers throughout the country are women. This, however, represents a major change during the past two decades (1970–1990). In the early 1970s, less than 2% of police officers were women (Eisenberg, Kent, & Wall, 1973).

Historical Development

Toward the end of the 19th century, police departments began to hire a very small number of women. This was not part of the social revolution or affirmative action. Policing had become so complex a community service that police executives believed certain jobs could be better served by women officers. Women were first hired to deal with policing problems involving juveniles and women. Women police officers at the end of the

19th century and the beginning of the 20th century enforced laws concerning women and children, supervised recreational centers where juveniles and women might get into trouble, and served as matrons in custodial settings.

In 1915, the International Association of Police Women was founded (Price & Gavin, 1982). Throughout the early 1900s, women continued to function as social workers, matrons, and custodial personnel. They were certainly not thought of as "real" police officers. Patrol work was considered to be far too dangerous and physically demanding for a woman.

It was not until the 1950s that women were allowed to compete with men for openings in police academies, for patrol jobs, and for promotion.

Police Women Today

After the 1950s, more and more women began to apply for jobs as law enforcement officers, and to challenge the myth that women were not capable of doing this job. Early prejudices decreed that women did not have the upper body strength to do police work, that they were overly emotional, and that they would be horrified by the kinds of things that police officers must face and must do. They were considered to be without objectivity and simply too "illogical" (Bell, 1982).

As more and more women entered the law enforcement workforce, studies began to emerge that demonstrated somewhat more objectively women's capacity to do the job. Indeed, the research has indicated over the years that policewomen tend to imitate male personality characteristics and even to go beyond their male partners in risk taking and aggressiveness to prove that they are capable (Kennedy & Homant, 1981; Lester, Gronau, & Wondrack, 1982).

The road has been rocky for women in seeking acceptance by their male counterparts. Male officers have traditionally protected (or overprotected) their territory. Women were at first and, to some extent today, considered "civilians" rather than "real cops." By and large, the policing styles and strategies of male and female police officers are more alike than they are different (Lord, 1989). Grennan (1987) reports that female police officers do not react any differently to violent incidents in comparison with male officers. He does point out, however, that among male officers there is a higher rate of weapons discharge in comparison with female officers. He suggests that the female officer tends to have a less aggressive personality and perhaps better negotiating skills. Despite great strides, however, the ranks of male police officers still tend to believe that female officers should "think like men, work like dogs, and act like ladies" (Martin, 1980).

It appears evident that women can attain levels of fitness and skill well within the demands of police patroling (Charles, 1982). Although some women are not suitable for police work, this is also true for large numbers of men. Modern policing requires the dispelling of some of the antifeminine attitudes within police organizations (Bouza, 1978).

THE FORESEEABLE FUTURE

The complexity of police work may be greater than that of any other profession, and it is likely to become even more complex. Public expectation (as well as the expectation of police themselves) requires the working police officer to be nurturing, caregiving, sympathetic, gentle, teaching, commanding, and demanding of respect; able to demonstrate courage, maintain control, and meet great hazards; and all while resisting hostile impulses. Police officers must control crowds, prevent riots, apprehend criminals, and chase speeding vehicles. They must deal with school traffic, illness, injury, delinquency, suicide, and missing persons. This is just the beginning (Levy, 1966). The mission of the police continues to be the preservation of peace, the protection of life and property, the detection and arrest of offenders, and the prevention of crime (Bouza, 1990).

To accomplish this mission requires men and women of unusual skill, talent, and perseverance. For psychologists to be useful in this important social institution, they must understand the complexity of the police job. Police officers are not simply "another patient target population." The men and women who serve the community as police officers are for the most part dedicated, admirable professionals. As the job of policing becomes more complex and demanding, psychological services can become increasingly useful in ensuring effective performance of duties as well as maintenance of personal quality of life. To help police officers, psychologists would do well to recognize them as skillful and dedicated professionals.

CHAPTER THREE

Psychological Services for Law Enforcement

In the 19th century Gilbert and Sullivan operetta *Pirates of Penzance,* one scene involves a squad of British police officers who sing "A Policeman's Lot Is Not a Happy One." What was written over 100 years ago about police officers is both true and not true. Sometimes the police officer's lot is a very happy one, and sometimes it is, indeed, quite miserable. The general public finds this range of satisfaction difficult to understand. As noted previously, police officers seldom reveal how they really view their jobs or how they feel about their profession except to other police officers. Even careful researchers who interview police officers rarely get the whole story or even the real story. Cop novels and television police dramas mislead researchers as well as the general public.

The police officer's job differs from place to place, and policing in the United States differs significantly from policing in other parts of the world. As was detailed in Chapter Two, American police officers are expected to take much more individual responsibility and to make more on-the-spot decisions than their counterparts in Europe and other parts of the world.

The police officer's mission, the community's expectations, the jurisdiction of the police department served, and the statutes of the state in which it operates make understanding the stresses and problems in the police officer's life an extremely complex task. There are times, however, when the police officer's lot is certainly not a happy one. To do their job effectively, police officers must be especially flexible and skillful individuals, able to tolerate enormous stress. They frequently need help as they begin to buckle under the strain. Psychology has been helpful and can become even more helpful in promoting the welfare of law enforcement officers and officials. This capability in turn would promote the welfare of the communities being served.

Psychologists did not enter into supportive or helpful roles with law enforcement until around 1950 (Hoover, 1989). Early efforts primarily involved selection of police recruits and family crisis intervention (Bard, 1970).

In 1968, the Los Angeles Police Department hired the first full-time, in-house staff psychologist. In 1973, the Police Task Force in their report of the National Commission on Criminal Justice Standards and Goals included a section detailing the needs for behavioral science resources in police agencies (Reiser, 1982a).

The Federal Bureau of Investigation, and in particular the Behavioral Science Unit of the FBI Academy in Quantico, Virginia, has been instrumental in the growth of interest and opportunities for police psychology. For many years, the FBI Behavioral Science Unit has applied psychological science and practice to the understanding of criminals, their *modus operandi*, and their apprehension. In more recent years, the unit has focused interest on the kinds of psychological stresses that plague law enforcement officers.

In the fall of 1984, the Behavioral Science Unit hosted a major conference at the FBI Academy concerning the police services that psychologists may render to local departments. Approximately 150 psychologists and law enforcement executives attended that meeting. Over 60 papers were presented describing the range of services that were being made available to law enforcement agencies around the country (Reese & Goldstein, 1986).

The initial conference was so successful that requests for an additional conference came from all parts of the United States as well as from more than 20 countries around the world. This led to the International Conference on Police Psychology, which took place, again at the FBI Academy, at the end of 1985. The participants spent 5 days exchanging information about the provision of behavioral science services to law enforcement agencies (Reese & Horn, 1988).

Continuing its support and seminal leadership, the Federal Bureau of Investigation's Behavioral Science Unit sponsored a third major conference in 1989 on critical incidents in policing (Reese, Horn, & Dunning, 1992).

The networks established at these meetings not only exist today but have been expanded considerably. Consulting psychologists to law enforcement agencies and those who are staff members in such agencies continue to meet, to correspond, and to exchange information.

Following the second FBI-sponsored meeting, several police psychological organizations were formed. The Council of Police Psychological Services (COPPS) and the Academy of Police Psychologists (APP) developed to continue the networking and to establish standards and guidelines for the provisions of psychological services to law enforcement agencies. Appendix B presents the Annual Report given at the APP meeting in April of 1991.

The number of roles served by psychologists working with police departments has increased rapidly since the early 1980s. Most large departments now have behavioral science units, and even small departments utilize the services of psychologists who work independently or in larger organizations (Fitzhugh, 1984; Hoover, 1989).

In some instances, agencies requesting psychological services follow a bidding procedure specified by the community and issue a *Request for Proposal* (RFP). The RFP designates exactly what services will be required and frequently indicates the number of hours that should be devoted to such services. Appendix C presents an RFP recently issued by a sheriff's department for psychological services. Psychologists seeking to be consultants to police agencies can expect this kind of competitive bidding procedure more and more in the future. Appendix D illustrates a proposal responding to the RFP in Appendix C.

On the other hand, psychological services sometimes are the outcome of the interaction between the psychologist and an individual member of the agency. The following letter, received from a psychologist who had taken a workshop in police psychology, illustrates this kind of interaction:

Dear Dr. Blau:

I have been meaning to write to you for some time to tell you that I really enjoyed the workshop you gave on Police Psychology last spring. You presented a lot of helpful information in a short period of time. As a direct result of taking your seminar, I have significantly increased my consultative work with the XXX Police Department.

My partner, XXX, MD, and I started doing preemployment psychologicals for the XXX Police Department in 1979. The screening process quickly evolved to what is in effect at the present time. Applicants for the XXX Police Department must have at least two years of college credit. The department identifies qualified applicants who are seen for psychological evaluation and medical evaluation prior to the final decision being made about hiring. A number of years ago, the department stopped using an Oral Board approach. Applicants are given MMPIs, CPIs (for positive personality characteristics), produce several writing samples, and are interviewed. Interviews address communication skills, ability to think clearly on their feet, motivation for law enforcement work, relevant attitudes, and judgment. In the past 12 years we have screened over 700 applicants. We periodically check our ratings to ensure there is no ethnic or sexual bias. By all accounts, the procedure has worked very well, and I have found it to be transportable. We have used the same procedure to select officers for the XXX, Florida, Police Department, a very small department, with good results. I hope sometime we will have the opportunity to have an in-depth discussion contrasting the selection procedure you use with the one we have developed.

At about the time I took your seminar, the XPD approached me about doing all of their Fitness-for-Duty evaluations. I had done a few of these in the past on special occasions. Most Fitness-for-Duty evaluations were done by XXX Counseling Clinic, a local group of psychologists and counselors who have held what is essentially an Employee Assistance Program (EAP) contract to provide therapy services to police department employees and their families for a number of years. Clearly, it was appropriate to separate the counseling from the Fitness-for-Duty evaluations.

After returning from your seminar, I met with the new Assistant Chief and the XPD's Administrative Supervisor to discuss ways we might increase my involvement with the department. Your seminar gave me a lot of good ideas and some "ammunition." Knowing that psychological selection and annual reevaluation of tactical team members was an "optional" under the accreditation standards, I brought that up for discussion. It was agreed that I would perform brief evaluations on applicants for openings on the TAC Team (negotiators, entry team, and snipers) and do annual reevaluations based on current MMPI-2s and brief interviews. This led to further discussion with the TAC Team commander (who happened to be a former student of mine when I taught at XXX more than a few years ago). He asked me to be a consultant to the TAC Team, to participate in any of their training that I wanted to attend, and issued me a bulletproof vest. I now am routinely called out with the TAC Team in either hostage or barricade situations. I have participated in training exercises (e.g., "shooting" recruits when they improperly search buildings), and two weeks ago I attended the FBI Hostage Negotiation Training Program.

Hopefully, the department will sponsor me to attend additional courses, including courses on offender profiling. One of the reasons I wanted to write was because I had been having so much professional fun with the new professional challenges. Attending your workshop helped me open some of the doors. Ours is a very large department, in a university town. In contrast to the situation where your becoming a sworn officer helped your credibility, my impression is that the department values my input because I am a psychologist and *not* a cop. Of course, a 12-year track record with the preemployment selection program earned me some degree of credibility with the department.

The second reason for writing is to inquire further about the Police Psychology interest group you mentioned in the seminar. Do you have more specifications on it?

Lastly, if you should decide to offer a longer, more in-depth training program in Police Psychology some time in the future, I would be very interested in participating.

Signature

Whereas early interaction between psychologists and law enforcement agencies tended to be reactive, in recent years, psychologists have reached out to be more helpful and more proactive through practical experience and research (Blanch, 1977; Ostrov, 1986a; Trotter, 1987).

STANDARDS FOR LAW ENFORCEMENT AGENCIES

Beginning in the 1980s, concerns about standards for law enforcement at the local level emerged. The Commission on Accreditation for Law Enforcement Agencies was formed and produced *Standards for Law Enforcement Agencies* (1989). These standards are of particular importance to psychologists, because they are the first formulated national standards for law enforcement that include expectations for psychological services.

The standards were originally developed by four major law enforcement executive member associations: the International Association of Chiefs of Police (IACP), the National Organization of Black Law Enforcement Executives (NOBLE), the National Sheriff's Association (NSA), and the Police Executive Research Forum (PERF). The purpose of the commission is to develop an accreditation process that would provide state and local law enforcement agencies with an opportunity to voluntarily demonstrate that they have met an established set of law enforcement standards.

In this compilation, over 900 standards are organized under 48 topic headings. Included are such areas as Law Enforcement Role and Authority, Relationships with Other Agencies, Organization, Direction, Promotional Issues, Training, Selection, Performance Evaluation, Law Enforcement Operations (Patrol, Criminal Investigation, Organized Crime and Vice Control, Juvenile Operations, Crime Prevention, Unusual Occurrences), and Operational Support (Intelligence, Internal Affairs, Inspectional Services, Public Information, and Community Relations). Standards were also developed to cover traffic operations, prisoner and court-related activities, and auxiliary as well as technical services.

The majority of the standards were considered to be "mandatory." Accredited agencies must comply with all applicable mandatory standards as well as with 80 percent of the nonmandatory standards.

The process of accreditation requires that an agency make application, complete a questionnaire, conduct a complete self-assessment, and successfully pass an on-site assessment by the Commission Review. It is a long process, generally taking several years. Accreditation is for a 5-year period; at the end of the 5th year, the individual agency must apply for reaccreditation.

The roles of psychologists are addressed directly and indirectly throughout the Accreditation Standards. Under "Selection," the standards speak to the selection processes using only those components that have been documented as having *validity, utility,* and *minimum adverse impact.* Any written tests used in the selection process must be documented as having utility, validity, and minimum affirmative action adverse impact. The standards further mandate a written directive within the agency stating that all tests will be administered, scored, evaluated, and interpreted in a standard and uniform manner. Test materials must be stored in a secure area and that the selection process be evaluated annually.

An "emotional stability and psychological fitness examination" using valid, useful, and nondiscriminatory procedures must be conducted on every police candidate prior to appointment to probationary status. The standards state specifically that psychiatric and psychological assessments are required to screen out candidates who might not be able to carry out their responsibilities as police officers or to endure the stress of the working conditions found in law enforcement.

The standards also mandate that only qualified psychologists or psychiatrists will be utilized by an agency to assess the emotional stability and psychological fitness of candidates. The primary purpose of this is to ensure proper interpretation and legal defensibility of the selection process.

Under "Special Operations," the standards indicate that officers assigned to Special Weapons and Tactical (SWAT) teams or decoy operations should be carefully selected, using psychological screening examinations. The standards further require that members of special units be tested annually by a licensed psychologist or psychiatrist to identify any symptoms that might be debilitating to the officer or the officer's mission.

In the section describing hostage negotiation operations, the standards specify special criteria for selecting officers who will serve on hostage negotiating teams. Included will be the passing of a psychological screening examination "including an MMPI test and a clinical interview with a licensed psychologist or psychiatrist."

The original goals of accreditation are to increase law enforcement agency capabilities for preventing and controlling crime, to increase agency effectiveness and efficiency in the delivery of law enforcement services, to increase cooperation and coordination with other law enforcement agencies and with other agencies in the criminal justice system, and finally to increase citizen and employee confidence in the goals, objectives, policies, and practices of the agencies. The psychological services delineated in these standards are an important part of the accreditation procedures.

Although psychologists should view the standards as a major step toward integrating psychological services within law enforcement agencies, they are really only a beginning. The standards address selection, special duty evaluation, selection for special assignments, and some reference to fitness for duty. Provisions are made for annual tracking and for having a psychologist available to help in emergency situations. The standards do not identify a wide range of psychological services currently being provided to police departments such as stress inoculation or treatment, critical incident counseling, employee assistance programs, peer-counselor training, investigative hypnosis, family and marital counseling, the psychological autopsy as an investigative tool, psychological profiling, morale surveys, and drug and alcohol treatment.

Appendix A presents the information from a brochure listing all the psychological services available in a medium-size law enforcement agency. This brochure describes more than 30 individual kinds of services. It is a good example of how professional psychological services become an integral part of an agency that has grown aware of their usefulness.

Although the initial interest in psychological services by law enforcement agencies was prompted by an effort to protect the agency in the event of litigation (Flanagan, 1986), current use by both large and small agencies has gone far beyond this purpose.

A SPECIALTY IN TRANSITION

Police psychology may well be the newest emerging specialty in professional psychology (Loo, 1986). A multitude of problems requiring the attention of psychologists have gradually emerged as psychologists gain experience in the law enforcement mission. For example, police psychologists have learned that police managers suffer stress in their decision making, in responding to time pressures and variations in work load, and in dealing with the uncertainties of the work environment. Many managers in law enforcement have major responsibilities with limited authority. This constriction often leads to role conflict, ambiguity, and great answerability regarding subordinates but little participation in organizational decision making.

As a specialty in emergence, police psychology can only be described in its current status. Further applications and utilization are bound to occur. The development during the 1980s and early 1990s of a variety of psychological services to law enforcement is likely to continue (Delprino & Bahn, 1988; Norton, 1986).

The sources or stimuli for new psychological services frequently come from individual law enforcement officers. Line officers make requests for marital counseling, family services, and individual counseling; whereas police managers seek help in strategic planning, the improvement of morale, and the establishment of more efficient hostage negotiation activities. Criminal investigators have begun to call on psychologists to provide investigative hypnosis, sensitivity and restraint training, and crime scene analysis.

THE PSYCHOLOGICAL CONSULTANT

At this time, most psychologists who work with law enforcement act as consultants or contract employees. The degree to which a consultant can be effective in police work depends a great deal on who the consultant serves and to whom the consultant reports. If the consultant has been retained and has initial contact with upper management, there will probably be a good deal of involvement in organizational diagnosis and development issues. The higher the level of interaction, the more likely the psychologist will be involved in evaluating the department's status and making recommendations for problem solving. This might include such issues as the street cop versus the brass, poor upward communications among rank levels, and overemphasis on negative discipline. Every consultant can expect a good deal of initial caution and hostility on the part of the people he or she works with. Suspicion and distrust accompany the stereotypes on both sides of the interface. Openness and sensitivity are required, and the psychologist must readily present these qualities. An attitude of humility and willingness to listen is helpful. The psychologist working as a consultant must be willing to accept and tolerate the slowness of change commonly found in bureaucratic institutions. One of the most important attributes for the consultant (or staff member, for that matter) is patience (Reiser & Klyver, 1987).

If possible, the consultant should report directly to the chief or the sheriff. By having a close association with the highest possible level in the organization, the consultant can obtain the support necessary to effect recommendations involving change and innovation.

The advantages and disadvantages for the psychologist who serves as a contract employee or a consultant might be summarized as follows:

Advantages

1. Autonomy and distance can be maintained.
2. There is somewhat less bureaucratic interference with the psychologist's job.
3. There is a minimizing of dual relationship problems.
4. The kinds of deliverable services tend to be broader and more flexible.
5. It is easier to maintain confidentiality.
6. There are fewer pressures for the psychologist to be all things to all people.
7. The psychologist has an opportunity to serve other agencies.
8. It allows for the introduction of broader applications and newer psychological techniques.
9. It is probably more lucrative.

Disadvantages

1. A "distance" or a barrier between the psychologist and the staff tends to exist because the law enforcement officers form a "closed society."
2. The range of services is generally capped at the narrowest level, for fiscal and administrative reasons.
3. Psychologists rarely get complete feedback on the services they provide.
4. The psychologist is viewed as an outsider and in some instances does not get the full story as to how and why services are being requested.
5. There is much less opportunity for the psychologist to make recommendations and suggestions to management based on full participation in the functioning of the organization.
6. There is less opportunity for research.

THE IN-HOUSE OR STAFF PSYCHOLOGIST

The psychologist who is a staff member in a law enforcement agency has certain advantages as a member of the establishment. There is a ready access to confidential personnel information. As a full-time staff member, the psychologist acquires hands-on experience with applications of a wide range of psychological services fairly rapidly. This exposure allows for a more rapid and more thorough generalization of the psychologist's skills. The psychologist who spends full time in a law enforcement agency acquires credibility and confidence as a member of the department.

The advantages and disadvantages of a psychologist being a staff member might be generally described as follows:

Advantages

1. Salary is predictable.
2. There are health and retirement benefits.
3. There is a sense of identification and involvement with the organization.
4. The psychologist knows the clear-cut lines of authority and his or her responsibilities.
5. The psychologist is closely involved with budgetary planning and has an opportunity to "campaign" for an increased behavioral science budget.
6. The psychologist learns the unspoken and unwritten rules that are necessary in exerting influence within a law enforcement agency.

7. There is ample opportunity for research.
8. It is easier to initiate new kinds of services by first exploring them informally.
9. The psychologist gets prompt informal feedback as to how services are being received and the development of positive and negative attitudes by officers concerning these services.
10. The psychologist is able to develop a network that helps in dealing with conflicts and opportunities.

Disadvantages

1. The psychologist is a staff member subject to the bureaucratic stresses and the antagonisms of entrenched staff members who may feel threatened by "psychology."
2. The staff member may be overwhelmed with requests and demands for service far beyond his or her realistic capabilities.
3. Along with other law enforcement staff members, the psychologist is subject to a host of minor criticisms, backbiting, and resentment.
4. There are limits on the flexibility of choice in working time, working conditions, and financial opportunity.
5. Dual relationship issues and ethical constraints are more likely to occur with the in-house psychologist than with the consultant.
6. It is all but impossible for the in-house psychologist to develop any kind of long-term therapeutic services for law enforcement officers and/or their families.
7. Continual stresses and pressures occur as the psychologist deals with expectations and demands of staff members that may involve serious ethical dilemmas.

These factors are not all-inclusive. These issues will be addressed in more detail in future chapters.

There are many more bureaucratic and administrative requirements for the in-house psychologist than for the consultant. The paperwork can be extensive. The in-house psychologist must follow a job description and revise it as the job changes. The job description on p. 54 is for a police psychologist in a county sheriff's agency.

In addition to satisfying the job description, most in-house psychologists must conduct a job task analysis (pp. 55–56) to meet the bureaucratic requirements of the agency.

JOB DESCRIPTION

JOB SPECIFICATION TITLE   DIRECTOR, BEHAVIORAL SCIENCE UNIT

FUNCTION

Work involves providing psychological expert guidance and consultation to line officers and management to enhance the general mission of law enforcement by the XXX Sheriff's Office. This work also involves development of psychological screening and evaluation instruments as needed. This position reports directly to the Undersheriff/Sheriff. Also included in responsibilities is the supervision of Postdoctoral fellow in Police Psychology.

CRITICAL TASKS

1. Offers initial consultation to officers and families seeking resolution of problems.
2. Conducts psychological autopsies, serial rapist profiles, and psychological profiles of serial murderers, as required.
3. Consults with Director of Personnel and personnel staff on testing procedures and results.
4. Offers crisis consultation to deputies and families following traumatic incidents.
5. Advises/serves on Hostage Negotiation Team.
6. Develops/implements stress relief programs.
7. Participates in continuing educational programs.
8. Performs related work as required.

MAJOR WORK CHARACTERISTICS

1. Knowledge of group process, social/psychological data, principles of learning, abnormal psychology, stress research, health and wellness psychology, neuropsychology, and forensic psychology.
2. Ability to conduct, train, and supervise psychological assessment, crisis intervention, individual and group therapy, identification of and treatment planning for chemical dependence.
3. Ability to provide management consultation.
4. Skills needed to prepare proposals and background briefing for research projects.

MINIMUM REQUIREMENTS (PREFERRED AND REQUIRED)

PhD in clinical psychology; one-year predoctoral and one-year postdoctoral clinical internship; possession of State of XXX License for the practice of psychology; expertise in police psychology.

WORKING CONDITIONS

Office environment. On call during crisis situations.

JOB TASK ANALYSIS

BUREAU/BRANCH _____Executive Bureau_____   **DATE** _____

DIVISION _____Behavioral Science Unit_____   **OTHER** _____

JOB CLASSIFICATION _____Director_____

DUTIES

To provide psychological services to the XXX Sheriff's Office and its employees. To train and supervise the postdoctoral fellow.

RESPONSIBILITIES

To oversee and ensure that the Behavioral Science Unit is operating effectively and efficiently. To fulfill requests for services in an ethical and professional manner.

Tasks—Prioritized in Order of Importance	Frequency of Tasks
1. Selection of interpretation for law enforcement applicants.	3–10 hrs monthly
2. Fitness-for-duty evaluations to establish an employee's psychological fitness to serve as a law enforcement or corrections officer.	1–6 hrs monthly
3. Critical incident counseling following traumatic events.	Depends on External Factors
4. Individual counseling as requested by agency employees.	1–5 hrs monthly
5. Family and marital counseling.	1–5 hrs monthly
6. Research projects. At present, the BSU is developing and implementing a preemployment psychological testing battery for corrections officers.	As time permits
7. Supervision. To supervise, evaluate, and review the services provided by the postdoctoral fellow.	20–30 hrs monthly
8. Special Testing. To provide psychological services to XXX spouses and families.	4–5 hrs monthly
9. Training. To train XXX employees in various fields that will facilitate and foster higher functional performance.	7–10 hrs monthly
10. Administrative Consultation. To advise administration, when requested, on matters with psychological indexes.	1–5 hrs monthly
11. Consultation with agency departments to assist with investigations.	4–10 hrs monthly

Tasks—*Prioritized in Order of Importance*	*Frequency of Tasks*
12. Consultation with external agencies as directed by the Sheriff/Undersheriff.	4–10 hrs monthly
13. Department administration and clerical activities.	6–20 hrs weekly
14. Continuing education and certification credits to keep abreast with advances in police and clinical psychology.	40–100 hrs annually
15. Field Work. To apply knowledge to field and to maintain proficiency in policing techniques.	6–10 hrs monthly
16. Investigative hypnosis and profiling to assist law enforcement personnel in furthering criminal cases.	5–10 hrs annually
17. Promotion Board. To assist in the decision-making process.	5–10 hrs annually
18. Smoking Cessation Clinics. To promote better health habits among XXX Sheriff's Office employees.	6–12 hrs annually
19. Library Research. To keep interested persons abreast with various topics by reprinting news and research articles from around the world.	4–10 hrs annually

MINIMUM LEVEL OF PROFICIENCY NECESSARY IN JOB-RELATED SKILLS

Must be versed in theory and practice of counseling, psychotherapy, testing standardization, testing procedures, data analysis, testing interpretation, and the law enforcement profession.

MEANS BY WHICH CHARACTERISTICS MAY BE ACQUIRED

1. Graduate school and related training.
2. Law enforcement academy.

MINIMUM QUALIFICATIONS

1. PhD in clinical psychology.
2. Certification as a law enforcement officer.

METHODS FOR MEASURING OR TESTING THESE QUALIFICATIONS

1. Peer review.
2. Appropriate documentation of qualifications.
3. Research.

ADDITIONAL COMMENTS IMPORTANT BUT NOT PREVIOUSLY MENTIONED

An additional way to assess services being provided is to review monthly reports. Psychological services are requested sporadically, sometimes surpassing 70 hours per week and at times being less than 35 hours per week.

CIVILIAN OR SWORN OFFICER?

In the preceding Job Task Analysis, one of the requirements was that the psychologist be a sworn officer. At this time, there are probably less than 100 psychologists working with law enforcement agencies who are also sworn police officers.

In the early days of applying behavioral science techniques to law enforcement, the work was done by sworn officers with minimal professional qualifications. It soon became evident that greater expertise was required in applying psychological methods to the law enforcement establishment, and psychologists were added as consultants and staff members. In many cases, this was a welcome change for the agency because it was considered prestigious to have a "doctor" of psychology on the staff or as consultant.

There was no great movement among police managers to encourage sworn officers to move toward obtaining advanced degrees in psychology, nor for psychologists to become police officers. In spite of superficial acceptance, there is still a strong underlying tone of suspicion and skepticism about using psychological science in conducting police business.

A police psychologist who is also a sworn officer, with experience in the department, has certain advantages:

Advantages

1. The psychologist–police officer has a great deal more understanding of the policing job than the consultant or staff member without police experience.
2. The capacity to form instant empathy is more likely with a psychologist who is or has been a police officer.
3. A psychologist–police officer has many characteristics of the peer counselor because of having experienced many of the things that the patient or client is likely to discuss, particularly critical incidents or stressful situations.
4. Trust between the police officer and the psychologist is more rapid and more thorough when the psychologist is also a cop.
5. The psychologist–police officer understands the clients' language much better than a consultant or staff psychologist without such experience; "cop language" may have to be learned as a second language by those who have not been on the job.
6. Police clients themselves express a preference for sworn personnel stating, "It takes one to understand the unique problems inherent in the job."

In some cases, there is a boomerang effect, and the police psychologist who is also a sworn officer may have certain disadvantages:

Disadvantages

1. Some police clients do not want to be interviewed or questioned by "a cop."
2. The psychologist–police officer has less of the mystique and specialness that may be helpful in establishing rapport.
3. It is probably easier for the police psychologist who has not been an officer to be objective in dealing with clients.
4. The psychologist who is also a department line officer, often takes up a space that could be filled by an officer doing standard police work full time.

Each role has advantages and disadvantages and lends itself to the job of police psychologist in special and individualistic ways (Franzese, 1987).

ORCHESTRATING SUCCESS IN PSYCHOLOGICAL POLICE SERVICES

Understanding and being prepared to help change the climate of the traditional police bureaucracy should be one of the goals of a concerned police psychologist. Most futurist thinkers in police science believe that police work can be improved by redefining the job from a relatively low-level occupation to that of a "profession" in the full sense of that term.

Changes cannot be brought about simply by working with the structure of law enforcement. The community, in general, must recognize that crime fighting is only one function of modern police work. The public must support the research and the training necessary to help police officers better utilize the powers granted in their commission, such as the choice of using deadly force under certain circumstances. There also is no question that increased educational background for administrators will enhance modern and professional policing. In pursuit of these goals, police psychologists must understand what police *really* do in day-to-day law enforcement (Bittner, 1990).

To do the best possible job of bringing behavioral science to the law enforcement agency, the police psychologist must fulfill four distinct roles:

1. Provider of traditional psychological services needed by individuals and by the establishment.
2. Trainer and educator.

3. Management consultant on innovation, attitude change, and morale.
4. Research and program evaluator with the appropriate feedback to encourage change.

Whether operating as a staff psychologist or as a consultant, it is almost always possible for a psychologist to have impact in these four areas (Loo, 1986).

Psychology has a great deal to offer any law enforcement agency—large or small. Law enforcement officers and their management structure face a considerable variety of problems, many of which can be addressed by knowledgeable and skillful professional psychologists. Whether psychological services can be effective depends on the degree to which police managers accept that understanding human behavior can further the goals and purposes of law enforcement.

Although there may be models where this spontaneously occurs, it is the rarity and exception rather than the usual and customary. Law enforcement officers, both at the ground level and at the management level, are often suspicious of new ideas that differ from the way they were trained and the way they think law enforcement should be operated.

The number one indication for determining whether a law enforcement agency can utilize professional behavioral science services is the receptiveness of the leader. If the chief of police, or the sheriff, or the director in the case of state and federal agencies, is narrow, limited, or hostile to the development of behavioral science services, a low level of opportunity and service delivery is likely to occur. Resources will not be allocated to behavioral science, and creative ideas that emanate from psychologists are likely to be rejected or sabotaged.

The director of the behavioral science unit should report directly to the senior manager of the department, except in the case of very large organizations where bureaucratic restraints may necessitate reporting to a deputy commissioner or a deputy director. Even in large organizations, it is likely that if the real boss is unaware of the roles, functions, and skills of psychologists within the department, full service cannot be delivered.

When law enforcement agencies first considered utilizing psychological services, they would often assign a low-level functionary to explore the concept—the personnel director, or a person at an even more subordinate level of administrative responsibility. The psychologist who is interested in providing a full range of professional services should gracefully and tactfully refuse to negotiate with a lower-level contact. Initial discussions may occur with such an intermediary, but early on, the psychologist should insist on a meeting with the chief, the sheriff, or the commissioner. This can sometimes be accomplished by offering to present a briefing or a colloquium on the roles of police psychologists, or the historical development of behavioral science units. The psychologist offering services to a law enforcement agency ought not to sign any contracts, or make any commitments without thoroughly understanding what management expects and what they know about psychologists and their services. It is possible to function within an agency where the top administrator knows the value of psychology and will support it, even though most of the department officials are ignorant of the value of such services or resistant to professional psychology. It's probably impossible to have a well-functioning unit where the top person is unaware of the value of such services, or is resistant to them. It is best to start at the top, a lesson learned through hard experience by industrial/organizational psychologists in the past.

Unfortunately, many police psychologists are relegated to limited roles because the police bureaucracy has a propensity to think in narrow terms. Thus some police executives consider psychologists to be experts at testing police recruits. Others view psychologists as stress counselors or as specialists in murder and rape profiling, or as experts in conducting forensic hypnosis for investigative purposes. A good many simply believe that psychologists have no place in police work.

A police psychologist who is also a trained and sworn officer may be expected to "toe the line" and to have a strict and regimented place in the hierarchy. The police psychologist who becomes a part of the department should seek the highest possible rank in order to address managers as peers. The ideal would be for the director of a police psychology or behavioral science unit to have the rank or equivalent rank of the third highest sworn officer in the department. He or she would then report directly to the number one person (chief, sheriff, commissioner, or superintendent) or this person's chief deputy (deputy commissioner, undersheriff, deputy chief, etc.). Such an arrangement negates some of the difficult, tedious, and disruptive territorial battles that tend to occur in a bureaucracy.

As the psychologist develops a variety of services within the agency, it is generally a good idea to state exactly what behavioral science can and cannot do. To this end, a detailed description of the behavioral science unit either as a separate pamphlet, or as part of the general orders of the agency can be quite useful. Appendix A describes a behavioral science unit that offers a wide variety of modern psychological services.

ETHICAL ISSUES

In a 1988 study, Zelig found that 55% of the respondents reported that they had encountered an ethical conflict while serving as police psychologists. Most frequently encountered ethical dilemmas included issues of confidentiality, conflicts between the ethical standards of the psychologists delivering the services and the needs of the agency, and dual relationships.

Weiner (1986) found that ethical dilemmas are frequently encountered when the police psychologist does psychotherapy with a police officer, or conducts an evaluation for special purposes. Here the rules of the organization, or of society, come in conflict with the usual and ordinary confidentiality and privileged communication that psychologists offer their clients in other institutions or in the independent practice setting.

In an effort to codify ethical issues in the delivery of police psychological services, D'Agostino (1986) proposed a series of principles for psychologists working in police settings. These principles, which closely resembled the ethical principles promulgated by the American Psychological Association, are described in the following sections.

Principle I—Responsibility

Psychologists should maintain the highest standards of their profession. They accept responsibility for the consequences of their acts, and make every effort to ensure their services are used appropriately. For the police psychologist, ethical decision making is influenced by the nature of police work and police organization. Power and control are central issues. Requests for services may appear to be legitimate when actually they are an effort by individuals or factions within the department to increase their own power. An example of this would be fitness evaluations or evaluations for emotional stability where the goal is not to help the officer but to use the results for discipline or harassment. Although functioning as an agent of the police organization as well as of the individuals within the organization, the psychologist should be aware of power struggles in order to avoid participating in the misuse of psychological knowledge. Any ethical errors that are made should be corrected as best possible by notifying the appropriate parties and ensuring that the error will not be repeated.

Principle II—Competence

All psychologists share the responsibility of maintaining high standards of competence in the interests of the public and the profession as a whole. Psychologists provide services and use techniques in which they are qualified by training and experience. In areas where standards are not yet recognized, psychologists take precautions to protect the welfare of clients. Psychologists maintain knowledge of current scientific and professional information. Because of the present lack of established standards for practice in the police setting, psychologists must be particularly careful in doubtful areas and communicate conclusions about competency and limitations of the current state of knowledge to police executives. Communication with other police psychologists in the field about these issues is of great importance.

Principle III—Moral and Legal Standards

In terms of their own behavior within the police setting, psychologists should be sensitive to the prevailing community standards and possible impact that conformity or deviation may have in the quality of professional service delivery. Police officers and executives tend to strongly support traditional values of family, conformance to the law, honesty, and integrity. They will carefully gauge the personal values of police psychologists and are likely to react negatively to unconventional moral values and behavior.

Principle IV—Public Statements

Psychologists in the police setting must represent accurately and objectively their professional qualifications, affiliations, and functions as well as those of the institutions or organizations with which the statements may be associated. There should be a full recognition of the limits and uncertainties of any evidence cited in such statements.

Principle V—Confidentiality

Psychologists have a primary obligation to respect the confidentiality of information obtained from persons in the course of their work as psychologists. Such information is revealed only with the consent of the person or the person's legal representative except where not to do so would result in danger to the person or others. The client should be informed of the legal limits of confidentiality. Within the police setting, a fundamental question is, Who is the client? This should be settled as early as possible. The multiple roles and functions of police psychologists lead to role conflicts and subsequently to ethical conflicts. Roles and responsibilities must be carefully defined. At the beginning of the contact, the police psychologist should make the client aware of what feedback the supervisor is expecting, and what will actually be given. The limits of the client's confidentiality should be determined and communicated to the client. This will give the police officer or the police officer's family member the option of choosing to continue to participate, or to withdraw.

Police psychologists should be aware of the exception to the confidentiality principle in "duty to warn" applicable to homicidal and suicidal individuals. Case law suggests that three conditions must exist before "duty to warn" is applicable:

1. There must be a special relationship between the person who is knowledgeable about another person's potential dangerousness and the dangerous person.

2. The therapist must make a reasonable determination based on professional judgment that the client is dangerous.
3. There must be a foreseeable victim.

Procedures should be established to make the responsibility of the police psychologist clear to clients.

Principle VI—Welfare of the Consumer

Psychologists are expected to respect the integrity and to protect the welfare of the people in groups with whom they work. When conflicts of interest arise, psychologists are expected to clarify the nature and direction of their loyalties and responsibilities and keep all parties informed of their commitments. Application of Principle VI in police settings is a complex and challenging task, particularly if the psychologist is counseling the police officer or a family member on marital conflict, family dynamics, or divorce issues.

Principle VII—Professional Relationships

Psychologists respect the prerogatives and obligations of the institutions or organizations with which their colleagues are associated. They act with regard to the needs, special competencies, and obligations of colleagues in psychology and other professions. Because police departments or public agencies receive close scrutiny from other governmental agencies as well as the general public, there is a special sensitivity and reactivity of police departments to public statements made by police psychologists. Any public discussion of police departments and the work of police psychologists should take place only with the prior approval of the employing agency. Psychologists should take special care not to undermine public confidence in police officers and police organizations.

Principle VIII—Assessment Techniques

Psychological organizations have developed many principles and "rules of the road" for the development, publication, and utilization of psychological assessment techniques. Psychologists make every effort to promote the welfare and best interests of the client while using these. They guard against misuse of assessment results.

Police psychologists have used assessment techniques for selection, fitness for duty evaluations, and selection of personnel for specialized units. Tests have even been used for the evaluation for promotion. These areas are well known, and industrial/organizational psychology has established guidelines and procedures to ensure ethical performance by psychologists doing assessment.

Police departments differ widely in policies and procedures relating to the use of psychological techniques. Psychologists must be alert to the possibility that their department may misuse assessment instruments by employing nonpsychologists in the application of the techniques. Psychologists in the police setting must be especially alert to the limitations of assessment techniques with these populations.

Deitz and Reese (1986) have developed a series of strategies to minimize role conflicts of psychologists offering services to police agencies. Their strategies are classified as follows:

Strategy #1

Provide the law enforcement agency with a copy of the principles of ethics of your discipline before accepting employment or a consulting assignment.

Strategy #2

Identify your profession and the client to anyone whom you interview, including suspects, defendants, victims, witnesses, and law enforcement personnel.

Strategy #3

Obtain fully informed consent for all interviews, tests, procedures, and treatment.

Strategy #4

Do not compromise the legitimate needs of the person interviewed, the community, or the client agency by offering greater confidentiality than is necessary or possible.

Strategy #5

Disclose to the client or agency the limitations of your expertise.

Strategy #6

Recognize the differences between the values and norms of mental health professionals and the values and norms of law enforcement professionals.

Strategy #7

Direct all communications to the appropriate level within the command hierarchy of the law enforcement agency.

Strategy #8

Obtain the permission of those in authority before speaking with the media or publishing any identifiable information about cases or agency activities.

Strategy #9

Recognize the warning signs of overidentification with law enforcement: excessive interest in police paraphernalia, unnecessary use of police jargon, and callousness.

Strategy #10

Participate actively in your parent discipline to avoid overidentification with law enforcement.

The preceding recommendations are likely to be reflected in future formalized standards.

To render the most effective services possible to law enforcement officers and agencies, the psychologist must be patient, sensitive, and tolerant. The very concept of psychology can be especially threatening to individuals who function in a closed bureaucratic system. It is sometimes difficult for professional psychologists to modify their usual and customary role as the authority figure in the assessment or treatment setting. Too often, psychologists are used to dealing with clients who come "hat in hand" for services. Although police officers need and often want help, their pride may result in defensiveness that appears as hostility or in some cases fawning obsequiousness. These attitudes can easily be misinterpreted and lead to an ineffective interaction between the parties.

A police officer's lot is not always a happy one, but there are indications that psychology may be in a position to improve it in the future (Blau, 1989).

PART TWO

Assessment

CHAPTER FOUR

Officer Recruit Selection

The earliest interaction between psychologists and law enforcement was probably Lewis Terman's use of a modified form of the Binet Intelligence Scale—the Stanford–Binet—to assist police selection in California in 1916 (Deitz & Reese, 1986). Psychological testing of prospective recruits is now the largest single activity conducted by psychologists within the law enforcement establishment.

When the United States entered World War I, the need to select and train large numbers of military personnel led to significant advancements in psychological instruments to help with this effort. Even before the United States' entrance into World War I, the *Journal of Applied Psychology* was formed. In early editions, Thorndike reported "rating scales for selecting salesmen" and other devices for predicting success on the job. It was during U.S. involvement in World War I that the concept of requiring a criterion extrinsic to the test construction itself was developed. Psychological tests of "intelligence" were extensively used in 1917 and 1918 to select men for officer training (vonMayrhauser, 1992).

Before mid-century, some early attempts were made to use "personality instruments" to predict job success in police work (Humm & Humm, 1950).

The use of psychological tests and interviews in an effort to select police officers who would succeed on the job was reported in 1950 (DuBois & Watson, 1950). In the years that followed, the use of psychological tests to predict police officers' suitability or performance gradually became an area of extensive research and practice.

In 1954, psychological and psychiatric screening procedures of all potential police officers became part of the selection procedures used by the Los Angeles Police Department. Their battery included a Minnesota Multiphasic Personality Inventory (MMPI), a group Rorschach, a tree drawing, and a brief psychiatric interview. These procedures were part of a five-step selection process that included a civil service written examination, an oral interview, a background investigation, and a complete physical examination. It is reported that about 10% of applicants were successful in the five-phase screening process, whereas 15% to 20% of these were eliminated during academy training for various reasons (Reiser, 1982b).

In 1973, the President's Commission on Law Enforcement and Administration of Justice included a recommendation in their final report that law enforcement agencies increase their quality of personnel selection and procedures to assure fair hiring practices. It was this commission that first directed that psychological screening be incorporated in the selection procedures by the year 1975 (The President's Commission on Law Enforcement and Administration of Justice, 1973).

Although efforts to make police selection more thorough and scientific accelerated during the 1970s, police departments were reluctant to undertake serious research concerning realistic performance criteria. Studies revealed it is extremely difficult to predict police performance because every year that officers are on the job, they are exposed to powerful influences that shape their ideas, philosophy, and behavior (Lefkowitz, 1977).

During the 1980s, police departments throughout the country began using a variety of psychological tests and interviews to predict the performance of police officer recruits. Police officials themselves began to see psychological screening as an important practice within the personnel selection procedure (McCreedy, 1974).

A comprehensive summary of police psychology in the mid-1980s by Ostrov (1986a) presented both positive and negative aspects of the developing practice of using standard paper-and-pencil tests as part of the law enforcement mission. Law enforcement agencies use four major categories of testing to support personnel decisions. At the entry level, recruits are tested either before or after academy training. Next, special testing can be done for lateral entry, whereby experienced police personnel enter from other police agencies. Third, promotional testing may help differentiate the merit of various candidates for advanced positions. The fourth category of testing is to select appropriate officers for special assignments. The testing may include measurements of physical agility, personality, intelligence, physical status, background evaluation, and performance rating by supervisory personnel (Whisenand, 1989).

The psychologist's role in recruit selection has become that of test administrator, interpreter, and interviewer. The Accreditation Standards required that personality testing and interviewing be part of the psychological battery used in recruit selection. Recent surveys of recruitment selection procedures in major law enforcement departments in the United States indicate that there is no standard for tests or interviews, and that an extensive variety of procedures and instruments are used (Strawbridge & Strawbridge, 1990).

The length of time spent in testing ranges between a half an hour and four hours in various departments. The most often used tests are group-administered paper-and-pencil tests in combination with interviews (Lefkowitz, 1977).

SELECTING OUT PATHOLOGY

As law enforcement managers began to see some value in using psychological tests to help select police recruits, they focused on tests to identify recruits likely to embarrass the department, or get into difficulties that would lead to expensive litigation (Blanch, 1977; McCreedy, 1974). Management began to count on psychologists to search out those recruits with a potential for being emotionally disturbed, rather than to find those recruits who would do a good job of policing (Reiser, 1982b).

Psychologists not only have gone along with this attitude and expectancy but have generally encouraged it. Most of the psychologists who work with law enforcement agencies are clinical psychologists, with experience and perhaps preference for personality test instruments that attempt to identify psychopathology.

IDENTIFYING TRAITS ASSOCIATED WITH GOOD POLICING

In the 1970s, personality screening techniques became more widespread. Their purpose was to eliminate those who did not satisfy minimum requirements for stability and in some cases intellect. Where patrol officers were studied several years after recruit training to evaluate the consistency of their personality patterns, it was found that significant personality, attitude, and adjustment changes occurred over a period as short as 2 years. The working officers showed more somatic symptoms, more anxiety, more alcohol-use vulnerability, and other traits that would have been considered significantly negative indicators at the time of recruitment.

Dunnette and Motowidlo (1976) found that the personality traits that are measured during recruit selection are of little predictive value, because the shaping influences that operate along an officer's career beginning with the academy and ending with the officer's retirement are very powerful. These influences affect the personality traits that may be measured at the time of selection. Such traits apparently change with experience.

Almost any police manager will expostulate extensively about what he or she considers the important personal traits and behaviors of the "good officer."

Honesty

Next to screening out pathology, police managers focus on the trait of "honesty" or "integrity." One of the primary purposes of the often used polygraphic examination is to determine whether the police recruit candidate is truthful or not.

Integrity tests have been available for many years. The quality of such tests is subject to many questions. Most of these tests show high false-positive results. Honesty tests tend to fall into two categories: the overt integrity test that directly asks questions about the applicant's honesty and attitudes about theft, and those tests that could be called personality based. These latter measure a broader range of traits. Any of these tests are only as good as the standardization procedures that are followed (and hopefully replicated). The failure rate is quite high, and there is an issue of basic fairness in the use of such instruments (Bales, 1988).

Part of the reason that psychological tests to evaluate honesty or integrity have become so popular is that polygraph examination has been banned in many settings. More than 40 integrity tests are available in the field today; however, few studies of these tests have been published in peer-reviewed journals. Test developers present studies that have not been reviewed and published to support the use of their tests. The wide range of integrity tests is a major obstacle to determining the usefulness of these instruments. Although more and more such tests are being made available, their use in law enforcement is decreasing in favor of broader psychological test batteries. On the other hand, the use of such tests in industry tends to be increasing (Adler, 1989; DeAngelis, 1991a).

Other Personal Traits Desired

In attempting to define the "good cop," police managers frequently list the following characteristics:

- Bravery or courage.
- Decisiveness.
- Consistency and reliability.
- Resistance to stress.
- Cooperativeness.
- Traditional values.
- Respect for authority.

There are few sound studies of the behavioral traits of "good" and "poor" police officers. Their behavior is often described, but esoteric traits such as "street smarts" unfortunately defy definition, measurement, and prediction (Charles, 1986).

Some efforts have been made to use industrial/organizational methods to develop reliable and valid police selection instruments. Ashton and his colleagues (1984) constructed an Entry Level Police Services Examination that was field tested with 5,000 applicants for law enforcement jobs in a variety of police departments and municipalities across Massachusetts.

In carrying out this study, they set four tasks:

1. Role-task identification.
2. Ability identification.

3. Role-ability linkage evaluation.
4. Ability evaluation.

The details of this extensive study are worth exploring:

Role-Task Identification. Seven primary areas of the police job were identified:

1. Patrol.
2. Providing services and rendering assistance.
3. Applying and enforcing the law.
4. Investigating.
5. Assisting in protection.
6. Documenting and reporting.
7. Miscellaneous.

Ability Identification. This section identified the reporting and cognitive abilities necessary for the academy and ultimately for job success. A master list of abilities was combined by reviewing cognitive ability areas that were retrieved from the psychological literature.

Master List of Abilities for the Police Job. The authors attempted to identify psychological abilities that would be necessary for success in policing. These included:

1. Listening.
2. Reading.
3. Speaking.
4. Writing.
5. Ability to think of many ideas concerning the subject.
6. Ability to think of clever descriptors.
7. Ability to remember new information occurring as a part of a task that must be remembered and noted to carry out the task.
8. Ability to recall a series of items after one or more presentations (such as license plates).
9. Associative memory.
10. Memory for relationships that have logical connections with previously learned items.
11. Memory for ideas.
12. Problem sensitivity.
13. Methodical reasoning using arithmetical word problems.
14. Basic arithmetic.

15. Productive reasoning (thinking of stated facts through to logical conclusions).
16. Information ordering.
17. Category flexibility.
18. Spatial orientation.
19. Visualization of objects.
20. Speed of recognition of unknown objects.
21. Speed of recognition of known objects.
22. Ability to perform acts from instructions.
23. Selecting the best path to go based on minimal cues.
24. The ability to interact tactfully with other human beings.
25. Interpretation of interpersonal conflict situations.

The preceding represent only a portion of the master list of abilities but are indicative of the approach.

Role-Ability Linkage Evaluation. This characteristic refers to the ability to collect and confirm job-analytic information. Efforts were made to link role ability to the seven specific job duties.

Ability Evaluation. Studies were undertaken to see if ability areas were consistently associated with important on-the-job behavior. Criterion-related validity studies were conducted, and the following factors were found to be significantly related to behavior:

1. Verbal reasoning.
2. Arithmetic skills.
3. Interpretation of tables.
4. Interpretation of hypothetical rules and regulations.
5. Reading comprehension.

This was a massive piece of work, to be followed by additional study to determine cutoff points. Very few law enforcement agencies have expended this kind of effort for proper development of psychological instruments that can be helpful in making reasonable selection decisions.

A complex study of patrol officer qualifications in relation to field performance was conducted in the Chicago Police Department under a grant from the Law Enforcement Assistance Act of 1965. Baehr, Furcon, and Froemel (1968) reported their efforts to identify predictors for overall performance of patrol officers and the relation between predictors and specific patterns of exceptional and marginal performance. They found that they could categorize Chicago patrol officers as "newcomers," "established patrolmen," and "old timers." Each of these could be placed into subgroups of "excellent performance," "good performance," and "poor performance." Criteria of performance included supervisors' ratings, absences, numbers of arrests, awards, disciplinary actions, and complaints. They report a number of interesting findings: Some patrol officers who showed quite good performance in numbers of arrests and awards also showed exceptionally poor performance in the areas of departmental disciplinary action, complaints, and internal affairs investigation. They tended to be unpredictable and undependable. Sometimes they were quite good, and sometimes they were quite bad. Such officers tended to be below average in their ability to cope effectively with ambiguity, to use withdrawal appropriately, and to deal effectively and realistically with concrete problems. They apparently suffered conflict between impulsivity and moral control. Because they were able to function effectively for a certain percentage of time, they might end up as being rated as "average" thus disguising more than what would be revealed by a more detailed analysis.

The researchers concluded that it would be possible to identify and provide a description of meaningful performance subgroups within a patrol officer population. Cutoff points and specific predictive scores were not possible. In general, they found that desirable attributes for patrol officers included control of purely impulsive and emotional responses, a "work" rather than a "social" orientation, and a realistic rather than a subjective or feeling-oriented approach to life. The researchers concluded that ideal attributes for success as a patrol officer are related to "stability." This would include stability in the parental and personal family situation, stability stemming from personal self-confidence and the control of impulse, and stability in the sense of maintaining a cooperative rather than a hostile or competitive attitude. They finally concluded that stability, in part, would derive from a resistance to stress and a realistic rather than subjective orientation toward life.

PSYCHOLOGICAL INSTRUMENTS IN CURRENT USE

In many respects, the use of psychological tests and techniques for the selection of law enforcement trainees is still in its infancy. Although some efforts to introduce psychological testing into the selection procedure have been going on for three-quarters of a century, the gap between what psychological research and methodology in the area of testing could do and what it is actually doing for law enforcement is significant.

Because the law enforcement administration hierarchy has a tendency to believe in traditional methods of selection and training, screening out of pathology still tends to be the most important goal in police recruit applicant testing. Again, because psychologists who are involved with selection procedures in law enforcement are most frequently clinical psychologists, a focus on personality testing has developed and continues to be the psychological testing most often done in the law enforcement venue.

Strawbridge and Strawbridge (1990) surveyed 72 major law enforcement agencies to determine the tests used for applicant selection. They found that 51% of these agencies did not use psychological tests at that time. (This is likely to change rapidly as major agencies seek accreditation.) Of the 49% that reported using psychological tests, the most commonly used instruments are shown in Table 4.1. The table shows that the majority of tests used are measures of personality.

Other tests that agencies have used include the Otis Quick-Scoring Mental Ability Test, the Nelson–Denny Reading Tests, the Otis–Lennon Mental Ability Tests, the Law Enforcement Personal History Questionnaire, the House–Tree–Person Test, the Empathy Scale Inventory, the Shipley Institute of Living Scale, the Bender–Gestalt Test, the Millon Multiaxial Personality Inventory, the Metropolitan Achievement Tests, the Wechsler Adult Intelligence Scale-Revised, the Wide-Range Achievement Test, the Stroop Screening Test, the Test of Attentional and Interpersonal Styles, the Rotter Locus of Control Tests, the Jenkins Activity Survey, the Holmes–Rey Stress Scale, the Maudsley Personality Inventory, the Quality-of-Life Inventory, the "Why I Want to Be a Policeman Test," and the Strong–Campbell Interest

TABLE 4.1   Psychological Tests Used by Major U.S. Law Enforcement Agencies for Applicant Selection (N = 72)

Test	Agencies Using	Percentage
Does not use	37	51
Minnesota Multiphasic Personality Inventory (MMPI)	33	46
California Personality Inventory (CPI)	11	15
Inwald Personality Inventory	5	7
Clinical Analysis Questionnaire (CAQ) Parts I & II	4	6
Sentence Completion	3	4
Culture Fair IQ	2	3
Human Figure Drawings	2	3
Wonderlic Personnel Test	2	3
Otis–Lennon School Ability Test	2	3
Rorschach	2	3
Cornell Index	2	3
FIRO-B	2	3
State-Trait Anxiety Inventory	2	3

Note: Data derived from A Networking Guide to Recruitment, Selection, and Probationary Training of Police Officers in Major Police Departments of the United States of America, by P. Strawbridge and D. Strawbridge, 1990, United Kingdom: New Scotland Yard.

Inventory. Appendix F provides addresses of companies supplying most of these tests.

Undoubtedly, different departments may use not only different combinations of these tests but other tests that have not been identified here.

A considerable amount of testing done in officer recruit selection procedures may not be under the supervision of psychologists. Many departments test handwriting, composition, numerical ability, spelling, general knowledge, intelligence, grammar, vocabulary, verbal comprehension, reasoning ability, and logic as part of the written examinations administered by the agency's personnel section. Some departments utilize well-standardized instruments, whereas other agencies have tests that are simply the empirical derivation of the individual or individuals who believe these are important areas to measure in selecting police recruits. The reliability and the validity of such instruments are relatively unknown (Strawbridge & Strawbridge, 1990).

Some of the psychological instruments most frequently used in law enforcement recruit selection will be considered.

INTELLECTUAL FACTORS

It is rare that a law enforcement agency would specifically request a psychologist to establish an intellectual evaluation procedure for recruit candidates. Ordinarily, the issue of qualification for training or service as a police officer is left up to the personnel department of the agency, or to the selection board of the academy to which the individual applies or is appointed. Because most psychologists are retained to screen out applicants who are likely to cause trouble or incur litigation as police officers, the focus is primarily in the area of clinical psychology, and specifically in the areas of personality and character.

Surveys of the testing procedures used by major U.S. law enforcement agencies indicate that a relatively small number regularly utilize such intelligence tests as the Culture Fair Test, the Wonderlic Personnel Tests, the Otis–Lennon Test of Ability, and the Wechsler Adult Intelligence Scale-Revised (Strawbridge & Strawbridge, 1990).

There are potential problems in using intelligence tests to select police officers. There may be issues of adverse impact on minority applicants, and the tests available for use may not be acceptable within the guidelines for Equal Opportunity Employment (Gordon, 1969).

There seems to be a trend toward using the Wonderlic Personnel Test more and more frequently in law enforcement agencies. The Wonderlic organization itself reports a 1983 study of police patrol officers ($N = 3,346$) and a cross validation in 1983 ($N = 875$) where the median raw test score was found to be 21 (Wonderlic, 1983).

The Wonderlic is a relatively simple test to administer and to score. There are 50 items, taken from earlier forms of the Otis Test. The applicant is allowed 12 minutes to do as many of the items as possible. A variety of percentile scores are available.

The range of Wonderlic scores and their Wechsler Adult Intelligence Scale equivalents are presented in Table 4.2.

At the end of this chapter, several examples (Figures 4.3–4.5) demonstrate how the results of the Wonderlic may be presented to a recruit selection board.

TABLE 4.2   Wonderlic Raw Score Equivalents of Wechsler Adult Intelligence Scale Full-Scale IQs

Wonderlic (Form A) Raw Score[a]	Wonderlic IQ Equivalent	Wonderlic (Form A) Raw Score[a]	Wonderlic IQ Equivalent
1	59	23	106
2	61	24	108
3	64	25	111
4	67	26	113
5	69	27	114
6	71	28	116
7	73	29	118
8	75	30	120
9	78	31	121
10	80	32	123
11	81	33	125
12	83	34	126
13	86	35	128
14	88	36	130
15	90	37	132
16	93	38	134
17	95	39	136
18	97	40	138
19	98	41	140
20	100	42	142
21	102	43	143
22	104	44	146

[a]Add to the raw score the following corrections for age: 0 for ages 16–29 years, 1 for ages 30–39, 2 for ages 40–49, 3 for ages 50–54, 4 for ages 60 and older.

Note: After "An Economical Method for the Evaluation of General Intelligence in Adults," by C. Dodrill, 1981, *Journal of Consulting and Clinical Psychology, 49,* pp. 668–673. Copyright 1981 by the American Psychological Association. Adapted by permission of the author.

Personality Evaluation

The emphasis on personality functioning in psychological testing of police recruit candidates is a trend that will probably continue. Screening candidates for evidence of psychopathology and/or personality traits that may interfere with acceptable performance as police officers is likely to be the standard until more extensive batteries of accurate psychological tests and procedures are available to predict performance. This narrow focus has not been without its critics (Loo & Meredith, 1986). For the predictable future, however, personality testing as a part of law enforcement recruit selection should continue to be the most frequently utilized psychological procedure in the selection process.

The Minnesota Multiphasic Personality Inventory (MMPI). The MMPI has been the workhorse of paper-and-pencil or "objective" personality assessment for half a century (Butcher, 1979; Dahlstrom & Welsh, 1960). Reiser (1982b) reports that since 1954, the MMPI has been a part of the selection process used with police applicants by the personnel department of the City of Los Angeles. In his report, it is suggested that profiles of successful applicants may tend to differ from one department to another. For the Los Angeles Police Department, selected candidates were significantly higher on the *L, K, D, Pd, Hy, Pa, Pt, Sc,* and *Ma* scales than a comparable group of "normals," as defined by Dahlstrom and Welsh (1960). Butcher (1979) reviewed the use of the MMPI in personnel selection for police candidates. In this review, he presents an MMPI-based rating form for evaluating police candidates. The efficacy of the MMPI for selection purposes has been reviewed extensively (Beutler, Storm, Krikish, Scogin, & Gaines, 1985; Nislow, 1988; Shaw, 1986).

When the MMPI is used to study police officers after their training and during their career, significant changes over time have been reported. Police officers tend to show more somatic symptoms, more anxiety, and more alcohol vulnerability after several years on the job. The profiles of such officers show significant elevations on *F, Mf, Pa,* and *Ma* (Butler, Meredith, & Nussbaum, 1988; Hyatt & Hargrave, 1988).

Neal (1986) found that officers with elevated *K* scores during the recruitment phase tend to be rated high in their performance years later on the job. This suggests that those recruits who are more guarded about revealing themselves at the time of recruitment tend to become the most successful police officers. The reported stresses that occur later in the job may be the price paid by officers who "hold in" well at the beginning.

The MMPI has been less successful in predicting adaptation or success of correctional officer candidates (Shusman & Inwald, 1991; Blau, Super, & Brady, 1993). Too often, police recruit candidates for whom no job is available are encouraged to become correctional officers. The differences between the police officer's job and the correctional officer's job is extensive,

TABLE 4.3 "Good Cop/Bad Cop" Performance Dysfunction Criteria

Number	Criteria
1	Number of "resisting arrests" filed by officer
2	Excessive absenteeism around holidays
3	Inappropriate use of force in arrests
4	Inappropriate use and display of weapon
5	Personal financial difficulties
6	Complaints of petty thievery by merchants
7	Complaints of sexual overtures against officers
8	Excessive use of alcohol or drug use
9	Deficiencies in report writing
10	Excessive sick leave
11	Ignorance of basic law or poor preparation for court appearances

Note: From "Good Cop/Bad Cop: The Use of the MMPI in Selection of Law Enforcement Personnel," by A. McCormick, 1984. Paper presented at the 19th Annual Symposium of Recent Developments in the use of the MMPI. Printed with permission of the author.

and it is unrealistic to assume that the same instruments are likely to predict success for these two different jobs.

In an effort to develop a profile predicting effective on-the-job performance, McCormick (1984) compared MMPI profiles of 120 officers against "Good Cop/Bad Cop" dysfunctional criteria, as illustrated in Table 4.3.

McCormick had watch commanders identify their 60 "best" and 60 "least best" officers. The groups were discriminated by elevations in the *Hy, Hs, Pd,* and *Ma* scales. McCormick replicated the study using officers from another community. *He* reported an 80% hit rate using the "Good Cop/Bad Cop" profile in predicting the performance dysfunction of about 40 uniformed officers. He recommended a cutoff *T* score of 60 for the significant MMPI scales. Blau, Super, and Brady (1993) replicated McCormick's study and found that the profile was equally effective in another jurisdiction.

The MMPI and Ethnic Differences. There has been some question or perhaps criticism of the use of the MMPI in police selection, suggesting that this instrument was developed and standardized on an essentially all-white population. Muller and Bruno (1988) administered the MMPI to 99 male police applicants matched by age, education, and residence. They were divided into white, Hispanic, and black triads. The standard validity and clinical scales of the MMPI were used. No significant differences were found among ethnic groups.

The MMPI-2. The MMPI-2 was developed in an effort to restandardize, update, and revitalize this traditional instrument. (Butcher,

Dahlstrom, Graham, Tellegen, & Kaemmer, 1989). Widely divergent views as to the usefulness of this revision have emerged (Butcher, 1992; Rodgers, 1992). Butcher states that the original MMPI asked embarrassing questions and offered potentially irrelevant and offensive items. He suggests that the original form might lead to legal difficulties because it includes questions now forbidden in employment selection situations. He cites research suggesting that even normals endorse too many problems in the old form. He suggests that the new form was much more carefully standardized than the old MMPI. Butcher further suggests that what this instrument really needs to identify is whether a particular respondent is different from people in general and by how much. Butcher does not address the issue of restandardization that is necessary for any new form of any test.

Rodgers counters by suggesting that the "new" MMPI may be a marketing ploy to give the publisher more control over the widely used MMPI. He points out simply that the MMPI-2 is not really a major improvement. Although admitting that the MMPI-2 eliminated sexist, religious, and crude content from the original MMPI, it is yet to be determined whether the changes in items have changed the effectiveness of the test in making discriminations. Rodgers believes that much is yet to be done before the MMPI-2 can be accepted with respect to the research that was necessary to make the MMPI a standard instrument for clinical utilization.

Levitt and Webb (1992) conducted a survey of MMPI-2 users. They found that the enthusiastic insistence by the authors of the MMPI-2 that the acceptance of the revised instrument would be widespread and immediate has not happened. They found that over twice as many respondents had continued to use the MMPI over the MMPI-2. Large numbers of respondents questioned whether the MMPI-2 was too new and had too little research about its clinical correlates to be used in place of the MMPI.

One of the authors of the MMPI-2, Grant Dahlstrom, compared the compatibility of 2-point, high-point code patterns from the original MMPI norms with the MMPI-2 norms for the restandardized sample. He found that although some code patterns proved to be stable across both norms, code comparability was generally lower in a community-based sample than was true for psychiatric samples. He states that the differences arising from the use of the MMPI-2 norms are appreciable and highlight the need for new empirical data on the correlates of coding patterns based on these norms (1992).

Levitt, Browning, and Freeland (1992) selected 29 special scales derived from the MMPI and scored them from the MMPI and the MMPI-2. They used a normal and a psychiatric sample. Resulting pairs of mean scores were compared and absolute differences were found to be small but statistically significant. They decided that most of the MMPI special scales probably can be scored and interpreted from MMPI-2 items although further research along this line would be necessary.

Hargrave, Hiatt, Ogard, and Karr (1993) administered the MMPI and the MMPI-2 to 166 police officers in one setting. The comparison indicated an overall concordance of 78 percent for the two tests when "normal" high-point and two-point codetypes were grouped together and compared. Half of the subjects produced the same high-point, one-third produced the same two-point code. Seventy percent produced normal profiles on both tests. The MMPI and MMPI-2 scales were highly correlated. On Scale Mf of the MMPI-2, women scored higher and men scored lower.

The Inwald Personality Inventory (IPI)

This instrument is gaining considerable favor with law enforcement agencies throughout the country. It is essentially a "screening-out" test. It measures potential emotional adjustment difficulties and potential anti-social behavior that might adversely affect job performance. Such characteristics as alcohol abuse, drug abuse, job difficulties, tendency to abuse leave time, interpersonal difficulties, phobias, legal problems, and societal problems are measured and reported.

The IPI is said to identify negative behavior patterns and personality factors that might lead to problems in handling responsibility in the workplace. Although not developed exclusively for law enforcement applicants, this is the area in which the IPI is most frequently utilized at the present time. Some industrial organizations also use this instrument to screen out undesirable applicants.

The IPI is a relatively new instrument. A considerable amount of research has been done, most of which has been reported in paper sessions and poster sessions at scientific meetings.

The publishers claim to have focused on "real" law enforcement issues in the development of this instrument. The administration time is usually under 45 minutes. They claim norms based on over 9,000 law enforcement officer candidates. The publishers are able to provide separate norms for white, black, and Hispanic men and women. Studies are available that relate the results of the IPI to other standard instruments such as the MMPI, the California Personality Inventory (CPI), the 16-Personality Factor Questionnaire (16-PF), and other personality measuring instruments. Inwald (1988) reports good prediction of law enforcement recruits who will be terminated over a 5-year period.

Shusman and Inwald (1991) in a study of 246 male correctional officers report that the IPI was more successful in classifying correctional officers as to "positive" or "negative" job performance behavior than did MMPI scales alone. They go on to indicate that a great percentage of correctional officers were correctly classified when all the IPI and MMPI scales were used in the prediction equations.

The California Personality Inventory (CPI)

The revised California Personality Inventory (Gough, 1991), a paper-and-pencil test of personality, is well known and well respected. Devised as a measure of the personalities of adult normals, the original purpose was to assess vocational and career goals of individuals being counseled. An additional utilization has been the appraisal of fitness for specific jobs or activities.

The average time to complete the CPI is 45 minutes to 1 hour. Like the MMPI and other paper-and-pencil tests, the validation scales account for confusion, exaggeration, or faking. A wide range of scales are available, as is true of other paper-and-pencil personality tests. Some of the measured traits are dominance, capacity for status, sociability, social presence, self-acceptance, independence, empathy, self-confidence, poise, social expertise and effectiveness, responsibility, socialization, self-control, good impression, communality, well-being, and tolerance. Other scales measure achievement motivation, psychological mindedness, and flexibility.

The construction of the scales is such that "cookbook" interpretations are possible, giving vivid and interesting descriptions of the individual making scores at any level on each of the scales. On an a priori basis, many descriptors would seem to be associated with desirable and undesirable traits of successful and unsuccessful police recruits.

The CPI is said to be useful in the selection of managers and leaders (Gough, 1984). Research with the California Psychological Inventory involving law enforcement officers (as well as criminals) suggests that as with other personality measurements in wide use, this instrument shows promise in selecting out those who are not appropriate for the law enforcement job (Megargee, 1972). Many psychologists who are consultants to law enforcement departments report using the CPI as one of the instruments in their recruit selection batteries. Extensive research, either situational or longitudinal, is relatively scarce in the literature regarding recruit selection and performance.

Hargrave and Hiatt (1989) examined the CPI profiles of 579 police academy graduates. The graduates were rated as "suitable" and "unsuitable" for law enforcement. The overall CPI profiles were more in the pathological direction for those rated "unsuitable." A second study by these authors compared preemployment CPI profiles against officers who were experiencing serious job performance problems. Those with serious problems scored lower on scales comprising Gough's Class II group of variables. Scales *So, Sc, Wb,* and *To* differentiated the groups.

The Sixteen-Personality Factor Questionnaire (16-PF)

Another well-known, respected test of normal adult personality is the instrument developed by Raymond B. Cattell and his associates. First published in 1949, this test has been revised regularly since that time (Cattell, 1991). The instrument is said to measure levels of warmth, intelligence, emotional maturity, dominance, impulsivity, superego strength, boldness, sensitivity, trust, imagination, shrewdness, confidence, radicalism, self-sufficiency, self-sentiment, and tension. Five "second order" factors provide measures of extroversion, anxiety, tough poise, independence, and control. Again, this instrument is used primarily to screen out undesirable candidates.

Studies indicate that successful police officers are low in Factor I (tending to be unsentimental, expecting little; self-reliant, taking responsibility, hard to the point of cynicism; few artistic responses, unaffected by fantasy, intending to act on practical logical evidence; tends to keep to the point; does not dwell on physical disabilities). Police were also found to be low on Factors QI and QII (conservative, respecting established ideas, tolerant of traditional difficulties, group-dependent socially, and acting as a sound follower) (Cattell, Eber, & Tatsuoka, 1970).

McEuen (1981) used the 16-PF in screening 1,405 applicants for the Atlanta Police Department during the years 1978 and 1979. Of this group, 111 officers were hired and were used as the subjects in his study. Comparing the performance of these officers against academy grades, dismissals from the department for cause, and individual and composite work evaluation ratings, he found that the 16-PF (and its derivative, the Clinical Analysis Questionnaire) were predictive of academy success, as well as of behavior that resulted in dismissal for cause. The 16-PF was not predictive of work evaluation ratings.

Law Enforcement Assessment and Development Report (LEADR)

This instrument was developed as a derivative of the 16-PF (Burnett, Johns, & Krug, 1981). The factors scored on the LEADR include performance potential, emotional maturity, integrity/control, intellectual efficiency, and interpersonal relations. The authors point out that these measures should be considered along with physical fitness information, educational background, training, experience, and other relevant data necessary in the police selection procedure.

LEADR is a four-page, computer-based analysis of the 16-PF questionnaire. The questionnaire has 187 items and is usually completed in about 45 minutes to 1 hour. A 6th- to 7th-grade reading level is required, according to the authors.

There are no cutoff scores on the LEADR factors. The authors state "these decisions must be left to individual agencies for a variety of reasons." It is strongly suggested that the results of the LEADR analysis be used in conducting interviews with candidates.

Ten studies are reviewed by the authors suggesting that a variety of police agencies have been successfully utilizing LEADR in recruit selection.

To date, there are no definitive or prospective studies using this instrument to predict either academy or on-the-job performance.

The Personality Assessment Inventory (PAI)

This self-administered paper-and-pencil inventory was designed to provide information on "critical clinical variables" among adults. The PAI contains 344 items. There are 22 nonoverlapping scales: 4 validity scales, 11 clinical scales, 5 treatment scales, and 2 interpersonal scales. In many ways, the PAI follows the developmental pattern of other pathology-measuring tests such as the MMPI, the CPI, and the 16-PF. It has been developed "from scratch" on a somewhat more sophisticated basis than the other instruments, with attention to more contemporary views of psychopathology.

The clinical scales reflect these contemporary concerns. Measurements include somatic complaints, anxiety, anxiety-related disorders, depression, mania, paranoia, schizophrenia, borderline features, antisocial features, alcohol problems, and drug problems. Treatment scales include aggression, suicidal ideation, stress, nonsupport, and treatment rejection. Two interpersonal scales—dominance and warmth—provide some insight into an individual's interpersonal style (Morey, 1991).

The PAI is not designed to provide a comprehensive assessment of the domains of normal personality. Screening for psychopathology is the primary focus of this instrument, particularly in respect to selection of police officers.

As a brand-new personality test, the PAI has not been used with any frequency in police selection. Studies by Kay (unpublished, personal communication from author) indicate that this instrument shows promise in equaling the selecting-out capabilities of earlier instruments, in a more contemporary and perhaps more appropriate format. Although the PAI appears to measure issues of great importance in police selection, such as stress, propensity to abuse alcohol, and abuse of drugs, it remains to be seen whether this instrument lives up to its promise in future research.

OTHER PSYCHOLOGICAL PROCEDURES IN CURRENT USE

Psychologists use a wide range of standardized instruments in providing psychological testing services for law enforcement departments who seek this service as part of their recruit selection or officer selection. Some of these are objective personality tests such as those mentioned previously in this chapter, while other clinical psychologists add or prefer projective techniques such as the Rorschach, Draw-a-Person, and Sentence-Completion instruments. Tests of achievement, interest, honesty, and other aptitudes are measured by small numbers of psychologists who serve law enforcement agencies. Some agencies rely on honesty tests (often scored and interpreted by mail). Goldberg et al. (1991) demonstrated that it is possible to achieve undesirable scores on honesty tests for a variety of reasons. They found it is also possible to achieve desirable scores by both honest and dishonest means. Undesirable scores were found to be statistically associated with undesirable criteria behavior, such as theft. The pattern of psychological traits that leads to the prediction of honesty is complex and as yet is poorly understood.

In 1964, Blum suggested that the Strong Vocational Interest Blank and the Strong–Campbell Interest Inventory II have scales that correlate with measures of performance in the law enforcement job. Baehr et al. (1968) concluded that interests tests are of questionable value in predicting the performance of police officers.

Some psychologists use a writing sample for analysis of verbal skills and in some cases personality. Most law enforcement agencies evaluate writing skills as part of personnel selection procedures.

Interviews

The Accreditation Standards of the Commission on Accreditation for Law Enforcement Agencies (CALEA) includes a requirement that a clinical psychologist conduct an interview as part of the psychological testing procedure. There are no specifications as to what should be included in the interview. Some police psychologists use an informal interview procedure, whereas others prefer a structured interview. Figure 4.1 presents a structured interview used in one behavioral science unit.

Biographical data can be useful in predicting success and failure in police officers. Spielberg, Spaulding, Jolley, and Ward (1979) found that variables predictive of successful performance in the police job included participation in high school athletics, fewer family moves, less need for job encouragement, and higher values for achievement and societal contributions. Based on their studies, Spielberg, Ward, and Spaulding (1979) have proposed a model for police selection that puts together research predictor variables in three categories: (a) physical, biographical, and demographic variables; (b) psychological assessment; and (c) situational tests.

STANDARDS AND CONSTRAINTS

The first set of proposed guidelines for preemployment screening of police recruits was proposed and endorsed by the International Association of Chiefs of Police at their annual Police Psychology Sectional Meeting in October 1986. In August 1987, at the 95th annual meeting of the American Psychological Association, the Police Psychology Section of the Division of Public Service issued an unedited version of these proposed standards. These recommended guidelines are on pp. 92–95.

PRESELECTION INTERVIEW FORM

NAME _____ DATE _____

POSITION APPLIED FOR _____

Why do you want to work into this profession?

_____

_____

		Circle Response	
Have you ever seen the inside of a jail? How many times?		Yes	No

_____

_____

I. *School Hx*

   A. Tell me about the education you have obtained?

     _____

     _____

   B. Were you involved in any school or after-school activities?   Yes   No

     _____

   C. Have you ever been suspended or expelled from school?   Yes   No

     _____

   D. Were you in any special classes or placement?   Yes   No

II. *Work Hx*

   A. Are you working now?   Yes   No

     _____

   B. Have you ever had problems with your boss/co-workers?   Yes   No

     _____

   C. Have you ever been disciplined at a previous job? How many times?   Yes   No

     _____

     _____

   D. Have you ever been fired or asked to leave a job? How many times?   Yes   No

     _____

     _____

   E. What is the longest time you ever had a job?

     _____

     _____

     _____

FIGURE 4.1   Structured Interview for Use in Recruit Selection

Circle Response

F. How many jobs have you had in the past two years? List and indicate the approximate number of months employed at each.

_____

_____

III. *Military Hx*

A. Have you been in the military?   Yes   No

B. What was your last rank? _____

C. Conditions of Discharge? _____

D. Were you ever disciplined? How many times?   Yes   No

_____

_____

IV. *Social Hx*

A. Do you have any hobbies?   Yes   No

_____

B. How do you spend your spare time?

_____

C. Do you exercise?   Yes   No

_____

D. Do you or your spouse have any past-due credit accounts?   Yes   No

_____

E. Have you ever been told you have a problem with your temper?   Yes   No

V. *Law Hx*

A. Have you ever had any felony convictions?   Yes   No

_____

_____

B. Have you ever committed a crime?   Yes   No

_____

C. How many vehicle code violations have you received (number of tickets)?

_____

_____

D. How many fistfights or shoving matches have you been in?

_____

E. When was your last fistfight? _____

F. Have you ever used a weapon in a fight?   Yes   No

_____

_____

FIGURE 4.1   *(continued)*

Circle Response

VI. *Addictive Behavior Hx*

    A. Do you or have you ever used illegal drugs?   Yes   No

    _____

    B. Have you ever smoked marijuana without other people?   Yes   No

    _____

    C. Have you ever smoked marijuana more than one time in
       a week?   Yes   No

    _____

    _____

    D. Do you consume alcohol?   Yes   No
       1. How many drinks do you have per week? _____
       2. How often do you get intoxicated? _____
       3. When do you get intoxicated? _____
       4. How many times have you driven while intoxicated?

       _____

       5. Have you ever been violent while drinking?   Yes   No

       _____

       6. Have you ever been in an accident while drinking?   Yes   No

       _____

       7. Have you ever been told that you have a drinking
          problem?   Yes   No

VII. *Physical Health Hx*

    A. Do you have any physical limitations or problems?   Yes   No

    _____

    B. List serious physical ailments and approximate time
       they occurred.

    _____

    _____

    C. Are you taking any medication?   Yes   No
       What medication? _____
       For what purpose? _____

VIII. *Mental Health Hx*

    A. Are you or have you ever been in counseling or therapy?   Yes   No
       For what? _____
       How long? _____
    B. What are your bad habits and faults?

    _____

    _____

    _____

FIGURE 4.1 *(continued)*

Circle Response

C. What are your good habits and assets?

_____

_____

D. Have you ever been hospitalized for mental, nervous,
   or stress problems?   Yes   No

_____

_____

E. Have you ever taken medication for your "nerves" or
   for a mental condition?   Yes   No

_____

_____

F. Do you experience any of the following conditions?

(Check the appropriate column)

	NONE	RARELY	LESS THAN AVERAGE	MORE THAN AVERAGE	FREQUENTLY	ALWAYS
1. Pain	____	____	____	____	____	____
2. Lack of energy	____	____	____	____	____	____
3. Suicidal thoughts	____	____	____	____	____	____
4. Poor memory	____	____	____	____	____	____
5. Expressing too much or too little anger	____	____	____	____	____	____
6. Problems concentrating	____	____	____	____	____	____
7. Financial problems	____	____	____	____	____	____
8. Dizziness	____	____	____	____	____	____
9. Family problems	____	____	____	____	____	____
10. Feelings of being misunderstood	____	____	____	____	____	____
11. Nervousness	____	____	____	____	____	____
12. Fear	____	____	____	____	____	____
13. Stress	____	____	____	____	____	____
14. Sadness	____	____	____	____	____	____
15. Eating problems	____	____	____	____	____	____
16. Sleeping problems	____	____	____	____	____	____
17. Anxiety in closed or dark places	____	____	____	____	____	____
18. Problems getting along w/certain "types of people"	____	____	____	____	____	____
19. Feeling overwhelmed	____	____	____	____	____	____
20. Difficulty remaining calm	____	____	____	____	____	____

FIGURE 4.1   *(continued)*

G. In 50 to 100 words, indicate why you would like a career in this profession.

IX. *Other*

A. Is there anything else that you feel should be known, positive or negative, which can have impact on your application or possible employment, if discovered later?

_____

_____

B. At this point, is there anything that was unclear or that you possibly mistook for which you would like to change your response?

_____

_____

C. I have answered all questions honestly and to the best of my ability.

I consent and understand that the information I provided may be used to assist in determining my application/employment status.

I further understand that intentional misstatements or false information could result in the denial or termination of my application.

_____   _____
Signature   Date

FIGURE 4.1 *(continued)*

RECOMMENDED GUIDELINES FOR PREEMPLOYMENT SCREENING FOR LAW ENFORCEMENT AGENCIES

The purpose of this document is to describe the components of a preemployment screening program for law enforcement agencies, and to serve as a guide in establishing new preemployment screening programs. The principles outlined in this paper are based on general guidelines accepted by APA governing the practice of psychology. Researchers and practitioners are expected to meet at least the minimum APA requirements for providers of psychological services.

I. QUALIFICATIONS OF PROVIDERS OF PSYCHOLOGICAL TESTING SERVICES

1. In accordance with the most current APA *Standards for Providers of Psychological Services* (APA, 1985), practitioners should meet the minimal qualifications for a Professional Psychologist. He or she should also be qualified according to the standards of the state in which they are operating. It is recognized that some states do not require that psychologists be licensed, and other states exempt some specialty areas such as Industrial-Organizational Psychologists, as well as psychologist working in State and Municipal settings. However, if the state requires a license for providers of psychological services, they should be licensed as psychologists in their primary state of service, and in good standing.

2. Psychologists who conduct psychological screening for law enforcement agencies should be able to offer evidence of adequate training and/or experience in the area of psychological test interpretation and psychological assessment techniques. This is in accordance with Section I, paragraph 1, of these recommendations, and in conformance with pertinent APA Standards. Practitioners should be familiar with the research literature available on psychological testing for law enforcement officers.

3. Psychologists supervising persons other than themselves (interns, students, staff, etc.) who provide services to law enforcement agencies should be responsible for the conduct of those individuals, and should see that their services conform to APA standards.

4. Providers of psychological services for law enforcement agencies should be familiar with the pertinent APA Guidelines covering psychological testing.

II. RECOGNITION OF THE LIMITATIONS OF PSYCHOLOGICAL
TEST DATA

Due to the many factors that can influence test results, administrators should be aware that psychological recommendations *should*
be used as only one component of a hire–no hire decision. Where
state law requires psychologists to make hire–no hire recommendations, or to make determinations of "psychological" or "emotional"
suitability, these decisions should be based on well researched,
documented and validated criteria.

Candidates denied employment based, even in part, on the psychological evaluations should be allowed an opportunity to appeal
the decision to the hiring authority.

III. RECOMMENDED COMPONENTS OF A PREEMPLOYMENT
SCREENING PROGRAM

A comprehensive psychological screening program for law enforcement applicants should contain the following elements:

1. *Job Analysis and Development of Hiring Standards.* Data on psychological attributes considered most important for effective behavior should be obtained using appropriate data-gathering
   techniques such as job analysis, interviews, studies of "critical
   incidents," surveys, etc. If possible, local hiring standards
   should be developed for each agency. However, if it is not feasi-
   ble to obtain local data to develop hiring standards, appropriate norms and data from similar populations should be used.
   Based on the best available data, *preliminary* hiring standards
   should be developed. Individual practitioners or agencies
   should make a continuing effort to refine and evaluate their selection techniques. In order to demonstrate validity between
   selection procedures (i.e., tests and interviews) and performance criteria, an ongoing review process should be conducted
   to validate the specific test/interview content to be used to
   screen applicants.
2. *Testing.* An appropriate test battery, which includes objective,
   validated, psychological instruments, should be administered to
   applicants.
   a. The psychological tests used in a preemployment screening
      test battery should be validated for use with law enforcement
      officer candidates. If possible, local hiring norms should be
      developed. In smaller departments, data comparing popula-
      tions and job requirements should be developed to support
      the carryover of validation studies from larger agencies.
   b. Test results should be available to the evaluator before any
      follow-up interviews are conducted.

    c. Provisions should be made for the security of all testing materials.

    d. In accordance with APA Ethical Principles, psychologists must respect the right of the applicant to have a full explanation of the nature and purpose of the assessment technique, or must secure a waiver of that right in advance.

    e. An appropriately trained professional should be given the primary responsibility for interpreting and verifying individual results if mail-order or computerized tests are employed.

3. *Interview.* It is strongly recommended that individual "face-to-face" interviews for all applicants be conducted by a qualified, licensed psychologist before a final evaluative report is made. The interview should be used to verify written test results, and to gather additional relevant information on the applicant. In those agencies where time and volume considerations preclude individual interviews, appropriate background information on each candidate should be obtained which can be used to verify written test results.

    a. A structured interview format should be employed. Wherever possible, the format should include, but not be limited to, questions about such things as employment history, drug usage, prior arrests, etc.

4. *Reports.* Written or verbal reports should be provided to the agency based on an analysis of all psychological material including available data, and test and interview results. If verbal reports are submitted, then the psychologist should maintain documentation of findings supporting the recommendations. The final report should include any reservations that the psychologist might have regarding the validity or reliability of the results. Efforts should be made to educate agencies about the benefits and limitations of the psychological assessment procedures.

5. *Recommendations.* As stated in Section II, psychological recommendations *should* be used as only one component of a hire–no hire decision. Where state law requires psychologists to make hire–no hire recommendations, or to make determinations of "psychological" or "emotional" suitability, these decisions should be based on well researched, documented, and validated criteria.

    a. In the evaluation, psychologists should point out potential job-related problem areas for those individuals whose psychological difficulties may adversely affect specific job performance.

    b. Specific cutoff scores should only be used when there is clear evidence that such scores are valid, and have been cross-validated in research studies in the agency where they are being used.

   c. Clear disclaimers should be made so that reports evaluating current emotional stability or suitability for a job in law enforcement will not be deemed valid after a specific time.

6. *Record Maintenance.* Psychologists should maintain all psychological test records in strictest confidence, and these records should be discussed only with those involved in the selection process.

   a. Retention of records. State Statutes should be followed regarding the length of time that preemployment psychological records should be maintained.

   b. In the absence of any binding regulations, the length of time that records must be maintained would be up to the discretion of the individual agency or practitioner. However, the agency or practitioner should have a written policy or plan outlining a timetable for removing old records.

7. *Follow Up.* Providers of psychological testing defend their procedures, conclusions, and recommendations if a decision based, even in part, on psychological results is challenged. In order to do this:

   a. Continuing efforts should be made to validate final "suitability ratings" using behavioral criteria measures.

   b. Agencies who use psychological testing as part of their preemployment screening should maintain adverse impact data by sex and ethnicity.

   c. The privacy of individuals should be protected. Preemployment test results should not be used for purposes other than making preemployment hiring decisions. If these data are used in follow-up research to validate test results, individual officers' identities should be protected.

AGENCY CONSTRAINTS, RESTRICTIONS, AND PROCEDURES

Each individual agency, local, state, or federal, is likely to have a set of procedures and requirements involving the use of psychological tests for pre-employment screening of applicants. In some cases these restraints or procedures are very specific, and/or limiting. The following represents the entire General Order relating to psychological testing in a local law enforcement agency:

> After the applicant has been provided with a conditional offer of employment, he/she shall be scheduled for psychological testing.
>
> 1. Psychological testing shall consist of the Minnesota Multiphasic Personality Inventory and the Law Enforcement Assessment and Development Report.
> 2. The psychological tests shall be administered by the Human Resources Division and the test answer sheets shall be mailed to a licensed forensic psychologist for scoring and evaluation.
> 3. The psychologist shall provide a written report to the Department regarding the clinical profile of the candidate and his/her medical opinion as to the suitability of the applicant for the position based solely upon test results.
>
> If no disqualifying factors are apparent following the psychological testing, the applicant will be scheduled for a physical examination and drug screen to determine if the applicant *currently* has the physical or mental qualifications necessary to perform the job and if the person can perform the job without posing a "direct threat" to the health or safety of him/herself or others.

In some agencies, particularly those that have received accreditation, the General Orders regarding psychological testing procedures may be quite elaborate. The following is taken from the General Orders of the medium-size local law enforcement agency:

> PURPOSE
>
> 1.1 ESTABLISHMENT—This General Order contains a description of the selection process. This agency shall use only those selection procedures and requirements which have been documented as satisfying the professional and legal requirements of reliability, validity, utility and minimum adverse impact. Any written test(s) or procedure(s) provided or administered by this agency, or any private sector organization involved in the selection process, shall meet those requirements.
>
> 1.1.1 RELIABILITY—The selection process and its component parts must be reliable. Reliability is a necessary precursor of validity. Before a

performance measure/test can be valid, it must first be reliable. There are several types of reliability. For selection purposes, the most important types are test-retest reliability and inter-rator reliability. Both types can be demonstrated by statistical analysis.

1.1.1.1 TEST–RETEST RELIABILITY refers to an individual scoring similarly on a performance measure/test over a time interval.

1.1.1.2 INTER-RATOR RELIABILITY refers to an individual's performance measured/test being rated similarly by two or more rators.

1.1.2 VALIDITY—Each step in the selection process shall be designed to predict job performance or detect important aspects of the candidate's work behavior, as it relates to the position for which application is made. There shall be demonstrable proof of the relationship of the particular step or procedure to the job. Research statistics, or other proof required by law and sound management practice, shall be documented and on file with the Director of the Personnel Section, except for those dealing with the results of the psychological screening processes, which shall be maintained by the Director of the Behavioral Science Unit. The selection process and each component part shall be validated using either criterion, construct or content related validational methods.

1.1.2.1 CRITERION RELATED VALIDITY refers to the effectiveness of a performance measure/test to predict an individual's behavioral performance in a specified situation or job. Concurrent validity and predictive validity are two types of criterion validity.

1.1.2.1.1 CONCURRENT VALIDITY uses a criterion measure which is obtained at approximately the same time as the performance measure/test.

1.1.2.1.2 PREDICTIVE VALIDITY is the main type of criterion validity used for personnel selection. Predictive validity refers to the use of performance measure/test to predict how an individual will perform on a criterion (job) at later time.

1.1.2.1.3 CONSTRUCT VALIDITY refers to the extent that a performance measure/test is said to measure theoretical constructs or traits such as honesty, integrity and fairness. It is established by professional judgment which is based on sound evidence from multiple sources.

1.1.2.1.4 CONTENT VALIDITY refers to the degree to which a performance measure/test samples the content area which is to be measured. A performance measure/test's content validity is primarily established by subject-matter experts who determine whether the performance measure/test's items accurately and thoroughly assess the skills, abilities and knowledge that are crucial to successful job performance. To ensure that performance/test items represent critical job behaviors, the selection of such performance measure/test items should be derived from a job analysis.

1.1.2.1.5 UTILITY—Each step in the selection process shall be of practical value, based on validity, selection rate, number of candidates to be selected, and the nature of the job. The research statistics, or other proof required by law and sound management practice, shall be documented and on file with the Director of the Personnel Section, except for those dealing with the results of the psychological screening processes, which shall be maintained by the Director of the Behavioral Science Unit. These files shall be maintained in such sufficiency and for such duration as to allow for proper data collection regarding research and legal defense.

1.1.3   ADVERSE IMPACT—The United States Supreme Court has ruled that statistics showing a discrimination and statistics in disparate cases must be linked to one or more specific employment practices that caused the disparity. Thus, each step in the selection process shall be measured to ensure that it does not result in a disadvantage to a race, sex, disability, or ethnic group. The statistics, or other proof required by law and sound management practice, shall be documented and on file with the Director of the Personnel Section. Adverse impact, if any, shall be minimized in the selection process.

1.1.3.1   The determination of the selection rate for each group shall be calculated as follows:

1.1.3.1.1   Divide the selections made by the number of candidates from each group.

1.1.3.1.2   When all selection rates have been determined, compare each with the highest group selection rate.

1.1.3.2   A selection rate for any particular group that is less than 80% of that for the highest group shall cause a review of the system and/or procedures to identify possible inequities. A lower percentage may not indicate discrimination, if the numbers are small and not statistically significant, or when recruiting has caused the pool of applicants to be typical of what normally is expected from the particular group.

1.1.3.3   A selection rate for any group that is more than 80% of that for the highest group may not provide proof that discrimination is not occurring, if the differences are significant in both statistical and practical terms, or when groups are systematically discouraged from making application.

1.1.3.4   All records and data used to monitor adverse impact shall be maintained by the Personnel Section. This documentation shall disclose the impact of the selection process on each identifiable group by race, sex, and ethnic origin.

1.1.4   All steps in the selection process shall be administered, scored, evaluated, and interpreted in a uniform, fair manner. All elements of the system shall be clearly set forth and carried out identically for each candidate.

1.1.4.1   Employees assigned to the Personnel Section shall be thoroughly trained in the content and use of all selection procedures through in-service training and formal certification that meets State Department of Law Enforcement requirements. To enhance the confidence of both candidates and the general public, wherever possible, employees assigned to the Personnel Section shall be representative of racial and ethnic groups in this County, and of both sexes.

1.1.5   Selection from among candidates for appointment to this agency shall be accomplished as specified in Section 3.0 of this General Order, pertaining to career service eligibility and transfer of agency employees.

1.1.5.1   Selection materials shall be kept in a secure area in the Personnel Section. Access to these files shall be granted on a limited basis.

1.1.5.2   Whenever selection materials are disposed of, disposal shall be performed in a manner that prevents disclosure of the information contained therein. Burning or shredding under monitored conditions are recommended.

1.2   ADMINISTRATION—The authority and responsibility for administering the selection process shall be vested in the Director of Personnel Section. The following procedures shall be used in the administration of the selection process.

1.2.1   A current listing of all vacancies by job classification by dates shall be posted on bulletin boards throughout this agency.

1.2.2   Job announcements shall include description of the duties, skills, and responsibilities; establish minimum educational level; state physical requirements, if any; state the filing deadline; announce that the position is under the protection of the Equal Employment Opportunity Act; and may be advertised through local mass media.

1.2.3   The eligibility qualifications for any position, including lateral entry, shall be found in the job description of the position to which the entry is made.

1.2.3.1   Lateral entry shall be available for specialist, managerial, and administrative positions.

1.2.3.2   When qualified personnel are available from within and outside this agency, the selection process shall favor agency employees.

1.2.3.3   Employees may apply by submitting a Transfer Request through the chain of command once the job announcement has been published. Applications shall not be submitted for transfer, if no vacancy has been announced.

1.2.4   A candidate previously denied appointment can reapply, be retested, and be reevaluated for an existing position, provided the following conditions are met:

1.2.4.1   To qualify for reconsideration after denial, a candidate shall wait at least 12 months after the date of the denial letter.

1.2.4.2   Reconsideration shall be initiated upon written request from the candidate, provided nothing in the candidate's background indicates an unfitness for appointment, based on CJSTC [Criminal Justice Standards Training Commission] standards.

1.2.5   All candidates shall be informed of the entire selection process, including written notice as to its expected duration. They shall also be informed of the reapplication process, by means of applicable information from the General Order; the Physical Assessment Test for Law Enforcement and Corrections Officers, the Application Process, and Reapplication Process Requirements.

1.2.5.1   Each candidate shall be informed as to the exact nature of each part of the process including, but not limited to, physical and psychological exams if applicable, polygraph tests, and background investigations.

1.2.5.2   Candidates shall be informed that due to the nature of public trust involved, they shall be subject to a very thorough background investigation, which includes the development of very sensitive and confidential information about their personal lives.

1.2.6   Disposition of all records of candidates who have not been selected for appointment to this agency shall be in accordance with applicable state and federal law. Sufficient data should be maintained to ensure continuing research, independent evaluation, and defense against lawsuits.

1.2.7   The oral interview portion of the selection process shall be accomplished by the Personnel Selection Unit.

1.2.7.1   The oral interview shall include questions appropriate to the position for which application is made. In addition, standardized questions shall be asked which relate to specific measurable personal attributes. These shall be rated on a uniform scale for all applicants.

1.2.7.2   The results of the oral interview shall be documented in the candidate's file.

1.2.8   Physical and age qualifications are found on Requirements for Deputy Sheriff/Corrections Officer.

1.2.9   Each candidate shall undergo a physical examination at his/her expense, to be conducted by an agency designated State licensed physician. The physician shall complete, sign, and date the Criminal Justice Standards Training Commission form CJSTC-39, Minimum Guidelines For Physical Examination. In addition, two tests shall be conducted at the expense of this agency, as indicated below.

1.2.9.1   Each applicant shall complete a drug analysis through the testing of his/her urine. This test shall be administered by a certified laboratory identified by the Director of the Personnel Section.

1.2.9.2   Each applicant shall successfully pass an eye test conducted by a licensed professional selected by the Director of the Personnel Section.

1.2.10   A strength and endurance assessment, as described on the Physical Assessment Test form, shall be administered to each candidate for a certified position.

1.2.11   This agency shall require each applicant for a law enforcement/corrections certified position to be examined by a qualified professional psychologist. Psychological screening will be conducted to evaluate job related characteristics. Records of the results of these examinations shall be retained on file in the Behavioral Science Unit.

Federal Constraints

In the past 20 years, the legislative and executive branches of the federal government have devoted much attention to establishing and clarifying the rights available to members of "protected classes" insofar as competing for employment positions in both the public and the private work sectors. Discrimination in employment, promotion, discipline, and compensation are forbidden. Discrimination is particularly defined in terms of gender, race, national origin, age, and more recently physical disability. In some ways, the complexity of the most current (1990) Americans with Disabilities Act (ADA) creates ambiguities in interpretation and application particularly in the area of police selection (Higgenbotham, 1991; Scuro, 1992).

The ADA took effect on July 26, 1992, for employers with 25 or more employees; on July 26, 1994, it will take effect for employers with 15 to 24 employees (Public Law 101-336, 1990). Preemployment medical inquiries, medical exams, and psychological testing will be prohibited except that a job offer may be conditioned on successful completion of a *postoffer* medical or psychological exam. All medical and psychological tests have to be done on a "pass–fail" basis. The Act requires that medical criteria be "appropriate." Each medical and psychological standard adopted by an agency may ultimately be substantiated through expensive court litigation (Litchford, 1991). The Act states that any disability the applicant may have must not detract from the individual's qualifications to perform the job, with or without reasonable accommodation by the employer. These federal requirements do not require that a disabled person be hired, but demand equal employment opportunity only if the person is capable of performing the essential functions of the job. The Act further requires that if an examination such as a psychological or medical examination be given, all applicants for the job must be subject to the same medical and/or psychological screening. Those characteristics measured by the psychological tests must be known to be related to the job and consistent with "business necessity."

There are varying opinions as to whether the preemployment psychological examination must be given *after* making a conditional offer of employment. If the screening is for the purpose of diagnosing mental illness based on a medical model, then the evaluations probably must be conducted after a conditional offer of employment has been made by the law enforcement agency. Equal employment opportunity employment regulations have stated that "impairment" does not include common personality traits such as poor judgment or a quick temper. Thus, preemployment evaluations of such characteristics prior to a conditional offer of employment may not be in violation of the ADA. The preemployment screening must not screen out an individual with a disability on the basis of the disability unless it can be shown that disability is job related for the position in question. The informed opinion at this point is that there is little dispute that physical fitness and mental stability are critical to effective police performance, and it appears that nothing in the ADA would impede continued utilization of job-related psychological screening (Flanagan, 1991).

Confidentiality

Psychologists are aware of and generally deeply concerned about issues of confidentiality in the work they do. The understanding that psychologists have concerning their relationship with clients and the protection such clients may receive from the restrictions of the APA Code of Ethics, or of state licensing boards, does not apply in preemployment screening situations with police applicants. In this case, the client is not the applicant, but the agency for whom the testing is being done. In recruitment screening, the applicant has limited rights except in the areas of discrimination and hiring practices, as noted in the previous section. The issue of confidentiality can be a thorny one (Weiner, 1986).

Psychologists who conduct recruit screening would be well advised to ensure that each applicant understands the purpose of the test, and agrees to participate, in writing. Figure 4.2 presents a simple informed consent form for such a purpose.

ANYTOWN POLICE DEPARTMENT
APPLICANT'S INFORMED CONSENT FOR PSYCHOLOGICAL TESTING

APPLICANT'S NAME _____
(Last)   (First)   (Middle)

I understand that I will be taking (a) psychological tests(s) as a part of my application for employment by the Anytown Police Department. I further understand that the test(s) will be scored and profiled in a standardized manner and that these results will be used by the selection board as a part of their decision process. I agree to answer all questions in a straightforward, direct, and honest manner.

_____
(Applicant's Signature)

_____
(Date)

Witness: _____

FIGURE 4.2   Informed Consent Form for Use in Recruit Testing

REPORTING THE RESULTS OF PSYCHOLOGICAL SCREENING

Too often, the reports of clinical evaluation of police candidates' emotional fitness contain rich descriptive accounts typical of the reports generally written by clinical psychologists in a practice situation. These reports may or may not be useful in weeding out candidates who will not make good police officers. In most instances, the screening procedure's "search for pathology" may not be the best help that psychologists can give law enforcement in selecting the best applicants for jobs (Lefkowitz, 1977).

The psychologist who does not have the advantage of a careful study of positive traits that relate to efficiency in the police job, or local norms for screening out undesirable traits that are detrimental to the police officer's position must whenever possible simplify the reports so that they are as useful as they can be, without being irrelevant, distracting, or confusing.

Figure 4.3 presents a limited kind of recruit screening done by a consultant to a small-town police agency. Part of the report is fairly objective, and other parts of it are based on clinical decision making.

Indeed, the report in Figure 4.3 is very simple. Questions can be raised as to the reliability and the validity of such reports. This format, however, is usually well received by members of the selection committee in a police

---

POLICE SCREENING INSTITUTE
APPLICANT PSYCHOLOGICAL SCREENING

NAME OF APPLICANT   Doe, John

DEPARTMENT   Anytown Police Department

REFERRED BY   Sgt. Brown and Chief Smith

DATE OF SCREENING   April 11, 1990

SCREENING PROCEDURES

Minnesota Multiphasic Personality Inventory (MMPI)
Wonderlic Personnel Test, Form IV
Writing Sample
Interview

RESULTS

Mr. Doe presents himself in a relatively rigid manner. He is about 6 feet in height and of moderately stocky build. He answers questions directly, and appears to be alert and responsive. He does not appear to be threatened by the testing situation and he answers all questions quite directly. When asked about any negative traits he might have for the job, he indicates his handwriting is relatively poor but he is working on this to make his writing more readable.

FIGURE 4.3 Sample Report of Preemployment Psychological Screening

INTELLECTUAL FACTORS

Mr. Doe's performance on the Wonderlic places him at the 82nd percentile in comparison with adults at all educational levels. This places Mr. Doe in the Bright range of intellectual capacity. This means that on this standardized test, in comparison with all males between the ages of 18 and 30 who have at least a high school education, he performs as well as or better than 82 out of 100.

PERSONALITY FACTORS

The personality tests suggest that Mr. Doe may at times be somewhat nonconforming and impulsive. He has a tendency to act independently and may have some minor difficulties with social expectation.

FINAL SUMMARY EVALUATION

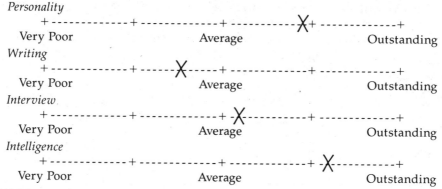

Personality

+ ------------- + ------------- + ----------- X + ------------- +
Very Poor   Average   Outstanding

Writing

+ ------------- + ------ X ----- + ------------- + ------------- +
Very Poor   Average   Outstanding

Interview

+ ------------- + ------------- + - X ----------- + ------------- +
Very Poor   Average   Outstanding

Intelligence

+ ------------- + ------------- + ------------- + - X ----------- +
Very Poor   Average   Outstanding

RECOMMENDATION

Psychological test results are advisory and should never be used as the sole basis on hiring or firing decisions.

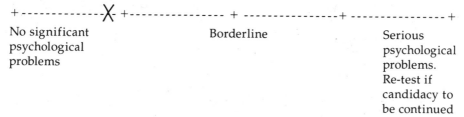

+ ------------- X - + ---------------- + ---------------- + ---------------- +
No significant   Borderline   Serious
psychological   psychological
problems   problems.
                                                         Re-test if
                                                         candidacy to
                                                         be continued

Mr. Doe is a bright law enforcement applicant. There are some indications that he is rigid and may have tendencies to follow the rules too closely in some instances. It is possible that with good Field Training and supervision, he will become more flexible. There are some small indications that he may use alcohol to relieve stress. This should be monitored and explored.

William Jones, PhD
Licensed Psychologist

FIGURE 4.3 *(continued)*

department because it is a straightforward statement of whether the psychologist thinks the individual has any serious problems that could lead to undesirable behavior should the candidate be selected, trained and put on the job.

In some agencies, efforts have been made to provide a more objective screening procedure, where issues of reliability and validity are considered in some depth. Some selection committees want more information about the individual's psychological status if questions are to be raised about the applicant's fitness for the police job. Figure 4.4 provides a format for a single-page psychological screening report based on research conducted in a local agency, using McCormick's "good cop/bad cop" profile (McCormick, 1984).

McCormick developed this profile in one agency and cross-validated it in a second law enforcement agency. In using this form, the Minnesota Multiphasic Personality Inventory, the Wonderlic Personnel Test, and a clinical interview constitute the basis on which the single page is filled out. Intelligence is described in terms of the percentile for high school graduates, ages 18 to 30. The four scales developed in McCormick's research were cross-validated by Blau et al. (1993) in their own department.

The form presents descriptors for each of the four "good cop/bad cop" negative indicators so that the selection board can get some idea as to the kind of behavior that can be expected from applicants whose scores exceed a T-score of 60 on the four critical scales. These descriptors are reported by Lachar (1974).

The report shown in Figure 4.4 commends itself by its simplicity. It provides relatively little information but still meets the need of selection boards to have "some idea" what the tests may mean.

Figure 4.5 presents a slightly different report form, where the results of the interview are included in a two-page report. There is no information available as to whether the longer or the shorter report is more effective or more desirable. The choice of report style and format still remains a matter of choice by the individual psychologist responsible for the employment screening procedure.

As can be seen in the two-page report illustrated by Figure 4.5, the candidate's behavior during the interview more or less confirmed the MMPI test results noted on page 1 of that report.

Figure 4.6 presents a somewhat different preemployment screening evaluation. In this case, the consulting psychologist was requested to conduct a third screening evaluation. The candidate had "passed" one and "failed" one with psychologists ordinarily used by this particular department. The psychologist conducting the third evaluation was asked to provide a "tiebreaker."

Report styles vary. Every psychologist who works with law enforcement agencies must choose the style that is most appropriate and acceptable to the individual organization.

LAW ENFORCEMENT OFFICER APPLICANT
PSYCHOLOGICAL SCREENING RESULTS

NAME _____ DATE TESTED _____

INTELLIGENCE

Comments _____

PERSONALITY

Hs ( )	Hy ( )	Pd ( )	Ma ( )
Below 60 [ ]	[ ]	[ ]	[ ]
60–74 [ ]	60–69 [ ]	60–69 [ ]	60–64 [ ]
Significant concern about body functions; Vague concerns about health; Emphasizes physical problems.	Experiences physical problems under stress; Naive; Self-centered; Lacks understanding of interpersonal relationships.	Independent; Somewhat nonconforming; Impulsive; Minor problems with societal rules and expectations.	Energetic and enthusiastic; May be too independent.
			65–69 [ ]
			Hyperactivity may reduce efficiency.
75–84 [ ]	70–75 [ ]	70–79 [ ]	70–85 [ ]
Prominent concerns over physical func-tioning; Many physical problems reported; Sour attitude.	Immature; Demanding; Egocentric; Gross social immaturity.	Rebellious; Resentful; Nonconforming; Low tolerance level; Impulsive-ness; Often goes undetected in bright people.	Maladaptive overactivity; Low tolerance level; Irritable, angry, and restless; Intense but short-range enthusiasm.

OTHER SCALES ABOVE 70 ____ ____ ____ ____
( ) ( ) ( ) ( ) ( ) ( ) ( )

RECOMMENDATIONS   [ ] No Apparent   [ ] Borderline   [ ] Serious
                       Problems   Problems
                                                             Possible

ADDITIONAL COMMENTS _____

_____

DATE OF REPORT _____ BY _____

**Psychological test results should never be used as the sole criteria
for hire/no hire or termination decisions. Results are advisory
to the administrators who make these decisions.**

FIGURE 4.4   Research-Based Psychological Screening Report

LAW ENFORCEMENT OFFICER APPLICANT
PSYCHOLOGICAL SCREENING RESULTS

NAME __Jones, Al_____ DATE TESTED __1/17/92____

INTELLIGENCE _____ Fell at the 11th percentile in comparison with males, high

Comments _____ school graduates, ages 18 to 30._____

PERSONALITY

Hs (70)	Hy (65)	Pd (78)	Ma (63)
Below 60 [ ]	[ ]	[ ]	[ ]
60–74 [X]	60–69 [X]	60–69 [ ]	60–64 [X]
Significant concern about body functions; Vague concerns about health; Emphasizes physical problems.	Experiences physical problems under stress; Naive; Self-centered; Lacks understanding of interpersonal relationships.	Independent; Somewhat nonconforming; Impulsive; Minor problems with societal rules and expectations.	Energetic and enthusiastic; May be too independent.
			65–69 [ ]
			Hyperactivity may reduce efficiency.
75–84 [ ]	70–75 [ ]	70–79 [X]	70–85 [ ]
Prominent concerns over physical func-tioning; Many physical problems reported; Sour attitude.	Immature; Demanding; Egocentric; Gross social immaturity.	Rebellious; Resentful; Nonconforming; Low tolerance level; Impulsive-ness; Often goes undetected in bright people.	Maladaptive overactivity; Low tolerance level; Irritable, angry, and restless; Intense but short-range enthusiasm.

OTHER SCALES ABOVE 70 ___K___ ___ ___ ___ ___ ___ ___
                       (76) (   ) (   ) (   ) (   ) (   ) (   )

RECOMMENDATIONS [ ] No Apparent   [ ] Borderline   [X] Serious
                      Problems   Problems
                                                             Possible

ADDITIONAL COMMENTS __Is not likely to bring credit to the job._____

_____

DATE OF REPORT __1/19/92__   BY __Z. Brown, PhD_____

**Psychological test results should never be used as the sole criteria
for hire/no hire or termination decisions. Results are advisory
to the administrators who make these decisions.**

FIGURE 4.5 A Preemployment Psychological Screening Report with an Interview
Summary

INTERVIEW

DATE ___1/18/92___   BY ___Z. Brown___

	Very Poor	Average	Outstanding

1. APPEARANCE   +....X... +........ +........ +........ +

   Came to interview wearing torn jeans and dirty sneakers. Shirt torn at the
   elbow. Smokes without asking permission. Needs haircut.

2. COMMUNICATION   +X........ +......... +......... +......... +

   Uses swear words continually during discussion. Has a nasal, rasping voice.

3. SOCIAL SKILLS   +........ X........ +........ +........ +

   Has some semblance of politeness when put under pressure.

4. CLINICAL IMPRESSION   +....X... +........ +........ +........ +

   This young man appears to be easily threatened and responds with
   aggressiveness and resentfulness.

FINAL SUMMARY EVALUATION

	very poor	average	outstanding
Personality	+.....X... +.......... +..........+ ....+		
Writing	+.....X... +.......... + ...+ ....+		
Interview	+X........ +.......... + ...+ ....+		
Intelligence	+X........ +.......... + ...+ ....+		

FIGURE 4.5   *(continued)*

PRESELECTION PSYCHOLOGICAL SCREENING

NAME Blue, Jack   DATE OF EVALUATION 9/10/92

ADDRESS P.O. Box 2330   DATE OF BIRTH   8/11/62

     Anytown, FL 32307 PHONE   (904) 123-4567

REASON FOR REFERRAL

Mr. Blue was referred for a psychological evaluation by Chief Brown. This is Mr. Blue's third examination. Results of the first examination indicated that Mr. Blue would not be a fit applicant for a law enforcement position. Results of the second evaluation contraindicated the first evaluation and suggests that Mr. Blue would be a suitable law enforcement candidate. The present evaluation will be used to evaluate Mr. Blue's suitability as a law enforcement officer taking into account the first two reports.

RESPONSE TO EVALUATION

Mr. Blue is approximately six feet two inches tall and weighs 245 pounds. He has a muscular build. He has brown hair and brown eyes. Speech is clear and slow. Hearing appeared to be within normal limits. Motor behavior was tense. It was noted that he gripped his pencil quite tightly. He is right-handed. Mr. Blue cooperated fully during the examination. He appeared to be able to shift mind-set between testing and interview. It was noted that Mr. Blue is a fingernail biter. He was well-groomed and dressed casually for the evaluation.

TESTS ADMINISTERED

Wonderlic Personnel Test-Form IV, Minnesota Multiphasic Personality Inventory (MMPI), Reitan-Indiana Neuropsychological Screening Test, Draw-a-Person Test (DAP), Clinical Interview, Behavioral Observations.

EVALUATION RESULTS

A. *Intelligence and Neuropsychological Factors*

On the Wonderlic Personnel Test, Mr. Blue obtained a raw score of 20. When compared against males of all educational levels, this placed him at the 40th percentile. This means that he exceeds 40 percent of all males of all education levels nationwide in terms of intellectual functioning.

On the Reitan-Indiana Neuropsychological Screening Test Mr. Blue's results were suggestive of mild cerebral disturbance, particularly in the right cerebral hemisphere.

In general, results of both intellectual and neuropsychological testing are within the broad range of normal.

B. *Personality Factors*

Mr. Blue appears to be quite candid and straightforward. Test results, however, suggest that Mr. Blue has a tendency to present himself in an overly optimistic or positive light. Testing and interview suggests that Mr. Blue's positive and amiable style of interaction may wane when the novelty of new endeavors begins to diminish.

FIGURE 4.6   A Preemployment Screening Evaluation in the Narrative Style

Mr. Blue has a tendency to have minor altercations with the law. This may be in the form of nonconformance to social standards. Mr. Blue has a tendency to be impulsive. This may result in him losing his temper and engaging in fighting behaviors.

He views himself as somewhat of a "macho" male. This may offend others around him. He has a tendency at times to view the behaviors of others as worse than they are.

Mr. Blue's past history clearly indicates that he has had problems with drinking and with fighting. Although these behaviors generally tend to wane with age, there is no indication that this has begun to occur.

CONCLUSIONS

The current psychological testing of Mr. Jack Blue suggests that he would not be an appropriate candidate for law enforcement training and service.

> Francis X. Smith, PhD
> Consulting Police Psychologist
> Florida Lic. # PY1234000

FIGURE 4.6 *(continued)*

Computer-generated psychological test reports are now almost standard procedure for many psychologists. Such tests are available for preemployment screening in law enforcement. Figure 4.7 (pp. 112–119) presents a computer-generated preemployment screening test report of the Inwald Personality Inventory.

Currently, there is no "standardized" form of report on preemployment screening for police officers. As more studies are done to relate standardized instruments to the police job, such a formalized report may evolve.

CONCLUSIONS

The importance of preemployment psychological testing is underscored by the tremendous cost-effectiveness of such programs. Recruiting, testing, hiring, training, and equipping replacement officers are expensive procedures (Pape, 1990). Cost analysis of the effectiveness of preemployment screening suggests that it costs a major city almost a half million dollars for each employment error in hiring an unsuitable officer (Fitzsimmons, 1986).

The process of screening applicants has received some attention but certainly represents only the beginning (Kanatz & Inwald, 1983). Serious questions remain as to the validity and reliability of such procedures. To some extent, psychologists have done a "good job" because most departments can tolerate a good many false negatives. The number of applicants for police jobs usually far exceeds the number of employment spaces open. Although this is somewhat unfair and should be rectified, most departments that have instituted preemployment testing still agree that screening has improved the turnover problem significantly. The remaining difficulties are being addressed (Ostrov, 1986a).

Researchers are beginning to explore some of the significant problems such as the changes that occur after a police officer passes through training and into active service. Measuring psychological traits prior to training may disregard the powerful shaping influences throughout a police officer's career, beginning at the academy and ending with retirement (Dunnette & Motowidlo, 1976). Fortunately, some researchers are applying traditional personnel research methods to develop comprehensive selection procedures for police departments (Ellison, 1986; Whisenand, 1989).

Currently, most psychologists serving local law enforcement agencies are following the procedure of selecting out negative traits to help law enforcement departments avoid problems that result from hiring officers with personal characteristics that are antithetical to good policing. Until such time as comprehensive batteries are available and can be fitted to local conditions, police psychologists are well advised to do the best they can, following the standards provided by the American Psychological Association, the American Educational Research Association, and the National Council in Measurement of Education (1985) in their *Standards for Education and Psychological Testing.*

HILSON RESEARCH INC.   IPI NARRATIVE REPORT
INWALD PERSONALITY INVENTORY
Agency 0000-1   Date 10/02/92   Case 75   Sex -M-   Race -W-

INTRODUCTION

This report is intended to be used as an aid in assessing an individual's emotional stability and suitability for a job in the public safety/security field. It is not intended as a substitute for a clinical interview, as a final evaluative report regarding a candidate's ultimate job suitability, or as a sole source for denying employment to an applicant. It has been developed with the purpose of providing relevant material to be further explored in individual interviews and investigations. These results are also intended to provide supportive material with regard to "post-conditional offer" hiring decisions. It is expected that the results will be used as one component in a comprehensive selection procedure, including other elements, such as written tests, interviews, and background investigations.

VALIDITY MEASURE

This individual has been candid in answering the items on this questionnaire. He has been willing to reveal minor faults and shortcomings.

"ACTING-OUT" BEHAVIOR MEASURES—SPECIFIC "EXTERNAL" BEHAVIOR

* He may be a habitual user of alcohol. He describes himself as a recreational drinker with a good alcohol tolerance. Check his drinking habits carefully.

** This person may be a habitual user of drugs. He is likely to use marijuana on a regular basis, and may also use other substances. A history of frequent drug usage and/or drug dependence may be indicated.

** He shows a significant history and/or pattern of motor vehicle infractions and driving difficulties. These are likely to include moving violations, automobile accidents, and, in some cases, driving while under the influence of drugs or alcohol. Such individuals may be immature, impulsive, and somewhat resentful of authority.

According to item responses, there is little evidence of significant work adjustment difficulty in this person's background. To verify this finding, it is suggested that an evaluation of his work record also be made.

** This individual shows evidence of clear antisocial tendencies. He shows a history of brushes with the law and societal norms. This may include arrests and convictions for criminal activities. Disciplinary problems in school or military service may also be indicated. Such individuals tend to be cynical and manipulative, unable to control their hostile impulses. If this person is being considered for a position of responsibility, a very careful background check is highly recommended.

FIGURE 4.7   A Computer-Generated Preemployment Screening Test Report
Reproduced by permission of R. Inwald, Hilson Research.

* He may show a somewhat casual attitude about work attendance and lateness. He may have difficulty meeting job responsibilities, and may tend to contract minor illnesses that keep him from working.

ATTITUDES AND TEMPERAMENT

* Items endorsed indicate this individual may be an impulsive risk taker who may tend to make "spur of the moment" decisions and try things for a "thrill." This may be associated with substance abuse tendencies.

This individual does not express a large number of antisocial attitudes, cynicism about society, or a sense that he feels justified in breaking rules in order to "beat the system."

** According to item responses, he may be an extremely impulsive, overactive individual who maintains an almost frantic pitch of activity and finds it difficult to slow down. He appears to make quick, spontaneous decisions that may be subject to sudden changes. He is restless, impatient, and likely to overreact to small emergencies. He may be seen by others to be volatile and/or aggressive. He also may lack the ability to plan ahead, and may live only for the immediate moment. Such individuals often experience interpersonal difficulties and show poor work adjustment. A pattern of asocial behavior may also be evident.

He does not appear to be an overly rigid, critical person, or to have fixed, stereotyped views of the world.

There is little evidence that this person is overly "driven" or competitive with regard to his career or life goals. He does not endorse items indicating similarity to "Type A" personalities.

INTERNALIZED CONFLICT MEASURES

He does not admit to a large number of physical symptoms or minor illnesses that might adversely affect job performance. He does not appear to be overly concerned about his health, and may not be particularly prone to physical conditions or illnesses.

This person denies having had past counseling for a problem, having participated in a formal treatment program, or having ever taken tranquilizers.

He does not show evidence of excessive anxiety, or a tendency to be a chronic worrier.

Based on item responses, this individual does not admit to symptoms or thoughts characteristic of people who have phobias or irrational fears that limit their functioning.

This person does not appear to be overly concerned with details, and does not show evidence of being particularly "obsessive" in his approach to life.

FIGURE 4.7 *(continued)*

He does not admit to symptoms of depression, and appears to be satisfied with his general progress in life.

There is indication that this individual spends at least some leisure time in the company of others, and desires outside social contacts. He does not appear to be a "loner," and may enjoy a support network of friends.

He has not admitted to a large number of unusual experiences or thoughts common to persons who suffer from a severe emotional disturbance or thought disorder.

INTERPERSONAL CONFLICT MEASURES

This person does not appear to have difficulty asserting himself when necessary. He expresses confidence in his ability to speak his mind, and may be able to face confrontations with others in a straightforward manner.

It appears that this individual does not have significant difficulty getting along with others. He may be adept at avoiding unnecessary arguments, and does not appear to alienate others through aggressive, impulsive, or moody behavior.

He does not seem to be unduly suspicious or skeptical of the motives of others, nor does he express a sense that others are likely to take unfair advantage of him.

* There is some indication of family problems in this person's background. He may harbor some degree of resentment toward his parents and/or relatives.

* He has endorsed some items suggesting possible difficulties relating to or working with members of the opposite sex. His attitudes might be more carefully explored in interview to determine if they might affect performance on the job.

** Difficulties in spouse/mate relationship(s) are strongly suggested. This may be part of an overall pattern of family conflict and interpersonal difficulty, and should be carefully evaluated in follow-up investigations.

IPI CRITICAL ITEMS FOR FOLLOW-UP EVALUATION

The following endorsed item(s) may provide useful leads for follow-up interviews and/or further investigation. Because individual items may have been endorsed in error, they should not be used alone as a basis for making decisions, and should be verified by the tested individual and/or by outside sources whenever possible.

TROUBLE WITH THE LAW

11. I have been suspended from school. (T)
36. I have had no fistfights since I was twenty years old. (F)
130. I have been involved in a fistfight in the past five years. (T)
159. I have been convicted of a crime. (T)
171. I was arrested in my youth over a minor incident. (T)
287. A bill collector has tried to find me. (T)

FIGURE 4.7 *(continued)*

ALCOHOL AND/OR DRUG USE

5. I enjoy a six-pack of beer, or four or five drinks. (T)
31. I have smoked marijuana without other people around. (T)
73. I smoke marijuana on social occasions. (T)
157. I could easily drink a six-pack, or four or five drinks. (T)
248. I have tried cocaine more than once. (T)
284. I have smoked marijuana more than two times in a week. (T)

TEMPERAMENT

172. I used to have a really bad temper. (T)

DEPRESSION

142. There have been times when I have lost my appetite, had difficulty sleeping, and lost interest in my usual activities. (T)

PHOBIC/STRESS/PHYSICAL SYMPTOMS

137. I am usually anxious about something. (T)

UNUSUAL SUSPICIONS/CONCERNS

44. Sometimes I worry about people thinking I am crazy. (T)

FAMILY CONFLICTS

106. I have been divorced. (T)
141. I am currently separated from my mate. (T)
195. I have had a child out-of-wedlock. (T)

Critical Item Total = 19 T-score = 73

FIGURE 4.7 *(continued)*

HILSON RESEARCH INC.   PSYCHOLOGIST RATINGS
INWALD PERSONALITY INVENTORY
Agency 0000-1   Date 10/02/92   Case 75   Sex -M-   Race -W-

PREDICTION OF LAW ENFORCEMENT PERFORMANCE RATING

The IPI prediction of law enforcement performance is a prediction of the rating a psychologist would assign to a candidate after administering a battery of tests and conducting a clinical interview. In a research study, psychologists (with no access to this IPI rating) rated individuals as "Low Risk" for future performance difficulty (52% of candidates), "Moderate Risk" (32%), or "High Risk" ("Do Not Recommend"—16%). Fisher's linear discriminant function equations for each of the rating categories were developed utilizing IPI scale scores.

In order to generate the predictions below, this individual's IPI scale scores were entered into the equations developed for each rating category. Equation totals were compared and the equation with the highest total was selected to make the prediction (see asterisk below).

Low risk for future performance difficulty	14.4
Moderate risk for future performance difficulty	16.4
*High risk for future performance difficulty	19.9

HIGH RISK FOR FUTURE PERFORMANCE DIFFICULTY: In a validation study of 3,464 public safety/security officer candidates, 53% of the candidates receiving this IPI "High Risk" rating were subsequently rated "Do Not Recommend" by the evaluating psychologist. For this group, 11% were subsequently rated as "Low Risk" by the psychologist based on tests and clinical interview data. In a cross-validation study of 2,332 additional public safety/security officer candidates, 52% were rated "Do Not Recommend" and 10% were rated as a "Low Risk" by the psychologist.

FIGURE 4.7   *(continued)*

HILSON RESEARCH INC.   PREDICTIONS OF PERFORMANCE
                    INWALD PERSONALITY INVENTORY

Agency 0000-1   Date 10/02/92   Case 75   Sex -M-   Race -W-

PREDICTIONS OF PERFORMANCE

Using Fisher's Discriminant Function Equations

*Late > = 3 Times	9.3
Late < 3 Times	7.4
Absent > = 3 Times	11.2
*Absent < 3 Times	13.5
Disciplinary Actions	−1.1
*No Disciplinary Actions	0.2
*Terminated	4.7
Not Terminated	4.4

Based on this analysis, it would be predicted that this individual is most likely:

1. To be late three or more times within one year (60% accuracy)

2. To have less than three absences within one year (61% accuracy)

3. To not have any disciplinary actions within one year (57% accuracy)

4. To be terminated within one year (67% accuracy)

Note: The above predictions are based on data obtained from an urban agency. Candidates predicted by the IPI to be terminated within one year who also show a Critical Item total score greater than 10 should be carefully evaluated before hiring.

FIGURE 4.7   *(continued)*

HILSON RESEARCH INC.   PERSONALITY PROFILE GRAPH
                          LAW ENFORCEMENT NORMS
        Agency 0000-1   Date 10/02/92   Case 75   Sex -M-   Race -W-

Raw	Tsc		10	20	30	40	50	60	70	80	90	100
5	35	GD	XXXXXXXXXXXXXXXX									
3	65	AL	XXXXXXXXXXXXXXXXXXXXXXXXXXXXXXXXXX									
5	87	DG	XXXXXXXXXXXXXXXXXXXXXXXXXXXXXXXXXXXXXXXXXXXXXXX									
5	67	DV	XXXXXXXXXXXXXXXXXXXXXXXXXXXXXXXXXXX									
3	50	JD	XXXXXXXXXXXXXXXXXXXXXXXX									
10	76	TL	XXXXXXXXXXXXXXXXXXXXXXXXXXXXXXXXXXXXXXXX									
5	60	AA	XXXXXXXXXXXXXXXXXXXXXXXXXXXX									
9	68	SA	XXXXXXXXXXXXXXXXXXXXXXXXXXXXXXXXXXX									
8	56	AS	XXXXXXXXXXXXXXXXXXXXXXXXXXX									
19	69	HP	XXXXXXXXXXXXXXXXXXXXXXXXXXXXXXXXXXXX									
4	39	RT	XXXXXXXXXXXXXXXXXX									
7	56	TA	XXXXXXXXXXXXXXXXXXXXXXXXXX									
0	40	IC	XXXXXXXXXXXXXXXXXX									
0	47	TP	XXXXXXXXXXXXXXXXXXXXX									
3	54	AN	XXXXXXXXXXXXXXXXXXXXXXXXX									
3	38	PH	XXXXXXXXXXXXXXXXX									
1	40	OB	XXXXXXXXXXXXXXXXXX									
3	51	DE	XXXXXXXXXXXXXXXXXXXXXXXX									
1	37	LO	XXXXXXXXXXXXXXXX									
2	50	UE	XXXXXXXXXXXXXXXXXXXXXXXX									
3	48	LA	XXXXXXXXXXXXXXXXXXXXXX									
3	49	ID	XXXXXXXXXXXXXXXXXXXXXXX									
4	48	US	XXXXXXXXXXXXXXXXXXXXXX									
6	63	FC	XXXXXXXXXXXXXXXXXXXXXXXXXXXXXXXX									
1	61	SC	XXXXXXXXXXXXXXXXXXXXXXXXXXXXX									
3	68	SP	XXXXXXXXXXXXXXXXXXXXXXXXXXXXXXXXX									

                          10   20   30   40   50   60   70   80   90   100

Scores over 69T are "significantly" elevated and point to areas for further
exploration. Each scale over 69T falls outside the "average range" and indicates
the person tested has scored higher than 97.7% of the norming group.

FIGURE 4.7   *(continued)*

Scores over 59T may point to areas for further exploration and indicate that the person tested has scored higher than 84.1% of the norming group.

Scale/Content Area Descriptions

GD	Guardedness	TL	Trouble with the Law and Society
AL	Alcohol		
DG	Drugs	AA	Absence Abuse
DV	Driving Violations	SA	Substance Abuse
JD	Job Difficulties	AS	Antisocial Attitudes
HP	Hyperactivity	LO	Loner Type
RT	Rigid Type	UE	Unusual Experience
TA	Type "A"	LA	Lack of Assertiveness
IC	Illness Concerns	ID	Interpersonal Difficulties
TP	Treatment Programs	US	Undue Suspiciousness
AN	Anxiety	FC	Family Conflicts
PH	Phobic Personality	SC	Sexual Concerns
OB	Obsessive Personality	SP	Spouse/Mate Conflicts
DE	Depression		

FIGURE 4.7 *(continued)*

CHAPTER FIVE

Fitness-for-Duty Evaluation

Policing tends to be a stressful and sometimes unpredictably dangerous vocation. Day in and day out, police officers must make difficult decisions concerning themselves and the citizens they are sworn to protect. The requirements for alertness, energy, and good judgment are high. The ability of a police officer to function properly at all times is subject to the effects of stress, family difficulties, injuries sustained off and on the job, financial problems, shift work, fatigue, depression, and an almost endless variety of other influences. Many of these difficulties are common to all police officers at one time or another during their careers.

When a police officer's performance is affected by internal or external factors, the issue arises as to whether the officer is "fit for duty." In general, a police officer is considered unfit for duty if his or her physical or emotional condition might result in danger to the self, to fellow officers, to citizens, or to the reputation and proper operation of the department.

Traditionally, fitness-for-duty evaluations have referred to physical examinations to determine whether the officer is physically fit to carry on the strenuous tasks of policing. In more recent years, police departments have come to depend on psychological or psychiatric evaluations to determine whether personal or emotional factors might prevent the officer from functioning properly.

At the present time, fitness-for-duty evaluation is usually requested when an officer's emotional or behavioral adjustment in relation to the job is cast into question by reported incidents or situations that suggest instability. At this point, a fitness-for-duty evaluation is ordinarily conducted at the request of the management of the agency (Inwald, 1990b). Many referrals for fitness-for-duty evaluation are made for officers who have done something or have been involved in something that may put the department or the officers in jeopardy legally. They may have been implicated in questionable behavior in which the public media has asked questions about police brutality or proper procedure. Sometimes, a citizen's complaint to the Internal Affairs Division results in an investigation that raises the question of an officer's emotional stability. Or an officer who was involved in a shooting may be suffering post-traumatic stress.

Many police administrators are reluctant to order a fitness-for-duty evaluation because, by definition, it suggests a suspected serious deficiency in the officer's ability to "do the job." Administrative complications and sometimes legal problems can follow such a referral. As a result, fitness-for-duty evaluations may sometimes not be requested when they would be quite appropriate (Saxe-Clifford, 1986).

Delprino and Bahn reported in 1988 that approximately 39% of the departments they surveyed used psychological examinations for suspended and problem police officers; 67% believed there was a need for such psychological evaluations; and 43% intended to institute such procedures.

LEGAL AND ETHICAL ISSUES

Psychologists generally understand that their relationships with clients are governed by a code of ethics that requires confidentiality. In most states, statutory provisions promulgated by licensing boards offer the client privileged communication in addition to confidentiality. When evaluating police officers in a fitness-for-duty assessment, psychologists must have a keen awareness of those aspects of confidentiality and privilege that apply and to which the officer is entitled.

In most fitness-for-duty evaluations, the officer has been a member of the agency beyond a probationary period and may have a variety of rights guaranteed by the rules of the agency, the collective bargaining unit for the agency, or in some cases state or federal law. Elaborate due process procedures may be required by the agency or by the union that represents the officer. The officer may have the right to restrict certain previous medical or psychological records from inspection by the evaluating psychologist. Contact with other members of the agency or outside individuals may be allowed, or may be restricted. The officer may have the right to read the report and dispute it in a formal situation. In some instances, an attorney may be permitted to attend the evaluation. With the increasing rights of law enforcement officers to engage in collective bargaining agreements, it is critical that psychologists conducting fitness-for-duty evaluations thoroughly understand the purposes, limitations, and legal implications of an evaluation.

Managing the directed referral of an officer for a fitness-for-duty evaluation is a complex and difficult task (Berberich, 1986). Confidentiality cannot be maintained in view of the source of referral and purpose of the evaluation (Archibald, 1986; Weiner, 1986).

Psychologists conducting fitness-for-duty evaluations have an obligation to explain their role in the proceedings to both the agency referring the officer, and the officer-subject. Differences in attitudes, values, techniques, and priorities can produce situations where the psychologist and the law enforcement personnel find themselves at odds. Certainly, psychologists working for law enforcement agencies must apprise their referral sources of the ethical principles under which they operate. Psychologists must also identify their professional role, credentials, and ethical constraints to the individuals they evaluate. Specifically, psychologists must define the limits of confidentiality and privilege (Deitz & Reese, 1986).

There are those who believe that a mandatory evaluation can be most efficiently done by an individual who is not directly connected with the department making the referral. There is no question that the referral agency is the client in these matters (Ostrov, 1987).

The acceptability of fitness-for-duty evaluations in supporting administrative sanctions against officers has been challenged in a variety of courts. In general, the fitness-for-duty evaluation has fared quite well both in the state courts (see *Redmond v. City of Overland Park*, 672 Supp. 473 (D. Kan. 1987)) as well as in appellate courts (see *City of Greenwood v. Dowler*, 492 N.E.2d 1081 (Ind. ABP. 1 Dist. 1986)).

Before the beginning of any assessment procedures, the officer must completely understand the purpose of the evaluation, the person or persons who requested it, and to whom the results will be addressed. As much as possible, the evaluation should be done for specific purposes, to answer specific questions. This will differ from one fitness-for-duty evaluation to another. Even after the psychologist has explained all of this, the officer should sign an "Informed Consent" form agreeing to the various conditions under which the evaluation will take place. Figure 5.1 presents an Informed Consent form used by the agency whose procedures will be described in Figure 5.2.

Legal issues become even more convoluted when the agency that first refers an officer for a fitness-for-duty evaluation later mandates that the officer, because of conditions found in the evaluation, needs to be referred for treatment. They may then refer the officer to the same psychologist who did the evaluation. When such a directed referral is made, it is usually, from management's point of view, to get the officer to "straighten up." The psychologist is supposed to "take care of this" in some manner. Most mental health professionals believe that when a treatment referral is "directed," the chances of success are quite limited (Berberich, 1986). For both ethical and operational reasons, the mental health professional who does the evaluation should not also do the intervention.

GUIDELINES FOR FITNESS-FOR-DUTY EVALUATIONS

Establishing guidelines for the agency's referral procedures is a vital step in ensuring that fitness-for-duty evaluations proceed in an ethical and efficient manner. These guidelines should specify what agency members are entitled to make such referrals and should spell out the

INFORMED CONSENT—FITNESS FOR DUTY

I, _____, having been referred to the Behavioral Science Unit of the Any County Sheriff's Office for a FITNESS-FOR-DUTY EVALUATION, understand that I will be interviewed by a department psychologist; I will be given a series of psychological tests; and that a report of the findings of this evaluation will be sent to the Sheriff and Undersheriff.

I understand that there will be no interpretation of the results of these tests to me, except as may be done by the Sheriff or the Undersheriff, in respect to the report submitted to them.

I further understand that the test materials will be kept in confidential files in the Behavioral Science Unit for the remainder of my employment with the agency.

I further understand that the report of the evaluation may be used by the Sheriff or the Undersheriff in any administrative matters involving my fitness for duty.

I have had the above explained to me and I agree to do my best in the evaluation process.

_____   _____
OFFICER   WITNESS

_____
DATE

FIGURE 5.1 A Form for Obtaining Informed Consent for Fitness for Duty

---

1. Only qualified psychologists and/or psychiatrists should be responsible for Fitness-for-Duty Evaluations.
2. If professional licenses are required by the state, they should also be required for the mental health professional conducting any Fitness-for-Duty Evaluations.
3. Mental health professionals who conduct Fitness-for-Duty Evaluations should be experienced in the field of police and/or public safety psychology and familiar with the research on testing and evaluation in this field.
4. Whenever possible, Fitness-for-Duty Evaluations should not be conducted by a mental health professional who also provides confidential counseling within the same department.
5. The primary "client" in Fitness-for-Duty Evaluations is the agency, not the officer/employee. Therefore, evaluators who have a dual relationship (e.g., as the officer's past therapist or counselor) should refrain from conducting Fitness-for-Duty Evaluations in these cases.
6. The exact level of confidentiality should be determined in writing through the mental health professional's consultation with the agency prior to conducting Fitness-for-Duty Evaluations.

FIGURE 5.2 Fitness-for-Duty Evaluation Guidelines From "Fitness-for-Duty Evaluation Guidelines: A Survey for Police/Public Safety Administrators and Mental Health Professionals," by R. Inwald, 1990b. Paper presented at the 1990 American Psychological Association meeting, Boston. Printed with permission of Hilson Research Inc., 1990.

7. A signed consent form advising of the limits of confidentiality should be obtained from the officer/employee prior to any assessment for fitness for duty.

8. A full description of the reason(s) for referral for a Fitness-for-Duty Evaluation should be obtained prior to any assessment.

9. Fitness-for-Duty assessments should include (a) at least one interview with the officer/employee, (b) a battery of standardized/written tests, (c) interviews with the supervisor, (d) family, (e) co-workers/associates, (f) therapist, (g) other involved individuals as deemed appropriate, (h) review of any past psychological evaluations, (i) review of any past medical evaluations.

10. Whenever possible, Fitness-for-Duty Evaluators should go beyond standard clinical testing and interviewing techniques to include a review of relevant background information such as personnel records, investigator's reports, as well as appropriate interviews with the officer/employee's associates and/or family members.

11. A full investigation of any specific incidents leading to the Fitness-for-Duty referral should be made before any Fitness-for-Duty recommendations are made to the agency.

12. If information, such as past psychological reports, are deemed necessary for review by the evaluator, yet cannot be obtained, any recommendations should include the comment that the evaluation is based on available data and might be affected by specific additional information that was requested but not obtained by the evaluator.

13. A written report documenting the findings of the evaluation along with specific recommendations regarding the officer/employee's ability to meet responsibilities of continued employment and/or retraining/rehabilitation suggestions should be provided to the agency.

14. Fitness-for-Duty evaluators should not make recommendations outside of their area(s) of expertise. Evaluation and treatment recommendations are appropriate for mental health professionals. However, administrative decisions, such as termination of an employee or the requirement of participation in a treatment program, should be left to the authorities of the referring agency.

15. The written report should provide clear documentation and reason(s) for any determination about an officer/employee's "Fitness-for-Duty."

16. Provisions should be made so that reports are shared only with those directly involved in decision making regarding the officer/employee's current work responsibilities.

17. A policy for providing the Fitness-for-Duty Evaluation results to the officer/employee should be developed with the agency prior to any evaluations. Whenever possible, the evaluator or another qualified mental health professional should be available to interpret results if they are shared with the officer/employee.

18. Detailed supporting test materials, reports, and notes gathered during the evaluation should be maintained by the evaluator for a period of at least three years.

FIGURE 5.2   *(continued)*

degree of confidentiality. The kinds of reports, verbal or written, should be outlined in some form within the agency's general orders. The psychologist, in turn, must be aware of how the assessment will be used and what decisions are likely to be based on the evaluation. When the guidelines are being established and written, the agency's attorney or another legal advisor should participate in the discussions (Saxe-Clifford, 1986).

Stone (1990) suggests that fitness-for-duty evaluations move through three phases: (a) making the officer aware of the nature of the assessment, (b) having the officer take various required tests, and (c) conducting an interview and making observations. From this input, the psychologist develops the evaluation report. Inwald (1990b) has recommended guidelines for fitness-for-duty evaluations based on a survey conducted among police/ public safety administrators and mental health professionals. Figure 5.2 presents Inwald's fitness-for-duty guidelines.

Table 5.1 reports the results of a small research study by Inwald (1990b) with only 25 respondents. It is included because it demonstrates a creative approach that could be used on a continuing basis to monitor and track the development of guidelines or standards for practice.

Fitness-for-duty evaluation referrals should probably never be made by line supervisors or intermediate level management. This provides too much of an opportunity for misunderstandings or misuse of the procedure. The referral should come from the very top or from the Deputy Chief or the Undersheriff. The evaluation request may be instituted by a director of a division or even a supervisor, but direct access to the power to call for the fitness-for-duty evaluation should be restricted to top management. Department regulations should include this stipulation.

Where the source of the referral is unknown or ambiguous, the psychologist should not proceed, but should schedule a consultation to clarify the source of the referral and the individual to whom the results will be directed. At this time, it is also important to determine exactly what questions are being asked.

Figure 5.3 presents a formal general order that prescribes the procedures to be used in a local law enforcement agency for the fitness-for-duty evaluation.

CONTENT OF THE EVALUATION PROCEDURE

Once again, as with selection procedures, psychology's testing traditions are brought to the fore with the fitness-for-duty evaluation. Although the evaluation may be formal or informal because few agencies place restraints on procedures (sometimes requiring only a psychiatric interview), psychologists are likely to administer and interpret a battery of psychological tests. Even in the short period of time that psychologists have been providing these evaluations, it has become somewhat traditional to administer tests, give an extensive interview, and make a formal

TABLE 5.1   Agreement with Fitness-for-Duty Evaluation Guidelines ($N = 25$)

Guideline Number	Agree with No Reservations		Agree with Some Reservations		Disagree		Omissions	
	%	No.	%	No.	%	No.	%	No.
1	52	(13)	12	(3)	36	(9)	0	(0)
2	84	(21)	16	(4)	0	(0)	0	(0)
3	92	(23)	8	(2)	0	(0)	0	(0)
4	72	(18)	24	(6)	4	(1)	0	(0)
5	84	(21)	4	(1)	12	(3)	0	(0)
6	96	(24)	0	(0)	4	(1)	0	(0)
7	68	(17)	24	(6)	8	(2)	0	(0)
8	60	(15)	24	(6)	12	(3)	4	(1)
9a	92	(23)	4	(1)	4	(1)	0	(0)
9b	88	(22)	12	(3)	0	(0)	0	(0)
9c	88	(22)	8	(2)	4	(1)	0	(0)
9d	48	(12)	36	(9)	16	(4)	0	(0)
9e	60	(15)	24	(6)	16	(4)	0	(0)
9f	60	(15)	28	(7)	12	(3)	0	(0)
9g	56	(14)	36	(9)	8	(2)	0	(0)
9h	80	(20)	12	(3)	8	(2)	0	(0)
9i	72	(18)	16	(4)	12	(3)	0	(0)
10	84	(21)	16	(4)	0	(0)	0	(0)
11	84	(21)	12	(3)	4	(1)	0	(0)
12	72	(18)	20	(5)	4	(1)	4	(1)
13	100	(25)	0	(0)	0	(0)	0	(0)
14	76	(19)	16	(4)	8	(2)	0	(0)
15	100	(25)	0	(0)	0	(0)	0	(0)
16	80	(20)	12	(3)	8	(2)	0	(0)
17	96	(24)	0	(0)	4	(1)	0	(0)
18	96	(24)	0	(0)	4	(1)	0	(0)

Note: From "Fitness-for-Duty Evaluation Guidelines: A Survey for Police/Public Safety Administrators and Mental Health Professionals," by R. Inwald, 1990b. Paper presented at the 1990 American Psychological Association meeting, Boston. Printed with permission of the author.

PURPOSE

The Behavioral Science Unit (BSU) performs psychological Fitness-for-Duty Evaluations on officers referred by the Sheriff and the Undersheriff. The purpose is to identify any psychological trait, factor, or condition that may interfere significantly with the officer's ability to carry out his/her mandated duties in a manner concordant with the rules, regulations, general orders, and traditions of the Anycounty Sheriff's Office (ACSO). Each evaluation focuses on questions posed in the referral. Psychological reports of Fitness-for-Duty are advisory only and should never be the sole basis for administrative decisions.

PROCEDURES

A. *REFERRAL*

A request for a Fitness-for-Duty psychological evaluation may be initiated by the Commander of any Division of the ACSO. The written request for the evaluation must come to the Behavioral Science Unit from the Sheriff and the Undersheriff. A formal referral should include:

1. Name of officer.
2. Date of referral.
3. Department of division making referral.
4. Specific questions or concerns, stated in terms of duty performance deficiencies or possible deficiencies.

B. *SCHEDULING*

When the referral is completed by the Undersheriff's secretary, an appointment will be made with the Manager or Assistant Manager of the Behavioral Science Unit. This will ordinarily consist of a 1-hour interview appointment and one or more 3-hour testing appointments.

C. *STRUCTURING*

The officer being referred should be told the reason his/her Commander is making the referral. On arrival for the interview at the BSU office, the officer will be told the following:

1. The nature of the testing sessions.
2. The purpose(s) stated in the referral.
3. That the report will address only the questions or issues noted on the referral (except as noted in #7).
4. The report will be sent in a CONFIDENTIAL envelope.
5. No report or interpretation will be made to the officer by the staff of the BSU.
6. The file of tests and materials will be maintained for seven (7) years and then destroyed.
7. The psychologists of the BSU reserve the right and duty to address significant issues of fitness for duty beyond the questions asked, should issues appear during the evaluation.
8. The officer being evaluated will be required to sign an authorization indicating that he/she understands the purpose and conditions under which

FIGURE 5.3   Fitness-for-Duty Evaluation Procedures

the Fitness-for-Duty Evaluation is being done and that he/she agrees to participate and have the report sent to the Sheriff and Undersheriff.

D. *INTERVIEW*

Each officer who is referred for Fitness-for-Duty Evaluation will be given a clinical interview. The interview will include some or all of the following:

1. The officer's education and work background.
2. Family background and current status.
3. The officer's views and response to the referral questions.
4. Mental health history.
5. Medical history.
6. Mental status examination.
7. Observation.

F. *REPORT*

The Fitness-for-Duty Report shall not be a lengthy traditional psychological report. Since the report is advisory to administration in respect to specific questions as to fitness for duty, the report will contain the following sections:

1. Identifying data.
2. Reasons and questions for referral.
3. Tests administered.
4. Officer's response to the evaluation.
5. Test findings.
6. Opinion regarding fitness for duty.
7. Treatment recommendations, where appropriate.
8. Additional conclusions, where indicated.

APPEAL AND REEVALUATION

In situations where the validity or reliability of the Fitness-for-Duty Evaluation is considered questionable or insufficient, another evaluation can be scheduled. Where therapeutic activity on the part of an impaired officer has been accomplished, a posttreatment Fitness-for-Duty Evaluation may be conducted to determine if the officer has become fit for duty. Where the objectivity of the BSU is questioned or where a conflict of interest is apparent, reevaluation by a psychologist unconnected with the ACSO will be recommended.

RECORDS

The file containing the test data and a copy of the report of the Fitness-for-Duty Evaluation will be kept in a special locked file in the BSU. A copy of the key will be deposited in a sealed envelope with the Administrative Commissioner. When the officer leaves the employ of the ACSO, the file will be destroyed, unless the termination may involve future litigation. Monthly lists of termination should be routinely supplied to the BSU together with indications of whether litigation is an issue.

FIGURE 5.3 *(continued)*

report (Saxe-Clifford, 1986). Where there is concern about future litigation or union challenges, the administration is likely to require a formal report.

The referral questions asked by management are often vague; the letter may simply say "psychological evaluation for fitness-for-duty." Psychologists should make every effort to have the appropriate administrator specify exactly what problems have arisen that cast doubt on the officer's fitness to serve.

Although each referral is different, psychologists have a tendency to conduct a somewhat standardized assessment. Very few departments have specific requirements for the fitness-for-duty test battery. It is a delicate matter to choose the content of the evaluation battery, including not too much and not too little.

Certain basic psychological techniques are generally suitable for the fitness-for-duty request. Some combination of the following will provide answers to most questions:

- Clinical interview.
- Collection of collateral information.
- Measures of intellectual efficiency.
- Evaluation of cognitive skills or neuropsychological deficit.
- Personality evaluation.

Among the data from the preceding procedures should be useful information concerning the officer's fitness. Occasionally, a special test may be advisable, such as a reading skills battery, where the referral is made because the officer is late in submitting reports, or the reports are indecipherable.

Clinical Interview

This interview is generally the first part of the fitness-for-duty evaluation. When the officer arrives for this appointment, the psychologist must identify himself or herself, state the specific reasons for the evaluation, the questions that will be asked, and the individual who will receive the final report. The officer must understand that confidentiality and privilege are very restricted. In addition to providing a verbal explanation, the psychologist should ask the officer to sign a statement itemizing all these constraints as an indication that he or she has given informed consent.

The psychologist may use a formal, guided interview or may prefer a more informal procedure. In either case, careful documentation is necessary. The psychologist may ask about the officer's family, both current and past, as well as about the officer's medical and mental health history. The officer should be asked for his or her views in response to the referral questions about fitness for duty. The psychologist may conduct a mental status examination during the interview and should take observational notes concerning the officer's response to this relatively stressful situation.

Collection of Collateral Information

For the psychologist to be comfortable in reaching conclusions about the fitness of a serving officer, converging information should be obtained from a variety of sources whenever possible. A fitness-for-duty evaluation has greater reliability and validity when it agrees with collateral information and with observations made during the interview.

Collateral information may be available from the officer's personnel file. In some situations, the psychologist may ask the officer's permission to interview family members. The same is true of supervisors and partners. In instances where drug or alcohol abuse is involved, the psychologist may ask permission to interview the officer's sponsor in an AA or other peer-counseling support group.

Although these efforts may pose difficulties at times, it is important that the psychologist be free to contact additional people during the evaluation. Where issues of drug or alcohol abuse occur, hospital records or an interview with the officer's doctor can be helpful.

Such collateral information seeking is somewhat unusual in psychological evaluation, but in the fitness-for-duty evaluation, it can be critical (Ostrov, 1986b).

Intellectual Efficiency

Many psychologists who serve law enforcement agencies include a standard measure of intellectual capacity in their fitness-for-duty evaluations. This may range from as simple a test as the Wonderlic Personnel Test, described in Chapter Four, or may be as extensive as a complete Wechsler Adult Intelligence Scale-Revised. This is a matter of choice and judgment, and no standard exists. Tests should not be given simply to conduct a test battery. There must be purposefulness in the choice of instruments, and if an intellectual measure is included, there should be some reason to believe that this may shed light on the officer's fitness for duty.

Cognitive Skills

This area, associated with the rapid development of neuropsychological screening batteries, becomes more important where an officer has either been in a situation where he or she was physically hurt, including head injuries, or where the officer has been acting in such a way as to suggest that there may be memory dysfunction, cognitive confusion, or deterioration in planning and organizational function. A wide range of neuropsychological screening batteries are available from which the psychologist can choose. There are now short forms of the Halstead–Reitan Neuropsychological Battery (Reitan, 1984) and the Luria–Nebraska Neuropsychological Battery (Golden, 1987).

Personality Evaluation

Where questions about the officer's judgment and behavior are at issue, personality tests are most likely to be utilized in fitness-for-duty evaluations. As with the psychological tests used in selection, the MMPI remains an instrument of choice in most settings. The use of other paper-and-pencil personality tests is rapidly growing. Because few data are available about the usefulness of any psychological tests in fitness-for-duty batteries, the MMPI must be given a certain degree of credibility—a number of studies suggest the reliability of this old warhorse (Wasyliw, Grossman, Heywood, Ostrov, & Kavanaugh, 1988; Grossman, Heywood, Kavanaugh, Ostrov, & Wasyliw, 1990).

As in the selection batteries for police recruits, psychological testing in fitness-for-duty evaluation tends to focus on pathology. Most often, the agency needs an answer to this question: Is there reason to believe that this officer cannot perform duties that require the power of arrest, the use of deadly force, and the judgment to make the hundreds or thousands of small decisions that are critical to the job of the serving officer? To date, there are no substantial studies of the relationship between pathological indicators on standard psychological tests and the capacity of officers to serve 20 or more years effectively and efficiently. Until these important but expensive and complex studies can be done, judgment, experience, and the generalization of research data will be the guiding influences in the psychologist's choices of instruments and procedures.

THE REPORT

Although there is no standard format in reporting fitness-for-duty results, the use of complex technical terms and vague psychological descriptors must be avoided. A standardized report may include the following sections:

- The dates when the referral was received, the evaluation was conducted, and the report was actually prepared.
- An introduction that states in one or two sentences why the referral was made and who made the referral.
- A description of the procedures used.
- A section labeled "Test Results." Where the officer is found to be fit for duty, a single sentence such as the following is sufficient: "None

of the psychological findings suggest that this candidate is not fit for continued duty in his/her usual and customary role within the Department." Where the officer is fit, there is no need to ramble on about psychological factors that may have nothing to do with the questions.

- A final section should be "Summary and Recommendations." In this section, the psychologist may simply state: "No reason not to return to duty." Where reasons have been found to indicate that the officer is not fit for duty, details in the summary may include such statements as "The intellectual measures show that thinking is fragmented and decision making tends to be inaccurate" or "The personality tests suggest that the officer is depressed, agitated, and subject to tangential thinking." Where such findings occur, it is the psychologist's responsibility to render an opinion such as "At this time, the officer is not able to conduct himself/herself appropriately in his/her customary duties."

- When the officer is found to be unfit, recommendations are warranted. The recommendations are limited by the experience of the examiner. The psychologist who knows little about the training, regulations, and departmental procedures of a law enforcement agency should avoid making recommendations that may be vague and confusing (i.e., "The officer's agitation as a result of the critical incident he experienced, requires some decompression and conflict-resolution"). Where the psychologist is familiar with the law enforcement agency making the referral, or understands law enforcement procedures, the recommendations may be more specific: "Although the subject is fit to return to duty, it is recommended that the Department's use of firearms safety procedures be reviewed and evaluated by the firearms safety instructor."

Even though fitness-for-duty evaluations and reports are not standardized, they should be sensible, practical, and relatively restricted. The psychologist must always remember that those who receive the reports are relatively unsophisticated about interpreting psychological data. Too much information about the test results may confuse the issue. The psychologist should also be aware that a long, rambling, nonspecific report may become the focus of conflict and/or litigation if the officer is dissatisfied with the report. Should a lawsuit be filed, the report is sure to come under the scrutiny of the officer's attorney, and in some cases the courts. Superfluous statements and generalizations that might be acceptable in an ordinary clinical evaluation can then become the subject of unfortunate misunderstanding, confusion, or distortion. For this reason, the psychologist who conducts fitness-for-duty evaluations must be familiar with the laws regulating such evaluations in the jurisdiction where they are being conducted.

As in all professional activities, but with particular emphasis on possible negative outcomes, the psychologist who conducts such evaluations must cut no corners and work with great care.

Some psychologists use a structured interview and/or rating scale after completing their fitness-for-duty evaluation. Appendix G presents a "Law Enforcement Fitness-for-Duty Questionnaire" that has been successfully used in a number of departments.

Aside from extreme situations or legal complications, the psychologist should understand that the fitness-for-duty report may become a part of the officer's permanent record. It can affect promotional opportunities. The psychologist should also remember that the officer will be reading this report and will be affected by it. The justification for a conclusion should be complete and straightforward.

The case of Patrol Officer William Jones illustrates a fitness-for-duty report done by a psychologist on the staff of a local law enforcement agency. Officer Jones entered into service with the Jenson Police Department in 1970. He functioned reasonably well as a patrol officer until 1981. At that time, he apparently hurt his back while assisting a motorist at the scene of a minor motor vehicle accident. Subsequent examinations revealed some spinal difficulties that were apparently related to this accident.

Patrol Officer Jones applied for disability on the basis of his physical difficulty and the psychological concomitants of his injury. A duty-related psychological disability was granted to him in 1982 and was reviewed on a periodic basis. Mr. Jones was referred for a psychological evaluation, to try to determine whether there was any possibility he could ever return to duty, in any capacity. Figure 5.4 presents the report that was submitted to management of his agency.

The report shows that the psychologist chose to review extensive records, interview the subject, and then conduct a series of examinations that included additional interviews, intelligence tests, neuropsychological screening tests, tests of malingering, and both objective and projective personality tests. The report is rather extensive. Some sections describe personality factors that are probably of little interest to those making the management decision as to whether Officer Jones will return to duty. By and large, it represents a fairly traditional fitness-for-duty report.

It is not unusual for a fitness-for-duty evaluation to be challenged either by the subject or by the department making the referral. In such cases, additional evaluations may be done. Ordinarily, a psychologist who is not connected with the referring department is chosen to be the tiebreaker.

The case of Patrol Officer Ted Bartlet illustrates this type of evaluation. Officer Bartlet was conducting routine patrol operations in the fall of 1989. He was driving in a patrol car, without a partner, as was the policy of his department. Answering a silent alarm, he came upon a burglary in progress. After calling for backup, he observed the burglar was leaving

---

FITNESS-FOR-DUTY EVALUATION
February 15, 1992

NAME   Jones, William   DATE OF EVALUATION   2/8 & 2/10/91
ADDRESS   1010 Elm Drive   TELEPHONE   (715) 342-5757
BIRTH DATE   8/13/39   AGE   51-5
EDUCATION   AA Degree   OCCUPATION   (Medically Disabled)
                                                            Police Officer

REFERRAL

Mr. Jones is referred for evaluation by Commander Albert R. Gilbert, Trustee of
the Jenson Police Pension Fund. Commander Gilbert states that Mr. Jones is
presently on a duty-related psychological disability granted to him in 1982.
Records of Mr. Jones's service and treatment are enclosed.

Commander Gilbert would like answers to the following questions:

1. Is Mr. Jones fit to return to duty as a patrol officer?
2. Could he be employed as a desk officer?
3. Is he psychologically fit for employment as a clerk in the Police Department?

REVIEW OF RECORDS

Various medical records were reviewed. Military records were also reviewed.
Selected documents from Mr. Jones's police personnel file were reviewed. A
casualty report filled out for the Jenson Police Department stated that Mr. Jones
was injured (his back) while attempting to assist separating two automobiles
involved in an accident. Various doctor's reports were reviewed. Dr. Stone
opined in August 1979 that Mr. Jones suffered a C-5 disc injury which left him
with degenerative disc problems of C-5 and C-6. The degeneration was
confirmed by other physicians. A report dated January 25, 1980, by Dr. Smithers,
about 13 months after the accident, indicates a slowed degeneration of C-5 and
C-6. The doctor opined that Mr. Jones was capable of returning to work if "he is
so inclined." The doctor saw no justification for a cervical operation.

Dr. James Brown opined in May 1980 that Mr. Jones is medically unable to
resume his position as a Police Officer in any capacity whatsoever at that time
or in the future. Dr. Sam Green opined in June 1980 that Mr. Jones is having a
significant posttraumatic depression secondary to his neck injury. Other
medical reports gave concurring or disagreeing opinions to varying degrees.
Reports of rehabilitation counselors were reviewed. Officer Jones was placed on
disability on December 4, 1981, by the Jenson Police Pension Board.

A psychological evaluation dated August 1989, performed by George A. Wash,
PhD, produced an extensive report detailing Mr. Jones's background history, the
history of his accident, and subsequent difficulties. Intellectual evaluation
placed Mr. Jones in the Low Average range of intellectual capacity (WAIS-R,
FSIQ 84). Dr. Wash opined that Mr. Jones suffered a Somatoform Pain Disorder

---

FIGURE 5.4   A Fitness-for-Duty Report by a Staff Psychologist

(300.81). Secondary to this, the doctor felt that Mr. Jones suffered depression and probably was abusing alcohol. Beneath the superficial symptoms, the doctor felt that Mr. Jones suffered a long-standing dependent personality disorder. A good many therapeutic recommendations were made.

CURRENT EVALUATION

Mr. Jones was first seen on February 8, 1991. He was interviewed and given a series of tests. His interviewing and testing were to continue on the 9th, but during the testing on the 8th he began to say that he was starting to feel bad and was not sure he could complete the testing. That evening he called and left word with the answering service that he would not be in for his appointment on the 9th and that he wished to be called and have this rescheduled. We acceded to his wishes.

On interview, Mr. Jones stated that he is totally unable to work. He is unsure whether he had a period of unconsciousness during the accident. His complaints currently include difficulties in expressive speech, buzzing in his ears, difficulty in writing because of the pain, dizziness, general pain, sensitivity to light, numbness in his arms, and headaches. He claims to sleep only two to four hours a night. He does sleep in the afternoon. He is very fatigued. He has blurred vision. He claims concentration difficulties and confusion. He believes he has no initiative. He states that other people tell him that he has a poor memory. He admits that he has always had some trouble with his memory. He has always had trouble organizing things. He doesn't drive because he becomes disoriented. His dependency has increased and his judgment is impaired.

Emotionally, he claims that he is agitated by his pain, always depressed, tense, and anxious. He has had a series of sexual problems since 1983 when he had a hernia operation. He always wants to be alone so that he is unable to socialize. He has a lot of irritability.

He gives an extensive history which is repetitive to the report noted above by Dr. Wash. He did discuss his Army career between 1956 and 1959. At the end of three years, he emerged as a private first class.

He says that he is currently under the care of Drs. Allen and Whitney (psychiatrists). He states that he tried Prozac and it didn't work. He stopped it because he couldn't afford to continue using it. He takes Tylenol, Nuprin, or generic ibuprofin daily.

He attempted to get a disability pension from the Veterans Administration but has been turned down.

He states that he smokes a package of cigarettes a day, but doesn't drink at all.

He has some friends where he now lives, mostly retired police officers. He watches TV, plays an organ, and attempts to set up a computer that he has bought. He doesn't socialize very much because he is afraid of getting pain and headaches. He says that he would like to take physical exercise, but he doesn't.

He discussed his two marriages briefly.

FIGURE 5.4   *(continued)*

EXAMINATION PROCEDURES

History and Interview, Wonderlic Personnel Test, Wechsler Adult Intelligence Scale-Revised, Indiana–Reitan Neuropsychological Short Form, Hand Dynamometer, Lezak–Rey 15 Item Test, Neuropsychological Symptom/Sign Course, Thematic Apperception Test, House–Tree–Person Test, Draw-a-Person Test, Sentence Completion Test, Minnesota Multiphasic Personality Inventory, FIRO-B, Edwards Personal Preference Schedule, Clinical Observations.

RESPONSE TO EVALUATION

Mr. Jones is about 5 ft. 11^1/$_2$ in. and weighs 194 pounds. He has dark brown hair and blue eyes. He walks with a limp. He wears glasses.

Speech is soft and clipped. He slurs and mumbles on occasion. Hearing appears to be within normal limits.

Mr. Jones is right-handed, is slow in movement, and complains of pain in his right arm. He socializes in a rambling, complaining manner.

His ideas are tangential. He cooperates fairly well. Confidence is low. He complains regularly of his money problems. He complains of pain. He is unable to finish the examinations in the time allotted and additional time must be scheduled. At the end of one session, he indicated that he might not feel well the next day and might not be able to come in to finish testing. Indeed, this occurred.

Mr. Jones submitted additional handwritten history because he felt "the doctor didn't ask me enough questions about my complaints."

RESULTS OF EXAMINATION

A. *Intellectual Factors*

Six subtests of the Wechsler Adult Intelligence Scale-Revised indicate that Mr. Jones performs in the Low Average range of intellectual capacity. He is particularly poor in new learning and the ability to pick out key ideas.

On the Wonderlic Personnel Test, commonly used for police selection, he achieves a raw score of 11. A minimum recommended score for this test for police recruits is 20. His score places him at the 10th percentile for males at all educational levels indicating that 90% of applicants are of better intellectual function than Mr. Jones.

B. *Neuropsychological Factors*

Mr. Jones was able to pull between 10^3/$_4$ kg and 12^3/$_4$ kg with his right hand and between 20 kg and 26^1/$_2$ kg with his left. This indicates significant weakness in the right hand. His productions on the Indiana–Reitan Neuropsychological Screening Test are characterized by distortion, rounded corners, and missing parts of the key figure. The results would be considered characteristic of individuals who have some moderate degree of intracranial pathology. A full neuropsychological evaluation would delineate this more clearly.

He is able to produce four out of five figures on the 15-Item Test indicating that it is unlikely that Mr. Jones is "faking" or malingering.

FIGURE 5.4   *(continued)*

C. *Personality Factors*

(1) *Interpersonal Activity.* At the first level on interpersonal activity, Mr. Jones showed a number of Need-Drives (above the 75th percentile for adult males) and Need-Avoidances (below the 25th percentile for the same group) as follows:

Need-Drives	*Need-Avoidances*
Succorance	Nurturance
Intraception	Exhibition
Deference	Affiliation

An analysis of Mr. Jones' responses suggests the following patterns of interpersonal activity: In general, his needs are to receive emotional support and sympathy from others. He tends to be introspective and reflective. It is fairly easy for him to be subordinate to others, and to conform to rules and regulations.

It is somewhat difficult for him to take care of others, and to be sympathetic. He doesn't usually try to draw the attention of others and to make his presence known. He will not usually go out of his way to enjoy the company and friendship of others.

In one-on-one interactions, Mr. Jones expresses little of his real inner thoughts and doesn't want to hear from others. He is an extremely dependent person, being drawn to strongly directive and controlling people. He is unable to make decisions himself. He has modest needs to exchange affection.

At a deeper interpersonal level, Mr. Jones is an individual with very simplistic and often unrealistic values. He is very self-focused. His usual approach to things is complaining and critical. He constantly focuses on physical symptoms and problems that may or may not be with demonstrable physical etiology.

He can be shy and hypersensitive to the evaluation of others. He has trouble accepting personal responsibility. At times he may be self-critical.

He often complains of weakness, lethargy and fatigue. He is generally tense, anxious, and irritable. He lacks self-understanding and insight. He has excessive worry. He overreacts to minor difficulties.

(2) *Anxiety Structure.* Mr. Jones is very anxious about not being taken care of. His self-esteem is quite low. He is fearful of authority figures. Whenever attention is not given to him, he becomes very anxious. When people do not meet his needs as he expects them to, he becomes anxious.

(3) *Outlets and Defenses.* Intellectual defenses include strong dependency on others, criticism, complaints, sympathy seeking, and somatic preoccupation. He tends to distort circumstances to meet his own needs. He sees himself as "crippled" to justify his current situation.

FIGURE 5.4   (*continued*)

Less intellectual outlets include a potential for alcohol addiction, depression, shallow relationships, suspicion and distrust, and significant passivity. Mr. Jones suffers a somatoform disorder, and has been a lifelong dependent personality.

CONCLUSIONS AND RECOMMENDATIONS

Psychological evaluation of Mr. William Jones indicates that he is a man of limited intellectual capacity who has a very severe psychological disorder. He focuses his entire attention on his physical complaints and his needs to be taken care of and to be attended to. His capacity to understand the psychological aspects of his difficulty is very limited. His potential for response to therapeutic treatment is poor. He might benefit from some short-term interventions when he is under significant stress. He is unlikely to achieve long-term benefits.

In response to the original questions, the following conclusions seem warranted:

1. Mr. Jones is certainly not fit to return to duty as a patrol officer.
2. It is unlikely that Mr. Jones could function in any reliable manner even as a desk officer.
3. It is certainly not recommended that Mr. Jones be employed as a clerk in the police department, since his constant complaining and demands for attention would not only interfere with any kind of productive work, but would be very disturbing to the people he works with and works under.

The likelihood that Mr. Jones is going to ever be able to understand the psychological nature of his difficulty is extremely limited.

Robert Binet
Staff Psychologist

FIGURE 5.4   *(continued)*

the premises with materials that appeared to be a product of the burglary. He reported this on his portable radio, drew his weapon, and accosted the burglar, in the usual and customary manner. Unbeknownst to Officer Bartlet, an accomplice was hiding behind a wall. This person attacked the officer from behind, stabbing him four times. The backup arrived, and the perpetrators were apprehended. Patrol officer Bartlet was taken to the hospital and given extensive emergency treatment. After his release from the hospital, he had to return several times for additional surgical repairs.

At the time of this incident he was having a number of family problems, and he was transferred to the job of serving warrants. He later requested return to his usual patrol duties. Following department procedure, he was sent to the department psychologist for evaluation. The department psychologist felt that he was not fit for duty and sent him to a therapist for counseling. The therapist didn't believe he needed counseling. He was returned to the department psychologist and then sent to another doctor for evaluation. The other doctor didn't think he needed help but scheduled some sessions to work through whatever problems might exist. On returning to see the department psychologist, he was again told that he wasn't fit for duty. Officer Bartlet made application with another city's police department and was cleared psychologically by its psychologist. He then applied to his superiors for another evaluation because his preference was to return to work in his own department.

The deputy chief of his department referred Officer Bartlet for a fitness-for-duty evaluation (Figure 5.5) with the following questions:

1. Does Officer Bartlet show any deficiencies that would prevent him performing as a patrol officer?
2. If there are deficiencies, what are they?
3. Should deficiencies exist, is there any therapeutic procedure that would be recommended to remedy these deficiencies?

Some psychologists may feel uncomfortable serving as an evaluator where there has been a difference of opinion among colleagues. On occasion, however, this is a necessary role for the police psychologist in the best interests of both the department and the individual officer seeking reinstatement.

Appointments were made for Officer Bartlet, and he was seen on two occasions for a total of 6 hours of interviews and testing. Preliminary to his appearance for evaluation, the psychologist conducting the fitness-for-duty evaluation reviewed all of Officer Bartlet's official records, the reports of the other psychologists, and the officer's supervisors' ratings. In addition, the psychologist conducted telephone discussions with Officer Bartlet's supervisors, Sergeant Williams and Lieutenant Pearson. All of this was done with the permission of both the officer and the department. Officer Bartlet was given a careful explanation of the purpose of the evaluation and the limits on confidentiality and privilege, and signed an informed consent that included permission to speak with supervisors, family, or partners.

Figure 5.5 (pp. 140–142) presents the fitness-for-duty evaluation that was submitted after the examination of Patrolman Bartlet.

These are but two examples of fitness-for-duty reports. As was stated previously, currently there is no standard for such reports. Good professional judgment, and adherence to the current ethics and standards for psychologists are the best guidelines.

POLICE SERVICES INSTITUTE
FITNESS-FOR-DUTY EVALUATION

NAME   Bartlet, Ted   DATES OF EVALUATION   3/24 & 3/26/91

ADDRESS   14 S. Elm St.   TELEPHONE   (217) 876-5432
              Belmont, IL 40170
                                        AGE   28-9

BIRTHDATE   6/21/62   EDUCATION   High School & one year

DATE OF REPORT   3/27/91   college

REFERRAL

Officer Bartlet is referred by Deputy Chief C. Grain, District I Enforcement
Operations Department. It is requested that a Fitness-for-Duty Evaluation be
conducted to answer the following questions:

1. Does he show any deficiencies as a law enforcement officer?

2. If deficiencies are found, is there any therapy to remedy these deficiencies?

INTERVIEW

Officer Bartlet appeared on time. He was neatly dressed and appropriately
responsive. He answered all questions directly.

He is 5 ft 10 in. in height and weighs 155 pounds. He has blue eyes and brown
hair. He has a long scar on his left wrist and hand, the result of the altercation
while on duty in 1989.

He speaks in a clear and articulate manner. Hearing is normal. He is right-handed.
He socializes in a polite, formal manner. He cooperates extremely well.

He indicates that he was stabbed in September 1989. As a result, he has had four
surgeries. At the time of the injury, he had some family problems. Apparently,
he is now working in warrants. He wants to return to patrol. He saw Dr. Geer,
department psychologist, who sent him to a social worker for counseling. She
stated that he didn't need counseling. When he returned to Dr. Geer, he was
then sent to Dr. Spinks. Dr. Spinks didn't think he needed treatment, but
scheduled six sessions to "work through any problems that might exist."

When Deputy Bartlet returned to see Dr. Geer, Dr. Geer didn't feel he was fit
for duty.

Officer Bartlet applied for the Inman Police Department, and was cleared
psychologically by its psychologist.

The officer's history was taken and nothing unusual was noted.

EXAMINATION PROCEDURES

Interview, History, extensive review of records and previous psychological
reports, Wonderlic Personnel Test, Graham–Kendall Memory for Designs,
Indiana–Reitan Neuropsychological Short Form, Hand Dynamometer,

---

FIGURE 5.5   A Fitness-for-Duty Report by a Consulting Police Psychologist

Nelson–Denny Reading Test, Thematic Apperception Test, Draw-a-Person Test, Sentence Completion Test, Minnesota Multiphasic Personality Inventory, Holmes Stress Scale, telephone discussions with Sgt. Williams and Lt. Pearson.

RESULTS OF EXAMINATION

A. *Intellectual Factors*

Officer Bartlet's percentile rank in comparison with male high-school graduates was 40.6. This places him in the Average range of intellectual capacity. No unusual responses were noted.

B. *Neuropsychological Factors*

Officer Bartlet was able to pull between $53^3/_4$ kg and $57^1/_4$ kg with the right hand and between $38^1/_4$ kg and 41 kg with the left hand. This is within normal limits for his age.

He fell within the "normal" range on both Memory-for-Designs and the Indiana–Reitan Neuropsychological Screening Tests. Results are contraindicative of any difficulty neuropsychologically.

C. *Reading Skills*

The results of the Nelson–Denny Reading Test indicate that Officer Bartlet reads quite competently, although somewhat slowly. He is well within normal limits and his reading skills are competent for his job.

D. *Stress Factors*

Exploration of stress factors covering the period from the present to three years ago indicates that his highest level of stress (moderate) occurred one to two years ago. During the past year, he has had a low level of stress. No indicators of excessive stress reaction.

E. *Personality Factors*

The results of the personality tests indicate no signs of psychopathology. The basic personality pattern is that of an individual who makes strenuous efforts to appear his best and be his best on the surface.

Officer Bartlet is slightly rigid, prefers to follow the rules, and has very great difficulty in cutting corners. His aspirations are not very high, but he prefers to do a good job and win the respect of those around him.

Officer Bartlet tends to work best under strong supervision, with a supervisor he can admire and imitate. He tends to be a very conscientious person.

Officer Bartlet does best when he is appropriately praised and given strong leadership. Indications are that he has strong motivation for a career at the basic level of law enforcement.

SUMMARY AND CONCLUSIONS

Complete psychological evaluation to determine Patrol Officer Ted Bartlet's fitness for duty indicates that he is a man of average intellectual capacity, with no neuropsychological deficits, competent reading skills, relatively low stress level, and no indications of personality psychopathology.

FIGURE 5.5 *(continued)*

As an individual, he tends to be a "good soldier" and will do well under strong supervision that he respects and toward whom he can model himself. His slight rigidity is likely to mellow with good supervision and experience.

No deficiencies were found to indicate that Patrol Officer Bartlet would not do well if he continued in law enforcement.

John Johnston, PhD
Consulting Police Psychologist

Note: Psychological test results should never be the basis for hiring or firing. They are advisory in nature to aid executive decision makers.

FIGURE 5.5   *(continued)*

CHAPTER SIX

Special Unit Testing

Policing is a demanding job, regardless of the department in which officers conduct their operations. Nevertheless, certain special units, largely in the major departments, have missions that tend to be more dangerous, more taxing, and all in all more stressful than routine police operations.

In recent years, there has been a growth of interest in both testing candidates for positions in special units, and for evaluating members of special units on a regular basis to determine whether their participation has resulted in any psychological condition impairing their capacity to serve. A brief review of these special units and their missions will be helpful to understand the special nature of the psychological assessment procedures that should be used with these groups.

Special Weapons and Tactics (SWAT)

These special units were first formed in 1964, in the Philadelphia Police Department. The department had become aware of a significant increase in bank robberies. The SWAT group was established as a special unit that could react quickly to bank robberies in progress. The characteristics of this special squad included considerable fire power, and the capacity for rapid response. The success of the Philadelphia SWAT unit led other departments to establish similar units.

The formation of such special squads by major departments represented a significant departure from traditional police activity. Upper level police managers recognized that specially armed, highly motivated, and well-trained teams of officers were a definite asset when dealing with heavily armed criminals or with dangerous situations that might require rapid and expert intervention. These teams have come to be a part of most major departments. Their missions have been to intervene during felonies in progress, to be on a standby basis in dangerous situations such as hostage taking, and to be available for such volatile occurrences as terrorist attacks.

The SWAT teams in most jurisdictions are trained with weapons and special equipment that allow them to make unorthodox, rapid, and confrontational entry into buildings and other settings in fairly unusual but effective ways. They may land by helicopter, use mountain-climbing equipment and paraphernalia, or detonate special explosive devices to effect entry into barricade situations. Their training and procedures are much in line with those of special units of the U.S. Army such as Special Forces, and the British Special Air Service and Special Boat Service.

Members of SWAT teams are selected according to a variety of criteria. Emphasis is frequently on having a "normal personality" and the ability to work well as a team member. A high level of physical fitness is required. Team members must tolerate stress and conditions of extreme fatigue and still respond effectively to variable confrontations.

A SWAT team generally consists of 12 members organized into an *assault group* and a *cover group*. The *assault group* has the mission of effecting entry into the dangerous situation while the *cover group* protects the perimeters within which the entire operation occurs. An explicit chain of command is established to ensure accurate communications between the SWAT team and the police department.

SWAT team members train regularly. They are on 24-hour call. SWAT teams are most frequently used in hostage situations, where negotiation fails; in sniper situations; and with barricaded suspects. SWAT teams are sometimes called on to help arrest subjects who are heavily armed and prepared to resist arrest. More recently, SWAT teams have been used as part of the security arrangements when important government officials visit a locality where such teams are available.

The teams train continually and usually establish a high *espirit de corps*. They not only train together but often socialize together as an elite group within the police family (Kolman, 1982).

Undercover Operations

Police undercover operations have become the "darlings" of television shows, movies, and popular novels. The hero or heroine is generally a person who doesn't "look like" a police officer, is often pretty "grubby," and appears to be part of an illegal operation, frequently involving narcotics. The role is presented as extremely dangerous.

The undercover operations depicted by the media are somewhat close to the reality. Most undercover operations fall into two types: *person* and *place* surveillance. *Person* surveillance occurs at a distance between the subject of the surveillance and the police officer. The officer may follow, wait for, or observe the subject to get information about his or her daily movements or illegal activities.

In *place* surveillance, the police officer appears to be "one of the group" whether it is as a gang member or as a participant with a lawyer, another police officer, or any subject of an investigation. A real relationship is simulated.

Police officers who participate in undercover operations must follow a relatively narrow corridor within the legal restraints against entering into deceptive long-term interactions with suspects. Some undercover operations are more intrusive than others. There have been frequent objections to undercover operations by those who believe that such police actions abrogate moral and constitutional rights to privacy.

The courts have generally ruled in favor of situations where the police have gained admittance to a private dwelling through deception. The Supreme Court ruled in *United States v. Baldwin* (621 F.2d 251 (1963)) that police do not require prior judicial approval in the form of a warrant before using an undercover agent. The Court determined that wrongdoers are not protected by usual Fourth Amendment constraints.

Many undercover agents are extremely skillful actors. The men and women who volunteer for such duty seem to relish the risk and acquire great skill at playing a role down to the smallest detail.

Undercover work can place the police officer in tenuous or dangerous situations. Rarely can the undercover officer call on backup, or a partner, when a situation goes sour. In spite of these grave dangers, relatively few undercover police officers have been seriously injured or killed on duty. Although this does happen occasionally, the frequency of such events is amazingly low in view of the many undercover operations that police agencies have mounted throughout the United States.

Police officers are selected for undercover work on the basis of their ethnic background, experience, apparent anonymity, or street smarts. Most commanders of undercover units agree that participation in undercover work requires a great deal of intelligence, self-confidence, determination, and judgment. The most dangerous undercover assignments involve efforts to infiltrate various elements of the narcotics trade. The largest percentage of officers who are hurt or killed on duty have been involved in undercover narcotics operations (Barefoot, 1975).

In the law enforcement community, the incidence of psychiatric disturbance and severity of symptomatology has been found to be highest among active undercover agents. The most disturbed officers were relatively young, with no prior undercover experience, who were engaged in long-term investigations. The degree of disturbance was not, by usual standards, exceptional (Girodo, 1991a).

One of the gravest dangers in undercover investigation of illegal narcotics traffic is the potential for the undercover officer to begin using narcotics. There is some reason to believe that greater use of drugs and alcohol by undercover agents may be more than a personality issue. The stress of such work appears to be an instigating factor. It was found, however, that agents who tended to have a "disciplined self-image" presented a lower risk for drug corruption without losing the high-energy, risk-taking motivational qualities necessary for successful undercover performance (Girodo, 1991b).

Using the Eysenck Personality Questionnaire, the Health Opinion Survey, the Symptom Checklist-90, and the Hilson Career Satisfaction Index, Girodo (1991c) studied 271 undercover agents. He found that the agents most likely to show mental health disturbances were Neurotic-Introverts, whereas those who were least likely to show such disturbance were Stable-Extroverts.

Hostage Negotiations

The general recognition of hostage situations as a special area for police training and development occurred during the 1970s. The hostage situation occurs when an individual defies efforts by the police to intervene by taking a hostage and making threats. Ordinary methods of resolution such as confrontation with the subject, or SWAT team activity sometimes led to disastrous results with loss of life and very adverse publicity. The concept of the *hostage negotiation team* was developed to attempt to deal more effectively with such situations and to resolve them without injury or loss of life to subjects, hostages, bystanders, or police officers.

The hostage negotiation concept developed from the realization that the life of the subject, a hostage, a person attempting suicide, an innocent bystander, or a police officer is of primary importance and concern. The members of the hostage negotiation team train very much as the SWAT team does, regularly, with simulated hostage situations. They often work in close coordination with SWAT teams. They practice specific procedures for establishing communication with the hostage taker or the threatening individual. The purpose is to deescalate the situation and resolve it without serious injury or loss of life. Chapter Eleven of this book is devoted to the psychologist's role in hostage negotiation activities.

Juvenile Crime

All departments, other than the smallest agencies, have one or more personnel designated as juvenile crime officers. Larger agencies may have specialized departments such as juvenile sex crimes, juvenile crimes against property, and juvenile family issues. The members of these departments generally receive special training, and sometimes supervision, in dealing with juveniles and their families.

An area of particular interest and growing activity is child-abuse investigation. The role that police play in this area may cover many areas such as physical abuse of children, neglect of children, sexual abuse of children, and acts of parents that may encourage delinquency in the children.

Juvenile misbehavior is an old area of activity for police officers, and the abuse of children has been going on throughout recorded history. Only recently, however, have officers been specially selected and trained to deal with these situations. Particularly in the area of child sexual abuse, officers are trained (sometimes very badly) in techniques of interviewing and evaluation using a variety of psychological tools such as anatomically correct dolls, drawings, and playroom activity. Originally, female officers were almost universally selected to work with juvenile problems. Contemporary practice is to attempt to select and train officers who have some special skill for relating well with children and troubled parents.

Sex Crimes

Most sex crimes are investigated by detectives in an agency's criminal investigation division. A more recent trend in policing is to form a special sex crime unit, with detectives who have special training in the investigation of felonious sexual behavior. The crimes investigated by such special departments include rape, assault and battery involving sexual interaction as a major aspect of the crime, prostitution (although in many departments this crime is subsumed under vice), and illegal sexual exposure.

Although some police departments have other special units, the preceding represent the bulk of those units using psychological techniques for selection of officers for work in special units or evaluation of officers' ongoing performance.

ACCREDITATION STANDARDS

The Commission on Accreditation for Law Enforcement Agencies (1989) describes some standards for the use of psychological assessment instruments with members of special operations teams. Such teams include SWAT, hostage negotiation, decoy operations, undercover surveillance, bomb disposal, and protection at special events. *Principle 47.1.5* states:

> Officers who are assigned to SWAT Team or decoy operations should be carefully selected. Special criteria for selection should be identified, such as a stipulation that the assignment is voluntary; prior law enforcement experience in a field assignment; physical fitness and agility; and passing a psychological screening examination. . . . Test scores should be kept on file for the duration of an officer's assignment to the operation.

In addition to selection criteria recommended by the Commission, *Principle 47.1.6* recommends ongoing psychological testing. Specifically, this directive states:

> Harmful side effects of stress resulting from high-risk and dangerous work may be manifested in officers assigned full time to tactical or undercover operations. Annual testing by a licensed psychologist or psychiatrist can identify these symptoms and their debilitating conditions.

These standards also address psychological testing of hostage negotiators in *Principle 471.1.10:*

> Hostage negotiators should be carefully screened and selected. Special criteria for selection should be identified, such as passing a psychological screening examination, including an MMPI test and a clinical interview by a licensed psychologist or psychiatrist.

The accreditation standards do not offer specific recommendations for ongoing evaluation beyond what has been noted here.

RESEARCH TO DATE

Although everyone seems to agree it is a good idea to have some kind of ongoing assessment of police officers who serve in these special roles, relatively little has been done to address the question of what tests have reliability and validity for the specific task played by the officer being evaluated.

Getty and Elam (1988) used the Minnesota Multiphasic Personality Inventory (MMPI) and the California Psychological Inventory (CPI) to obtain a personality profile of hostage negotiators and compared this with a control sample of municipal police officers. They found that they could describe a scoring key for each of the two tests used that would differentiate successful hostage negotiators from line police officers. Their results indicated that hostage negotiators would be described as being above average in ability to communicate effectively with others, self-confident, good at divergent thinking, and helpful and sympathetic in their dealings with other people. Baruth (1988) has recommended routine mental health checkups and special activities for law enforcement personnel who deal with hostage and terrorist incidents.

Farkas (1986) found that the effects of undercover policing were extensive and predictable. His research underscores the importance of psychological monitoring of undercover personnel to determine whether the stress of participation in these special assignments has resulted in sufficient emotional turmoil to warrant a change in assignment.

DEADLY FORCE EVALUATION

Ordinarily, if a police officer is involved in a deadly force situation where it becomes necessary to take an individual's life, an evaluation is requested only to determine the officer's fitness for future duty. On some occasions, a psychologist conducts a psychological evaluation of the officer's mental state in respect to the deadly force situation and tries to determine whether the officer used reasonable judgment at the time of the incident.

There are no established standards for such an evaluation. It may even be questionable whether psychologists have the tools and knowledge base to make such an investigation. Ranking with such issues as the insanity defense and the psychological autopsy, the psychological evaluation of deadly force incidents is based on the nature of the request and the available instruments.

The questions asked of psychologists who conduct deadly force evaluations vary considerably and are generated, in most instances, by administrative or legal proceedings. The request may be made in respect to a department's investigation of the officer's use of deadly force. The evaluation may be made in conjunction with a criminal or civil action against the officer.

In the case on pages 152–159, the request was made preliminary to an officer's appearance before a grand jury to determine whether there was sufficient basis for a true bill or an indictment. An attorney representing the Police Benevolent Association was appointed to defend the officer. In preparation of this defense, the attorney requested a deadly force evaluation. The psychological report represents that evaluation and contains all the facts of the case.

In this case, the psychologist was asked to appear before the grand jury and present his findings. He made an appearance, and in spite of sharp questioning by the District Attorney who conducted the proceedings, and who attempted to restrict the scope of the psychologist's testimony, the grand jury members themselves asked that the psychologist be allowed to describe his evaluation in full detail. At the conclusion of their deliberations, the grand jury found no cause for indictment.

RECOMMENDED TEST BATTERIES

It is impossible at this time to be specific about the test batteries that would be most useful in both selecting officers for special teams, and evaluating the continuing stability and efficiency of those officers who work on such teams. The most commonly used instruments are the Minnesota Multiphasic Personality Inventory and California Personality Inventory. The variety of examination procedures used by psychologists who do such special evaluations is considerable. In the area of hostage negotiation, the most productive efforts have been those directed toward identifying the personality characteristics of negotiators who will operate more successfully than line officers. In other instances, including the tracking of officers who serve on special teams, the role of the psychologist is to "screen out" pathology or potential inadequacy as in recruit selection. The purpose of the battery is to determine whether the officer has ceased to function adequately because of some degree of emotional distress. Cutting scores and guidelines do not exist at this time. Each individual police psychologist makes the determination as to each officer's fitness for duty. This area will require considerable exploration before more objective guidelines can emerge. In the meantime, psychologists assigned to conduct such evaluations must follow the ethical principles, standards for practice, and standards for the use of psychological tests promulgated by the American Psychological Association (American Psychological Association et al., 1985).

THE ASSESSMENT CENTER

With the passage of the Civil Rights Act of 1964, there have been many challenges to traditional practices used in selecting personnel, particularly for promotion. Industry and government began to rely on a method developed during World War II called the *assessment center* (U.S. Office of Strategic Services, 1948).

The assessment center is a method for making selection decisions that focuses on "simulations"—exercises in which the applicant is observed doing a variety of directed activities. The assessment center may include such techniques as leaderless group discussion, the "in-basket" exercises, and other methods to evaluate operational capacities of individuals (Grant, 1984).

Assessment centers usually consist of a combination of standardized tests and the structured exercises. The individual may be evaluated over a 1-, 2-, or 3-day period, either by himself or herself, or as part of a group (Bernstein, 1989).

In the in-basket exercise, the participant is provided with a basket of memos, phone messages, letters, directives, and so forth. The examinee is asked to role-play a manager on a new job who has to respond to these items. The contents of the material are selected to evaluate reactions of the participants. To enable standardization, all the applicants in the assessment center receive the same materials. Scoring is done in a standardized manner. These results lead to evaluations of decisiveness, communication skills, ability to delegate, skills in problem solving and so forth.

Role playing is an important part of the assessment center. Participants are asked to play specific roles appropriate to the job for which they are being considered. Observation is done by carefully selected observers who are familiar with the job under consideration and are trained in objective evaluation.

When the assessment center is completed, the staff evaluates each participant on the behavioral dimensions that the center was designed to serve (Bray, Campbell, & Grant, 1984).

Pynes and Bernardin (1989) studied the use of the assessment center in evaluating police performance. They point out that one of the great difficulties in using this tool is the problem of measuring and describing police performance. In spite of this, assessment centers have been considered useful, especially in the area of promoting police officers into leadership positions.

Many other psychological tools can be helpful in selecting police officers for special duty, for promotion, or for other roles, but these have not been used very extensively. Industrial psychologists have been little involved in these issues. Once the need becomes more apparent, it is likely that the appropriate research will be done to ensure that these modern methods become more available to law enforcement.

RUBERT BOB SMITH, PhD

Diplomate in Clinical Psychology
American Board of Professional Psychology

PSYCHOLOGICAL REPORT
DEADLY FORCE EVALUATION

NAME	White, Charles	**DATE OF EXAMINATION**	5/19/83
ADDRESS	Narcotics	**TELEPHONE**	463-8587
	State Police	**OCCUPATION**	Police Officer
	Division 5		(Sergeant)
DOB 3/15/42	**AGE** 41	**EDUCATION**	12

REFERRAL

Richard Cook, Esquire, refers this case. By telephone, he states that Sgt. White, a police officer, while on duty on February 5, 1983, in a drug raid in which 10,000 units of LSD and various drugs were seized, shot and killed Jack Gardner. The facts of the case have been such that Prosecuting Attorney is considering Grand Jury review. Sgt. White is cloudy about his thinking following the time he killed Mr. Gardner with his service revolver.

Questions for evaluation include:

1. Did Sgt. White have intent to kill at the time of the incident?
2. Was Sgt. White's response self-protective, reasonable, and responsive to the situation?
3. Would any psychological instability noted in Sgt. White suggest defective judgment?

At the time of the incident, the deceased had concentrations of opiates in his blood in the range associated with overdose, and could be toxic. He was known to be a mentally disturbed person. Mr. Cook wonders whether these circumstances could explain the deceased's disobedience of the police officers' orders, which led to the homicide.

REASON FOR EVALUATION

Sgt. White participated in a police action in which a suspect was killed. Sgt. White fired the weapon that killed the subject. As part of the investigation of the circumstances of this death, psychological assessment to determine Sgt. White's psychological state, his intent, his state of mind, and his response to the circumstances is requested.

PROCEDURES

Review of all pertinent records regarding the shooting during the narcotics arrest, pertinent events previous to and subsequent to this, laboratory reports, reports of witnesses, criminal records of defendants, and other material. History and interview with Sgt. White. Review of Sgt. White's records. Minnesota Multiphasic Personality Inventory, Holmes Stress Scale. Review of pertinent research relating to deadly force and its use by police officers. Review of dangerousness and violence research.

ESSENTIAL FACTS OF THE CASE

On February 5, 1983, Sgt. White led a team of agents of the State Police to accomplish the arrest of a number of suspected drug dealers. During the course of the procedures, Sgt. White became concerned for the safety of his undercover men who were inside the house preparing to make the initial arrests. He led a team of officers who used bolt-cutters to open a locked, wrought-iron gate and then broke through a door in order to assist the officers inside the house. Upon entering the front door of the house, the agent immediately preceding Sgt. White found one of the suspects disobeying a police officer's orders to stay against the wall. He pushed this suspect (Gardner) against the wall and instructed him to remain there. As Sgt. White came through the door, he noticed that this subject was not obeying the officer's commands, again. As he moved toward this suspect to ensure safety of himself and his men, the suspect suddenly turned to Sgt. White and moved quickly toward him. Sgt. White, in a position of readiness, was taken quite aback and assumed a proper defense posture. Before the move by the suspect, Sgt. White had his weapon at a 45-degree angle from his body which was usual for such circumstances. As the suspect came at him, both surprising and threatening Sgt. White, Sgt. White attempted to move backward, in the limited space available, while at the same time, his partially raised weapon began to arc downward into a usable, protective position, as would be natural under such circumstances. At that point, Sgt. White discharged his weapon. The shot killed the suspect. Sgt. White reports a somewhat fragmented perception of events from that point until he made the telephone call requesting the proper personnel to deal with the death that had occurred during this police action.

SGT. WHITE'S PERCEPTION OF THE EVENTS

On interview, Sgt. White states that when he entered the door of the house he saw Officer Chavez put the suspect to the wall. He saw the suspect start off the wall. Suddenly, the suspect was "on top of me." Sgt. White says, "I was moving toward him with my gun at 'ready.' This would be about a 45-degree angle. He scared me. My heart was in my throat. I stopped and started to pull back, and pulled the trigger instinctively. I didn't "see" this. Suddenly, there was something there. I didn't know what he was doing. After the shot, he suddenly disappeared. I said to myself, "Where did he go?" For an instant, it surprised me. Then it dawned that I had shot my gun. I looked down and there he was. I thought to myself, "We've got a shooting." I remember going to the counter and starting to unload my gun. I realized they would need it for evidence. I called and advised the office of the shooting. I didn't even tell them who had been shot. I then called Lt. Flemming and told him."

Sgt. White remembers the officer who preceded him through the door shoving Mr. Gardner against the wall. He remembers feeling "I better get him under control" when he saw Gardner come off the wall. It was later noted that this man was wearing a hat. Sgt. White does not remember the hat. He states he never saw the suspect's hands. Suddenly, he had the feeling of this man's "presence" upon him. He does not remember any physical contact but he does remember that he did not know what was "going on" (the defendant's intent in moving off the wall) and he reacted instinctively (automatically taking a defensive-protective action). When asked about his memory, Sgt. White stated that for at least 30 minutes after this he was in a "daze," in a state of shock. He remembers going out of the front door and seeing the people with the bolt cutters who opened the wrought-iron door. He cannot remember saying anything from the time he shot the suspect until the time he used the phone. He says that some of his fellow officers said that he had said some things.

In discussing the events leading up to this, Sgt. White noted that 1 to 2 weeks previous to the event described here, in the *Segalla* case, he was in a similar situation where surveillance contact was lost. He had deep concerns for the safety of the officers who were involved in an arrest that was going on. He became extremely tense. Because of the communication problems, his two agents had to make the arrests by themselves. Although nothing serious happened, he was extremely upset by this, being fully aware of the grave dangers that occur during the initial phases of narcotics arrests. He was acutely aware that this is the time that an officer is likely to be injured or killed by a perpetrator facing arrest. In the current incident, he states that the radio reports that he was monitoring upset him considerably. Hearing what he heard, he said to himself, "These guys are in trouble." His actions after that point were based on the concept that it was his responsibility to ensure that this police action would not result in injury or death to any of his agents.

BACKGROUND FACTORS

Sgt. Charles White, 41-year-old police officer with 17¹/₂ years of experience in the State Police, was born in California but raised in Oklahoma. His mother and father are both living and well. His parents divorced when he was very young and his mother remarried in about 1945. He himself was raised by his grandmother on the mother's side as well as his father's mother and a great aunt. The great aunt was particularly important in his early life. He was raised in a very religious home with strong traditional standards.

He has three brothers and a sister. He always considered his stepfather as his father and they got along well. The stepfather died a year and a half or two years ago.

Graduating from high school in Oklahoma, Sgt. White worked at a number of jobs including the Safeway Stores, the oil fields, as a carpenter, and as a worker in a baking company. He entered State Police training at the age of 23. After 9 weeks of recruit training, he was assigned to Las Cruces Station and remained a trooper until 1979. He served in a variety of locations. Twelve years of his service have been in the Narcotics Division, on and off in uniform. He entered Narcotics after 6 years on the force.

He had training in hand-to-hand combat and the use of firearms on the basis of one hour per day for 9 weeks in his early training. Since that time he has had to qualify in the use of arms on a regular basis as is the policy of the State Police. He has special training as a first aid instructor, in search and seizure at the FBI School, and a three-week training course leading to a Certificate of Competency from the U.S. Department of Justice Bureau of Narcotics and Dangerous Drugs in the enforcement of narcotics and dangerous drugs. He has been to management school, a variety of State Police in-service training schools including electronic intelligence.

Sgt. White is in good health. He has no physical condition of untoward nature at the present time. He has taken a total of 10 days of sick leave while on the State Police Force. He uses tobacco, smoking about a pack a day. He rarely uses alcohol, confining himself to an occasional beer. He is in relatively good physical condition.

His work is very demanding and he has relatively little time for himself. There is a good deal of pressure on him and his family. He enjoys being around the home. At one time, he fished but he does not have the time nor the availability of facilities. He owns a motorcycle and enjoys doing his own mechanical work. He and his wife like to ride the cycle, attend movies, go to town, and go to the Flea Market. He enjoys working in the yard.

His first marriage occurred when he was 18 years of age, and he stayed in this for 15 years. There are two sons and two daughters to this union. His second marriage occurred when he was 34 years of age. His wife at the present time had been formerly married. She has two children from the former marriage, which he considers his own and which he has raised as his own. They see him as their father.

He has discharged his weapon a total of six times in his $17^{1}/_{2}$ years in police work. There have been many incidents where he restrained himself from discharging his weapon in spite of the fact that the situation was dangerous.

PSYCHOLOGICAL EVALUATION

The history of Sgt. White is not untoward in any way. Having early family problems is frequently found in the histories of successful police officers and other persons who enter dangerous social service occupations. His focus on his strong early religious upbringing again is a factor often found in the family history of successful police officers.

Analysis of the Minnesota Multiphasic Personality Inventory indicates that Sgt. White falls completely within the normal personality range. No eccentricities, evidence of instability, poor judgment, inappropriate behavior, or other disturbance is noted.

A description of Sgt. White's personality would indicate that he has a tendency to overlook faults in himself, his family, and his circumstances, although this defensiveness would be considered quite mild. His cautious personality is standard for police personnel. Impulsive and grossly inappropriate expression of feelings would not be expected in this man. It can be expected that he will be energetic, active, and in general, an overworker. His highest scale on the MMPI is that scale generally found to be highest among successful police officers.

When faced with stress, Sgt. White is the kind of person who will tend to internalize it rather than to express it. He tends to be a controller of tension.

The personality is that of an individual who expresses strong conformist, traditional attitudes but who will tend to enter an occupation where he is required to deal with people who are marginal or dangerous. The personality pattern is that which we find in successful police officers, combat commanders, and such individuals. Personality research suggests that such individuals tend to have more dissociative phenomena than those persons who do not have this profile. This personality profile is that of individuals who tend to be aggressive and extrapunitive in their reaction to stress and frustration. There is no psychiatric diagnosis or disorder for such a person and they are considered to be completely normal.

The Holmes Stress Scale was administered to Sgt. White. This scale evaluates the significant life changes that occur in an individual in order to determine the degree of stress under which they normally operate. Stress is a measure of the changes in a person's life that intensify their pace of living and lead them into situations where they are likely to experience more illness and more overreaction than the average individual. An analysis of Sgt. White's activities in life in the past 18 months results in a stress index that would be rated 326 conservatively and 411 when including items that are somewhat equivocal. The research shows that individuals whose stress index falls below 120 suffer very little stress and are generally able to function in a wide range of situations without any type of overreaction or propensity to suffer illness as a result of the stress. Between 120 and 300, a 50-50 chance of overreaction or stress reaction can be expected. When a scale exceeds 300, the chances are 89 or more out of 100 that the person will have stress reactions. Certainly, Sgt. White can be considered to be under considerable stress at the present time, excluding the incident under consideration. This in itself is not unusual; people in his type of dangerous work, which requires rapid, aggressive decisions, are generally found to suffer high levels of stress. This accounts for the significant and unexpected occurrence of hypertension and other somatic diseases in police officers at relatively early ages. It also probably helps account for the extremely high rate of suicide that occurs among police officers.

The psychological evaluation indicates that Sgt. White is a man of normal personality, ideally suited for his job as a police officer operating in stressful and dangerous situations, conscientious, and concerned about those serving under him. He is a man who is likely to act in what he considers to be the best interests of those he is responsible for. He, like most people under pressure, has a higher propensity for mild, brief dissociative reactions than the average.

DEADLY FORCE AND DANGEROUSNESS RESEARCH

There is a large body of research concerning the use of deadly force on police officers and by police officers. An average of 102 police officers a year are killed by civilians, and approximately 275 legal interventions by police officers result in a civilian death.

In pursuit of their mandate to preserve life and keep the peace, police do kill or maim suspected lawbreakers. One of the most important indicators of whether such events will occur in a police force has been found to be the social or community propensity of the city's armed criminal suspects to act with assaultiveness and aggressiveness toward police. This differs from one town to another.

The research indicates that the better the police force in terms of training and selection, the higher will be the fatality rate from discharged weapons. For instance, the Los Angeles Police Department, considered to be the most carefully selected and best-trained police department in the United States has a fatality rate of 37% for weapons discharged other than in training. The "hit" rate for officers' weapons discharged is 62%. By contrast, in Chicago, where selection and training procedures are considered to be extremely lax and where the police department has suffered a great deal of criticism, the "hit" rate has been 18%.

Police officers are aware of the dangers of their profession. Three law enforcement officers are murdered annually for every 10,000 officers in the United States. The more than 21,000 police departments in the United States respond to a great many dangerous events that police officers are aware may confront them in the line of duty.

The research shows that, although police officers become much more cautious and concerned when they are aware that suspects may have a weapon, this is not particularly helpful in protecting themselves. In the research, it was found that 71% of officer victims knew or had good reason to believe that the suspects were armed before any shooting started. This indicates that although officers may be forewarned by their perception of a dangerous situation, they remain at very high risk. The research shows that officers in tactical units are seven to nine times more likely than patrol officers to become involved either as shooters or as victims.

The largest study of the use of deadly force concludes "the use of deadly force by the police is concentrated within an environment of community violence in general." Thus, it is a community's culture of violence, or the neighborhood of the community in which the police officer is operating that determines the likelihood of a police officer shooting or being shot.

There is a general myth, commonly believed by civilians, that most police officers are shot by "unstable" individuals. The research indicates that this indeed is a myth. Police officers are in greatest danger and most likely to be killed by rational criminals who are attempting to flee the scene of the crime. Their intention is secondary to their attempts to protect themselves from capture. Thus, the strongest signal to a police officer that he or she is in danger, is a suspect who appears to be making an effort to escape (Geller, 1982).

Dangerousness and violent people have been carefully studied during the past 25 years. The number one fact emerging from all of this research is that danger cannot be accurately predicted. Those people who are most dangerous are those who have a history of being dangerous, those who associate with individuals having a history of being dangerous, and those who live, work, or recreate in settings where dangerous, violent behavior has occurred. Violence is a basic human propensity. It is ordinarily used as a defense measure, but in modern society, violence and dangerousness are often used for political purposes, personal gain, vengeance, and so forth.

Law enforcement officers must evaluate and gauge individuals in terms of their propensity to be violent and dangerous. All persons involved with violence become activated by the closeness of dangerous situations. In social/psychological research, the concept of "buffer zone" has emerged.

The probability of a violent act occurring increases geometrically with the decrease in distance between two potentially dangerous subjects. This is true for dangerous criminals, and it is true for law enforcement personnel in dangerous settings. In police training, this is referred to as the "critical defense zone." Dangerousness is defined as the capacity to use deadly force. This is part of the training and part of the requirements of all law enforcement officers on active duty. It is inconceivable that a law enforcement officer who would be hesitant to use deadly force in an appropriate situation could function or be trusted by the personnel working with him or her. If one cannot accept the concept that law enforcement personnel must have the capacity to be violent in appropriate situations, one must reject the entire concept of law enforcement.

The buffer zone is considered to be 24 to 48 inches. In dangerous situations, violence is likeliest to be activated as the distance between the stimulus individual and the response individual decreases. Given a police officer with a capacity to be violent in appropriate situations, this violence is likeliest to be activated when a dangerous stimulus moves physically closer to such a police officer, particularly as the distance decreases from 48 inches downward (Hays, Roberts, & Solway, 1981).

SUMMARY AND CONCLUSIONS

The following conclusions are based on the psychological evaluation of the personality of Sgt. Charles White, his background history, and the circumstances surrounding the incident, as well as the research appropriate to the use of deadly force, dangerousness, and violence:

1. Sgt. White shows no psychological pathology.
2. Sgt. White's personality is that which is expected and found among successful officers.
3. Sgt. White works in a unit of law enforcement that is considered among the most dangerous.
4. In the narcotics trade, it is rare that weapons are not present where drugs are transferred or sold.
5. In the preceding incident, Sgt. White was in charge of the situation and responsible for his men.
6. In addition to the ordinary anticipation of danger to himself and to his men, Sgt. White had a recent experience where he was concerned for the safety of his men because of communication difficulty.
7. In the current situation, a similar miscommunication occurred, and he heard information over his radio that led him to believe that his men might be in difficulty.
8. Sgt. White's record, his history, and his previous performance indicate that his actions were concurrent with a law enforcement supervisor taking the responsibility of protecting the men of his unit on a dangerous assignment.
9. Psychologically, his state of mind at the time of the preceding occurrences was that of an individual under a great deal of stress, taking

appropriate action under time-stressful circumstances, with his men's lives at stake.

10. On entering the scene noted earlier, Sgt. White was aware that one of the suspects was disobeying the orders of one of Sgt. White's officers.

11. Sgt. White moved in, properly, to neutralize the suspect who again disobeyed the police orders.

12. The suspect suddenly made sharp movements threatening Sgt. White's defense zone, and Sgt. White reacted in a proper, instinctive, trained manner as any law enforcement officer would be likely to do under similar circumstances.

13. Sgt. White's reaction immediately following the incident in which he does not remember details of what he may have said to other officers or in their presence is well in keeping with a minor, not unexpected dissociative response:

   A sudden temporary alteration in the normal integration functions of consciousness. A sudden inability to remember important personal information. A localized amnesia following a severe psychological stress. The termination of the amnesia tends to be abrupt and in less than an hour. (American Psychiatric Association, 1981)

Nothing in our psychological evaluation indicates that Sgt. White has ever had a propensity to unusual violence, malicious intent, or propensity to overstep his professional mandates. The evaluation suggests that an experienced officer dealing with a known dangerous situation had his buffer safety zone suddenly and intensely violated, and reacted accordingly with a defense-of-life shooting.

Rubert Bob Smith, PhD
Consultant in Clinical Psychology

Attachment 1—References

Attachment 1 to
Psychological Report
White, Charles

REFERENCES

American Psychiatric Association. (1981). *Diagnostic and statistical manual.* Washington, DC; Author.

Geller, W. A. Deadly force: What we know. *Journal of Police Science and Administration*, 1982: 10, (2).

Hays, J. R., Roberts, T. K., & Solway, K. S. (Eds.). (1981). *Violence and the violent individual.* New York: S.P. Medical and Scientific Books.

PART THREE

Intervention

CHAPTER SEVEN

Critical Incident Counseling

To illustrate the unusual kind of stresses under which police officers operate, and the conditions that sometimes lead to the death of an officer, the following newspaper article is quoted from the Tampa, Florida, *Tampa Tribune*, December 10, 1992.

TEEN CITES PEER PRESSURE IN PULLING GUN

By Orval Jackson
Tribune Staff Writer

TAMPA—"I stuck the gun to her head. I didn't say nothing to her."

So testified a Tampa teenager on trial Tuesday for attempted first-degree murder of a Tampa police officer during a July 4 confrontation in a housing area north of Ybor City.

But Eugene Williams, 16, said he feels bad about what he did, saying he had been drinking and wasn't thinking when he pointed the gun at the head of Officer Lisa Bishop.

"I was trying to feel like a part of the crew I was with," Williams said. "I was trying to be someone, be a big man."

The case is expected to go to the jury today.

Bishop said she was interviewing a man whose car had been struck by gunshots when she suddenly was pushed from behind and onto the hood of her police car.

"I heard a scuffle behind me and the next thing I knew, I was bent over the hood," Bishop said. "I remember feeling a body against me and a hard object pressed to the back of my head behind my ear. I heard someone say 'Don't move,' and I heard a click. At that instant, I froze."

Bishop said the man she was talking with grabbed the gunman's hand and began struggling with him. She ran to the back of her car and radioed for help. The officer said she saw the gunman running away. A .25-caliber handgun was found nearby.

Williams, who was arrested on July 6, said another boy handed him the gun as he started toward the officer. He said he was egged into his action by a third boy who was angry because Bishop had shined her flashlight in his eyes earlier.

Williams said the gun was not loaded and he never tried to pull the trigger, even though his finger was on it. Three weeks after his arrest, Williams wrote a letter to Bishop asking for her forgiveness.

Had there been a live round under the firing pin in the pistol, something the accused could not really know, Officer Bishop would now, in all probability, be dead.

Although it is estimated that 90% of law enforcement officers are affected by one or more critical incident stress situations during their careers (Conroy, 1990), psychological services for such incidents have only recently become a generally accepted procedure, at least in larger police departments (McMains, 1986).

The entire concept of professional intervention is to some degree repugnant to law enforcement officers. As was outlined and described in Chapter Two, the law enforcement community is a complex, established social grouping with many performance expectations, and relatively little flexibility. The concept of "being helped" is abhorrent to most police officers. To the line officer, someone who "needs help" is inadequate, insufficient, incompetent, or a "screw-up." It is a situation to be avoided at all costs, even denied or covered up. To "need help" means that the officer is no longer reliable, would not make a good partner, or is not worthy of the respect and good will of colleagues. This respect and goodwill is a reward and benefit that experienced law enforcement officers will do almost anything to preserve.

To many police managers, an individual who "needs help" suggests inefficiency, bureaucratic problems, paperwork, and the worst of all situations—litigation against the department. In some departments, police managers are more than willing to abrogate their responsibilities after an officer is involved in a critical incident by willingly turning the situation over to a grand jury for review (particularly where deadly force is involved). This sends a message to the officer that he or she is guilty until proved innocent, no longer has the support of the department, and is probably tainted forever (Scuro, 1982).

In spite of the attention critical incidents get from the popular media, the working police officer has no interest in being involved in "shoot-outs," murder and mayhem, and other events that may lead to critical incidents. Yet, these things to happen in the life of the police officer. Rarely does a police officer retire after 20 years without having experienced some kind of critical incident that has had a significantly stressful effect on the officer's life.

THE NATURE OF A CRITICAL INCIDENT

A critical incident is probably most easily defined as a psychologically distressing event outside the range of usual human experience. This definition, the linchpin of the diagnosis *Post-Traumatic Stress Disorder* has been defined in the *Diagnostic and Statistical Manual of Mental Disorders* (Third Edition, Revised) (DSM-III-R). Within this classification, the American Psychiatric Association (1987) has established some fairly specific criteria for an emotional response to a sudden and terror-inducing experience. Although there may be changes in specifics in the definition of the Post-Traumatic Stress Disorder in future diagnostic systems, the essentials are likely to remain constant. They include the following:

1. The individual has experienced an event outside the range of usual human experience that would be markedly distressing to almost anyone.
2. The traumatic event is reexperienced, usually persistently, in the form of recurrent recollections, distressing dreams of the event, the sudden feeling that the traumatic event is recurring again (flashback), or intense distress when the individual is exposed to events or situations that resemble the original traumatic event.
3. The individual tends to avoid stimuli associated with the trauma (the neighborhood, the people, the circumstances, the time of day) or experiences a numbing of general responsiveness that wasn't present before the event. This can include amnesia for important parts of the trauma, circumventing activities that might arouse recollections, sudden and marked disinterest in usual and ordinary life activities, feelings of detachment and estrangement, restricted range of emotion, and pessimistic feelings about the future.
4. Certain psychological symptoms are likely to go along with this including sleep difficulties, outbursts of irritability, concentration difficulties, overreaction, and other anxiety symptoms.

The law enforcement community is unique in terms of an officer's potential exposure to especially traumatizing experiences. Such things as traffic accidents, abusive language, efforts at assault and battery by individuals being arrested, and a wide range of other activities may become "usual and customary" experiences of the seasoned patrol officer. There are, however, other especially traumatizing experiences that most officers seldom or never experience during a career. For a law enforcement officer, a critical incident would be a threat to the individual's survival or continued functioning, a threat of such intensity that it is likely to produce significant symptoms or reactions in the average law enforcement officer. (Wells, Getman, & Blau, 1988.) The common characteristics of a critical incident are:

1. The event is likely to be sudden and unexpected.
2. The event is a threat to the officer's existence or well-being.
3. The event may include an element of loss (partner, physical ability, position).

4. The event may result in an abrupt change in the officer's values, confidence, or ideals.

CRITICAL INCIDENTS UNIQUE TO THE
LAW ENFORCEMENT COMMUNITY

Deadly Force

The most severe traumas experienced by police officers are associated with one of the significant elements of the law enforcement officer's responsibilities—*deadly force*. Two aspects of the law enforcement officer's job are unique in respect to every other occupation. The first is the power of arrest. Every sworn police officer is duty-bound to prevent crime wherever possible, and to apprehend and take into custody the perpetrators of a crime. In connection with this responsibility, law enforcement officers are permitted to use deadly force in discharging their sworn duties. At the same time, officers are restrained from using deadly force to apprehend a criminal whenever this is possible. Thus, police are caught between one citizen group that demands the use of deadly force to prevent crime and apprehend criminals, whereas another large group assumes too much deadly force is being used by police. These latter critics exert a great deal of political pressure to reduce armed police intervention (Scharf & Binder, 1983).

Almost all police officers are armed. About half of major police departments require officers to remain armed while they are off duty and be prepared to intervene if a felony comes to their attention. The other 50% of departments *permit* officers to carry off-duty guns and strongly urge them to be available to intervene, even though off duty, while in their own jurisdictions. There are no indications that off-duty officers who are armed increase community violence levels (Fyfe, 1982).

While pursuing their duties, police officers are targets of felons who are armed with firepower equal to or exceeding that possessed by the police officer. As a result, cops are killed. In the decade 1980–1989, 801 law enforcement officers were feloniously killed in the line of duty (Major, 1991).

During this decade, 783 of the officers killed were men; 18 were women. The dead included 515 between the ages of 25 and 40, and 327 who were killed while attempting to make an arrest. Firearms killed 735 officers, and of these, 120 officers were killed by their own weapons, taken away during a scuffle with the felon. The victims included 157 who were killed while wearing protective body armor. Two-thirds of those killed were patrol officers.

The issue of deadly force—its occurrence and the conditions under which it occurs—has been extensively studied and reported (Blau, 1986; Geller, 1982; Lundstrom & Mullan, 1987; Manolias & Hyatt-Williams, 1986; McMains, 1986; Meredith, 1984; Meyer, 1986; Reiser, 1982a,b,c;

Weiss, 1989). When a police officer is killed in the line of duty, an average of over 100 survivors (relatives, partners, shift cohorts, friends, supervisors, etc.) are traumatized and are in need of counseling. This suggests the need for such services is for 10,000 or more survivors a year.

In addition to the traumatizing effects on survivors of an officer's death, there are the traumas that accrue to an officer who kills or wounds another person. In a sense, this is considered a "failure" on the part of the officer, who has not "controlled" the event to bring about a successful and bloodless resolution. The officer is certainly going to face administrative and possibly legal action that can be extremely disruptive. This will be considered later in this chapter.

Other traumatic events involving deadly force include the officer who is wounded, the officer who is "nearly killed" as noted earlier in this chapter, and the officer who is severely beaten in an altercation. All of these can have significant emotional effects, not only on the officer who is involved, but on those officers who are close to that person.

Trauma to partners, friends, and family results not only when officers are killed but after officers are wounded. There are no accurate wounds-suffered data available because various departments have different reporting techniques. Hospitals and emergency centers do not identify the occupation of those who are treated for assaultive wounds.

As best can be reckoned, police officers kill about 375 subjects a year. There has been a general downward trend in justifiable homicide by police over the past 20 years. This is probably a result of more sophisticated police training and tactics. Recent laws and regulations prohibiting the use of deadly force in situations not involving clearly dangerous offenders or imminent threats to the lives of officers or others have also been responsible for the decrease in deadly force by police officers. There are now two fairly standard rules: Deadly force may be used in defense of life, or to apprehend dangerous and violent fleeing felons (Fyfe, 1989).

With over 260 million citizens in the population of the United States, annual deaths caused by police officers number under 400. On the other hand, the citizen population is killing 100 to 150 officers a year, with a population of sworn officers under 600,000. Thus the citizens enjoy a strong lead in the use of deadly force.

Other Traumatic Situations

Police officers are human beings. They are subject to the circumstances that are traumatic for all human beings. The kinds of critical incidents during a police officer's career that have profound effect on the officer or those close to the officer include the following:

1. The tragic death of a family member.
2. Divorce or separation.

3. Participation in a community disaster (cyclone, earthquake, hurricane, riot).
4. Suicide of a family member or a fellow police officer.
5. Observation or participation in the investigation of ghastly crimes such as mutilated victims of homicide.

The degree to which an officer may be affected by these incidents depends on the officer's personality, experience, the degree of support or lack of support that the officer receives, and many other factors.

All in all, law enforcement officers (together with but more so than other public service personnel such as firefighters and emergency medical service people) have a much higher probability of being exposed to critical incidents than people in almost any other job category.

THE EFFECTS OF A CRITICAL INCIDENT

The effects of a critical incident on a police officer cannot be predicted with great accuracy. Stress may be cumulative. If the officer has had stressful experiences from other sources prior to the incident, the reaction is likely to be greater. As was specified previously, many factors influence the degree of reaction to a critical incident in addition to previous stress experience. The officer's reputation, status, conditions under which the critical incident took place, peer responses to the incident, responses of senior officers, and the response of the public media and the community to the event, can all have significant influence on the officer (Baruth, 1986).

The effect of any shooting incident is drastic. Approximately 80% of officers who are involved in a shooting will leave their departments shortly thereafter. The aftermath of a traumatic event for a peace officer can be devastating and disruptive in all facets of the officer's life. In life-threatening situations, the officer not only deals with surviving and maintaining basic integrity but must be concerned with his or her department's reaction to the event, the community's reaction, the family's reaction, and the response of friends. The critical incident may be the last straw that breaks the officer's coping ability, and the degree of stress of the incident itself can be secondary (Blak, 1986).

Officers go through three phases of reaction following a traumatic event: *the impact phase, the recoil phase,* and *the post-traumatic phase.*

During the *impact phase,* which follows the traumatic event, the following conditions and reactions can be expected:

1. It begins with the traumatic event and continues until the stressor no longer has a direct effect.

2. It may last a few minutes or several days.
3. The officer's focus of attention is on the present and on the traumatic event. This phase lasts longest in the event of an officer's death or in cases of an officer's use of deadly force. The traumatized officer or surviving partners in the case of an officer's death may experience repetitions of the event in the form of flashbacks during investigations and other discussions. Interrogation by senior officers and questioning by the media and lawyers may require officers to continue focusing on the traumatic event for days, weeks, or even months.
4. Reactions by the traumatized officer may include feeling or acting stunned or bewildered. There may be a blurring of attention, isolation of emotion, or automatic behavior with bland emotions. The more that the events following the traumatic incident continue to stress the officer, the longer and more intense this phase is likely to be.

A highway patrol officer made a routine stop of a vehicle for exceeding the speed limit. While questioning the driver, the officer became suspicious of materials that he saw on the back seat of the car. He asked the driver to step out of the car, in a routine manner. The driver got out of the car and immediately assaulted the highway patrol officer, struck him to the ground, pulled the officer's pistol, and shot him dead. A massive search for the culprit began within an hour of the time of the homicide. At the end of approximately 12 hours, the culprit was discovered and arrested by officers of the local sheriff's department. An officer in the arresting party, a lieutenant, requested psychological services the next morning. He stated as follows:

> I don't know why I'm here, but I know that I ought to be here. We arrested this scumbag at about 2:00 this morning. He was jabbering away and admitted killing Bill. (The lieutenant had known the deceased highway patrol officer.) We put him in the back seat of a patrol car. Sam Jones was on one side of him and I was on the other side. As I sat looking at him, cuffed and docile, I had a tremendous urge to pull my pistol and shoot the bastard. He had simply snuffed out the life of a young cop with a wife and two children. The vehicle was loaded with narcotics. He was the scum of the earth. He didn't deserve to live. I knew I couldn't do this. It was all I could do to restrain myself.
>
> I haven't been able to sleep. I have felt confused. I can't keep my mind on stuff. All I can think of is that poor kid being shot in the head by this scumbag. I don't know if I did the right thing in restraining myself. I went to work this morning, and I did what I had to do but frankly I can't remember what I did. Something is wrong and I need help.

This officer was suffering a post-traumatic reaction of a severe nature. He was operating within the *impact phase*. Crisis consultation procedures were immediately instituted, and within two weeks, the lieutenant appeared to be comfortable and symptom free.

Following the impact phase, the *recoil phase* begins. This lasts until the officer is able to return to routine duty and daily living. This period may range from several days to many weeks. The *recoil phase* is characterized by the need to retell the story in an attempt to master the traumatizing event. This phase may also include a tendency to be overreactive to ordinary events, as well as a need to share and receive support from other officers. The officer may experience acute emotional reactions such as depression, impotent rage, withdrawal, anxiety, bad dreams, sleep disturbances, and somatization.

Following this phase, the *post-traumatic period* begins. It usually appears after the officer returns to a regular routine. On the surface, the officer may appear to be stable and then the long-range effects of a traumatic critical incident may begin to appear. There may be periodic episodes of depression, feelings of hopelessness, sleep disturbances, bad dreams, or a continuation of the reexperiencing (Wells et al., 1988).

In addition to these symptoms and effects, if the officer has had even a mild head injury, there may be some symptoms of this trauma such as confusion, disorientation, and poor judgment as well as memory difficulties (Reed, 1986).

TABLE 7.1   Officers' Reactions Following Their
Shooting a Subject in the Line of Duty (*N* = 86)

Officers' Reaction	Percentage
Heightened sense of danger	58
Anger	49
Nightmares	34
Isolation/Withdrawal	45
Fear and anxiety about the future	40
Sleep difficulties	46
Flashbacks	44
Emotional numbing	43
Depression	42
Alienation	40
Guilt/Sorrow/Remorse	37
Problems with authority figures	28
Family problems	27
Fear of loss of control	23
Sexual problems	18
Alcohol/drug use	14
Suicidal thoughts	11

Note: From "Post-Shooting Traumatic Reactions: A Pilot Study," by R. Soloman and J. Horn, in J. Reese and H. Goldstein (Eds.), *Psychological Services for Law Enforcement,* 1986, Washington, DC: U.S. Government Printing Office, Superintendent of Documents.

Solomon and Horn (1986) studied postshooting traumatic reactions in 86 police officers who had been in a line-of-duty shooting (53% killed a culprit and 47% wounded the subject). The kinds of reactions reported are indicated in Table 7.1.

These results confirm that all officers who experience a critical incident do not respond in the same way. The range can be considerable, more intense in some than in others (Ayres, 1990).

Figure 7.1 presents a simplified post-traumatic stress syndrome checklist that can be used to determine whether an officer is experiencing such a reaction.

NAME _____ DATE _____
TRAUMA DATE _____

A. *INCIDENT* _____

_____

_____ 1. Outside range of human experience.

_____ 2. Markedly distressing to almost anyone.

B. *REEXPERIENCED* (1+)

_____ 1. Distressing, recurrent, intrusive recollection.

_____ 2. Recurrent distressing dreams of events.

_____ 3. Sudden reliving of the event (flashback).

_____ 4. Intense distress at exposure to events symbolizing event.

C. *AVOIDANCE OF STIMULI ASSOCIATED WITH THE TRAUMA OR NUMBING* (3+)

_____ 1. Avoids thoughts or feelings associated with the event.

_____ 2. Avoids activities or situations that arouse recollections of the trauma.

_____ 3. Inability to recall important aspects of the trauma.

_____ 4. Markedly diminished interest in significant activities.

_____ 5. Feelings of detachment or estrangement from other people.

_____ 6. Restricted range of emotion.

_____ 7. Sense of foreshortened future and expectations.

D. *INCREASED AROUSAL* (2+)

_____ 1. Difficulty falling or staying asleep.

_____ 2. Irritability or outbursts of anger.

_____ 3. Difficulty concentrating.

_____ 4. Hypervigilance.

_____ 5. Startle response.

_____ 6. Physiological reactivity when at a place or event symbolizing or resembling the trauma.

FIGURE 7.1   Post-Traumatic Syndrome Checklist

The numbers beside each of the subheadings *B, C,* and *D* in the figure are the cutoff points recommended in the *Diagnostic and Statistical Manual* (Third Edition, Revised) (American Psychiatric Association, 1987).

INTERVENTION PROCEDURES

There is literally total agreement that early intervention is critical in treating post-traumatic incidents (Baruth, 1986; Reiser, 1982c). All law enforcement departments should be prepared for critical incidents among their officers because these incidents are bound to happen even though occurrence may be fairly infrequent in small departments.

INTERVENORS

Not all intervenors are helpful. There is no way to prevent certain potentially negative influences following a critical incident. The press is bound to be involved, and an investigation team will interview and evaluate the officer's performance. Those who can be of greatest help to the victims and survivors of critical incidents include (a) those who are close to and accepted by the victims/survivors, and (b) those who have the skill and experience to be of service. The most effective intervenors may have either or both of these characteristics. The most commonly involved intervenors are:

1. *Fellow Officers.* Generally highest in acceptance by victims and survivors, fellow officers vary considerably in counseling skills and/ or experience. The potential to help is high, while the potential to worsen the situation is relatively low, except in the case of those fellow officers with insensitive or destructive personality styles.
2. *Immediate Supervisors.* Supervisors offer the same potential to be of help as fellow officers. In addition, they can also arrange smooth transitions and attend to the necessary administrative details with the least stress on the traumatized officer.
3. *Unit Commanders.* As an authority figure of considerable significance in the lives of all concerned, the commander of the unit in which the traumatic incident occurred is in a position to counsel, give general support, and set a standard and model for helpful behavior. The unit commander can also ensure that the immediate supervisor takes care of all administrative matters. The unit commander can give the supervisor support and guidance during all phases of the traumatic incident process.
4. *Peer Counselor.* A police officer who has been trained as a peer counselor can provide continuing support, monitoring, or follow-up intervention where effects of trauma are long-term or chronic.

Contacts between the peer counselor and victims should be confidential.

5. *Chaplain.* In most law enforcement departments, the chaplain is seen as the most neutral and accessible source of understanding and support. Spiritual counsel is especially helpful when the trauma involves a death.

6. *Mental Health Professionals.* Psychologists, psychiatrists, and other professionally trained mental health workers may be helpful if they have experience in counseling law enforcement personnel and their families. Without this familiarity, the mental health professional may be unaware of or insensitive to the embarrassment, shame, distrust, or emotional distance that most highly functional and practical people like police officers initially tend to feel in respect to "shrinks." A mental health professional who has also been a law enforcement officer can be especially effective.

7. *Other Officers' Family Members.* Spouses and other family members of fellow officers can be particularly helpful in lending support to the families of slain officers or of officers who have suffered other traumatic incidents. Most law enforcement agencies have an informal network of officers' spouses who are ready and able to help out in emergencies.

8. *The Media.* Newspapers and television reporters, editors, and producers can have powerful effects—positive or negative—following a critical incident. Traumatic events involving law enforcement personnel usually are of major interest to readers and viewers. Whether the reporting of such incidents is sympathetic and supportive or, as in some instances, distressing or even destructive to victims and survivors, depends on a variety of motives, bureaucratic requirements, and personalities of media representatives. In most instances, reporting the story—not its impact on the traumatized officer or survivors—will be the priority of the media.

9. *The Citizenry.* In the United States, perhaps more than in any other country in the world, citizens contact law enforcement personnel directly with opinions, evaluations, and commentary. Following a critical incident, the communications received from concerned, interested, or opinionated citizens can have a significant effect on the reaction of the officer and his or her family to the event.

Intervention Points

Help should be available and rendered at all appropriate times following a traumatic critical incident. The range of possible intervention times is from immediately following the event to as long as a year later. In general, the earlier the appropriate intervention, the more effective it is likely to be.

1. *At the Scene.* Conflict control, stabilization, and support immediately following the critical incident can make the difference between a short-term, acute reaction or chronic post-traumatic stress. The most influential intervenors at the scene are likely to be fellow officers, immediate supervisors, unit commanders, the media, and civilian bystanders.

2. *The Investigation.* Regardless of the individual(s) or specific emotional trauma involved, mandated departmental regulations and procedures must be carried out. The traumatized individual, partners, other officers, or even family members may be required to give testimony. The immediate supervisor and unit commander are the key intervenors in this phase.

3. *The First 24 Hours.* During the *impact phase,* and as the officer enters the *recoil phase,* the peer counselor, the immediate supervisor, and the mental health professional are most likely to provide positive intervention.

4. *Week 1.* As the officer-stress victim moves from the *recoil phase* to the *post-traumatic* period, the immediate supervisor, the peer counselor, and the mental health professional continue to be the first-line intervenors. The unit commander may also be of assistance.

5. *Weeks 2–4.* As the officer returns to duty and familiar routines, his partners, fellow officers, and immediate supervisor are in the best position to monitor and intervene if stress reactions continue or develop. Where necessary and appropriate, the peer counselor or mental health professional may continue with crisis consultation or support.

6. *Months 1–6.* Where stress reactions (job-related or family-related problems) continue or appear in this time period, professional help is indicated. Although the peer counselor and supervisors may be supportive, stress reactions extending for this period of time may have deeper roots that should be explored in a professional health setting.

There may be slight modifications of these recommended intervention points, but most departments that have operational response teams follow this general outline (McMains, 1986; Wells et al., 1988).

Intervention Techniques

Intervention is probably best conducted by a psychologist who is already familiar with the officer, if such a person is available. A psychologist who is knowledgeable about police procedures would be the second choice (Baruth, 1986).

Some intervention techniques can be used effectively by almost any intervenor, whereas others require special training or qualifications. The inappropriate use of some intervention techniques can be in some cases dangerous (untimely clinical exploration, interpretation). The effectiveness of any intervention technique to help relieve post-traumatic stress is governed by the timeliness, tone, style, and intent of the intervention. Some of the more commonly favored techniques for the relief of post-traumatic stress include:

1. *Attentive Listening*. This technique can be used by any intervenor and is usually helpful in any stress-relief effort. Good eye contact, an occasional nod, and genuine interest without comment are the essential mechanics of this technique.

2. *Being There with Empathy*. Simply "being there" and indicating availability, concern, and awareness of the turbulent emotions being experienced by the stressed individual add reassurance and hope. The fellow officer or peer counselor who has experienced a similar traumatic incident can be most empathetic. In addition, it is helpful to let the traumatized officer know what he or she is likely to experience in the days to follow.

3. *Reassurance*. This technique is valuable only if the reassurance is reality oriented. It should take the form of reassuring the victim that routine matters will be handled, premises and property will be secured, family will be protected, and the victim's responsibilities will be handled by others. It is vital for the traumatized officer to realize he or she is not alone. Organizational support from command personnel can be an important reassurance for the officer-victim. Such support may include describing what the department will do and how the incident is viewed by superior officers, and providing local assistance where appropriate.

4. *Supportive Counseling*. This technique requires formal training. Using procedures such as *effective listening, restatement of content, clarification of feelings, reassurance, community referral*, and *networking*, counselors can help the victim prepare for a return to less stressful circumstances. Peer counselors are particularly skilled in these techniques.

5. *Group Grief Sharing*. In death-of-an-officer incidents, holding meetings of family, partners, associated law enforcement personnel, and others closely associated with the dead officer can help prevent or relieve excessive stress responses by allowing the participants to vent their emotions fully.

6. *Interpretive Counseling*. Peer counselors or mental health professionals can use this intervention technique to stimulate the victim to search for and discover the underlying emotional stresses that intensify a naturally stressful traumatic event. This procedure should be used when the victim's emotional reaction is significantly greater than the circumstances of the critical incident warrant. Interpretive counseling

may reveal emotional difficulties that require more extensive professional help than that which can be provided in the context of crisis consultation.

7. *Clinical Exploration.* The victim of a traumatic critical incident may develop a series of stress reactions that do not abate with the crisis procedures described earlier. When this happens, the victim may suffer a chronic post-traumatic stress disorder. Extended post-traumatic stress is debilitating and requires referral for clinical exploration of the condition. Psychologists, social workers, psychiatrists, and/or other mental health professionals who have experience and training in working with law enforcement personnel are the consultants of choice.

A Post-Traumatic Syndrome Interview form such as the one presented in Appendix H may be useful in the *clinical exploration* phase.

Conditions of Intervention

Intervention techniques and skills must be applied in appropriate ways following a traumatic critical incident. The following are some of the most important conditions:

1. *Immediacy.* Intervention during the hours immediately following a critical incident is crucial. All techniques other than interpretive counseling and clinical exploration tend to be most effective in the first 12 to 24 hours after the trauma.
2. *Brevity.* All the preceding techniques are likely to work best with a minimum of verbiage and repetition. Language should be concise and communication brief.
3. *Privacy.* Except for group grief sharing, intervention techniques are best provided to the victim in as private a setting as possible.
4. *Respect.* The traumatized victim of a critical incident may respond in unusual or unexpected ways. The intervenor who expects to render effective help must be prepared to tolerate unusual behavior and continue to respond with acceptance and respect. It is destructive for an intervenor to become distressed by a victim's behavior and criticize or attempt to control the victim's responses by being authoritarian or by demanding that the victim "shape up."
5. *Support.* The intervenor in a traumatic critical incident situation must be supportive. Whether in earlier or later stages, intervention is more likely to be successful if the victim sees the intervenor as fully supportive, on the victim's "side," and willing to do anything within reason to ease the victim's burden.

Making Critical Incident Procedures Operational

Each law enforcement department must develop its own standardized procedures for responding to traumatic events. Written regulations and procedures tend to be rigid, but in the case of procedures developed and specified for dealing with traumatic events, the application of the required actions should be subject to the judgment and availability of the intervenors. Larger departments should have available trained peer counselors and mental health staff or consultants. Smaller law enforcement units should develop close ties with larger departments so that trained and experienced intervenors can be "borrowed" when an emergency situation arises. In general, critical incident response procedures can be codified in departmental regulations or orders that include the following:

1. *Activation.* Regulations dealing with official response to traumatic incidents should begin with clear-cut descriptions of the events that would require a critical incident response from the department.

2. *Crisis Team Manager.* Department procedure manuals should designate the individual(s) who are to be contacted as soon as a critical incident occurs. These individuals should be senior staff who are trained and experienced in responding and managing rapidly and efficiently.

3. *Crisis Team Members.* Specific members of the department should be designated on a duty roster as a crisis team cadre. The crisis manager should select members for the response and management team who have experienced traumatic incidents, as well as newer team members who would profit from the experience of serving with more seasoned crisis intervenors.

4. *Press Liaison.* Some departments have a permanent public information officer. Others have no formal press contact personnel. Media professionals can be significant intervenors—helpful or unhelpful—in a critical incident situation. One member of the crisis management team should be prepared to meet with the press. This team member should provide accredited press representatives with the following:
   a. All the facts consistent with the law, department policy, and the best interest of the ongoing investigation.
   b. A briefing as to the concerns about victims and survivors and how the press may be most helpful as intervenors.
   c. Around-the-clock availability to answer questions and provide a single-source liaison between the press and the crisis manager.

5. *Initial Assignments.* Department procedural manuals or regulations should provide specific information on assignments for the crisis

manager and crisis team members for the various kinds of critical incidents likely to occur.

6. *Meetings and Reports.* The department's procedural manual should specify when the crisis management team should meet with respect to the different kinds of crises likely to be encountered. The types of formal and informal reports to department management should be specified in detail.

The details with which each procedure is described will depend to some extent on the size and resources of any specific department (Wells et al., 1988).

Law enforcement agencies operate on the basis of fairly rigid policy and the organization's General Orders. Figure 7.2 presents an example of

---

Line-of-Duty Death. The death of an officer in the line of duty affects all members of the department, as well as the fallen officer's family and friends. The entire community is likely to feel the loss. When the partner or the supervisor of a fallen officer becomes aware of or is notified of a line-of-duty death, the following procedures are to be followed:

1. The chief of the department is to be notified forthwith.
2. The designated crisis team manager is to be notified and dispatched immediately to the scene.
3. The crisis manager is to report his or her presence to the supervisor at the scene.
4. The crisis manager will designate a crisis team member as staff leader at headquarters to establish communications with the crisis manager at the scene and to assemble the crisis team members designated by the crisis manager. The staff leader will be directed by the crisis manager to contact the fallen officer's partner, best friend, the chaplain, and where appropriate, the fallen officer's former training officer, all of whom should be apprised of the details of the situation and placed on alert.
5. When the crisis manager has established the relevant details of the incident, he or she should formulate an action plan to accomplish the following:
   a. Notification and support of family survivors.
   b. Continuing communication with senior staff.
   c. Press liaison.
   d. A 24-hour plan for utilization of the crisis team.
6. This preliminary plan should be cleared immediately with the senior officer at the scene and with the chief.
7. Once cleared, the plan should be implemented. The crisis manager should assign a crisis team member to the scene and immediately return to headquarters to supervise the crisis plan implementation.

FIGURE 7.2   General Order for a Reaction to Line-of-Duty Death

one department's crisis management and intervention plan for line-of-duty deaths.

In this particular department, the crisis manager is generally a lieutenant or a captain, preferably from the department to which the fallen officer belonged. The crisis team member designated as staff leader is either the staff psychologist or a peer counselor trained in these procedures.

The department policy must be set up before a critical incident occurs, since once the incident has happened, there is usually no way to establish procedures. The demands of the situation preclude discussions and planning.

An FBI study of post-traumatic shooting reactions (Solomon & Horn, 1986) recommended the following for the treatment of an officer involved in a line-of-duty shooting:

1. Give compassionate response to involved officers at the scene.
2. Avoid judgmental remarks.
3. Provide physical and mental first aid.
4. Remove officer from the crime scene.
5. Replace officer's weapon.
6. Arrange contact with officer's family and provide support.
7. Provide a psychological break for officer before detailed interview.
8. Place officer on administrative leave (not suspension).
9. Provide mandatory counseling within 1–2 days.
10. Screen incoming telephone calls to the officer.
11. Advise employees of basic facts of the incident.
12. Screen office for vicarious thrill seekers.
13. Provide independent legal counsel for officer.
14. Allow a paced return to duty.
15. Consider the officer's interests in media releases.
16. Expedite the completion of administrative and criminal investigations and advisement of the outcomes to the officer.

In essence, dealing with the survivors of critical incidents in the law enforcement community requires the application of current knowledge about crisis consultation with post-traumatic stress disorders. These principles must be applied with a knowledge and understanding of the unique characteristics of police officers and their families.

TRAINING AND USING PEER COUNSELORS

The first use of peer counselors in the law enforcement community was in groups dealing with alcohol problems in major police agencies. Special

Alcoholics Anonymous groups, made up entirely of police officers, developed when it was found that police officers rarely attended AA meetings because they felt themselves to be a "different breed" from the civilians at such meetings. A significant degree of success was achieved by establishing groups made up entirely of serving or retired police officers, run by other officers who had successfully dealt with alcohol problems. This process will be explored in detail in Chapter Nine.

In critical incident stress counseling, peer counselors who are serving police officers (or in some cases firefighters or emergency medical service personnel) receive from 16 to 50 hours of training. These counselors often operate in teams. The primary activities of most peer counselors focus on "debriefing" personnel who are exposed to incidents that cause extraordinary emotion. The techniques taught to peer counselors include free expression that focuses on fears and concerns in a supportive environment, encouragement of insight by helping the victim to reframe the event in different perspectives, and continuing support. There are no standards for the training of peer counselors at this time (Conroy, 1990).

Wells et al. (1988) report the training of counselors who have themselves been victims of a critical incident, received counseling, and then volunteered for training as peer counselors. A 40- to 50-hour training program was developed to give these volunteers the appropriate information and supervised training to work effectively with critical incident victims. The training program used in this project is presented in Appendix I.

Figure 7.3 presents a checklist used by the graduates of the aforementioned project to ensure that they follow the appropriate steps once they are called to render assistance at a critical incident situation.

An informal peer counseling group was formed in 1953 called "Concerns of Police Survivors Inc. (COPS)." This national peer-support, self-help group has focused on the emotional needs and support needs of law enforcement families, friends, and co-workers who have lost a loved one in the line of duty. In addition to giving support to survivors, they work with law enforcement departments to ensure awareness of how important it is to be prepared to deal with line-of-duty deaths (Sawyer, 1989).

REFERRAL

When critical incident counseling is not sufficiently effective to deal with all the consequences of a critical incident, the officer should be referred for additional professional help. In spite of excellent and timely critical incident counseling, some officers develop a chronic post-traumatic stress syndrome. Other officers continue to be distressed and develop drug or alcohol problems. In some cases, the officers suffer other emotional difficulties. When this occurs, referral is necessary to continue treatment.

PROCESS CHECKLIST

DATE _____ TIME _____ CALL FROM _____ DEPT _____

OFFICER _____ SCENE _____

INCIDENT _____

___

___ Approval to help by _____
___ ID to senior officer at scene/
        structure
___ ID to officer/victim
___ Precounseling statement
___ Catharsis session
___ Support and reassurance
___ Officer to contact family/partners
        ___ Accepted ___ Rejected

___ Media statement to senior
        officer
___ Offer to meet with other
        officers in group
___ Follow-up at officer's home
___ 2-day contact
___ 3-day contact
___ 1-week contact
___ 4-week contact

NARRATIVE SUMMARY AND RECOMMENDATONS _____
_____
_____
_____
_____
_____
_____

Counseling completed _____ BY _____

FIGURE 7.3   Deadly Force Peer Counseling Process Checklist

The fully trained police psychologist is in a position to act as an employee assistance counselor. This will be taken up in some detail in Chapter Eight. If an officer continues to show the effects of exposure to extreme stress in a critical incident, the police psychologist is likely to discover this in the follow-up contacts that should be standard procedure after such incidents.

In making the referral, the police psychologist should try to recommend professionals who are familiar with law enforcement procedures. The psychologist must be sure that the officer understands the importance of the referral, and agrees to participation and continued treatment. In some instances, it will be necessary to face the officer with the reality that a fitness-for-duty evaluation is necessary since the officer's reaction is likely to interfere with regular duties. This delicate and difficult task must be faced directly and implemented expeditiously.

Some police psychologists have developed sufficient experience in these matters to be able not only to make a referral but to devise a treatment plan.

DEPARTMENT OF PUBLIC SAFETY

TREATMENT PLAN

RE: John Q. Smith (hereafter employee)

1. Employee will enroll in and comply with all of the requirements of the program at Local Hospital including but not limited to the following:

   Program attendance requirements (attendance to begin within nine days of date of signature below).

   AA-CA meeting requirements (usually 90 visits in 90 days post discharge).

   Psychotherapy, family therapy, or chemotherapy.

   Spouse abuse treatment.

   Approval from attending physician when obtaining prescription for medication that may have intoxicating side-effects.

   Inpatient detoxification and/or treatment requires abstinence from all intoxicating substances while in the program, testing (of bodily fluids or otherwise) for presence of substances.

2. Employee agrees to maintain abstinence from all nonprescribed intoxicants (including alcohol in all forms) for a period of two (2) years from the date of signature below. Thereafter, he agrees to not use any illegal intoxicant while in the employ of City. He also agrees to comply with any and all requests for random witnessed drug tests for two years from the date of signature below if he continues to be employed by City.

3. Employee agrees to initiate and maintain monthly (or more frequent at his or her election) contact with the psychologist until formally relieved of this requirement by the psychologist. This to be renegotiated at a later time, at which point an addendum to this plan will be made.

4. Employee will bear financial responsibility for all treatment.

5. Employee is aware that failure to fully comply with the terms of this plan in the absence of a reasonable and verifiable excuse, will result in employee's being declared unfit for duty. In addition, employee is aware that, for this reason, psychologist will contact the Office of Professional Standards (OPS) which may, in turn, initiate possible disciplinary action against him or her. In particular, the contact between OPS and psychologist:

   Will describe the employee's substance use history.

   Will note the fact that the employee was granted confidentiality under City and Departmental policy.

   Is noncompliant with treatment.

   Is a danger to himself or others (if in a sworn position).

   Under this provision, an attempt will be made to notify employee prior to communicating his fitness status to OPS.

6. Employee recognizes that item 5 (next above) constitutes a contingent limited waiver of the privilege of confidentiality. So long as he or she is in compliance with treatment, confidentiality is offered within the limits specified under the City Ordinance.

_____   _____
Employee   Date

_____   _____
Witness   Date

FIGURE 7.4 Treatment Plan Referral for an Officer Requiring Treatment beyond Critical Incident Counseling. Courtesy of Anthony Stone, PhD, MHP.

Figure 7.4 shows a treatment plan developed for a police officer who became involved in chronic abuse of alcohol after a critical incident experience.

Where an officer has been mildly or severely injured during a critical incident and there are indications that he or she has suffered a concussional syndrome, referral for neurological and neuropsychological evaluation is indicated (Reed, 1986). In such circumstances, fitness-for-duty evaluations may have to be done by professionals outside the department who have not been involved in the critical incident counseling of the officer.

RECORD KEEPING

In critical incident counseling, record keeping is a delicate matter. Confidentiality is of the utmost importance. On the other hand, there will be many pressures for the counselor to give testimony in the department investigation, in the grand jury hearings, and in any litigation, criminal or civil, that frequently follows the critical incident.

It would be impossible for a critical incident counselor to remain effective if the person giving support and services to the officer-victim could also become a witness against the officer. For this reason, all contacts and records must fall within the code of confidentiality and privilege that applies to the clients of psychologists in the particular jurisdiction where the critical incident counseling takes place. This important issue casts some doubt on utilizing peer counselors. Unless counselors are licensed mental health professionals, statutory and ethical constraints against revealing information from contacts with the officer-victim are unlikely to apply. The more the incident involves legal issues and investigative procedures, the more important it is that the critical incident counselor be a fully licensed professional.

The development of such specialized crisis consultation services in law enforcement is still in a nascent stage; standards and procedural constraints are yet to be developed. There is no question, however, of the importance of these procedures and the likelihood that they will become even more sought after in the future.

CHAPTER EIGHT

Stress: Prevention, Inoculation, and Counseling

THE NATURE OF STRESS

The term *stress* has so infiltrated the vernacular that it now ranks with descriptors such as *motivation* and *nervous* in identifying a variety of subjective perceptions or observations. In its simplest and most superficial form, stress is defined as some kind of strain or pressure. It is frequently used as a contraction of *distress*.

In medicine, stress is more narrowly defined as "any stimulus or succession of stimuli of such magnitude as to tend to disrupt the homeostasis of the organism" (Gennaro, Nora, Nora, Stander, & Weiss, 1979). Most current views of stress and the effects of stress have emerged from the pioneering work by Selye (1956) that resulted in his General Adaptation Syndrome theory. Selye pointed out that when an organism is subjected to unusual or unexpected demands of the environment, the adrenocortical system responds on an emergency basis to relieve the imbalance. Selye found that if the stressors continue to affect the organism, physiological deterioration, and eventually death, will occur. Understanding of the nature and effects of stress on human beings moved forward a quantum step in the work of Holmes and Rahe (1967). These researchers attempted to place numerical values on certain *life events* that apparently had strong negative effects on human beings. They were surprised to find that not only negative events but presumably positive events could be stressful. Such occurrences as marriage, marital reconciliation, gaining a new family member, promotion on the job, improvement in financial status, and outstanding personal achievement could trigger stress that in turn would increase the individual's chances of suffering a stress-related physical illness.

Using "death of a spouse" as the baseline measure of extreme stress, and assigning a weight of 100 to this event, Holmes and Rahe rated 43 life events that would have some effect or consequence for the individual. Table 8.1 lists

TABLE 8.1   **Stress Values for Various Life Events**

Event	Stress Points
Death of spouse	100
Divorce	73
Marital separation	65
Jail term	63
Death of a close family member	63
Personal injury or illness	53
Marriage	50
Terminated from job	47
Marital reconciliation	45
Retirement	45
Change in health of family member	44
Pregnancy	40
Sexual problems	39
Gain of new family member	39
Business adjustment	39
Change in financial state	38
Death of a close friend	37
Change to a different line of work	36
Change in number of arguments with spouse	35
Mortgage over $20,000	31
Foreclosure of mortgage or loan	30
Change in responsibilities at work	29
Son or daughter leaving home	29
Trouble with in-laws	29
Outstanding personal achievement	28
Wife beginning or stopping work	26
Begin or end school	26
Change in living conditions	25
Revision of personal habits	24
Trouble with supervisors	23
Change in work hours or conditions	20
Change in residence	20
Change in schools	20
Change in recreation	19
Change in church activities	19
Change in social activities	18
Mortgage or loan less than $20,000	17
Change in sleeping habits	16
Change in number of family get-togethers	15
Change in eating habits	15
Vacation	13
Christmas	12
Minor violations of the law	11

Note: From "The Social Readjustment Rating Scale," by T. H. Holmes and R. H. Rahe, 1967, *Journal of Psychosomatic Research, 11,* 213–218. Copyright 1967 by Pergamon Press Ltd., Oxford, England. Reprinted with permission of the publisher.

the sources of stress originally proposed by Holmes and Rahe and reported by Petrich and Holmes in 1977.

Petrich and Holmes found that the outcome of increased accumulation of stress points resulted in negative physiological consequences in the form of illness. This was confirmed in extensive studies with a considerable variety of subjects in many cross-cultural settings (Holmes, Amundson, & Hart, 1986).

Table 8.1 shows these are fairly objective descriptions of life events. Dohrenwend, Dohrenwend, Dodson, and Shrout (1984) emphasized that focusing on environmental aspects of stress helped keep the concept independent of such psychological response variables as personal perceptions or personal appraisals. Some have strongly objected to this approach, suggesting that psychological response variables and personal appraisals are necessary to measure and understand stress (Lazarus, DeLongis, Folkman, & Gruen, 1985). Cohen, Smith, and Tyrrell (1993) conducted an interesting exploration of this conceptual conflict. They selected 394 healthy subjects who were intentionally exposed to a common cold virus and then quarantined. The subjects were monitored carefully for the development of a biologically verified clinical illness. These subjects were given three stress scales: the Stressful Event Scale after Holmes and Rahe, a scale of perception of stress, and a negative affect scale. The results indicated that those with higher levels of stress on the stressful life events scale had a significantly greater biological illness response than those who perceived themselves as stressed, or experienced negative affect.

The cutoff points in the Holmes and Rahe research (Holmes et al., 1986) suggest that subjects who collect 300 or more stressful life event points in the course of a year have an 80% or greater chance of a stress-related illness in the immediate future following the year of these events. With a score of 150 to 299 stressful life events units, the individual will have a 50% chance of a stress-related illness. Those who collect less than 150 stressful life event units have 30% or less chance of developing a stress-related illness in the months following the achievement of this level.

In 1992, the American Psychological Association and the National Institute of Occupational Safety and Health jointly sponsored a conference entitled "Stress in the 1990s." The participants agreed that stress has become a critical issue in the workplace during the past 10 years. Over 300 participants in the conference also agreed that stress is best defined as a psychological reaction to an excessive stimulation in comparison with an individual's resources for coping. Both internal and external stress factors were considered (Denton, 1993).

THE EFFECTS OF STRESS

Workers all over the world report that they suffer stress on the job. In the United States, more than 45% of all salaried workers say that they experience excessive stress as a direct result of the conditions of their employment (DeAngelis, 1993).

Work Quality

Anecdotal reports of many studies indicate that workers "feel" that stress decreases the quality of their work. They report that they work less rapidly, less correctly, and less efficiently. Work quality and quantity have not been studied extensively in well-designed research studies except for the effects of shift work, which will be addressed later in this chapter.

Somatization

The greatest amount of work on the effects on stress has been done in this area. Familiar to most clinicians is the concept of the *Type A personality*. Type A persons are characterized by extremes of competitive striving, time urgency, and aggressiveness. This personality appears to be at risk for cardiac effects of stress (Glass, 1977). Studying a variety of young healthy male service personnel in the United States and in Norway, Glass found that there was a significant correlation between the number of Life Change Units and illness, particularly cardiac difficulties.

In a massive study conducted at the Karolinska Institute in Sweden, using the entire adult population of Sweden, occupationally related stress was found to be closely related to muscular, cardiovascular, sexual, and gastrointestinal problems (DeAngelis, 1993).

Unresolved antagonism and "unfair" conflict on the job tend to create significant increases in blood pressure (Goleman, 1992).

In comparing day-working and shift-working police officers, with the latter reporting more stress than the former, the prevalence rates of complaints for musculoskeletal symptoms, disturbances of appetite, indigestion, respiratory infections, and autonomic nervous system symptoms was significantly higher for the stressed groups (Ottmann, Karvonen, Schmidt, Knauth, & Rutenfranz, 1989).

Other Effects of Stress

Although the primary effects of stress appear to be a lessening of the capacity to fight off a wide range of diseases, other effects are reported. Workers who are stressed seem to have a much higher probability of significant marital problems (Madamba, 1986), alcohol use (Pendergrass & Ostrov, 1986), and discontrol in the form of unrestrained outbursts or suicidal behavior (Danto, 1978). The effects of stress in the workplace have been well studied and reported (Abram, 1970; Cobb & Kasl, 1977; Cooper & Payne, 1978; Lazarus, 1976; Margiolis, Kroes, & Quinn, 1974; Rose & Levine, 1979; Simon, 1990).

STRESS AND LAW ENFORCEMENT

No other area of concern for police managers and academics with an interest in law enforcement has received as much attention as the nature of stress in the law enforcement job (Bratz, 1989; Reese & Goldstein, 1986; Reiser, 1982a).

Sources of Stress in Police Work

Stress in police work is a broad and general concept. Some law enforcement researchers suggest that stress sources can be divided into *external stressors* (court system, court scheduling, the media, community attitudes, local government decisions, poor social referral sources, and recidivism) and *internal stressors* (poor training, poor supervision, poor career development opportunities, inadequate reward, offensive department policies, excessive paperwork, poor judgment, lack of job security, and politics). This generalized view of sources of stress underlines the difficult position in which most police officers find themselves—great expectations from the community, rigid demands from management, relatively little support, and limited appreciation (Bratz, 1989; Violanti, 1988).

Sewell (1983) proposed a 144-item scale of critical life events, developed after the method of Holmes and Rahe. Sewell's stress units ranged in value from 13 (completion of a routine report) to 88 (violent death of a partner in line of duty). Low-ranking items included such events as working a traffic accident (23 stress units), working on a holiday (26), overtime duty (29), and an interrogation session with a suspect (33). Mid-level stressors included press criticism of department practices (47), written reprimand by a supervisor (50), wrecking a departmental vehicle (55), oral promotional review (57), improperly conducted corruption investigation by another officer (60), and riot control situation (61). Highest levels of stress were reported for such incidents as pursuit of an armed suspect (71), suspension (72), murder committed by a police officer (78), violent death of another officer in the line of duty (79), taking a life in the line of duty (84), and dismissal (85).

A little known yet highly significant potential source of stress lies in the unfortunate and embarrassing fact that a large number of officers who are shot in the line of duty are shot by fellow officers or by their own guns. Studying the Chicago Police Department and the New York Police Department over a 10-year period, Geller (1993) found that approximately 43 percent of officers who were shot fatally or nonfatally were struck by bullets fired by themselves or other officers.

Geller also points out that black officers face a double jeopardy. They (and black men regardless of occupation or station in life) find themselves vastly more likely than whites to be unfairly mistaken for criminals because they were in the wrong place at the wrong time and were of the wrong skin color. In addition, he notes that undercover police officers are 10 times more likely than their uniformed colleagues to shoot someone and/or be shot. Traumas, and the anticipation of traumas, together with the consequent stress, follow police officers throughout their career.

Shift Work

Rotating shift work is common and necessary in police work. Occupational stress studies show that shift changes can affect eating patterns, sleep patterns, lifestyle, domestic patterns, and psychological and physical health (Hurrell, 1986). Tepas (1990) reviewed the literature on shift work, its stress effects, and workers' behavior. He concluded that the eating and drinking behavior of night-shift workers differed significantly from that of day-shift workers. Night-shift workers ate fewer meals, had poorer appetites, were less satisfied with their eating habits than day workers, and ate at different times of the day. It was impossible to determine whether there was any difference in the effectiveness of special diets or dietary recommendations.

Akerstedt (1988) summarized the physiology of shift work and its relationship to circadian rhythmicity and sleep–wake phenomena. Individuals on a rotating three-shift (or similar) system work the night shift at the lowest phase of the circadian rhythm. On retiring to bed in the morning, they fall asleep rapidly but are prematurely awakened by their circadian rhythm and exhibit severe sleepiness, and reduced performance capacity. In comparison with the morning shift, the circadian psychophysiology of night-shift workers makes it difficult for them to sleep deeply as early as needed during the day. When it is time to get up, they have difficulties awakening because of the sleep loss and circadian rhythm, which at that point is at its lowest. This causes their work shift to be characterized by sleepiness and reduced performance. Apparently, as workers become older, their work is characterized by higher-than-average adjustment problems.

Ottman et al. (1989) suggest that much of the research on shift work may be inconclusive because of faults in research design and subject selection.

Management Style and Job Environment

The organizational structure of law enforcement agencies is such that supervisors and managers tend to be somewhat insensitive to the stresses suffered by the line officer. Because most ranking officers themselves have "come up through the ranks," they have a tendency to assume that whatever they experienced, other law enforcement officers should be willing and able to tolerate.

Ayres (1990) studied management practices and organizational charac-teristics in a variety of law enforcement settings. He concluded that 11 management practices created stress among patrol officers:

1. Autocratic, quasi-militaristic models of management.
2. Hierarchical structure.
3. Poor supervision.
4. Lack of employee input into policy and decision making.
5. Excessive paperwork.
6. Lack of administrative support.
7. Role conflict and ambiguity.
8. Inadequate pay and resources.
9. Adverse working schedules.
10. Boredom.
11. Unfair discipline, performance evaluation, and promotion practices.

Retirement

Although almost all law enforcement officers, from the beginning until nearly the end of their career, speak in positive ways about the pension and the benefits of retirement, stress appears to build up exponentially as they approach this point. In studying this phenomenon, Violanti (1990) found that police officers see themselves as members of a large club in which they have made their mark and are thoroughly accepted. They feel respected, they get along with their colleagues in most cases, and they can be dependent on their partners and be depended on. At retirement, the officer suddenly loses such interactions and social support. The rule is "when you're gone, you're gone." Many officers try to hang on by staying in social contact with their former partners. Because the rule in police work is 100% commitment to one's partners, it is difficult if not impossible for a working police officer to maintain any kind of serious contact with a former partner who has retired. In a real sense, this would take away sup-port from the current colleagues.

Other Sources of Stress

As was pointed out in Chapters Two and Three, the law enforcement voca-tion is unique in many respects. Law enforcement officers are always under public scrutiny, and they rarely have the opportunity to openly express their feelings—to the press, to the general public, to neighbors, or to casual acquaintances. This seems to result in a career-long propensity to internal-ize some of their strongest emotions. Consequently, police officers tend to suffer the well-known psychological effects of excessive internalization.

EFFECTS OF STRESS ON LAW ENFORCEMENT OFFICERS

There is generally no disagreement that law enforcement work is stressful, and that officers tend to be stressed continually. Farkas (1986) studied a group of 82 law enforcement officers before they went on undercover assignment, during their assignment, and afterward. He reported a wide range of effects of the stress these officers suffered on regular patrol duty as well as during their undercover assignments. He also provided valuable data about stress that continued to disturb officer's functions following their undercover assignment. Table 8.2 presents some of the data from this study.

Undercover assignment is a stressful role for police officers. Even before such assignment, there is a high incidence of loneliness/isolation, marital problems, nervous tension and anxiety, and oversuspiciousness. These symptoms increase significantly during the assignment. Some

TABLE 8.2 Percentage of Officers Experiencing Stress-Induced Symptoms before, during, and after Undercover Assignment ($N = 82$)

Symptom	Before Undercover Assignment (%)	During Undercover Assignment (%)	After Undercover Assignment (%)
Not sleeping well	6.1	28.3	7.0
Loneliness/isolation	19.4	37.0	37.5
Excessive use of alcohol	3.7	19.7	12.5
Drug abuse	0.0	1.2	1.4
Relationships/marital problems	11.3	27.6	14.2
Lack of energy	2.4	10.0	7.0
Sadness	7.3	13.3	5.4
Low self-esteem	7.2	13.5	4.1
Crying spells	0.0	2.4	2.7
Nervous tension or anxiety	13.3	39.0	9.6
Guilt	7.2	11.0	6.9
Feeling of emptiness	3.7	12.3	7.0
Self-doubt	6.1	18.5	1.4
Confusion	7.3	19.7	4.3
Experiencing self as "unreal"	7.7	21.2	2.8
Disorientation	2.5	13.7	1.4
Oversuspiciousness	15.2	44.0	19.5
Suicidal thoughts	0.0	0.0	0.0
Poor concentration	0.0	26.2	4.2
Poor memory	1.2	21.0	2.7
Hearing voices	1.2	0.0	0.0

Note: From "Stress in Undercover Policing," by G. Farkas, in J. Reese and H. Goldstein (Eds.), *Psychological Services for Law Enforcement*, 1986, Washington, DC: U.S. Government Printing Office, Superintendent of Documents.

disappear after the officer returns to regular duty, whereas some seem to continue (loneliness/isolation, excessive use of alcohol, oversuspiciousness). Data are not available as to how long these responses may last after the officer returns to regular duty, but there is no immediate return to previous levels of symptomology.

The most extensive research on the effects of stress on law enforcement officers has been done in the area of shift work. In a study based on the responses of over 2,600 shift-working and 1,300 day-working police officers, Ottmann et al. (1989) found that shift workers showed a significantly higher number of autonomic nervous system complaints, musculoskeletal disturbances, appetite and indigestion problems, and respiratory infections than did day workers. Some data in this study suggested that as the police officer becomes older, he or she is less affected by shift work. Shift workers' most frequently reported symptoms in this study were disturbances of sleep, flatulence, backache, headache, colds, pains in the limbs, heartburn, nervousness, inner restlessness, premature tiredness, stomachaches, hunger pains, lack of appetite, and outbreaks of sweating.

Peacock, Glub, Miller, and Klune (1983) compared police officers' responses to 8-hour shifts and 12-hour shifts in a rotating shift cycle. The 12-hour shift workers showed an improvement in blood pressure, sleep duration, sleep quality, and subjective measures of alertness over the responses to 8-hour shifts.

The likeliness of officers falling asleep on night shift is higher than those who are working during the daylight portion of their shift cycle (Akerstedt, 1988).

O'Neil (1986) found that police officers on shift work in comparison with day-working officers seemed to suffer from chronic mental fatigue with social, psychological, sleeping, and eating patterns that disrupted their physiology. His data suggested that night work rather than rotation of shifts appeared to be responsible for more nervous disorders among shift workers than among day workers. Symptoms included general weakness, insomnia, and overly aggressive behavior.

Not all police officers seem to be seriously affected by shift work. Lester (1986) in his study of municipal and state police officers found that almost half enjoyed shift work despite the disruption of family and social life.

There are no really good data about the effects of stress on police officers' marital relationships. Anecdotally, police officers are said to be more likely to be divorced than those of their age cohorts in the general population. No specific studies support this concept. Madamba (1986) found that police officers with marital problems report them in the same way as those who have marital problems in the general population. These problems seem to be a combination of stress and cultural beliefs, as well as marital role relationships that yield satisfactions or dissatisfactions. Madamba found that the officer's cultural background appears to be significant in determining the way he or she handles marital conflicts.

There is a popular impression that police officers are heavy users of alcohol. The use of alcohol and drugs is attributable to stress. Well-documented information is sparse and conflicting. There is some evidence that police do not differ in incidence of alcohol abuse from the general population. One report suggests that about 2% of police employees report receiving a diagnosis of "alcoholism" as a health problem. Alcoholism is defined as the consumption of 5 or more ounces of ethanol a day. This would be about 9 or more shots of whiskey or about 15 twelve ounce beers. Male officers tend to consume more alcohol than female officers (Pendergrass & Ostrov, 1986).

As with alcohol abuse, suicide and other self-destructive behaviors are popularly believed to exist among police officers in percentages far in excess of their cohorts in the general population. Allen (1986) reports that various studies show various degrees of support or rejection of this concept. He points out that the conceptual complexity involved in determining causal relationships between stress and suicide makes it almost impossible to partial out causes. He found no single profile that encompasses the diversity of suicidal behavior among police officers. He did find that suicidal officers tended to have high dependency needs and great difficulty in expressing such needs. Allen further suggested that the clues to intended suicide included the making of a will and giving away of cherished personal items, marked increase in indirect self-destructive behavior, unexpected changes in behavior, marked levels of depression and anxiety, sudden withdrawal from emotional ties, increased isolation, increased alcohol consumption, increasing erratic behavior, recent or impending divorce or separation, and retirement. Terry (1981) believes that police suicide is a much greater social problem than previously imagined and requires focused research efforts in the future.

The concept of *burnout* has come to represent organizational perception of long-term effects of stress. Blau (1988) has pointed out that long before burnout occurs, the individual suffers *overload*. Overload represents all the factors previously discussed as stressful events that accumulate and make themselves manifest through symptoms. Symptoms of overload include sleeping difficulties, irritability, difficulty in "getting started" at work, decreasing recreation, increasing family difficulties, inattention, and inefficiency. If burnout follows overload, the individual is likely to find it difficult, or even impossible, to return to work.

Golembiwski and Kim (1990) studied burnout in police work and suggested that actual burnout is characterized by depersonalization, reversed personal accomplishment, and emotional exhaustion.

Childers (1991) studied an interesting form of burnout that he labeled *plateauing*. He described this as a milder form of burnout that begins when an officer is promoted after a number of years and the challenges of working the street are gone. Paperwork and citizens' complaints become overwhelming, and the job is simply dull. There is a loss of a sense of challenge, and frustration is high. The condition that results is not psychologically or physiologically as intense as burnout and probably represents a special form of overload.

REDUCING SOURCES OF STRESS IN LAW ENFORCEMENT

Because shift work has been the most extensively studied source of stress for police officers, there have been a number of specific recommendations for reducing the officer's working hours as a source of stress. Dunham and his group discovered that the degree of stress versus the degree of satisfaction that accrued from different work schedules depended on the individual officer's attitude, particularly in respect to whether the organization was operating effectively and responsively (Dunham, Pierce, & Castaneda, 1987).

Hurrell (1986) reviewed the research on various police shift patterns and suggested that rotating shift work *clockwise* (day, evening, night) facilitates physiological adjustment more effectively than counterclockwise (night, evening, day). Orth-Gomer (1981) found that quality of sleep improved with the clockwise rotation of shifts. In addition, some favorable effects of this pattern over a counterclockwise pattern included normalization of lipids, glucose, uric acid, and blood pressure. Systolic blood pressure as well as catecholamine excretion rates were decreased during the clockwise rotation as compared with the counterclockwise shift.

Peacock et al. (1983) studied police officers' responses to 8- and 12-hour shift schedules. They found that when city police forces were changed from an 8-hour, 12-day shift cycle to a 12-hour, 8-day system, cardiorespiratory fitness, blood pressure, sleep duration, sleep quality, and subjective level of alertness measures showed improvement.

Not all studies support such changes. DeCarufel and Schann (1990) reviewed studies on the impact of compressed work weeks on police job involvement. They found that some studies indicated moving to 10-hour shifts produced unbalanced beats (coverage) and shifts of officers who were unlikely to meet the increase in calls for service and in crimes without some sacrifice in response time.

The Potential for Administrative Changes to Reduce Sources of Stress

In most industrial organizations, management style has a considerable effect on the happiness, longevity, and productivity of workers. The law enforcement community gives lip service to this need, but the essential rigidity of the system makes it difficult to introduce concepts of workers' involvement to police managers. It is likely that the more employees participate in decision making and planning, the lower will be the stress levels (DeAngelis, 1993). In these studies, such worker-participation in planning even resulted in a significant drop in cholesterol levels of employees.

Denton (1993) found that management could reduce stress by increasing decision latitude to include line officers, decreasing work load, stabilizing work schedules, avoiding shift work whenever possible, offering flex time and job sharing, and decreasing ambiguity at all levels of the organization. Management can also decrease stress by career development promotion, specific guidelines about career security, and ensuring whenever possible that the job avoids narrow, fragmented tasks that have little intrinsic meaning. Denton further recommended that participation and control by workers should be promoted to decrease the production of stress within the department. In an extensive review of ways in which management could prevent stress among line officers, Ayres (1990) proposed seven management strategies to create a healthier workplace:

1. Examining the nature of the workplace to determine interferences with function.
2. Believing in the mission of making life better for the line officer.
3. Living the organizational values and presenting appropriate models.
4. Encouraging upward communication.
5. Decreasing autonomy among superior officers.
6. Ensuring fairness.
7. Caring about the line officer.

The Ayres study furthermore recommended the following specific techniques for ensuring upward communication:

1. Create advisory groups from a representative sample of employees.
2. Organize brainstorming sessions involving line officers.
3. Career planning for each employee should include self-assessment, goal establishment, time inventories, action plans for personal life, and so forth.
4. Provide increased opportunities for employees' suggestions, opinions, and concerns to reach management anonymously and expeditiously. The chief or the sheriff should be a direct recipient of such messages.
5. Command and supervisory staff meetings should be attended by the chief, the sheriff, or the deputy chief and the undersheriff.
6. A department newspaper increases communication.
7. At staff meetings, various individuals should be rotated in playing "devil's advocate" on important issues.

8. Electronic mail should be instituted for rapid transmission of information throughout the chain of command.

9. Each department should have a peer-elected council of employees representing every division of the organization. Members should be rotated quarterly.

10. There should be executive–employee breakfasts, lunches, and coffees.

11. The higher ranking executives should make regular and unannounced visits to the field.

12. Executives should visit union meetings.

13. Executives should spend part of their time working on line jobs.

14. Every employee who leaves the organization should have an exit interview. The results should be made available to management on a regular basis.

15. There should be clear-cut, available grievance procedures.

16. Each component of every department should have an inspection process conducted annually with a written report.

17. Each department should have a labor management committee.

18. Top management should develop open-door availability.

19. Teams of employees should work in quality circles where they share common duties. They should meet voluntarily on company time to discuss pertinent issues.

20. During their probationary period, recruits should have a personal interview with a ranking executive concerning their perceptions, opinions, and ambitions as police officers.

21. There should be regularly scheduled retreats.

22. Morale surveys should be conducted regularly.

These recommendations are ambitious and might meet with some resistance in an already-functioning police organization.

INOCULATION TRAINING

Although administrative changes have the greatest potential to reduce stress (DeAngelis, 1993), law enforcement departments can institute certain training programs and procedures that have proven to be successful in teaching police officers to prevent and lessen stress circumstances in the policing job.

The simplest procedure to identify and make officers aware of sources of stress is to administer the Schedule of Recent Experiences developed by Holmes and Rahe. After the officers take this inventory and score it for themselves, they can have a discussion period and then be given a recommended series of preventive measures (Holmes et al., 1986). These suggestions include:

1. Each officer should become familiar with the life events and the amount of change they require.
2. The Schedule of Recent Experiences should be shared with the family so that they can see the events that build up stress points.
3. The officers should be told that with practice they can recognize when a life event happens.
4. They should be instructed that thinking about the meaning of the event for their own personal lives leads to feelings, and these feelings should be experienced and identified.
5. They should be helped to think about the different ways they can adjust to these events.
6. They should be encouraged to slow down, take their time arriving at decisions, anticipate life changes, and plan for them.
7. The officers should be encouraged to pace themselves in spite of the demands and pressures of the job.
8. They should be trained that the end of a work period is not a time for "letting down" but simply a "stopping point."

Some psychologists have found that simply providing this information to police officers is insufficient. A system worked out in one department which has had significant results has been a 4-hour training program entitled "Stress and Stress-Reduction Training." This begins with the presentation of three "symptom scales." Each of these is filled out by the officers after they have been told that this is a way of understanding others through understanding themselves. Figure 8.1 presents the "Stress Symptom Scale." Figure 8.2 presents an "Alcohol Abuse Potential Scale." Figure 8.3 shows a "Spouse Abuse Potential Scale."

Appendix J presents an outline for a 4-hour stress inoculation training program.

The 4-hour program can be given as a 4-hour workshop. It can be split into *two 2-hour* workshops. Sometimes law enforcement continuing education is offered for this. It can even be split into 16 15-minute sessions given at roll call for each shift.

At the end of the workshop, the officers are given a Stress Prevention Scale to help them to plan to participate actively in inoculating themselves against the stresses of the job (see Figure 8.4).

Although attention to the individual officer's needs is important, it should never be forgotten that the most important reductions in stress can take place through operational changes in the organization that improve communication and awareness of the stressful effects of inadequate management procedures.

Each of the following signs or symptoms may reflect the effects of stress. Check each one that applies to you on a fairly regular basis. This exercise will sensitize you to what to look for when evaluating an individual who may be a victim of excessive stress.

_____ 1. Very hard to get up to go to work.

_____ 2. More and more critical of small things lately.

_____ 3. Periods of depression deeper or longer than usual.

_____ 4. Recent unplanned loss or gain in weight.

_____ 5. Withdrawal from usual social contacts.

_____ 6. More nervousness than usual, lasting longer than usual.

_____ 7. Trembling.

_____ 8. Dizziness.

_____ 9. Pounding heart.

_____ 10. Inability to slow down or relax.

_____ 11. Troubled breathing.

_____ 12. More and more worried "up-tight" feelings.

None of these is a certain indicator of excessive stress. They are all signs that something is not as it should be physically or mentally and should be explored further.

FIGURE 8.1   Stress Symptom Scale for Police Officers

Each of the following conditions or behaviors has been found to be associated with alcohol abuse or problem drinking. Check the ones that apply to you. This exercise will sensitize you to what to look for when evaluating a person for alcohol abuse potential.

_____ 1. Drinking alone regularly.

_____ 2. Needing a drink to get over a hangover.

_____ 3. Needing a drink at a certain time each day.

_____ 4. Finding it harder and harder to get along with others.

_____ 5. Memory loss while or after drinking.

_____ 6. Driving skill deteriorating.

_____ 7. Drinking to relieve stress, fear, shyness, insecurity.

_____ 8. More and more family and friends worrying about drinking habits.

_____ 9. Becoming moody, jealous, or irritable after drinking.

_____ 10. "Binges" of heavy drinking.

_____ 11. Heavy weekend drinking.

_____ 12. Able to drink more and more with less and less effect.

None of these represents a certain indicator of alcohol abuse or problem drinking. They are all signs that problems may be developing, or already exist.

FIGURE 8.2   Checklist of Alcohol Abuse Potential for Police Officers

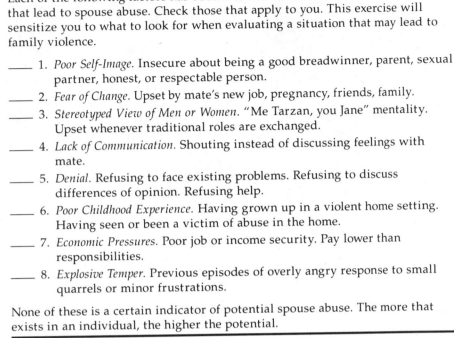

Each of the following factors has been found to contribute to the circumstances that lead to spouse abuse. Check those that apply to you. This exercise will sensitize you to what to look for when evaluating a situation that may lead to family violence.

____ 1. *Poor Self-Image.* Insecure about being a good breadwinner, parent, sexual partner, honest, or respectable person.

____ 2. *Fear of Change.* Upset by mate's new job, pregnancy, friends, family.

____ 3. *Stereotyped View of Men or Women.* "Me Tarzan, you Jane" mentality. Upset whenever traditional roles are exchanged.

____ 4. *Lack of Communication.* Shouting instead of discussing feelings with mate.

____ 5. *Denial.* Refusing to face existing problems. Refusing to discuss differences of opinion. Refusing help.

____ 6. *Poor Childhood Experience.* Having grown up in a violent home setting. Having seen or been a victim of abuse in the home.

____ 7. *Economic Pressures.* Poor job or income security. Pay lower than responsibilities.

____ 8. *Explosive Temper.* Previous episodes of overly angry response to small quarrels or minor frustrations.

None of these is a certain indicator of potential spouse abuse. The more that exists in an individual, the higher the potential.

FIGURE 8.3   Spouse Abuse Potential Checklist for Police Officers

TREATING STRESS

Although some of the greatest benefits in reducing stress can come from the reorganization of tasks and work organization using worker participation, this is not always possible. There are some programs, however, that can put into the hands of individual police officers certain special skills and knowledge to prevent or to lessen the effects of job-related stress.

Brief Counseling

DeAngelis (1993) reports a fairly extensive pilot study in England where a group of 250 workers received stress counseling and a matched control group of 100 workers were not counseled. Four or five counseling sessions were given, and referral was made to a mental health professional if more treatment was needed. The groups were evaluated 6 months before and 6 months after the experiment. The group that received stress counseling showed less depression, less anxiety, and less somatic concerns. There was also a 66% decline in sickness absence. It was found that the program was very cost-effective. Every 175 people counseled in

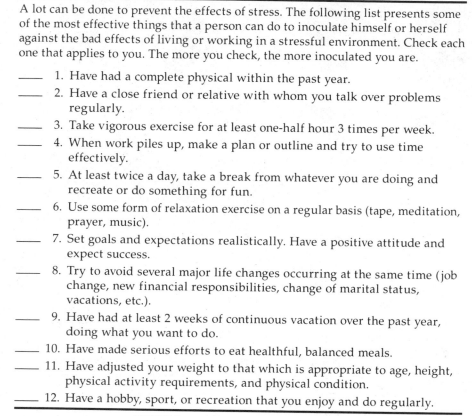

A lot can be done to prevent the effects of stress. The following list presents some of the most effective things that a person can do to inoculate himself or herself against the bad effects of living or working in a stressful environment. Check each one that applies to you. The more you check, the more inoculated you are.

_____ 1. Have had a complete physical within the past year.

_____ 2. Have a close friend or relative with whom you talk over problems regularly.

_____ 3. Take vigorous exercise for at least one-half hour 3 times per week.

_____ 4. When work piles up, make a plan or outline and try to use time effectively.

_____ 5. At least twice a day, take a break from whatever you are doing and recreate or do something for fun.

_____ 6. Use some form of relaxation exercise on a regular basis (tape, meditation, prayer, music).

_____ 7. Set goals and expectations realistically. Have a positive attitude and expect success.

_____ 8. Try to avoid several major life changes occurring at the same time (job change, new financial responsibilities, change of marital status, vacations, etc.).

_____ 9. Have had at least 2 weeks of continuous vacation over the past year, doing what you want to do.

_____ 10. Have made serious efforts to eat healthful, balanced meals.

_____ 11. Have adjusted your weight to that which is appropriate to age, height, physical activity requirements, and physical condition.

_____ 12. Have a hobby, sport, or recreation that you enjoy and do regularly.

FIGURE 8.4   Stress Prevention Scale

this minimal way represented a savings of about $200,000 in sickness absence. The most effective use for the individually oriented counseling approach seemed to be with marital difficulties and other personal problems. About 40% of the stress difficulties that were addressed in counseling had to do with work-related problems.

The police psychologist, either as a staff member or as a consultant, is the likeliest individual to provide such brief counseling for officers. In the event that the topic discussed concerns supervision or administrative stressors, issues of privilege and confidentiality become paramount. In some cases, the consulting police psychologist is a more appropriate source of service than the in-house psychologist.

A retirement counseling, career guidance program for officers about to retire may be advantageous for their future, as well as their feeling of goodwill for the department. Such a program would provide brief counseling on topics such as retirement benefits, insurance, job-seeking techniques, the psychology of retirement, financial management, and maintaining social contacts (Violanti, 1990).

Relaxation Training

Biofeedback procedures have proven effective in reducing stress in a wide variety of settings. Efforts to establish biofeedback opportunities for police officers have generally resulted in failure because of the limited time available for anything other than the officer's duties. To be helpful, relaxation exercises should be used on a regular basis.

A group of psychologists have developed a 12½-minute stress reduction tape that was standardized with a large number of police officers (Psychological Seminars, 1992). This tape, which follows traditional relaxation procedures, is used with a colorimeter that allows the officer to test his or her stress level before and after a session.

This tape is best given to officers after they complete the 4-hour stress identification and inoculation course. It can be provided on an individual basis following counseling for officers who request some relief from stress that they are experiencing.

Health and Wellness

Much success can be expected in reducing stress in officers who are encouraged and trained to include proper diet, sleep, exercise, and recreation in their lives.

For shift workers, certain recommendations that have proven to be helpful:

1. The officer should sleep immediately after a night shift rather than before it.
2. The officer should eat three regular meals a day.
3. Caffeine should be avoided within five hours before sleep.
4. Recreational and socialization links should be forged with other shift-working families.
5. During sleep time, there should be no telephones, doorbells, or domestic appliances that can go off and awaken the sleeper.
6. The bedroom should be made as quiet and as dark as possible using heavy curtains and thick carpets.
7. Alcohol should not be used as a sedative because subsequent sleep would be light and disrupted.

In dealing with shift work, the real issue is the circadian rhythms and the jet-lag type of symptoms that result when these rhythms are disrupted.

During shift work it is vital that the worker do everything possible, with the cooperation of his or her family, to continue social and domestic factors—eating, sleeping, and recreation—in spite of the shift.

Shift workers as well as officers on regular shift should be encouraged to maintain a schedule of regular exercise. In general, police officers have a positive attitude toward physical conditioning. Encouraging officers to spend between 5 and 10 minutes stretching and doing exercises immediately upon awakening can be a useful treatment for the effects of stress. Officers should be cautioned to "warm up" through stretching exercises, particularly as they age, to avoid strains that will turn the advantage into disadvantage. Such exercises as trunk range of motion (shrugging of shoulders), side bending, toe touching, trunk rotation, and shoulder extension are good starting points. Lower back flexibility exercises that include foot stretches and bends, leg lifts, and hip extensions are well known and useful.

It is well worthwhile to develop a set of recommended food habits for distribution to all officers. Such recommendations are readily available from a variety of sources and generally focus on high-protein, low-carbohydrate, low-fat diets. This is difficult for the circumstances faced by most patrol officers who "eat on the run." Anything that can be done to encourage officers to attempt to follow a proper diet regime will help reduce stress.

Recreation is an important area of stress reduction that police officers frequently ignore. Too often, they would much prefer to sit in an easy chair, drink beer, and watch television. This is understandable considering the conditions of their everyday work. Regular recreation is in an officer's best interest and should be encouraged. The department itself can cooperate by creating recreational facilities and group interactions such as softball teams, bowling leagues, recreational running, and golf tournaments.

Support

Emotional support or the lowering of the perception of work stress and strain both within the police organization and in the officers' outside life, have significant effects in reducing stress (Graf, 1986; Simons & Barone, 1991).

When officers either plateau or prepare for retirement, stress can be reduced where departments take an interest in reeducating the officer, counseling the officer for retirement, allowing lateral transfers, and above all, acknowledging work well done (Childers, 1991).

Referral

Stress counseling is brief, intensive intervention. Not all situations that arise with police officers can be handled this way. More intense and long-term professional assistance may be necessary. For drug and alcohol treatment and suicidal behavior, family and cohort support may be extremely helpful (Allen, 1986), but in severe cases, referral to a mental health professional for more intensive treatment may be necessary. When this happens, particularly when inpatient hospitalization is required, the department needs to respond in a supportive manner. Supervisory staff can help by not stigmatizing the suicidal police officer, or the officer with a drinking or drug problem. When the officer returns to duty, the behavioral science staff member or consultant should be available to assist with reentry and readjustment. To enlist the cooperation and participation of police management, the psychologist must stress the significant monetary savings that result from instituting such support programs. This is an ongoing battle against the traditional attitude of police officers that emotional matters are best hidden.

CHAPTER NINE

Individual and Family Counseling

The services offered to a police department by a psychologist, either as a staff member or as a consultant, depend on a number of factors. The first issue is the psychologist's background, training, and expertise. The narrowly focused clinical psychologist may be able to offer only limited clinical services. The generalist who can work with a wide range of human problems will find many instances where a variety of skills are required for individual and family counseling.

The second factor, and perhaps the most important one, is the issue of trust and the degree to which the psychologist is accepted by police department personnel. Usually, the department's first contact with a psychologist will be the result of a decision to institute selection testing or to require fitness-for-duty evaluations. Assuming the psychologist can provide useful service during the initial contacts and establishes personal contact with both police managers and line officers, requests for a variety of services are likely to follow.

A third and more subtle aspect of the match between what psychologists can do and what a police department may require is the general attitude (spoken or unspoken) about psychology, psychologists, and mental health held by senior members of the department. Strongly positive or strongly negative attitudes will filter down throughout the department and result in an increased seeking of services, or a consistent avoidance of mental health facilities. From the time a psychologist first makes professional contact with a police department, whether a variety of services are sought and accepted, depends on these interpersonal factors. The psychologist can do much to facilitate the growth of trust and acceptance. This has been discussed previously and is always a significant issue. Regular contact and positive interaction between the psychologist and police officers at all levels is essential for a developing and continuing relationship between a behavioral science unit, and the department.

204

No matter how much bridge building a psychologist may do to establish goodwill and acceptance within a police department, individual and family counseling will not succeed without a clear-cut policy of confidentiality and privilege. Individual police officers and their families who consult with the psychologist must be confident that such consultation will not cause embarrassment, confrontation, or loss of any kind of privilege. Without spelling out and maintaining confidentiality restraints, the psychologist is likely to receive very few requests for service.

COMMON REFERRAL PROBLEMS

Evaluation and intervention involving selection and fitness for duty are initiated by the law enforcement organization of which the officer is a member. In those cases, confidentiality and privilege are not a problem because the organization is the client.

The psychologist who gains credibility and goodwill in the organization will be approached to deal with more personal, individual problems. Most of these referrals will require relatively short-term contact. Of great importance in considering common referral problems is that, in many instances, the presenting problem is very different from the underlying or more significant source of distress. The individual's target complaints during the early interviews where help is sought may be quite unlike the kinds of problems that are brought up during therapeutic intervention (Sorenson, Gorsuch, & Mintz, 1985).

White (1987) reported the results of a 1986 survey of 366 municipal, county, and state police agencies in the United States that employed 200 or more people. These agencies were mailed survey questionnaires. An overall response rate of 77.9% was received. The results of the survey indicated that 65.1% of the agencies provided a mental health program for police personnel. Many of those agencies with no programs at that time (1986) reported that they were planning to institute such programs.

In-house counseling was provided in 57.9% of the responding agencies, whereas 82% of the agencies indicated that they had outside agency counseling. Just under 50% of the agencies had a combination of in-house counseling and outside referral options.

Hospital in-patient programs and drug/alcohol rehabilitation centers were where referrals were most frequently made. Over 70% of the respondents reported that their mental health services were available not only to sworn and nonsworn employees but also to their family members. Almost 80% of the organizations indicated that the mental health services were available on a round-the-clock basis.

Agencies that had mental health services available rated alcoholism, marital/family problems, and mental health problems as being more serious in their agencies than raters in agencies that did not have mental health services. Apparently, those agencies without services were simply unaware of the problems that existed. Following these three major problems, absenteeism, drug abuse, tardiness, low productivity, and low-quality performance were rated as important mental health problems.

This study also found that the first reported in-house counseling program was implemented in 1943 by the Portland, Oregon, Police Department. Outside agency counseling was first established in 1950 in the Metro Police Department of Washington, DC.

Group counseling programs, except for post-shooting trauma, have begun to make their appearance only recently. Such group programs include divorce adjustment, adolescent counseling, and police officer spouse adjustment groups. The least utilized service was found to be group counseling of adolescents. This is consistent with the difficulty in establishing such groups in general practice (Blau, 1991a).

All four of the treatment resources that were evaluated (in-house counseling, private consultants, hospital inpatient programs, and drug/alcohol rehabilitation centers) received high ratings of satisfaction. Of the respondents, 98.3% rated their mental health services as cost-effective. The most frequent reason given for not instituting mental health services in an agency was "financial."

In those agencies with mental health services, almost 22% had staff mental health workers who held supervisory ranks as sworn officers. Something over 32% of the total staff members of mental health components in law enforcement agencies were sworn officers. The results indicate that the larger the agency, the more likely a mental health program will exist. The title of such programs in over 50% of the cases was "employee assistance program."

The need for mental health services would appear to be highest among those law enforcement officers who have been undercover agents. The need for such services apparently occurs both while the agent is operational and during the postoperational career. Girodo (1991a) found that symptom clusters for operational agents matched very closely symptom clusters of psychiatric outpatients as measured by the Health Opinion Survey and the SCL-90, both self-report measures. Nonundercover officers were significantly below undercover agents in all symptom areas. Postoperational undercover agents, returned to regular police duties, fell between the two groups, suggesting that some aftereffects of undercover work affect mental health status.

There is little disagreement that police officers have mental health problems and symptom clusters similar to those in the adult population, although frequency is a matter still at issue. There are no indications that the existence of traditional mental health difficulties is any greater in a police population than in a general population. In point of fact, such symptoms and conditions may be less. That sort of epidemiological research is yet to be done.

Family Problems

Anecdotal reports as well as research studies indicate that police work creates stress that affects the police officer's family (DeAngelis, 1991b). Over 75% of spouses of police officers have been found to report stress from their mate's jobs.

To the mates and children of police officers, regardless of the officer's rank, age, sex, or duty assignment, police work seems unfair. The officer who works shift hours; witnesses human pain and distress; carries a gun; and is subject to the frustrations of a convoluted court system, excessive paperwork, negative public feedback, and unresponsive management is bound to carry the effects into the home. Police officers seem unique in the amount of daily frustration that they experience and the reactions from which the family cannot seem to escape (Bell, 1988).

The effects of police work on the children of police officers can be profound. Children and adolescent members of police families are caught between feelings of loyalty and pride in their mother's or father's work role, and anxieties about peer rejection because of popular, pejorative attitudes toward police. A common joke among children, going back almost 100 years, involves a playmate saying to another playmate in the presence of the child of a police officer they wish to tease, "Does your father work?" To which the second playmate responds, "Naw, he's a cop." Such attitudes are bound to result in serious conflict for the children of police officers.

The conflicts that result from the parents' roles intensify the usual and customary difficulties experienced by children and adolescents in trying to develop self-esteem and mechanisms for seeking success as they grow toward maturity. In many cases, this results in the children of police officers having the usual kinds of problems with school, social relationships, sibling rivalry, and conformity to a more intense degree than the children of parents in nonlaw enforcement occupations.

Marital interactional problems are common among those in police work. The mate must face all the stresses faced by the children. In addition, the question of the mate's loyalties to partners, or possible sexual involvement with other police officers, plagues many police mates. A simple illustration of this and the frequent insensitivity of the officer to the mate's needs is illustrated by the following dialogue between a sheriff's deputy and a police psychologist.

DEPUTY: I'm not sure if there is anything you can do, but I wanted to talk to somebody about this thing of my wife getting a divorce. I've done everything I can but she has filed and doesn't even want to talk to me. I feel really rotten about it because I don't understand it. She won't talk to me and I don't know what to do.

PSYCHOLOGIST: What's been happening at home?

DEPUTY: Nothing much—we've been married for nine years. It's her second marriage and my first. I thought we were getting along good. There are no sex problems other than when I'm tired and working on the graveyard shift. She takes care of the kids and the money and I don't interfere much there. I just don't understand.

PSYCHOLOGIST: Have there been any arguments?

DEPUTY: On and off, we fuss about things like all married couples do. I think, though, she resents my partner.

PSYCHOLOGIST: How's that?

DEPUTY: About a year ago, when I had just come off a surveillance, I was all "hyper" and jumpy. I couldn't sleep. About midnight, I got up and started to get my clothes on. I was worried about something we did on the surveillance that we didn't put into the report. I didn't know whether we should have put it in or shouldn't have put it in, but I was worried about it.

PSYCHOLOGIST: Did you tell your wife about this?

DEPUTY: She asked me, "What's wrong—where are you going?" I told her that I had a problem at work and couldn't get it off my mind and I had to talk about it. She said, "Tell me about it." I kinda looked at her—what does she know about this? I didn't want to hurt her feelings, so I said, "I can't talk to you about this, I gotta talk to my partner."

PSYCHOLOGIST: And so what happened?

DEPUTY: I went out and talked to my partner and came home about an hour later. She had locked the bedroom door and had a pillow and a blanket on the floor so I guess she wanted me to sleep on the couch.

PSYCHOLOGIST: Did you talk about this afterward?

DEPUTY: No, too much was going on and I just forgot about it.

This situation is not rare. It illustrates that communication difficulties are especially important sources of conflict between the police officer and her/his mate.

Drug and Alcohol Abuse

There are no accurate data as to the number of individuals in the United States who abuse alcohol or drugs—licit and illicit. Indeed, the definition of "abuse" is subject to a fair degree of controversy. Without question, a certain number of police officers among the over one-half million full-time sworn law enforcement officers in the United States use alcohol and drugs to the point where their life functions and their attention to duty are negatively affected. The dividing line between ordinary use of alcohol and drugs and the excessive use of these substances is often closely related to the degree of stress the individual suffers. Almost all those who begin to use alcohol and drugs excessively have histories of work stress. This is certainly true among law enforcement officers (Machell, 1989). Stress may be in the form of obvious pressures brought about by the intensity of policing

TABLE 9.1   Signs of Alcohol Abuse as Reported by Alcoholic Police Officers and Their Supervisors

Supervisors' Observations	Alcohol-Abusing Officers' Signs
Leaving post temporarily	Hangover on job
Drinking at lunchtime	Morning drinking before work
Red and bleary eyes	Absenteeism; day or half-day
Mood changes after lunch	Increased nervousness, jitteriness
Lower quality of work	Drinking at lunchtime
Absenteeism; day or half-day	Hand tremors
Unusual excuses for absences	Drinking during working hours
Loud talking	Late to work

Note: From "Signs of Developing Alcoholism" by Seafield 911, in *Supervisor's Training Manual*, 1991, Davie, FL, Seafield 911.

tasks and of unexpected occurrences, or it may be the result of overload and burnout (Childers, 1991). Freudenberger (1984) has suggested that the inappropriate use of drugs or alcohol in the workplace may be the individual's effort, conscious or otherwise, to "self-treat" stress symptoms. Officers in treatment for abuse of alcohol or drugs will often cite the stress and pressures they have faced in criminal and civil litigation as a source of their downfall (Scuro, 1985).

Signs of a developing drinking problem both from a supervisor's point of view, and from responses of alcoholic police officers (Seafield 911, 1991) are presented in Table 9.1.

As with other emotionally based problems faced by law enforcement officers, referral for evaluation or treatment of an alcohol or drug problem is likely to come long after the individual needs help. The propensity of police officers to deny and for supervisors to aid in the denial is well known, and constitutes a major barrier to providing adequate and timely mental health services for law enforcement officers.

Smoking Cessation

Since the Surgeon General's Report of 1964 first stirred the awareness of the American public about the dangers of tobacco smoking, there has been a steady decrease in the number of individuals who use tobacco regularly. In this last decade of the twentieth century, although over 40 million Americans have ceased smoking since 1964, approximately 28% of men and 31% of women still smoke (U.S. Department of Health and Human Services, 1988). This report further claims that cigarette smoking is responsible for more than one out of every six deaths in the United States and remains the single most important preventable cause of death as well as the major cause of stroke and the third leading cause of death in the United States. Although these data may be subject to some debate, more and more people, police officers among them, have begun to view tobacco smoking as an unquestionable health hazard and have become sufficiently concerned to seek professional help in breaking this habit.

Psychologists have been in the forefront in developing counseling programs for smoking cessation. These programs vary considerably, but more and more police departments are offering such services.

Gay and Lesbian Issues

A decade ago, for Behavioral Science Services in police departments to deal with alternate sexual lifestyles would have been unthinkable. In today's more enlightened society, gay and lesbian issues are now a matter of concern in the workplace in many settings. Contrary to expectation, gay and lesbian police officers have been found to be functionally competent, and to be accepted by a good many of their colleagues in police work (Blumenthal, 1993).

Hiatt and Hargrave (1994) compared psychological profiles (preemployment screening) and measures of job performance for gay, lesbian, and heterosexual samples. They found no difference in selection rates or ratings of job performance. Compared with heterosexual men, gay men scored higher on the MMPI scales 5 and F, whereas on the California Psychological Inventory, they scored higher on scale Sa. Gay men scored lower on the California Psychological scales Wb, Sc. No significant MMPI or CPI differences were found for lesbian and heterosexual women.

The New York City Police Department, with almost 30,000 sworn officers, has about 800 police officers who openly admit their alternate sexual lifestyle. Although there is, as elsewhere, still a good deal of homophobia in the police world, more and more police officers are finding that an alternate sexual lifestyle does not really interfere with performance of duty. Since 1980, policy in the New York Police Department has been to be intolerant of any kind of harassment because of sexual lifestyle.

In spite of the growing acceptance, gay and lesbian police officers—both those who have announced their alternate sexual lifestyle and those who are still "in the closet"—suffer a certain degree of rejection and as a result suffer additional job stress. More and more department psychologists are receiving requests for counseling services to deal with these issues.

EVALUATION

The amount and kind of evaluation conducted by the police psychologist will depend on the nature of the referral problem, the time that is available, and resources that can be committed to the process. The breadth and depth of evaluation services will also depend on the police psychologist's skills and background in the area of assessment. Evaluation techniques can range from a simple interview (listening to the problem and then deciding on a course of intervention), to an elaborate psychological evaluation that involves many hours of interviews, testing, and the collection of collateral information. Some behavioral science units serve only as a way station in the process of providing mental health services; they review the problem and then decide on the appropriate referral. In other agencies, the behavioral science unit acts as a community mental health center, specifically organized for police officers, other staff, and families.

The Troubled Police Officer

Police officers who ask for a consultation with the staff or consulting psychologist are seeking some kind of mental health service even though they may not know exactly what they want. A first interview should always precede any kind of decision as to further evaluation or immediate referral. In crisis situations, evaluation may consist simply of a clinical assessment during the first interview followed by appropriate crisis intervention techniques. Where the issue seems more complex, the psychologist may wish to have several interviews before deciding the extent of evaluation that is necessary.

Every interview should begin with the statement of the degree of privilege and confidentiality that the officer can expect according to the laws of the state, the ethics of the profession, and the agreements that have been reached with agency management. This notification of rights and limitations should also be in written form, signed by both the officer and the psychologist, and placed in the file. The officer should be reassured about where the files are kept, and who has access to them.

Once the preliminaries are out of the way, and the officer tells his or her "story," the psychologist must then decide on the next steps in the process. In some cases (such as alcohol abuse or drug addiction), immediate referral to a treatment facility may be made. In other cases, the psychologist may wish to conduct a full-scale evaluation consisting of psychological tests of intellect, neuropsychological status, achievement, interests, marital adjustment, and personality. In most instances, the officer will have taken some tests at the time of recruitment. These are probably available to the psychologist so that comparisons can be made between the officer's performance at that time, and during the current assessment.

Where a psychological assessment is scheduled, appointments should be made for feedback, which this chapter will address in more detail in the section "Intervention."

Family Problems

The most common referral received by psychologists working with police has to do with dissatisfaction between the husband and the wife regarding the work situation, finances, the children, and unfulfilled promises. In some instances, the psychologist may believe that a full marital evaluation, with testing for both parties, is indicated. Very few departments have such facilities. A full marital evaluation plus follow-up interviews amounts to somewhere between 40 and 80 hours of the psychologist's time. This may not be a cost-effective procedure for many departments, even though the resolution of marital problems probably results in considerable savings of money in terms of lower sick leave, better performance on the job, and less liability for errors that could result in litigation. Where the problem is complex and a full marital evaluation appears necessary, referral to an appropriate individual or agency is indicated. This will be addressed later in this chapter.

Children of Officers

Children and adolescents in the families of police officers are often the focus of parental concern. The problem may be marital strife demonstrated through the children's behavior.

The provision of child assessment and evaluation services for police officers and their families is an extremely useful mental health offering that is likely to have long-range benefits for the children, the family, and the department.

Where the child or the adolescent is the focus of a family problem, a full evaluation is indicated. This would include history taking with the parents and examination of the youngster's intellect, neuropsychological status, academic achievement, and personality, as well as any special measures that may be indicated. With younger children, developmental scales are useful. The Basic Psychological Examination for children and adolescents is outlined in detail by Blau (1991b) and has been used successfully with police families.

As with assessment of the officer, interpretation of results and further counseling are almost always indicated and will be addressed in detail in the next section.

Evaluation of children and adolescents in the family almost always leads to recommendations for the parents and further counseling. Again, the size of the behavioral science unit and the resources of the department will determine how much evaluation service can be given and what must be referred elsewhere.

INTERVENTION

Although the mental health intervention procedures offered by an in-house psychologist are to a large extent determined by the available resources together with the philosophy of upper management regarding mental health services, most police organizations prefer to send most of their officers and staff requiring such services to outside consultants. There are a number of practical reasons for this philosophy:

1. Issues of privilege and confidentiality are much simpler when intervention is done by a psychologist who is not directly associated with the agency.
2. Record keeping becomes a simpler matter and is less likely to mistakenly fall into the hands of unauthorized personnel.
3. The officer is likely to feel that the services are more professional and more confidential if he or she is able to make appointments away from the building that houses the police administration. Being "seen" at an administrative building is something that few officers find comfortable.

The range of things that a psychologist can "do" to help police officers and their families is extensive. At some point, all of the work that a psychologist may do as a staff member in a police agency or as a consultant must come down to what is actually provided in the way of resolution service to the client. Inevitably, problems are raised and the psychologist is sought as a problem solver, a "healer," or as a counselor to guide the individual in ways that will make the situation better.

Long-range therapeutic contacts are impractical in the law enforcement setting, and in truth, rarely do law enforcement officers seek long-range therapeutic services. When this does occur, referral is the most appropriate procedure. On the other hand, short-term interventions are both sought after and generally effective.

The interventions that can be provided, such as the child evaluation in the last section of this chapter, are dependent on the support of the organization, and the skills of the psychologists. Some of the most common interventions that have been found to be effective in working with police officers and their families follow.

Interpretation of Testing

Testing is psychology's birthright; the field has been exploring this area for more than 100 years. Psychologists test almost every human attribute. Too often, the worth and value of tests are restricted to a narrow and specific area such as selection testing. This can be true in the law enforcement setting unless the psychologist realizes that testing offers an opportunity for significant intervention.

Whether the testing is for a marital problem, an individual who feels depressed, or a family member who has difficulties that affect the entire family, only when the psychologist completes the evaluation and then provides interpretation and information to the individual or to the family is the testing procedure really useful. The amount of information that can be provided is sometimes not only considerable but significant. Whenever possible, all testing should be followed by at least one interpretation session and possibly several to give the individuals feedback about their performance in the evaluation, advice and recommendations, and an opportunity to plan implementation.

The following illustration represents the interpretation sessions held with a police detective and his ex-wife concerning their 7½-year-old son. The boy, living with his mother and stepfather, but seeing his detective father at regular intervals, was doing poorly in school. All kinds of questions had been raised by school personnel, but no solutions had been offered. The detective asked the psychologist what might be done, and a full-scale psychological evaluation was conducted. The mother and the father were in agreement about the need for such an evaluation and both seemed to be quite cooperative. This case occurred early in the police psychologist's career, and he wisely saw it as an opportunity to provide an intervention that not only would be useful to the detective and his family, but would develop departmental understanding of what psychologists can uniquely do to improve the lives of police officers.

The evaluation took approximately 9 hours of time including interviews and testing. The first interpretation lasted almost 2 hours, and the parents were given a tape recording of the interpretation. The second interpretation took place about 2 weeks later.

The First Interpretation Session with Albert's Parents

A verbatim account of the first interpretation session with the significant adults in Albert's life is presented here to illustrate the process. The first interpretation session was scheduled approximately 2 weeks after Albert's testing was finished. The clinical child psychologist used Albert's psychological report as the basis for the interpretation.

Both of Albert's natural parents and his stepparents had planned on being at this first session. Because of a change in shift schedules, the stepmother could not be present. This illustrates another good purpose for taping the sessions, since the tape enabled her to hear exactly what was said about Albert at a later time.

At several times during the session, a parent interrupted to ask a question or to make a comment. These interruptions are not included in the verbatim dialogue so that the presentation can have uninterrupted continuity. The clinical child psychologist should, however, encourage these interruptions and answer questions as they arise. Experience dictates that interruptions seldom occur during the first interpretation session.

After the two natural parents and the stepfather were comfortably seated in the consultation office, and were served beverages, the psychologist proceeded as follows:

I am glad to see all of you here today. Sorry that we all couldn't be here, but we're going to tape this session so that you'll have a chance to go over the results, and everyone can think about what I have to say at their leisure.

We're making a tape because what I'm going to tell you is very complicated. We've done a very thorough examination of Albert and found many interesting things about him. At the beginning, you asked a number of questions about Albert, and I think we have answered most of them. Let me start by telling you what we've done, what we found, what it means, and what we recommend.

We originally saw Albert because Dad was somewhat concerned. He had been told that Albert was not doing too well in school, and that he might be "hyperactive" or perhaps having a "learning disability." It was agreed among both parents and stepparents that a complete psychological evaluation would be helpful. We all met, and I took an extensive history.

We found that both parents have divorced, but have remarried. I must tell you that the children of divorce in almost all cases suffer consequences affecting their schoolwork, their self-concept, and their behavior for many years after the divorce. I am going to give you some special literature to read to help you understand the kinds of things that Albert is facing as a child of divorce. This will help you to lessen the effect.

A number of questions were raised, including "Is Albert hyperactive?" "Is he learning disabled or abnormal in any other way?" and "What can parents and stepparents do to help Albert in his adjustment?" Mother in particular wanted to know, "How can Albert's attention span be improved?"

We took an extensive history and learned that Mother is a 32-year-old executive secretary with a high school education. She describes herself as a person who is happiest when Albert is on his best behavior. She tries to be fair and to correct Albert constructively. Recently, she has remarried to Bill, a 29-year-old insurance executive. He describes himself as an "easygoing" person. He thinks he gets along pretty well with Albert.

The natural father, Jack, is a 38-year-old detective. He describes himself as kind of a stern guy. He does say that he and Albert have a good time and that they spend quite a bit of time together. They play and laugh a lot. Stepfather enjoys a more quiet relationship with Albert, watching TV and helping him with his homework.

Stepmother is relatively new to the scene. Mary is a 31-year-old correctional officer who has a short temper but believes herself to be honest.

There is a newcomer on the scene—Bill, a half brother who is almost 1 year old. All of you say that Albert seems to love his brother and there are no obvious signs of sibling rivalry.

Albert gets to see his grandparents, both on the natural side and on the stepparents' side on a pretty regular basis. He seems to get a lot out of these relationships. He also has a chance to see the mother's sister (his aunt) and her children (his cousins). They all get along pretty well.

Mother has the formal custody of Albert, but the families are very comfortable with shared responsibility, and natural father and stepmother see Albert frequently. There has been no stress about this.

The parents were divorced when Albert was about 2¹/₂, and Mother remarried when Albert was about 4. Dad remarried when Albert was about 6.

I have to tell you that you present almost an ideal cooperative situation for a divorced child. You are not angry at each other, you have very little or no unfinished business, you're very cooperative, and you all seem to be anxious to help Albert.

Our history showed that Albert was a big boy at birth, over 8 lbs, and that his early growth and development seemed to take place within normal limits. His pediatrician, Dr. Jason, finds him in good health. Albert broke his clavicle at age 2. He's had some sinus problems and nosebleeds. He had a lot of aches and pains, but they stopped last year.

There may be some mixed cerebral dominance or left-handedness within the family, and we will check that out with Albert.

Albert had preschool and he did well. During the first grade when he was at the Willow School they said he was hyperactive. He seemed to do pretty well academically. Now that he is in the second grade they say that he still seems fairly hyperactive.

You report that Albert makes friends easily and he tends to be a follower. At Mother's home he has his own room and he's put up a lot of posters. He's had some friends sleep over with him, but he has not slept over with his friends. You've told me that Albert likes the movies, TV, soccer, and riding his skateboard. He collects stickers. He's been a picky eater, and discipline has been very mild. Dad uses deprivation, and Mother does the same. Mother also will occasionally spank Albert.

Albert has been to day camp and he enjoyed it. He had an allowance for a while but this has been stopped. It's unclear to me why this was so, but I have some recommendations later to deal with this.

His bedtime is about 8:30 during school nights and he gets up at about 6:30. He does have chores at both houses.

You report that Albert has always sucked his thumb, and he wet the bed on and off since the age of about 3. He has occasional tantrums. He has been generally uncooperative and has a high energy level. You believe that he lacks self-confidence and is overly sensitive.

His performance at school is considered by everyone to be below his potential. You find that he's socially embarrassing. His emotional behavior is variable, sometimes seeming to be mature and sometimes childlike. He has occasional periods of irritability where there is no apparent cause. He does cause conflict in the family. He is impulsive, stubborn, cannot complete projects, has trouble following directions, but you notice that he is a kind youngster and doesn't have any bad responses to animals or small children.

I have to tell you that most of the things that you've mentioned are perfectly normal for first-born male youngsters between the ages of 5 and 9. I know that these behaviors are troublesome, but they do come and go, and every indication is that they will pass from Albert's life.

Well, with this history we would say that the information is "equivocal." This means that it may mean something and it may not. To really get at the answers, we gave Albert a very comprehensive psychological examination that we call the Basic Psychological Examination.

We gave him a large number of tests of his intellect, his neuropsychological brain-behavior interactions, his achievement, and his personality.

As you all know from many years of living, the human being is an extremely complicated creature. There is the outside individual that you see and respond to. I'm working at that level now. I wear clothes in a certain way, talk in a certain way, and present myself. All of you sitting here and listening are functioning at a middle level. You're listening, weighing, judging, and evaluating what you hear. There is a third level, sometimes called the unconscious or the subconscious. It causes us to do things without our thinking. For example, some mornings you wake up irritable and if you are asked, "Why are you irritable?" you will probably answer, "I got up on the wrong side of the bed!" Well, you got up on the same side you always get up on. We don't really know why certain reactions occur, but they do. In my interpretation I'm going to try to tell you all the levels of Albert's psychological life. The more you understand about him, the easier it's going to be to help him.

I'd like to start with the way Albert looks to us. This is called the "clinical picture." We don't think it means very much, but people are very concerned about the way they look on the outside. People spend billions of dollars a year on clothing, hairdos, contact lenses, and so forth. So let's start with that.

We noticed that Albert seems tall for his age. He has blond hair and blue eyes, and has several front teeth missing. This is perfectly normal for his age. During the examinations he would suck his thumb occasionally. He speaks in a high, kind of crackly voice, which is characteristic of 7-year-old boys. His hearing is within normal limits. We did notice, during all of the examination sessions, that Albert had a tendency to drink an unusually large amount of water. I've talked to all of you about this, and you agree that he is always drinking water. We want to suggest that Dr. Jason be informed about this, but I'll talk to you about this when we talk about sending copies of the report to appropriate people.

We found that Albert was a friendly youngster, but in some ways he seemed immature for his age. Sometimes he would cooperate extremely well, and sometimes he would be so agitated and jumpy that it was hard for him to pay attention to what we were doing. When we accepted this and allowed him to move around the room, he calmed down quickly and did better. If we set limits too strictly, he would tend to regress, and several times he came close to tears. We quickly found that criticism was not the way to work with Albert. We gave him a lot of positive regard and he did much better. It seems that his confidence is pretty limited and he gets upset easily. We have the feeling that Albert is a needful child who has to have some pretty clear evidence, on a regular basis, that he is loved and accepted.

He really doesn't look too much different from a lot of second-grade youngsters we've seen. I can understand how some of his teachers might think of him as hyperactive. He does have a lot of exuberance and energy. In my opinion, he is no different from a lot of intelligent youngsters who have more energy than they can use, and who may be somewhat worried about things.

That's what he looked like. Now I would like to get into the actual examination and what we found about Albert psychologically. The first thing we'd like to look at is intelligence. We like to think of this as "horsepower." How much energy does the youngster have that requires stimulation and opportunity to learn? The first thing I'd like to do is ask you to try to get rid of the concept of "IQ." One single number can never really describe a child. Even a youngster of 7 is quite a complicated individual, and, to understand him well, I'd like you to think of another concept that we have for describing children. It is called "percentile." A percentile is not a percentage. It is a way of characterizing any human trait in a very exact way. Let me give you an example: If an adult male is 5 ft 7½ in. tall, we could say that he is "average." That would be okay, but "average" in height for adult males might range between 5 ft 4 in. and 5 ft 10 in. To be more exact, we could say that our man who is 5 ft 7½ in. tall falls at the 50th percentile. This would mean that if we randomly selected 100 adult males, off the street, and lined them up military fashion from the shortest to the tallest, our man would be taller than 50 of the 100 and shorter than 50. He would fall at the *50th percentile.* I would like to use this concept throughout, comparing Albert with youngsters his age and his grade.

Looking at 11 different tests of his ability to learn and do things, we found that Albert fell at the 94th percentile. This means he is in the superior range of intellectual capacity. Only 5 out of 100 youngsters could do these tests as well as Albert did them.

We found that in some things he was able to perform at a much more competent level than in others. In none of his tests did he fall below the average range. Let me go through the 11 subtests of the Wechsler Intelligence Scale for Children—the Revised version—and tell you how he stood in comparison with other 7-year-old youngsters.

In his ability to collect general information, he was at the 63rd percentile. This is within the average range. In his ability to do analogous reasoning and make comparisons, he was at the 84th percentile. Arithmetic reasoning fell at the 99th percentile. His vocabulary skills were found to be at the 50th percentile. This was the lowest level to which Albert's intellect fell. Now, the 50th percentile is average, but for a boy of superior ability, this is somewhat low. Verbal comprehension, the ability to understand concepts through the use of words, fell at the 75th percentile. Albert's attention span, his ability to focus and use short-term memory, fell at the 50th percentile.

He was able to pick out key ideas equal to or better than 91% of youngsters his age. His social intelligence and his ability to predict his own behavior in comparison with others according to his age fell at the 75th percentile. Eye-hand coordination and design ability were at the 75th percentile. Albert's ability to manipulate large objects into a meaningful array fell at the 91st percentile. His ability to do small motor movement and new learning fell at the 98th percentile.

You can see that using IQ to describe a youngster leaves an awful lot out. In this description I just gave you, we see that Albert is an absolute whiz in arithmetic reasoning, assembling of objects, picking key ideas, new learning, and small motor movement. He is average, which is far below his basic ability, in vocabulary and his ability to concentrate. These results suggest that Albert may have some difficulty with immediate memory and expressive language skills.

To do a kind of cross-check on Albert's intellectual function, we gave him the Peabody Picture Vocabulary Test. In this, he didn't have to use any words. He simply had to point to one of four pictures that best described a word that was given by the examiner. On this he fell at the 50th percentile. This is very far below his excellent results on the Wechsler scales. This suggests that Albert's intellectual efficiency fluctuates and sometimes he is "on" and sometimes he is "off." He may also be the victim of distractibility, which influences the quality of his intellectual performance. This kind of response is not unusual for youngsters at this age. Albert is in a stage of considerable physiological growth. You can expect on-and-off response throughout his growing years. Sometimes it's better and sometimes it's worse.

We gave Albert a number of neuropsychological tests. We found he could pull between 11 and 12 kg with his right hand and between 11 and 13 kg with the left hand. Even though he is right-handed, the lack of difference in strength with the dominant hand and with the nondominant hand suggests that indeed he is in a stage of growth. We thought he might have mixed cerebral dominance. We gave him several tests of this and found that he is left-brain-dominant, which essentially means right-handed. On a test of visual memory, he showed some slight difficulty. We found this pretty consistent for his age, which, as I said, is an age of growth. In short, we found no reason to believe that Albert has any kind of neuropsychological deficit.

To determine whether Albert has a specific learning disability, we gave him a standardized achievement test to measure the three basic elements of his academic world: reading, arithmetic, and language. On the test that we gave him, compared with youngsters beginning the second grade, his reading fell at the 38th percentile. This is within the average range, but quite low for a youngster as bright as Albert. It is consistent, however, with the lowered intellectual factors on vocabulary and attention span that we found on his Wechsler scales. In arithmetic, where Albert showed himself to be extraordinarily skillful on the intelligence tests, he fell at the 2.3 grade level, which placed him at the 52nd percentile. Albert's language skills were at the 46th percentile.

His test results are within acceptable limits for his grade placement, but they are considerably below his potential. We evaluated each of the tests and found that in the reading tests, he lacks the vocabulary skills that are required to read at the level of his own potential. He also had trouble with literal-specific reading and inferential-specific reading. These may reflect his difficulty in vocabulary, and that's something that we want to address later on when we make recommendations.

The final area that we examined very thoroughly was Albert's personality. Personality is a very complex thing, as we all know. It involves "Who am I?" "What influences brought me to where I am?" "What things frighten me?" and a host of other questions. Personality is one of the psychological areas that really makes individuals different from each other.

We gave Albert a number of tests including projective techniques. A projective technique is an opportunity for the youngster to express things in personality that are at the lower levels of awareness.

I'd like to go through all the levels that we found. I've taken all of the tests and divided them into four elements. The first is interpersonal activity. Here, we'll talk about Albert and how he appears to people. At the second level we'll look at early identifications. Here, we'll try to determine the effects and the impact of his exposure to the important people in his life—you. In the third portion of the personality analysis, we'll look at his anxiety structure. These are the energies that Albert has delivered to him daily, and with which he must do something. We'll finally look at outlets and defenses, where we have measured what Albert does with the energies that he has. We will show you what he does that works in his best interests, and what he does with his energies that work against his best interests.

First let's look at his interpersonal activity. At this first level, we found that Albert appears at first to be a demanding, active, jumpy youngster. He tends to be pretty challenging as he becomes comfortable. It's as though he's testing his environment. His aggressiveness seems pretty indiscriminate—it can be toward adults or toward children, males or females. As one gets to know Albert, one finds that beneath his outside aggressiveness, Albert has a great fear of setting goals for himself and not reaching them. He has what we call a low level of aspiration. When he faces new things, Albert expects the worst. So we might say that Albert approaches life with a certain pessimism.

Next let's examine Albert's early identifications. In looking at our projective techniques, we attempt to find what we call identification and love objects. The identification object is the person whom the youngster seeks to imitate, and to whom the child looks as a model of what he's likely to be when he matures. The love object is the person he is drawn toward, feels safest with, and will eventually tend to mate with.

We found that primary identification for Albert was with a father figure. I'll tell you what we found, and then you can decide which of his father figures has had the greatest influence. The unconscious picture of the father figure as expressed in the projective techniques is that of a rather oral-aggressive person. That means an individual who says what he thinks when he thinks it and doesn't much mind who's listening. He sees the father as being somewhat of a temperamental person. He is seen as somewhat anti-intellectual, seeing people with a lot of education as not particularly practical. He himself is very practical and very aggressive. In spite of this picture of outer aggressiveness and roughness, the father is also seen as able to step in and do some mothering when the youngster is with him—feeling his head to see how much fever he has, cautioning him to be careful, taking care of him when he's hurt, and feeding him. The father is seen as loving his child, but the father has never been seriously invested with tiny details of child rearing. [At this point the mother and the stepfather looks smilingly at the natural father, who was grinning sheepishly and nodding his head.]

The mother figure is seen as a love object. The unconscious picture from the projective techniques is that of a person who has some trouble seeing the inner needs of the child. What she sees on the surface is what she responds to. Like the father, she can be verbally aggressive. He sees the mother as a security-minded person who is always worried about details of being safe. He sees her as having trouble being spontaneous in her nourishment or giving of warmth and affection. There are some indications that it may be because she herself had some difficulty establishing a warm and nourishing relationship with her own mother. We see this frequently—one learns to mother from one's own mother [at this point the mother began dabbing at her eyes with a tissue as she became teary]. Mother is clearly the motivator in the family, asking "Wouldn't you like to do this?" or "Why don't you give it a try?" She seems to be the one who has set the goals in the family. She is seen as a person who has very strong affection needs and is seriously uncomfortable if these are not met.

This information does not indicate specifically who has given him this impression of mothers or fathers. Albert himself would be surprised that we got this much information. We did not ask him, "What is your mom like?" or "What is your dad like?" These images came from the test results. [At this point there was a discussion of how accurately these descriptions fit the natural mother and the natural father.]

What I have described about the personality so far is essentially "yesterday." The last two portions of the personality relate to "today" and "tomorrow." Let me take up Albert's anxiety structure. Anxiety means the energies that are developed as a person sees something wrong in his or her environment. Anxiety is a warning signal that something ought to be done to change things. When the anxiety is realistic, it helps us. You certainly want Albert to be anxious about crossing the street without looking. On the other hand, anxiety about things that are not very realistic can be very painful. It does not help Albert a great deal to be afraid that monsters will break into his room at night and kidnap him. I would like to look at Albert's anxieties and tell you what I believe they represent, and then we will see what he does about them. I want to clearly emphasize the point that anxiety by itself is not a bad thing. A certain amount of anxiety is very normal, and very necessary for healthy growth and development.

Albert's deepest sources of anxiety relate to the fractured family situation, and in this he is like all children of divorce. I will give you some things to read about this when we finish. He is fearful of the loss of attachments. He is afraid that everyone in the family is angry at him and that most of the difficulties that Mom and Dad have experienced are his fault. I want you to understand that this is the most common thing we find in children of divorce. It is unrealistic, and it does not make sense to a lot of parents, but the child believes that whatever happened was his or her fault. He tends to feel very discouraged. He is frightened that he will be replaced in the affection of his mother by the new half brother. This again is very normal, but is painful to Albert. Many children his age overdo the "loving" behavior toward a new sibling to disguise or deny this anxiety.

We also found that Albert is very tense about poor school performance. He is afraid that he won't do well. He is frightened now that he has discovered that many things that adults tell him are not the truth. Until recently, he has believed every single thing his mother, father, stepmother, stepfather, and teachers have told him. It is at about age 7 that children realize that parents do not always tell the truth. This comes as a shock to some parents. You must remember that when the telephone rings and you say "If it's Mr. Jones, tell him I've left already," this may seem to you a perfectly acceptable fib. To the child it is a behavior that he has been told is absolutely unacceptable—lying. It is very difficult for young children to discriminate shades of gray. The brighter the child, the more confusing this can be. Albert is a very bright child and he is confused about this behavior.

Albert is unsure of the limits of his environment, so he is always testing them. He doesn't know really what is expected of him.

Albert often feels creative. He wants to build things, draw things, and make new things. In some ways, he is very embarrassed about this and tries to hide it. This makes him quite tense.

He has strong, natural, healthy sexual interests for his age. You must remember that he has a mental age that is about 2 years greater than his chronological age. He is thinking of some things like 9- and 10-year-old boys. He is quite frightened by these thoughts and feelings. He clearly has not had sufficient sex education. We will give you some material to ease this situation for Albert.

Albert has a great deal of difficulty with the concept of anger. He does not understand that anger is a natural part of everyone's life, and it occurs when a person is fearful and is unable to do anything about the fear. That in effect represents all of Albert's angers. Most of them are perfectly normal for his age. That does not mean they aren't painful.

Now let's look at what he does with the emotional energies that are delivered to him. We'll look at his outlets and defenses.

Albert tries to rid himself of intolerable tension through his assertive manner. He follows the policy of "when unsure, attack." In this he is very much like his Dad. He tests limits to try to understand new environments and new situations. Sometimes Albert is frightened of what people think of him, and he tries to get them angry at him by shocking them. This way he can be relieved of the fear that someone is thinking badly about him and not saying it.

Albert is pretty pessimistic about his life and very cautious about the future. As we can see, he has relatively few of what we call intellectual outlets and defenses. These are ones that he can organize and control.

Most of the outlets for anxiety that Albert has are what we call "labile." They come out suddenly, and they relieve tension quickly. They generally distress the people around Albert. These labile outlets include outbursts of anger, and strong oral-dependency, which includes his demands for candy, ice cream, food, and drinks. When he feels very guilty he will become quite phobic. I noticed that he is afraid of lightning, thunder, and "boogeymen."

Albert is desperately trying to hold his anger inward and is beginning to show the signs of early depression. This happens quite early in bright children. He is trying to display some of his angry feelings to power objects, such as fantasies of driving powerful vehicles, and he is beginning to attach himself to science fiction presentations on the TV. In this he is certainly more like a 9- or 10-year-old. He is moving into the next stage of development, and very much seeks the company of youngsters his own age, particularly boys, to express his feelings and to seek approval. He hasn't had a lot of chances to do this yet, but when he does, he is going to feel much better.

Well, that's the story of Albert. What does it all mean? Let me put it all together briefly and then tell you about some of the things we recommend.

Essentially, we find that Albert is a youngster who has potentially superior intellectual capacity. His intellect varies considerably, and this is probably based on developmental changes that are occurring. There are some indications that Albert is going to be a very big boy. Some of his stress and tension are based on the pressure under which he operates. So he has up-and-down performance, as well as up-and-down emotional responsiveness. Sometimes he does very well, and sometimes he spoils his own responses.

The personality structure is that of a very tense, pressured youngster who is suffering the aftermath of being a member of a fractured family. The parental models have had troubles of their own, and there has been no real chance to enrich Albert's strong intellectual and creative needs. He blames himself for the failures of the family.

To help Albert, I have a number of recommendations, and I would like to split them into individual things that each of you can do and things that you can agree on and do together. I'd like to start with Dad. Dad has a limited amount of time with Albert. I would like to suggest certain things that can be done that can be really helpful for the youngster. First of all, Albert needs sex education. I have here a booklet called "All About You." I would like you to read this book to Albert and then set up some times that you can talk about this, using the book to illustrate your discussions. You should mostly listen. Once you read the book to Albert, he will know what's in it.

Second, I'd like you to start some competitive games with Albert, but be sure that they are games at his level. If you would play cards, eventually teach him to play poker, but start with simple games such as "Go Fish." Dominoes, checkers, and other such games will be helpful.

Third, I'd like you to take Albert to the go-kart track. You can tell Albert you're teaching him to steer and compensate in preparation for the age when he can get a license. This will have an enormously positive effect on Albert.

When you have to change Albert's behavior, I would like you to use behavior management techniques. This essentially means accentuating the positive and eliminating the negative. When he does something you like, give him a lot of praise and support. When he does something you don't like, turn away. I'm going to give you some literature to read which will help you to understand how it works.

I think it's important that the father should have specific expectations for academic work, for Albert's behavior, and for chores. I think you should make it clear what you expect of him, but do it in a supportive, kindly manner.

Father is the identification object, and I think you must always be careful, as much as possible, to tell Albert the truth about things. Even in little things, deception is painful to Albert.

When Albert is with you, having a regular, consistent schedule is very important. The more predictable breakfast, lunch, dinner, and recreational activities are, the more comfortable Albert is going to be.

I know it's not easy for you to give spontaneous assurance. I think you must try to work with yourself to develop the ability to give Albert as much support and approval as possible.

Finally, I would like you to get a couple of calendars with some theme such as Star Trek so that he can have one in his room at your house and one in his room at home. If there can be some piece of furniture, a bulletin board, or other things that give him a sense of territoriality, this also will be helpful. You will notice that I gave Albert two pictures of himself with Harry the Bear when he first came. This is a way of establishing territoriality that gives children security. [At this point the parents very enthusiastically said that Albert asked to have both pictures framed and put up in his two rooms.]

I would now like to talk to Stepdad. Your role can be extremely important as a model for Albert. You are not a replacement for Dad, but you're an additional important male figure that can provide the security and confidence that Albert really needs. There are some specific things I'd like to recommend. First, I'd like you to reinforce the sex education given by Dad. I'm going to give you a copy of the same book. Second, I'd like you to follow through with games of competition. At your house I'd like you to be the one that sets the limits on when Albert goes to bed, and what he must do and must not do. He is getting too old for any kind of physical discipline. It would be much better if you set the limits clearly and then follow them with behavior management techniques. I'd like you to set a regular homework schedule for Albert and make sure that this schedule is followed. I think it should be 5 nights a week, Sunday through Thursday. I think it should be from 7:00 P.M. to 8:00 P.M. I think it should be in 10-min segments, with 5 min between each segment. You might want to have a kitchen timer set so that when the bell goes off he takes his breaks and when the bell goes off again he goes back to his homework. Often he won't have homework, but I'd like you to have him read for pleasure, at his desk, to get used to the idea that this is the place and time that he will do his schoolwork.

I think it's important that you provide him a regular allowance on Monday morning. At this age, 50¢ a week is enough. If you want to associate it with chores at home, that would be okay.

I'd like you to give him 10 or 15 minutes every evening when you and he can be alone. Try to get Albert to talk about what he has done. In all instances, provide him with as much reassurance and positive regard as you can.

I'm going to give you some booklets on behavior modification so that you can learn how to shape Albert's behavior to increase positive responses and decrease the things you don't like.

Mother is going to be very important. You are the traditional provider of security, warmth, and philosophy of life. I think it's very important that you take the position that Albert needs a lot of unrestricted positive regard. Compliment him as often as you can. Accentuate the positive. When he is stressed, give him reassurance. I would like you to try to avoid discipline whenever possible except when carrying through what father has set down as the limits. As I mentioned with Dad, you must always tell Albert the truth. That's harder to do than you think, and you may have to practice this. We as adults don't realize how literally children take our words.

A regularity of schedule is going to be vital. Every effort should be made to have the family eat at least two meals together. These should not be rushed or pressured times. Try to make mealtime a positive, friendly, supportive experience. Bedtime and other responsibilities should be scheduled pretty strictly so that Albert knows just what's going to happen.

I'd like you particularly to provide some creative opportunities for Albert. Whether it be finger painting, modeling with clay, or going to a children's creative workshop at one of the local community centers, I believe that Albert has really got to have a chance to see how creative he is.

I think it would be easier for Albert if you could help your husband to be the setter of limits and the masculine image. You've worked very hard with Albert, and it may be time for you to lean back a little and let your husband do some of the work as stepdad.

Stepmother is the most recent adult figure in Albert's life. I'm sorry she isn't here, but I will talk to you directly on the tape, Mrs. Doe. I hope you can realize that every child of every divorce situation has a fantasy of the parents reuniting. This should not be held against Albert. Now that Dad has married you and you are the stepmother, his myth and hope are pretty well shattered. You happen to be the last one to clinch the end of the marriage. That puts you in sort of a difficult spot for a short period of time. This can be overcome, and you can be really helpful. I think, first of all, by ignoring Albert's efforts to get you angry you will do a lot of good. Give him a lot of positive regard and avoid all discipline and criticism. I am going to give you some of these materials on behavior management and behavior modification. If you will read these booklets you will see how to change Albert's behavior without resorting to discipline or criticism. I hope that you can take part in arranging a fairly predictable schedule for Albert so that he knows what is going to happen.

There are some general recommendations I want to give that apply to Albert. Some of them may be practical, and some may require some consensus or negotiation. I am going to give these and then let you think about them. If they raise any conflicts, we will try to work these out and do those things that are most comfortable for all parties. First, I'd like you to take Albert to his pediatrician so that he can check to see if there is any basis for this excessive water drinking that we have noticed.

Second, I would hope that you could enter Albert into the Cub Scouts. That program gives a lot of opportunity for creative work, and Albert certainly needs this.

Third, I think Albert would profit from competitive physical activity. Your community offers a number of competitive swimming clubs for youngsters of Albert's age. Some of them operate all year long and others start in the spring. I would recommend that you start Albert in this activity. He's at the right age and he has a long, thin body, so he might do quite well in this sport. That would certainly build his confidence and use up a lot of his energy.

I think that next summer Albert is going to be ready for a camping experience away from home. As much as 4–6 weeks would be helpful. If you decide on this, I'd be happy to help you look at the camps in your area and select those that are likeliest to be helpful for Albert.

Albert doesn't have a place to keep his money, and I think he should have a little lockbox or bank in both of his homes.

Many of these recommendations may put some pressure on you. If any of you believe that you're running into a difficulty that can't be settled with a phone call, I would urge you to be willing to come in for a session to look over the situation, see where the difficulty is, and work out some solutions.

I've got a lot of material for you. These little pamphlets will give you the latest that we know about how to bring about the best kind of circumstances for your youngster. I've got a booklet called "Your Child from Six to Twelve." This will tell you a lot of things that are happening now to Albert and will show you that in some ways he is behaving in a manner more like a 9- or a 10-year-old. Here are some booklets on sex education that I mentioned. Here are several things on behavior modification that will help you to plan behavior management projects that will increase the behavior that you want Albert to show and decrease the behavior that is annoying to you. I also have some literature here on the kinds of things that children of divorce seem to feel as a group, and some things that can be done about this.

There is probably a total of about 3 hours of reading in these pamphlets. If you read all of them, you're going to be better informed about children and what you can do with children than 99% of parents. You have a very bright and capable youngster. It should be a pleasure and a rewarding experience to raise him. These materials will help you.

Finally, I believe that Albert ought to be reevaluated at the end of the sixth grade. If all is well at that time, you might want to consider selecting a special junior high school experience for him. If he has finished his development through the 12th year as we expect, he might be ready for some extra stimulating experiences. At that time we can tell you what he is ready for and make such recommendations.

I really don't know what's going to happen in the future. I've given you more recommendations than are necessary to straighten things out. I think the answers to your questions are clear. Albert is a normal, healthy boy of superior intelligence, and is not hyperactive. He is not abnormal, but he is like almost all of the 60% of youngsters who live in the residuals of a fractured family. The answer to your third question is clear: Each of you can help Albert in his development. Your concern about his attention span should be resolved as you institute these recommendations, and as Albert becomes more comfortable. A certain amount of patience will be required because some of Albert's so-called "problems" have to do with development. These will take care of themselves with time.

I hope that you will have a chance to play this tape two or three times between now and our next appointment. Make a note of any questions that you might have, and we will try to answer them at that time. Please feel free to call me between now and then if anything specific comes up. Perhaps at this point you would like to ask some questions that have arisen during my presentation.

The family interrupted in only a few instances during this presentation. After the presentation, they all made remarks suggesting that the picture of Albert that was presented indeed was an accurate one, and they were amazed at how much emerged from the psychological tests. They seemed enthusiastic, and it was suggested that they try some of the recommendations in the 2-week interim period before the second interpretation session. Plans were made to ensure that a second copy of the tape was made so that each family could have one. The families left on a very positive note.

During the 2 weeks between the first and the second interpretation sessions, one call was received from the stepmother, who asked a technical question about a behavior management project. She was distressed about Albert's jumping up from the table. She was counseled by telephone and seemed enthusiastic about carrying forth the behavior management project.

The Second Interpretation Session with Albert's Parents

All four parental figures attended the second session. They chatted pleasantly before the conference began, and seemed to be pretty excited about the program.

They reported that they had tried a number of the recommendations, and they were delighted. The mother was particularly excited about how easily Albert was willing to give up TV in the evening and start his study program under the guidance of the stepfather. They found a swimming club, and Albert was enrolled. He was already enthusiastically participating. Plans to start Cub Scouts in about 2 weeks had been made.

The family had no specific questions concerning the evaluation. An extremely positive tone emerged from each of the parents and stepparents. They requested that a full report go to the pediatrician. They agreed that a letter to Albert's second grade teacher, summarizing the intellectual findings and the achievement test findings and giving a brief statement about his stage of development, would be sufficient. Interestingly, they asked that a similar letter go to his first-grade teacher who continued to show interest in Albert.

The appropriate letters were sent, and copies of these were provided to the parents. The parents were also given a copy of the report of the BPE.

About 6 months later, the father called to tell the clinical child psychologist that Albert was doing exceedingly well and appeared to be at the head of his class. He had won a number of ribbons as a member of the swimming team, and had made some new friends. He was now going overnight to his friends' homes.

A letter was received from the natural mother reflecting much of what the father had said by telephone. She was particularly pleased with Albert's academic progress and his rising position as a leader in the class. Interestingly, she gave much of the credit to her new husband for creating a stable environment that gave Albert a great deal of security.

About 7 months after the assessment, a call was received from Albert's teacher. She mentioned how pleased she was with Albert's progress, but she specifically wanted to say that she had never received a letter from a professional person who had been consulted by one of her students. She appreciated this gesture and referred a family of one of her other students.

The case of Albert represents the kind of situation that is quite common in the practice of the clinical child psychologist who conducts Basic Psychological Examinations in the community.

Interpretation of test results and follow-up of initial contacts are excellent ways of intervening to help police officers and their families to solve problems. Follow-up is particularly important. The officers themselves may be reluctant to schedule an additional appointment after a first contact. Whenever the psychologist believes that such a follow-up appointment would be useful to "see how things are going" the appointment should be suggested. Officers are usually quite appreciative of this continued interest. In the previous example of Albert, the detective's son, the 6-month follow-up was a result of the psychologist's requesting an opportunity to review what had happened.

Brief, Intensive Counseling

Once behavioral science services are established in a law enforcement agency, officers seem to be more willing to seek appointments for counseling services if "the word" among officers is that the psychologist is "OK." Counseling may be requested after evaluation, in response to a telephone request, "walk-in," or during a casual meeting on or off duty.

On rare occasions, the police psychologist may be sought out by a disgruntled or manipulative officer as an unknowing accomplice to achieve a hidden agenda (retirement, disability benefits, change in shift or duty assignment, disciplinary action against a supervisor, or other goals). For the most part, an officer who seeks counseling has thought about this step long and carefully. Although frequently unsure and tentative, the need for help is strong.

The first meeting between psychologist and officer should follow a structure likely to create a safe and comfortable ambience. Such a structure cannot be rigidly followed but should probably include:

1. Positive regard for the officer's choice to seek help.
2. A clear description of the psychologist's responsibilities and limitations in respect to confidentiality and privilege.
3. An invitation to state the officer's concerns.

The following dialogue between a road deputy corporal and the agency's staff psychologist illustrates the initiation of brief-intensive counseling.

PSYCHOLOGIST: Come in Corporal. Glad to see you. (Shakes hands.)

OFFICER: How're ya doing. We met last year when you did the stress training for District 2.

PSYCHOLOGIST: Oh yeah! The hostage thing at the convenience store.

OFFICER: Yeah . . . we were all shook up about that. One of my section officers was in the bunch that were hostages. He still feels bad about it—Jack Barnes.

PSYCHOLOGIST: It was pretty rough. I remember Jack. Good guy.

OFFICER: Yeah, we used to be partners. He said you were OK. That's one of the reasons I decided to talk to you.

PSYCHOLOGIST: I'm sure it wasn't easy. Until you get to work with a psychologist, most people worry about it—how safe it is—how confidential.

OFFICER: Yeah . . . I thought about that.

PSYCHOLOGIST: Let me tell you a little about that. By law, whatever we talk about is confidential, which means I say nothing to nobody unless you give me written permission. You also have privilege which means what goes on here can't be used in civil or criminal court. There are a couple of exceptions: my records and I can be subpoenaed if you claim psychological defects in a civil or criminal action. Also, by law, I have to report any information about child abuse or *intent* to commit a felonious act or danger to yourself or others.

OFFICER: (Laughs.) I may be bad but not that bad!

PSYCHOLOGIST: I just like to make it clear that this is a place to get help and not be hurt by doing this.

OFFICER: I was worried about doing this. Jack told me it was private.

PSYCHOLOGIST: The Department has agreed to this, and they know my files are under my lock and key. Not available to them. The Sheriff signed a special order on that. Do you have any questions about this?

OFFICER: No, I don't think so.

PSYCHOLOGIST: Well, tell me a little about what I can do for you.

OFFICER: I don't know. I'm kind of fed up and I've been thinking about quitting.

The principles that apply to brief counseling contacts in the law enforcement setting are sometimes referred to as rational emotive therapy, behavioral management, and cognitive therapy. A number of therapeutic approaches share in common elements of briefness, focus on specific symptomatology or conflict issues, and direct operational efforts to re-solve the conflicts or to reach a satisfactory conclusion.

A straightforward approach to brief-intensive counseling would in-clude the following elements:

1. *The Psychologist Creates a Sanctuary.* In the setting for brief-intensive therapy, the psychologist does everything necessary to reassure the officer that it is safe to talk about problems in this setting, and that confidentiality and privilege protections are real.

2. *Focus on Critical Areas of Concern.* The psychologist helps the officer to narrow attention and discussion on the problems that concern the officer and interfere with full functioning.

3. *Identify Desired Outcomes.* Immediately following the focusing on critical areas of concern, the psychologist must help the officer iden-tify gaps between what is going on and what should be going on, what the officer is experiencing and seeks to experience, and in gen-eral the outcomes that are desirable.

4. *Review of Assets.* The psychologist must help the officer identify those aspects of his or her personality, duty assignment, family situ-ation, friendships, attitudes, and abilities that could be useful in moving toward the desired outcomes.

5. *Developing an Overarching Plan.* In reviewing the desired outcome and the officer's assets, the psychologist should encourage the officer to plan some steps that in general will result in as many of the desired outcomes as possible.

6. *Identify Practical Initial Implementations.* In reviewing the overarching plan, the psychologist should help the officer narrow on specific, fairly immediate, practical steps toward implementing the plan and achieving the desired outcomes. This selection should include some of the simplest and most practical options.

7. *A Review of Self-Efficacy.* Once the psychologist and the officer have agreed on general goals, immediate specific goals, assets the officer has, and steps for initiating the implementation of the plan, the psy-chologist should review with the officer the concept of *self-efficacy* (Bandura, 1977; Prochaska, DiClemente, & Norcross, 1992). In this situation, the psychologist asks this officer to focus on the question, "Do I really want to accomplish these things?" If the answer is in the affirmative, the psychologist should then help the officer to decide in practical terms whether the officer is capable of doing what has been planned. If the officer is confident of this capability, the psy-chologist should lead the officer to the third step in self-efficacy, "I will do it."

8. *Set an Appointment for Review, Reassurance, and Further Implementation.* At this point, the officer has developed a set of "marching orders"

with the psychologist's help. An appointment should be set up so that the officer can report back on the progress of the plan and can receive further counseling and assistance in implementing further steps toward his or her goals.

In the counseling example presented earlier in this chapter, the officer told the psychologist during the first session that he was discouraged. Further discussion indicated that the discouragement was fairly profound and he had been suffering a good bit of depression. He thought about quitting law enforcement and going into some other kind of work. Further exploration revealed that his enthusiasm had waned after he failed the Sergeant's Examination for the second time. Discussion about this indicated that the corporal had done extremely well on oral examination, had a good record, but placed poorly on the written examination. Further discussion suggested that he'd had some difficulties in reading the verbal material on the written examination.

An overall plan to discover the source of the corporals's difficulty and to take steps to pass the examination before deciding whether to leave law enforcement or not were the agreed on outcomes of the first session. Another appointment was made. Between the first and the second appointment the psychologist retrieved the records of the officer's recruit selection test battery. The officer had scored at the 70th percentile intellectually, and showed no pathological indications in the personality testing. During the earlier discussion, the officer had indicated that he rarely reads for pleasure and may be a "little slow" since he did not finish all the test items on both of his efforts toward passing the written examination.

During the second appointment, after some discussion, the psychologist suggested administration of a reading test. The corporal agreed and it was found that his vocabulary, comprehension, and speed of reading were all at the junior high school level. His reading skills were barely sufficient to do his job. He reported difficulty in writing out reports and reading general orders was a tedious task. A plan was made to have the corporal attend a developmental reading class at the local junior college. With some reluctance, the corporal agreed to do this. Going into the course, his reading comprehension was at the 6.5 grade level, his vocabulary at the 7.0 level, and his speed of reading at the 6.0 level (110 words per minute). On completion of the 10-hour developmental reading program, the officer had post-high school vocabulary and comprehension skills and was reading at 325 words per minute.

In a counseling session subsequent to completion of the developmental reading course, the officer indicated that he had more confidence in his reading and was beginning to enjoy it. He was still concerned about the Sergeants' Examination. As it approached, the psychologist provided the corporal with some information about test-taking attitudes and encouraged him to use a relaxation tape before the exam. The officer took the examination, placing second among all the candidates. Shortly thereafter, he was promoted. Only five sessions were devoted to this particular brief-intensive counseling. Aside from the very specific recommendations, a good deal of support was given, the officer's frustration was reflected and clarified, and he was helped to deal with a very specific problem in a practical and successful manner.

Not all brief-intensive counseling results in focusing on a clear-cut individual problem. Not all brief-intensive counseling sessions are as successful as this one. In some cases, counseling has led to an awareness of deeper personality difficulties that resulted in referral for long-term therapeutic intervention. Some of these situations will be addressed in later sections of this chapter.

Peer Counseling

The concept of developing operational police officers into mental health counselors began in the 1950s at the Boston Police Department where stress programs focused on alcohol-related problems and the provision of opportunities for officers with such problems to meet with cohorts who had been through the problem and had some training in helping others to deal with these issues. In 1955, the Chicago Police Department began such a program, again with alcoholism. The New York Police Department established a similar program in 1966, and shortly thereafter the Los Angeles Police Department followed with a similar program. Peer counseling has been successful and popular. The training of officers to be peer counselors is usually done by a clinical psychologist together with a police officer who has a degree in behavioral science. Somewhere between 20 and 40 hours are devoted to the training procedures (see Appendix F). The rationale behind the provision of such services by cohorts is that cops tend to feel more empathy and closeness with fellow cops. They are likely to seek help earlier if they feel that peer counselors are available. Peer counselors are trained to deal only with that which they know about and to refer more difficult or complex mental health problems to the psychologist (Klein, 1989).

Another reason peer counselors can be useful is that recovering alcoholic police officers may tend to enter back into their symptomatic behavior and suppress this with professionals who are not cops. Machell (1989) suggests that the availability of peer counselors may be helpful in preventing this kind of recidivism.

There are other indications that peer counselors can be helpful where more traditional professionals will fail. This appears to be particularly true where peer counselors are the leaders in group counseling (Linden & Klein, 1986).

Peer counseling has been extended beyond provision of services to officers with drug and alcohol problems. Klyver (1986) reports an evaluation of the Los Angeles Police Department's peer counseling program over a 3-year period. Specific methods of training had been developed. As of 1983, there were 200 trained peer counselors conducting almost 5,000 hours of counseling with over 2,000 individuals in the Los Angeles Police Department. They dealt primarily with job concerns, family relationships, disability issues, deadly force issues, alcohol and drug abuse, and financial problems.

Peer counseling will never be a substitute for a fully functional behavioral science program in a law enforcement agency. Peer counseling can be an invaluable adjunct to any broad program of psychological services to law enforcement.

Family Counseling

With the divorce rate approaching 50% in the general population, the range of family problems faced by police couples are those that tend to occur in many marriages. Certain areas of conflict appear more consistently than others. Borum and Philpot (1993) have analyzed the law enforcement officer's "high risk life-style" and the family problems that result. Special problems that occur in police families reflecting the vocation of one spouse or the other (or both) include the police system, which facilitates solidarity and isolation; the authoritarian or insensitive response patterns developed by police officers, which are brought home to the family; the fear and anxiety experienced by the family of a man or a woman in a highly dangerous occupation; irregular schedules; rotating shifts; overtime work; physical exhaustion; and the significant dilemma of having weapons in the home.

Borum and Philpot further point out that police officers tend to be overinvolved with their co-workers. They develop an "us and them" mentality that may preclude strong ties within the family. Aggression may be displaced to the home. Alcohol abuse may be more frequent in police families than in families where the wage earners work in a more stable setting. A further concern is marital infidelity.

In some cases, both partners are in law enforcement. Such couples do have some advantage in that there are fewer conflicts about the special social contacts that police officers make within the department. Each can understand the problems and pressures of the partner. They can discuss and communicate about police role influences at home. Unfortunately, if the spouses are both officers and work closely together, there is a potential for job problems being carried home. Where both spouses are officers, shift work can become a more significant issue than when one spouse has a stable work routine or is a homemaker.

Borum and Philpot strongly urge all counselors to become familiar with the police job, preferably by arranging to participate in a "ride along program" with a local police department. The counselor can meet some

police officers, get a closer look at what they do, and have a better understanding of how they can relate to police officers who seek help. Learning
some of the language of police officers can be helpful (see Appendix E).
The counselor should engage in communication on the officer's terms.

In most family counseling situations, the officer presents a crisis situation that should be dealt with as has been discussed previously. Once the
crisis is over, longer term counseling can be more effective.

Borum and Philpot present a series of goals and strategies for treatment. Goals may include strengthening the boundaries around the couple
relative to the departmental boundary, reducing "triangulation" through
elimination of external forces and encouragement of the couple's direct
communication, and helping the couple increase intimacy and bonding.
Further goals include increasing positive feelings toward the marriage,
building a sense of "connectedness" that is satisfying to both partners,
and helping the couple to gain some insight into larger systemic influences in their relationship.

The counselor should make efforts to motivate the couple for change.
This may include teaching the couple basic communication skills. An important emphasis in the counseling situation is to help the couple make
more time for themselves, openly discuss stresses in the relationship that
seem to be caused by the job, and in general be more communicative. In
their study, Borum and Philpot recommend a number of specific strategies and techniques to accomplish these goals. Stuart (1980) has also developed a variety of techniques for helping couples to change. Kaslow
(1986) has developed a training model for family therapy intervention
techniques.

Another approach to dealing with family problems has been developed
at the Manatee County Sheriff's Office in Bradenton, Florida. As part of
strategic planning, this organization has developed a *family cohesiveness
training program*. Participation is required of all sworn officers, from patrol
officers up through the sheriff himself. The program consists of two 2-
hour sessions in which the officers learn about a wide variety of situations that affect family interactions, the kinds of problems that may come
about in a marriage, how to identify difficulties, and how to get help. Figure 9.1 presents the outline of the family cohesiveness training program.

Health and Wellness Intervention

Recommendations concerning health and wellness are standard intervention procedures for individuals who are suffering stressful reactions.
There is a growing understanding that the benefits of health and wellness
programs for law enforcement agencies are tangible and broad based.
Such programs reduce injuries, boost morale, and in general foster a more
effective crime-fighting force. Police executives are finding that this can
be a cost-effective component of a department's overall health care policy
(Jones, 1992).

PURPOSE

In compliance with the Sheriff's expectancy that the Agency will function at the highest level of efficiency, integrity, and public service, this program of education, prevention, and intervention is presented. Its purpose is to deal with the special stresses and common pressures that occur with the families of law enforcement officers and the officers themselves.

The program is designed to indoctrinate all officers as to the special psychological conditions under which they operate. Further, the course is designed to help families work together to prevent undue stress, to identify developing interpersonal conflicts within the family, and to take the proper steps to resolve conflicts.

Family Cohesiveness Training will be offered in a block of two units, each of which will be two hours in length. Special materials and exercises will be included to help each officer achieve the objectives of the program.

OBJECTIVES

At the completion of two 2-hour sessions, each participant will:

1. Comprehend the size and scope of the problem of spouse abuse in the United States.
2. Identify at least three aspects of law enforcement work that add to ordinary job stresses.
3. Identify eight family resources and how they may be used effectively or in some cases abused.
4. Understand the primary bases for creating a marriage that works.
5. Identify and understand 10 sources of marital conflict.
6. Identify major sources of stress.
7. Identify methods of preventing major categories of stress-production.
8. Learn and practice one or more methods of stress reduction.
9. Identify at least three methods of obtaining professional help.
10. Identify the factors connecting alcohol use with spouse abuse.
11. Learn at least five signs of problem drinking.

SESSION ONE

1. Spouse abuse
   a. Occurrence
   b. Sources
   c. Relation to job
   d. Special aspects of law enforcement
2. The nature of stress
   a. Change
   b. Cumulation
   c. Overload
   d. Environmental factors
   e. Health factors
   f. Circadian rhythms
   g. Cultural factors
   h. Family factors
   i. Other
3. Marriage
   a. Why people marry
   b. Why some stay together and others don't

FIGURE 9.1   Family Cohesiveness Training Program

c. Love and affection

d. Marital roles

e. Changes and stages in marital development

f. Normal conflict

   (1) Unmet expectations

   (2) Miscommunications

   (3) Mismatched personalities

   (4) Children, in-laws, relatives

   (5) Religion

   (6) Finances

   (7) Recreation

g. Highly stressful and dangerous conflict

   (1) Drugs and alcohol

   (2) Illness

   (3) Jealousy

   (4) Depression

   (5) Cultural imperative

   (6) Loss of esteem

SESSION TWO

1. Warning signs

2. Preventing stress

3. Preventing overload

4. Stress inoculation

5. Stress awareness

   a. Colorimeter

   b. Holmes Stress Scale

   c. Relaxation and biofeedback

6. Family council

   a. Role playing

7. Support group

   a. Demonstration

8. Crisis consultation

9. Kinds of professional help available

10. Prevention directions

   a. Exercise

   b. Eating

   c. Recreation

   d. Relationships

   e. Other

11. Special materials

12. Discussion

FIGURE 9.1 *(continued)*

In almost every situation where the psychologist provides behavioral science services for officers or their families, health and wellness considerations should be part of assessment and intervention activity. In general, medical screening should be recommended as a regular part of the officer's life. Where the officer does not have an exercise program that includes cardiovascular training, this should certainly be suggested. The department should be encouraged not only to support such exercise programs, but to introduce fitness assessment as part of annual evaluations.

The provision of regular training programs and information on health and wellness is something that the psychologist can recommend to the department and can help to formulate and implement.

In cases that the psychologist counsels, where stress is an issue and is likely to continue, the recommendation of a health and wellness program involving exercise, recreational time, proper nutritional habits, and stress reduction techniques should be part of the intervention.

Smoking Cessation Programs. With the growing awareness of the health hazards of smoking, a variety of government imperatives have increased the awareness of people about the benefits of smoking cessation. Although the bulk of people who stop smoking "quit on their own," smoking cessation clinics have enjoyed some popularity and success.

Smoking cessation counseling procedures, which are done in a group format, generally take a total of 4 hours. The psychologist forms a smoking cessation group by announcing that there will be a "Smoking Cessation Clinic" on a specific date. Individuals are invited to sign up. The smoking clinic consists of two sessions. The first one is introductory and didactic. The second session focuses on reports by the various members as to what they experienced when they quit, and how they are doing. The second session should be approximately one week after the first session. Figure 9.2 presents an outline of the first session of a smoking cessation clinic. The follow-up session of two hours is spent in a fairly traditional group counseling mode. Each member is asked to report his or her experiences and plans are made for activities to support the continuation of abstinence. If requested, the group may meet a third time.

Employee Assistance and Referral

It is unlikely that any law enforcement department will be able to develop and support a full range of mental health services for the needs of all its officers. As was noted in a previous section of this volume, about 70% of medium-size and larger law enforcement agencies label their behavioral science and mental health facility as an "employee assistance program." This almost always includes a referral system.

The current use of the term "employee assistance program" (EAP) suggests that it is a service available to all employees of the institution. Usually one individual is designated as the employee assistant counselor. The system usually offers one or more sessions to allow the individual worker to present a picture of the problem being faced. The counselor, who may be a fully trained social worker, psychologist, or psychiatrist, or a mental health professional from some other discipline, then makes a tentative diagnosis or determination of the focus of the problem. It is then the job of the employee assistance counselor to find a place to send the worker.

Individual mental health professionals and treatment facilities are retained by the organization. A contract is usually required in which the individual or organization accepts certain third-party payments or very specific fees that are frequently much less than the common fee charges for such services within the community. In some instances, the fees are fully covered, and in others, the officer or the officer's family member must pay a portion of the fee. Ordinarily the list of eligible providers is developed by the Health Maintenance Organization (HMO) or the Preferred Provider Organization (PPO) and referral is limited to this list.

SESSION 1

A. *History of Tobacco*

B. *Costs*
1. $600/yr.—pack per day
2. Cosmetic
3. Interpersonal
4. Model for children
5. Health

C. *Benefits*
1. Tranquilizes or awakens
2. Taste
3. Socialization

D. *Who Smokes?*
1. 32% female, 29% male
2. Heaviest 16–35
3. Father and brother smoked
4. Peers
5. Military
6. Female in modern world

E. *Ways of Quitting*
1. Smokenders and other groups
2. Devices
3. Substitute pipes, cigars, smokeless
4. Nicorette and other chemicals/drugs
5. Behavior Modification
6. Hypnosis
7. Cold Turkey—Self-efficacy

F. *Committing Cold Turkey*
1. Accept it as desired habit—not addiction
2. Choose reason to quit
3. Choose to quit and forgo habit
4. Announce
5. Destroy all smoking materials
6. Prepare for life without the habit
7. Get teeth cleaned—tell dentist

G. *Possible Effects*
1. Not everyone
2. Most who do—mild
   a. Craving for habit
   b. Restlessness
   c. Irritability
   d. Some increase in appetite
   e. Lower blood pressure
   f. Lower heart rate

H. *Aids*
1. Danger of denying self-efficacy
2. Stress card for curiosity
3. Stress tape for craving/irritability or restlessness
4. Family support
5. Group follow-up

I. *To Continue in Group*
1. Give up today or next week
2. If not—don't come back

FIGURE 9.2   Outline for the Presentation of a Smoking Cessation Clinic

Some departments establish their own referral systems using their staff or consulting psychologist to screen and develop a referral network. This process involves obtaining a directory of social services for the community, lists of HMO and PPO facilities available in the community, and lists of individual practitioners who provide the kind of mental health services likely to be needed by officers and their families.

To develop a meaningful referral list, it can be helpful to send out a questionnaire to all the potential providers, requesting basic information. Figure 9.3 presents the kind of evaluation form that might be used to develop preliminary information.

PROVIDER NAME _____ THIS DATE _____

ADDRESS _____

_____ TELEPHONE _____

SERVICES AVAILABLE (check)

____ Crisis Consultation   ____ Individual Psychotherapy

____ Marital Counseling   ____ Grief Counseling

____ Alcohol or Drug Counseling

____ Emergency Services (nights, weekends)

____ Psychiatric Consultation

____ Psychological Testing: ____ Children   ____ Adolescents   ____ Adults

STAFF (number)

____ Mental Health Counselors   ____ Psychiatrists

____ Psychologists   ____ Social Workers

Other: _____

FEES

$_____ per hour. Other: _____

Do you accept?   ____ Health Insurance   ____ Medicare

Would you be interested in exploring a Preferred Provider arrangement? _____

SPECIAL SKILLS

Have any of your staff been specially trained in (check):

____ Working with police officers or other public safety personnel

____ Disaster counseling

____ Hostage negotiation   ____ Critical incident counseling

FURTHER CONTACT

Would you be interested in our contacting you to further possible referrals?

____ Yes   ____ No

If yes, person we may call _____

FIGURE 9.3   Employee Assistance Program Provider Evaluation Form

From this list, the staff or consulting psychologist can arrange visits to evaluate the facility and determine how referrals should be made and whether the individual or the organization can be useful to those in need of such services. The psychologist may then wish to offer some brief training to the mental health professionals who show an interest in providing services to law enforcement officers. Part of this interaction can be arranging for the professionals to spend some time riding in patrol cars so they can learn about the police officer's job.

A psychologist who intends to do a thorough and continually effective job in establishing a referral system, should try to follow up any referrals, not only with the organization, but with the individual officer or family member who has received services. When enough data are collected, it should be possible for the psychologist to match the professional evaluation of services provided by the individual or the organization rendering treatment with what the patients themselves say about the quality and helpfulness of that treatment.

Although there are clear financial and operational advantages to using an external referral system, there are some specific problems. An individual who seeks service ordinarily does best when the person they tell their story to is the person rendering the treatment. This is impossible in any employee assistance program. The clients are going to tell their story to the employment counselor. They'll tell their story to an intake worker at the institution or facility that offers the treatment, and they'll probably tell their story a third time to the individual assigned to do the assessment. They may tell their story a fourth time to the individual assigned to provide treatment. Such repetitious delays are not in the best interests of an individual who is frightened, stressed, and seeking sanctuary and support (Blau, 1988).

Many facilities which provide mental health services for law enforcement officers have emphasized their own preferred services rather than evaluating the needs of the individual patient. These organizations focus on what they preconceive to be the significant problems of police officers (alcohol and drug abuse, post-traumatic stress difficulties, depression, adolescent rebellion, and so forth). This is a negative aspect of managed care. The idea that there is a reliable and valid picture of the problems that exist among police and that these problems are fairly universal is unfortunate as well as invalid. The best mental health treatment and intervention takes full cognizance of individual differences, and managed care systems are not likely to do this.

The interest in providing mental health services, particularly on an inpatient basis, for law enforcement officers, has been growing in recent years. The following descriptions of several well-known programs indicate how this treatment option is being developed:

InterPhase 911, 23120 Sandalfoot Plaza Dr., Boca Raton, FL 33428. (800) 728-3267.

This is one of the older programs and is specifically dedicated to law enforcement officers. It has both residential and outpatient facilities. It is modeled after the Seafield Center in West Hampton Beach in Massachusetts. It has been designed to provide effective specialized therapy for the rehabilitation of law enforcement officers and their families who are suffering from alcoholism and other substance abuse. Program services include medical evaluation, medically supervised detoxification, psychological testing, individualized treatment plans, group/individual therapy, stress analysis and management, education, nutrition and wellness programs, family programs, continuing care, and support group activity. This organization is accredited by the Joint Commission on Accreditation of Health Care Organizations. There is a primary emphasis on stress-related substance abuse.

CENTURION ARC. 8614 Harrison Bay Road, Harrison, TN 37341. (800) 233-3737.

This group describes itself as the first program of its kind specifically designed to assist law enforcement officers and their families in coping with the stress of law enforcement. They indicate that they are prepared to respond to the problems of police stress that result in alcohol and drug abuse, financial problems, insomnia, depression, obesity, physical illness, stress reactions to shootings and other traumatic incidents, flashbacks, marital and family problems, divorce, burnout, sexual dysfunction, deteriorating job performance, aggressiveness, and suicidal risk. They try to respond to the needs of law enforcement officers by providing each participant with a clinically trained counselor who has personally experienced the stresses of law enforcement. The program includes complete medical evaluation, stress management training, biofeedback, nutrition counseling, education about stress, alcohol and drug abuse treatment, trauma groups, death and bereavement groups, depression groups, post-traumatic stress disorder groups, family groups, referral for financial counseling, Parent Effectiveness Training, and recreation and exercise therapy.

CPC BREA CANYON HOSPITAL. 875 North Brea Boulevard, Brea, CA 92621-6299. (714) 529-4000.

This is a psychiatric hospital accredited by the Joint Commission on Accreditation of Health Care Organizations. Founded in 1990, it is a 150-bed multiservice psychiatric hospital. Primarily focusing on alcohol-dependent peace officers, the hospital is staffed to treat dual-diagnosed patients who may be suffering post-traumatic stress disorder and other psychiatric diagnoses that may or may not involve substance abuse. They stress the importance of continuing recovery through self-help groups following hospitalization. A family program is provided. The program features both day care and inpatient services. They provide an exclusive physical environment that is occupied by police people and their families. Services include medical evaluation, individualized treatment plans, occupational activities therapy, stress management, medically supervised detoxification, chemical dependency treatment, education, nutrition and wellness programs, support group activity, specialized family programs, and one year of continuing follow-up care.

THE GUARDIAN CARE PROGRAM. Care Unit Hospital of Ft. Worth, 1066 West Magnolia, Ft. Worth, TX 76104. (817) 336-2828.

This traditional psychiatric hospital has a special program with a full range of psychological and psychiatric services in evaluation, treatment, and continuing care consultation for chemical dependency, acute and chronic stress, post-traumatic stress, and other psychiatric problem areas. The program is designed and managed by peace officers and police-related professionals, especially for public protection clients. There is a strong emphasis on spirituality as well as traditional mental health services.

These programs are typical of the kinds of facilities that seem to be springing up all over the United States to provide inpatient and outpatient services for employee assistance referrals of police officers. The degree of effectiveness of such programs is probably best determined by psychologists in the law enforcement community who make referrals and then conduct follow-up evaluations. It is quite likely that every police psychologist will to a larger or lesser extent make referrals of this sort.

PART FOUR

Consultation and Operational Assistance

CHAPTER TEN

Direct Operational Assistance

$\mathbf{A}$ll the various services that professional psychologists can provide to law enforcement agencies help to support the police mission. This help has traditionally been relatively indirect. Such psychological activities as recruit selection, fitness-for-duty evaluations, assessment of officers for special teams, counseling for police officers and their families, and training and research all contribute to the enhancement of the police mission. In recent years, as law enforcement officers and executives have come to know psychologists and have gained respect and confidence for psychological methods, there has been a growing tendency to request *operational assistance*. This has to do with the provision of psychological information or psychological service in *direct* support of the police mission.

The police mission is essentially to prevent crime, to solve crimes that have occurred, to pursue the probable perpetrators of crimes, to arrest these perpetrators and deliver them for processing by the criminal court system.

Traditionally, the policing job is never quite done. Pursuit of criminals is always, unfortunately, far behind the apprehension, conviction, and punishment of these perpetrators. One of the most demanding aspects of the police officer's job is "closing cases." Almost every working police officer is overloaded with demands to curb crime and to catch criminals.

The traditional approach to good police work is standard procedure. Police are trained to identify probable crime situations, to intervene where appropriate, and to begin the investigative procedure after a crime has occurred. Every trained police officer understands what must be done by the first responder to a crime scene. Skillful investigators know how to go about collecting information, interviewing witnesses, collating information, and closing an investigation. The key to crime solution is frequently information that can be provided by a confidential informant. Such information is weighed and judged by police officers, and is sometimes extremely helpful in the solution of crimes and the apprehension of perpetrators. Investigative officers are always ready and willing to receive information that might be useful in the pursuit of their goals.

HELP FROM BEHAVIORAL SCIENTISTS

The idea of behavioral scientists helping police to catch criminals is hardly a new one. A. Conan Doyle, in his Sherlock Holmes stories, developed and expanded the idea of an individual providing scientific help to police to augment their traditional methods of solving crimes and apprehending criminals (Doyle, 1987). Although much of gentleman detective Sherlock Holmes's fictional activity had to do with the chemistry and etiology of substances, there were frequent references to the behavioral characteristics of perpetrators that resulted in apprehension.

MacDonald and Michaud (1987) have developed a series of procedures to help police officers interrogate suspects as well as a typology of criminals to help in understanding their motivation. Baker (1992) has presented a systematic approach to the classification of criminals in an effort to aid in their apprehension. Bennett and Hess (1991) have proposed a cognitive interview procedure to enhance witness recollections during interrogation. Fisher (1990) has described a training module to help school resource officers identify risk factors for adolescent suicide, so that intervention procedures may be instituted. Blau and Blau (1988) have evaluated the capabilities of children as witnesses to crimes, and how they may be best interviewed.

Sometimes behavioral science research detracts from rather than adds to the methods and techniques for forwarding the police mission. Kassin and McNall (1991) studied the common interrogation technique of *maximization* and *minimization* during criminal interrogations. It is common for police officers to exaggerate the strength of the evidence and the magnitude of the charges in a case to encourage a subject to confess. The second technique mitigates the crime and plays down the seriousness of the offense in an attempt to get the subject to admit involvement. Kassin and McNall studied five situations where these techniques were used, and they found serious question as to whether minimization and maximization are useful methods of interrogation.

PSYCHOLOGICAL INTERVIEWS

A relatively new utilization of professional psychologists is in the interviewing and evaluation of suspects immediately following serious crimes. Knowing that in capital crime cases as well as other serious offenses, the insanity defense may become part of the judicial procedure, some police departments have arranged for the arrested suspect to be interviewed and evaluated by a clinical psychologist immediately after apprehension. In most instances, the issue of the sanity of the perpetrator is taken into consideration months or even years after the criminal act. By having the individual evaluated shortly after the act, a record is made of the mental state of the individual relatively proximate to the commission of the crime. The following represents such a clinical interview:

TO: Detective Ned Jones
FROM: Inspector T. Bear
SUBJECT: Interrogation of Mr. R. L. Brown

On 8 January 1988, I observed your interrogation of Mr. R. L. Brown. My observation began at 7:28 P.M. and ended at approximately 8:15 P.M.

Throughout your interrogation I evaluated the psychological status of Mr. Brown based on his verbalizations, his response to your questions, the questions he asked you, and his general demeanor throughout the interview.

EVALUATION

Mr. Brown was oriented as to time, place, and person. He was able to give his birth date and his age appropriately. His emotional affect was appropriate for the circumstances. He was cautious but responsive.

I would evaluate his intellectual level as in the low average range. This is based on his verbalizations, and his responses to your questions.

Neuropsychologically, I found that his communication was characterized by accurate receptive and expressive speech. He was cooperative. Although quiet and evasive, denying all knowledge of the charges against him, he responded appropriately. He later, in your interview, admitted to some things that he had previously denied. He seemed well in control of his thoughts and ideas and was very self-protective. While you were out of the room on several occasions, he was observed on the TV monitor looking in the files that were on your side of the table. On one occasion, he examined the room, particularly the windows, as though he were investigating options that were open to him.

During the initial part of the interview, he insisted that his name was "Eddie." Later on, he admitted that his identity was Bobby Lee Brown. He was able to identify people that he knew from photographs that you showed him.

He denied carrying a gun. At one point, he insisted that the investigator was intimidating him when the questioning became close and specific. He claims that his girlfriend lied in her statements to you.

Mr. Brown exhibited no odd, peculiar or strange behavior. There were no signs of hallucinations or delusions.

All of my observations suggest that at the time of my evaluation, Mr. R. L. Brown did not suffer from any insanity, lunacy, imbecility, or other incompetence.

The psychologist's letter to the detective was made part of the criminal case folder to be used in the event that the insanity pleading was raised.

NEUROPSYCHOLOGICAL SKILLS

Many of the opportunities for the clinical psychologist to be of assistance in police activity tend to be serendipitous. The psychologist happens to be there and is approached by an officer who has worked with the psychologist. Their mutual interest in psychological matters leads to the opportunity to use psychological skills or information. In the following case, the use of a police psychologist and neuropsychological information helped to resolve a homicide investigation:

A CASE OF HOMICIDE

FACTS OF THE CASE

At 5:15 P.M. in the afternoon, the dispatcher received a telephone call from a man stating that his roommate had shot himself. The homicide team responded. The roommate, a 32-year-old man, stated that he was in the bathroom when he heard a shot. He went into his friend's room and found the roommate had shot himself in the back of the head. He saw some movement and immediately called an ambulance.

The ambulance responded as did the homicide team. The scene was a two-bedroom apartment in a midtown adult apartment complex. Investigating officers found a 61-year-old male showing some vital signs, with a .38 caliber Charter Arms pistol lying under his left hand. The victim was lying on his bed, face upward. There was a massive wound in the right occipital area of the head, and a considerable amount of blood staining the pillow and bedclothes. There was very little blood spatter.

The victim was removed to the emergency room where he was put on life-support systems but only lived until approximately 9:15 P.M.

On interrogation, the roommate stated that he had been living with the older man, the victim, for several years. He states that the older man had been somewhat despondent because his mother, an 82-year-old woman, was deteriorating rapidly in a nursing home at some distance from the city where the homicide occurred. He stated that he had been having difficulties with his roommate, because of his roommate's change of behavior. The roommate had become "sloppy," unmindful of the needs of other people, depressed, and unwilling to be cooperative. He was also argumentative. The younger man had threatened to leave, and indeed indicated that he was planning on moving out in the forthcoming week.

THE VICTIM

The victim, a 61-year-old retired man, had made an appearance at the local hospital some three times in the previous 2 weeks complaining of chest pains and difficulty breathing.

Interrogation of neighbors indicated in general that these two men were isolates, drank a good deal of beer, sat out on their patio and smoked many cigarettes, and left the grounds of the apartment only to go to local stores to get more supplies of beer and cigarettes. No one in the complex knew the pair very well.

THE INVESTIGATION

The crime scene was cordoned off in the usual and customary manner, and all the necessary collection procedures were followed. A piece of a lead bullet, of approximately 30 grains was found in the folds of the pillow among the blood stains. Another gun, a .25 caliber weapon, was found in the apartment, as well as two boxes of shells for a .38 caliber pistol. Five bullets were missing from the two boxes. The gun itself had been fired once, and there were four remaining live rounds in the chambers. The ammunition was old (approximately 1955) and of German manufacture. Speculative causes of death that were considered from the beginning included:

1. The wound was self-inflicted by the victim.
2. The wound was inflicted by the roommate who then claimed the victim committed suicide.

A decision to label this event a self-inflicted wound was made difficult by the unusual condition of the victim. At first it was thought that there was an entry wound in the mouth, and the large area of destroyed brain casing in the occipital lobe was an exit wound. Once the victim was in the hospital it became clear that there was no wound in the mouth, and that the blood had drained from the sinuses as a result of the wound. The entry wound was just to the right of the midline in the lower occipital lobe. X ray indicated that the remaining portion of the bullet was lodged in the left supraorbital area over the left eye. CT scan indicated only one track for the bullet, leaving many questions as to where the large fragment that was found in the pillow might have originated.

In reviewing the scenario of a self-inflicted wound, it was clear that the victim, very thin, very tall and lanky, could have easily reached to the area in which the entry wound occurred in the rear of the head. One scenario was that he was lying on the bed face up, head turned to the left, pistol in the right hand, perhaps crying, and in making the decision to kill himself, brought the pistol to his head, which would bring it to a natural angle at the point where the actual entry occurred. The hypothesis that suggested the possibility of the roommate having killed the victim would require the concept that the roommate came upon the victim sleeping, placed the muzzle of the gun to the rear of the victim's skull and fired. This would not account for the gun being found under the victim's left hand.

Because the victim was still alive when investigating officers arrived, the hypothesis emerged that the victim did indeed shoot himself, remained alive, rose up in response to his self-inflicted wound, dropped the gun to his left side, and then fell back with his left hand on top of it.

AUTOPSY

In the autopsy performed the following morning, it was found that the shell had struck the occipital bone, which "sheared off" a small portion of the bullet. This was the object found on the pillow. The remainder of the bullet entered the occipital lobe and moved laterally to the left, striking the interior of the skull at a point behind the left ear, and then ricocheting around the edge of the interior of the skull until it came to a rest in the supraorbital area. This could account for why the patient remained alive several hours after the massive gunshot wound—the bullet actually destroyed very little cortical or subcortical tissue and did its main damage in the occipital lobe with massive bleeding.

During the autopsy, the police psychologist/neuropsychologist noted some neuropathic indications as the medical examiner sliced through the frontal lobe of the brain. When asked about this, the medical examiner indicated that the tissue abnormality indicated a stroke that had occurred within the past two or three years in the left frontal area.

NEUROPSYCHOLOGICAL CONTRIBUTION

The neuropsychologist provided the investigating officers with a review of the likely sequelae after a stroke affecting the left frontal areas. Impulsiveness, poor planning ability, disregard for usual and customary hygiene, and a tendency to be somewhat irrationally argumentative and uncooperative were the behaviors brought to their attention. This matched so closely with the roommate's description of the behavior of the victim that it seemed clear significant personality changes had taken place, corroborating the roommate's description of the events leading up to the suicide.

Further investigation indicated that the following conditions preceded the homicide:

1. The victim had been significantly depressed, more so during the 3 weeks previous to his death.
2. The victim was lamenting the anticipated loss of his mother.
3. The victim had come into significant conflict with a roommate and possibly a lover of long standing.
4. The threat by the roommate to leave was perceived as another desertion.
5. The victim had acted perturbed during the previous several weeks.
6. It appeared that he felt that "no one cared" and he had no social support system except for the roommate.

From a psychological and neuropsychological point of view, the evidence clearly supported the decision to view this as a self-inflicted wound and a suicide. Subsequent laboratory tests and further interrogation of all parties supported this conclusion.

Some of the assistance that psychologists provide to law enforcement agencies has become more formalized. Chapters Eleven through Fifteen present in some detail the ways in which psychologists offer operational assistance.

CHAPTER ELEVEN

Hostage Negotiation

Since the 1970s, hostage taking has increased significantly. This in turn means that the probability that a police officer will be involved in a hostage-taking situation during his or her 20-year or more career also has increased.

A hostage situation is defined as one in which a person or persons seize another person or persons and hold the individual or the group prisoner. They usually follow this act by making demands and creating a barricade situation to defy law enforcement authorities.

At one time, direct or indirect assault on the barricade was the primary police method of response, but in recent years, negotiation has been the procedure of choice. The hostage negotiator is a person who mediates between the hostage taker or a barricaded subject and law enforcement officials. In current usage, the negotiator does not have the power of decision. The negotiator's role is to buy time (Gallagher & Bemsberg, 1978).

Certain quite well known background characteristics of hostage takers suggest the stressors that may operate to bring about a hostage-taking situation. It has been suggested that male dominance is associated with hostage taking. Individuals who take hostages often lack family or social support systems. Most hostage takers choose to develop a confrontation with law enforcement (Fuselier, VanZandt, & Lanceley, 1991).

Although hostage-taking situations vary immensely, traditional law enforcement response has included a number of fairly standard procedures and styles:

1. There must be sufficient personnel to command the scene.
2. A chain of command is established.
3. Early efforts are made to gain media cooperation.
4. A communication network is set up.
5. Charts and lists are created to identify personnel easily.
6. A staff center or action center is established nearby the hostage scene but secure from the perpetrator.
7. Efforts are made to identify the hostages.

8. The negotiator does not meet the perpetrator's request to bring relatives or friends to the scene.
9. Every effort is made to avoid a show of force.
10. The negotiator will not negotiate for weapons, alcohol, narcotics, or anything that is likely to increase the threat to the hostages.
11. Location of the negotiation team is not shifted.
12. Every effort is made to communicate instructions to the hostages to ensure their safety.
13. As much information as possible should be obtained from the perpetrator.
14. Detailed information about the hostage site and surrounding areas must be obtained as quickly as possible.
15. The negotiator should be an individual with interpersonal sensitivity, tolerance of ambiguity, low authoritarianism, interviewing experience, past experience in stressful situations, excellent verbal skills, flexibility under pressure, and a strong belief in the power of verbal persuasion, bargaining, compromise, and conciliation.
16. The use of force and specialized teams must be a part of the plan but should be implemented only as a last resort (Myron & Goldstein, 1979).

Russell and Beigel (1982) have defined six types of hostage situations:

1. Criminals who plan to use hostages to ensure escape or get ransom money.
2. Criminals who do not plan to take hostages, but who become trapped inside an establishment they intend to rob. They are blocked in their escape, and they seize hostages in order to get out. This is the most common hostage situation.
3. Hostage situations in jail or prison riots.
4. A mentally ill person who seizes hostages in response to disturbed thinking.
5. Normal people under severe stress who may be intoxicated. Sometimes a parent under these circumstances may take a child hostage in a custody dispute.
6. Hostages taken by political terrorists, usually to get publicity for their cause, to gain revenge, or to force a release of political prisoners. Generally, these situations can't be readily handled by local police. The likelihood of killings during these situations is much higher than in others.

A recent innovation is hostage situation training for first responders (patrol officers who are first on the scene of a crime). Ordinarily, first responders do not participate in hostage situations. The reality of their being first on the scene has resulted in attention to this issue. Noesner and Dolan (1992) have proposed guidelines for the training of first-response officers. These include the following:

1. The officer should ensure his or her safety at all times.
2. Any contact with subjects should be used to calm and distract them and to gain information and time.
3. The first responder should avoid soliciting demands.
4. The first responder should listen carefully for clues regarding the emotional state of the subjects.
5. At all costs, the first responder should avoid bargaining or making concessions.
6. The first responder is encouraged to reassure subjects that the police will not storm the building.
7. The first responder should not offer any of the subjects anything, nor should the first responder give orders to the subjects.
8. If discussion takes place, the first responding officer should minimize the seriousness of the subject's crime.
9. No reference should be made to anyone in the building as "hostages."
10. Under no circumstances should the first responder try any kind of "trick" or be dishonest with the hostage taker.
11. The first responder should be taught never to say "no" to a demand. By the same token, the first responder should be cautious with any "yes" response.
12. The first responder should be cautioned not to be creative by making suggestions.
13. Under no circumstances should outsiders or family members be allowed to talk to the subjects.
14. The first responder is taught that an officer never exchanges himself or herself or anyone else for a hostage.
15. The officer should be trained to ask subjects if their intention is suicide if this seems to be the case. If the answer is yes, the first responder should be positive and encouraging that help is on the way and things can be worked out.
16. Under no circumstances should the first responder become vulnerable to injury by making personal contact or exposing self to the suspect.

Changes in the way hostage situations have been approached by police since mid-century have been the result of changes in the *outcome focus*. Originally, the primary goal was to resolve the hostage situation, even if it meant a pitched battle with the perpetrators. Modern developments include the awareness of the value of human life, not only of the hostages, but of bystanders, police officers, the hostages, and even the perpetrators. Litigation issues have become important because the circumstances surrounding hostage-taking situations can often lead to civil liability for the police department, the citizens who own the property, or the community itself.

Of equal importance currently is the attitude of the media. Public opinion, as expressed by the media, whether or not this is a reliable and valid expression, focuses on police activity that results in injury or death. Media attention is inevitable, and modern law enforcement agencies try to help media personnel understand the complexity and unavoidable dangers in hostage situations.

PSYCHOLOGICAL ASSISTANCE

McMains (1988) suggests that there are three roles for psychologists in hostage negotiations. The first role is that of the *professional*. As a professional, the psychologist brings to hostage negotiations a wealth of applicable behavioral science information. When providing this information as well as consultation to police within the scope of the professional role, the psychologist is bound by certain ethics and legal ties to certain standards.

The second role for the psychologist is as a *consultant*. In this role, the psychologist may help design and implement selection procedures and a training program for negotiators, including training materials and useful exercises. In this role, the psychologist provides special expertise and knowledge to administrators and supervisors as well as trainers. The psychologist does not interact with negotiators or commanders.

In the third role, the psychologist may be a *participant/observer*. To function in such a role, the psychologist must have a clearly defined attitude toward power and authority. He or she is not in control of the hostage incident and must recognize the authority of law enforcement personnel. Establishing trust between the psychologist and hostage-negotiation commanders and officer-negotiators is important. Being on call 24 hours a day is a necessary commitment for psychologists who work as participants in hostage-negotiation teams.

Psychological Aspects of the Hostage Situation.

Psychologists can contribute to the work of the hostage-negotiation team by clarifying the nature and attitudes of the hostage taker and the psychological aspects of the hostage situation. Psychologists familiar with the literature on hostage situations are aware that the hostage taker is often holding someone with whom he has a romantic involvement. It may be a family member, or it may be someone met on a casual basis. Psychological research suggests that hostage takers usually have relatively poor family or social support systems. Psychologists should know that in certain situations, subjects may be trying to arrange a "cop suicide." In such situations, the psychologist can help the negotiators to understand that getting the perpetrator to verbalize the intent to commit suicide is the first step in defusing the situation (Fuselier et al., 1991).

It is of particular importance that the law enforcement personnel know something about the terrorist hostage taker. Indications are that line police officers are likely to be first responders in terrorist hostage situations because such situations are becoming increasingly common in the United States.

Most of the early terrorist organizations were trained and based outside of the United States. The teams were essentially leftist groups. Each team had a leader (male or female) usually between 25 and 40 years of age, from a middle-class, urban/sophisticated background. This individual tended to be a perfectionist and was often college educated. More recently, terrorists have been representative of radical fundimentalist groups.

Most terrorist teams included one or more opportunists or criminals, usually between 20 to 30 years of age. Such individuals generally demonstrated strong, aggressive personalities and histories of criminal activity.

The team frequently had a third group who were "followers." They were young, 18 to 25, middle-class, male or female participants, dedicated to a cause, but with relatively weak personalities.

In recent years, fewer criminal opportunists have been members of the team. The skills of the criminal opportunist (driving, obtaining materials, planting bombs, and so forth) currently appear to be handled by the follower, who now tends to be from a lower-class family with limited dedication. Followers may or may not have been active in criminal street gangs in their own countries before they joined the terrorist team.

Some terrorists are at the opposite end of the political spectrum from the original left-wing terrorists. Right-wing terrorist groups often have a college-educated leader, 30 to 50 years of age, urban/sophisticated, and often a well-trained perfectionist. This leader tends to have a strong, controlled, paranoid personality. Criminal elements are often included in the right-wing gang. Followers in the right-wing terrorist group tend to be white, male, Protestant, 20 to 50 years of age, of lower-middle-class and lower-class origins, and unsophisticated. They often share with the leader paranoid personality traits (Strentz, 1988).

For a psychologist to be a useful consultant to a hostage-negotiation team, an understanding of the pertinent literature is critical. Careful study and attendance at workshops is a preliminary to the psychologist's making a significant contribution in this important area of police operation.

Most hostage-negotiation teams spend a great deal of time in training. Most supervisors of such teams are more than willing to receive psychological information that might be helpful to members in performing their complex duties.

The psychologist can develop and organize some information that can be useful to the hostage-negotiation team. Figure 11.1 presents an outline of a training program for hostage-negotiation team members.

The material in this outline is taught to hostage negotiation team members in either three $1^1/_2$ hour sessions, or one 4-hour session. Between each of the major segments of the workshop, time is allowed for questions and exchange of experiences among the hostage negotiators. After a hostage incident, the entire negotiating team should be debriefed by the psychologist and any difficulties that were experienced should be worked out.

Psychologists have studied characteristics of hostage negotiators in an effort to develop selection models, and to determine efficacy of methods. Getty and Elam (1988) used the Minnesota Multiphasic Personality Inventory and the California Personality Inventory with experienced hostage negotiators and a control sample of police officers not trained in hostage negotiation. They found that the successful, experienced hostage negotiators were significantly higher than the sample of police officers in verbal fluency, self-image, reasoning ability, and sensitivity to others.

Borum (1988) compared trained hostage negotiators with mental health professionals and untrained deputy sheriffs. The groups were tested on multiple-choice scenarios involving decisions about the most effective strategy to use with a particular hostage taker. The results of the study showed that hostage negotiators scored more correct responses than either the professionals or the line officers. The results suggest that skill and expertise in the mental health professions do not guarantee a transfer of such skill to hostage negotiations with mentally disturbed hostage takers. Although not tested, it would seem probable that mental health professionals with law enforcement experience or law enforcement officers with mental health training would be the most effective negotiators when dealing with a mentally disturbed hostage taker.

There is relatively little support for the idea that psychologists should serve as hostage negotiators. Ebert (1986) has suggested that psychologists should serve as the primary negotiators. He proposes that neither psychologists nor police officers will be successful negotiators without specialized training in hostage crisis management. He does state that psychologists have many of the desirable qualifications of a good negotiator.

Myron and Goldstein (1979) propose that the hostage negotiator should be thoroughly aware of certain negotiation strategies that have proven to be effective in the past. The following should be considered in all hostage situations:

1. The negotiator should be sure that all parties avoid precipitous acts.
2. The role of the negotiator is to establish a problem-solving context and a negotiating climate.

I. *WHO TAKES HOSTAGES?*

  A. *The Political Terrorist*

    1. To get publicity (primary goal).

    2. To show public the government is helpless.

    3. To cause the government to overreact.

    4. To gain release of other terrorists.

    5. To create civil discontent.

  B. *The Criminal*

    1. Usually trapped while committing a crime.

    2. Hostage taken to ensure criminal's safety, escape, or additional money.

  C. *The Mentally Disturbed Person*

    1. This accounts for 52% of all hostage situations.

    2. Paranoias, depressions, character disorders, inadequate personalities, drug and alcohol abuse are most common conditions.

    3. Hardest to handle.

    4. May be responding to hallucinations or delusions.

    5. May be trying to prove adequacy to someone.

    6. May be suicidal (intentional or unintended).

  D. *Prisoners*

    1. Usually seek media exposure.

    2. Want bargaining power.

    3. Standard negotiating techniques effective as long as a prolonged incident is tolerable to participants.

II. *HOW CAN PSYCHOLOGICAL SERVICES BE BEST USED?*

  A. *Selection of Negotiators*

    1. Good social skills.

    2. Able to present a pleasant, authentic social presence.

    3. Intelligent.

    4. Able manipulator.

    5. Excellent verbal skills.

  B. *Providing Information to Help Guide Negotiation Strategy*

    1. The apparent versus possible hidden motivation of the hostage taker.

    2. The personality of the hostage taker.

    3. Identifying and helping to deal with Stockholm Syndrome.

    4. Tracking the mental status of the hostage taker and victims.

  C. *Dealing with the Aftereffects of the Situation*

    1. Hostages.

      a. Achieve catharsis.

      b. Regain sense of mastery.

FIGURE 11.1. A Training Module Outline for Teaching Psychological Factors in Hostage Negotiations

    c. Reassess values.

    d. Reestablish close attachments.

    e. Some have no apparent aftereffects—those with mostly rural, simple values.

  2. Negotiators.

    a. Varies with degree of trauma, length of incident, who are involved, stability of negotiator, number of stress factors.

    b. Stress inoculation training helpful.

    c. Stress reduction training following the incident.

    d. Post-traumatic stress counseling where indicated.

III. *STRESS*

  A. *The Nature of Stress*

    1. Pressures brought about by change or unusual situations.

    2. Some is natural.

    3. Can seriously affect health, job, family.

    4. Common sources:

      a. Personal loss.

      b. Illness or injury.

      c. Change in job, income, lifestyle.

      d. New family members.

      e. Family members leaving.

      f. Changes in love attachments.

      g. Retirement.

  B. *The Effects of Stress*

    1. Vague fears.

    2. Repetitive or prolonged anxiety.

    3. Depression—signs:

      a. Fatigue.

      b. Sleeplessness.

      c. Boredom or restlessness.

      d. Lack of interest in food, sex, recreation.

      e. Feelings of worthlessness or hopelessness.

      f. Normal response for short periods.

    4. Traumatic stress reactions may include:

      a. Nightmares.

      b. Startle reactions.

      c. Suspiciousness.

      d. Night terrors—reexperiencing.

FIGURE 11.1. *(continued)*

3. In addition, the negotiator should be prepared for and willing to enter into an interaction of compromise with the hostage taker.
4. The negotiator should ensure that all parties avoid forcing or coercion.
5. The negotiator or those being advised should avoid a soft-bargaining negotiation strategy.
6. The negotiator should be flexible.
7. When the hostage taker is a professional criminal, the negotiator should emphasize rational techniques, problem solving, and compromise.
8. With the disturbed perpetrator, emotional techniques such as reflection of feeling should be utilized.

Myron and Goldstein further insist that the primary task of the negotiator is to calm the perpetrator. Calming techniques recommended include:

1. The negotiator should show understanding.
2. The negotiator should display calmness to the perpetrator.
3. The perpetrator should be encouraged to ventilate.
4. The agitated perpetrator should be distracted from the source of concern.
5. Everybody who makes contact, visually or audibly, with the perpetrator should avoid aggressive stances.
6. Nothing should be done to provoke the perpetrator.
7. Delay is of the essence, and the negotiator should stall for time. This should be understood by all parties, especially the tactical weapons team.
8. Being open and self-disclosing is a useful style for the negotiator.
9. The negotiator should not hesitate to show high levels of warmth.
10. Everything possible should be done to help the perpetrator save face during the negotiations. Nothing should be done to "talk down" to the perpetrator. Under no circumstances should the negotiator criticize the perpetrator.

Myron and Goldstein's volume represents an excellent training manual for hostage negotiators or negotiation team trainers.

Dealing with the Aftermath

After a hostage situation has been resolved, residuals may require the services of the clinical psychologist. Most of the sequelae involve post-traumatic stress. Those who most frequently require psychological aid include:

1. The survivors, partners, and friends of officers killed or wounded during the confrontation.
2. Officers who have been wounded or who have been taken hostage.
3. Civilians who have been taken hostage, or who have in some way participated in the event.
4. Relatives, friends, and associates of hostages who have been killed or injured.
5. Hostage-negotiation team members or SWAT team members who have in some way been traumatized by the events.

The appropriate procedures to deal with traumatic events have been addressed in detail in Chapter Seven. Immediate counseling opportunity at the scene or shortly thereafter is critical. Follow-up with those who have been counseled immediately after the hostage event may be necessary.

A peculiarity that sometimes occurs during a hostage situation is the "Stockholm Syndrome." First identified after a hostage situation that took place in Sweden, this description refers to a possible reaction of hostages after an extended hostage experience. Spending a considerable amount of time with the hostage takers sometimes leads the hostages to begin to identify with the individual perpetrators, the perpetrator's ideals or goals, or the hostage taker's position as an underdog. Many are surprised by this kind of identification reaction. Psychologists understand "identification with the aggressor" and other psychodynamic processes whereby an individual in a stressful situation may perceive things in an inappropriate or irrational manner. Victims of the Stockholm Syndrome usually require both immediate and long-range professional help to resolve their emotional conflict and discomfort.

Psychologists who are either consultants to or part of the hostage-negotiation team may or may not be in the best position to offer services after resolution of the hostage situation. Most hostage-negotiation teams go through debriefing immediately after the hostage situation is resolved. This often includes counseling by the department psychologist. Post-traumatic counseling for those suffering the residuals of a hostage-negotiation situation must be planned well in advance. To attempt to provide such services in the aftermath of such a complex illegal event on an *ad lib* basis is unwise. Police business takes place after such a situation. People are arrested, witnesses are questioned, statements must be signed, and other logistical considerations will take place. Ordinarily, counseling has a low priority at this time. The staff psychologist or the psychological consultant should work closely with the hostage-negotiation team and the police executives in charge of such incidents before they occur. Planning for post-traumatic stress counseling well in advance, with the approval of police executives, is a worthy effort and should be implemented by police psychologists in every department.

CHAPTER TWELVE

Psychological Profiling

This investigative technique is sometimes called *offender profiling* or *psychological criminal profiling*. Reiser (1982c) dates the beginning of the development of this psychological tool to the early 1970s. He indicates that the police psychologist has a unique opportunity for direct involvement in police work and investigation by applying psychological knowledge and experience in a variety of unusual policing circumstances.

Reiser describes psychological profiling as an arcane art in which psychodiagnostic assessment and psychobiography are combined with case evidence and probabilities from similar cases to draw a picture of a likely offender. Suspected personality variables and psychodynamics are inferred from the available evidence and from victim characteristics. Reiser further points out that contrary to hopes and expectations for a scientifically derived investigative tool, psychological profiling is merely an inferential process analogous to a psychological evaluation done with an ordinary client.

Criminal personality profiling as further defined by the Behavioral Science Unit of the Federal Bureau of Investigation at Quantico, Virginia, involves the study of unsolved crimes in an attempt to provide the behavioral and personality characteristics of unidentified offenders (Horn, 1988).

The process is basically a method of helping to identify the perpetrator of a crime based on an analysis of the nature of the offense and the manner in which it was committed. The process attempts to determine aspects of a criminal's personality makeup from the criminal's choice of action before, during, and after the criminal act. The personality information is combined with other pertinent details and physical evidence and then compared with characteristics of known personality types and mental abnormalities. From this, a working description of the offender is developed.

The origins of psychological profiling are subject to conjecture. Even as early as the beginning of the 19th century, there were some descriptions in the literature of such procedures. Efforts to do similar kinds of profiling appeared in the field of criminal anthropology early in the 1800s.

There is no question that criminal profilers have been influenced by the work of Arthur Conan Doyle who endowed his detective Sherlock Holmes with a tremendous capacity to understand the personality and habits of criminals from the way they smoked, walked, chose clothing, and behaved in other respects. Some of the behaviors suggested by Doyle's fiction, such as "the criminal returns to the scene of the crime," have been found to have some validity in modern application (Tetem, 1989).

DEVELOPMENT OF PSYCHOLOGICAL PROFILING

The most concentrated efforts to standardize the technique of psychological profiling have been the work of the behavioral science unit and its staff at the FBI Academy. As an outgrowth of this unit's program of instruction in abnormal psychology for its agents, the FBI attempted to assist the law enforcement community in the preparation of psychological profiles in selected unsolved criminal cases. The FBI profilers give credit to the work of the Office of Strategic Services, which employed a psychiatrist to help develop profiles of world leaders during World War II (Ault & Reese, 1980).

Criminal profiling has been productive most frequently in cases in which an offender has demonstrated repeated patterns of the same crime (Douglas, Ressler, Burgess, & Hartman, 1986).

In their original work, the FBI researchers studied serial murderers. They found certain characteristics that defined the *disorganized offender*. This individual was likely to be the first or last born child. The father usually had an unstable work history. The individual was treated with hostility as a child. The perpetrator tended to be sexually inhibited, ignorant, had sexual problems in relation to the mother, and was probably aversive to sexual behavior. Such a person would be described as frightened and confused at the time of the crime, was likely to know the victim, tended to live alone, and was likely to commit the crime in the victim's home.

The FBI research group defined the *organized offender* as an intelligent person in a skilled occupation, likely to think and plan out the crime. Such an individual is likely to be angry and depressed at the time of the murder, is likely to have a precipitating stress, and usually followed reports of the crime in the media. This individual would be likely to change jobs or leave town after committing the murder.

FBI researchers believed that one of the foundations of profiling would be that different offenders in different locations tend to commit similar crimes in similar ways because of similar personalities (Horn, 1988).

APPLICATION

Although there are some differences of opinion, profilers in general agree that, to be appropriate for profiling, the offenses should feature some form of overt sexual activity or severe emotional disturbance on the part of the perpetrator (Tetem, 1989). The most commonly profiled cases are assaults and homicides.

In homicide cases, the profiler must first determine whether the offender is an *organized* or *disorganized* individual. The end result is a composite behavioral sketch of a personality type and not a specific person (Horn, 1988). The work of Ressler and Burgess suggests that a small percentage of criminals may be responsible for a large number of homicides (1985). Such perpetrators are now defined as "serial killers." In homicide cases, the victim is not able to give direct verbal reports of the perpetrator, and the crime scene analysis must speak for the victim.

In sexual assaults such as forcible rape, sexual molestation, and repetitive indecent exposure, the victims are valuable resources in criminal profiling because they have had close contact with the perpetrator. The profiler is able to obtain information about the offender's verbal, physical, and sexual behavior that can be helpful in deducing motive and personality (Horn, 1988).

After developing profiles of serial murderers, the FBI researchers concentrated their attention on the serial rapist. They found that half of rapes are premeditated, and the remainder are impulsive or opportunistic. Their research suggested that the commonest approaches by a rapist have been "the con," "the blitz," or "the surprise." Minimal or no force is used in the majority of instances. About half the victims resisted. The most common reaction by perpetrators to resistance was verbal threat (Hazelwood & Warren, 1990). Hazelwood and Warren (1989) carefully studied 41 serial rapists who had been tried, convicted, and incarcerated. From their interviews, they developed details of the serial rapist's family structure, sexual history, current sexual behaviors, and types of victims chosen. Table 12.1 presents the data developed by Hazelwood and Warren (1989) on the family structure of serial rapists.

Following their work on serial murderers and serial rapists, the FBI investigators developed psychological profiles of "nuisance offenders." These were essentially serious obsessive-compulsive individuals who tended to commit such crimes as repetitive exhibitionism, pyromania (arson), kleptomania, voyeurism, obscene phone calls, "poison pen" letters, and other ritualistic crimes (Reese, 1979).

Profiling research has explored the personalities and methods of a variety of arsonists and bomb setters (Rider, 1980; Douglas et al., 1986). Rider points out the scope of this problem by reporting that a total of 125,513 arrests for arson were made between 1969 and 1978. Approximately 90% of those arrested were males.

Rider further reviews the research on the personality and lifestyle of pathological arsonists and concludes that they demonstrate the following cluster of characteristics:

1. Usually are under 25 years of age.
2. Often are victims of pathological and distressed rearing environments.
3. Most frequently come from a father-absent home.
4. Are mother-dominated.
5. Tend to be academically retarded.
6. Are of slightly below-average intelligence.
7. Are emotionally and psychologically disturbed.
8. Are socially and sexually maladjusted.
9. Are usually unmarried.
10. Are notably insecure.
11. Tend to have histories showing them to be cowardly.

The purpose of profiling is to help catch a criminal. In an unusual proactive application of these procedures, Hagaman, Wells, Blau, and Wells (1987) developed a family homicide profile that could be used to predict such an occurrence, and possibly to prevent the homicide.

Analyzing a series of family homicides, using traditional profiling procedures, these researchers determined that a family homicide is more likely to occur when the following situations arise:

1. Drugs or alcohol are in use at the time of the event.
2. There are cultural pressures for the perpetrator to save face.
3. The perpetrator has made previous threats of suicide.
4. The perpetrator has shown recent deep depression.
5. There has been a recent failed love relationship.
6. The perpetrator has been recently separated from the family unit.
7. The perpetrator has made a series of vengeance threats recently against the family.

Following the study, strategies for preventing family homicide were developed including:

1. Early arrest of perpetrators of family violence or abuse.
2. Identification and recording of repeated incidents of family abuse and requests for help.
3. Court-mandated counseling for repeated offenders.
4. Public education about the danger signs, where help can be obtained, and opportunities for treatment.

A number of social agencies were enlisted in this pro-active program; police officers were trained in the danger signs; and liaison was established

TABLE 12.1   Family Structure of Serial Rapists

	N	Percentage (%)
Assessment of Socioeconomic Level of Subject's Preadult Home (N = 41)		
Advantaged	7	17
Comfortable, average	15	37
Marginal, self-sufficient	11	27
Submarginal	8	20
Variable	—	—
Dominant Parental Figures (N = 40)		
Mother	20	50
Father	16	40
Other	4	10
Quality of Relationship to Mother or Dominant Female Caretaker (N = 39)		
Warm, close	14	36
Variable	12	31
Cold, distant	2	5
Uncaring, indifferent	4	10
Hostile, aggressive	7	18
Quality of Relationship to Father or Dominant Male Caretaker (N = 39)		
Warm, close	7	18
Variable	10	26
Cold, distant	12	31
Uncaring, indifferent	3	8
Hostile, aggressive	7	18
Evidence That Subject Was Physically Abused by Parents/Caretakers (N = 40)		
Yes	15	38
No	25	62
Evidence That Subject Was Psychologically Abused by Parents/Caretakers (N = 41)		
Yes	30	73
No	11	27
Evidence That Subject Was Sexually Abused (N = 41)		
Yes	31	76
No	10	24

Note: From "The Serial Rapist: His Characteristics and Victims," by R. Hazelwood and J. Warren, 1989, FBI Law Enforcement Bulletin, 58, 18–25.

between the social agencies and the police. Crisis line workers were trained in evaluating a potential for family violence and/or homicide. Figure 12.1 presents the Family Violence Interview that was developed for use by crisis line workers from the family homicide profiling research.

This interview form is designed for use by trained crisis workers receiving telephone calls from troubled citizens who are involved in or observers of potential family violence.

After the worker has established rapport and gained the confidence of the caller, basic information such as name, address, and telephone number should be recorded. This form should be filled out as soon as the worker ascertains that the caller is reporting a violent family episode in progress or about to happen.

FAMILY VIOLENCE INTERVIEW

By _____

Caller's Name _____ Date _____ Time _____ AM / PM

Telephone _____ Address _____

Relationship to Instigator _____

Instigator's Name _____

Address _____ Telephone _____

*HIGH RISK

I. *HAS THE INSTIGATOR BEEN VIOLENT BEFORE*

Has instigator caused trouble or hurt like this before?

YES *___ NO ___ DK ___ Details: _____

II. *INVOLVEMENT WITH LAW ENFORCEMENT*

Has instigator ever had the police or sheriff come to settle him down or arrest him before?

YES *___ NO ___ DK ___ Details: _____

III. *PREVIOUS MENTAL HEALTH RECORD*

Has instigator been mentally ill in the past?

YES *___ NO ___ DK ___ Details: _____

IV. *RECENT DEEP DEPRESSION*

Has instigator been recently low, discouraged, or depressed?

YES *___ NO ___ DK ___ Details: _____

V. *BACKGROUND HISTORY*

Has instigator had a recent family breakup?

YES *___ NO ___ DK ___ Details: _____

FIGURE 12.1 Family Violence Interview

PSYCHOLOGICAL PROFILING PROCEDURES

Horn (1988) suggests that psychological profiling involves seven steps:

1. A careful evaluation of the criminal act.
2. A comprehensive analysis of the crime scene.
3. A comprehensive analysis of the victim.
4. An evaluation of the preliminary police reports.
5. Evaluation of the medical examiner's autopsy protocol in homicide cases.

VI. *SEPARATION FROM FAMILY UNIT*
Has instigator recently moved out or been separated from the family unit?
YES *____   NO ____   DK ____   Details: _____
_____

VII. *THREAT*
Has instigator made any threats that you know of (suicide or homicide)?
YES *____   NO ____   DK ____   Details: _____
VIII. Is anyone antagonizing or hassling instigator now?
YES *____   NO ____   DK ____   Details: _____
_____

IX. *ALCOHOL OR DRUGS*
Is instigator using alcohol or drugs?
YES *____   NO ____   DK ____   Details: _____

(SCORE)   No Threat ____   Nonspecific Threats ____
Vengeance-Based Threat *____

Decision Checkpoints	( ) means "use own judgment"	Action
1 or 2 * checked:	NO CLEAR INDICATION	E + (C) + (D)
3 * checked:	VIOLENT SITUATION MAY BE DEVELOPING	C + (D)
4 * checked:	EMERGENCY—VIOLENCE PROBABLE	A + B
5 * checked:	EMERGENCY—VIOLENCE PROBABLE	A + B
6 or more * checked:	ACUTE EMERGENCY—IMMINENT VIOLENCE	A + B

A—CALL POLICE OR SHERIFF TO INVESTIGATE.
B—TELL INFORMANT TO AVOID INSTIGATOR. GET CHILDREN OUT.
C—REFER TO CRISIS LINE. CALL BACK IF SITUATION INTENSIFIES.
D—MAKE APPOINTMENT FOR FAMILY COUNSELING.
E—CONTINUE WITH USUAL HELP-LINE PROCEDURES.

FIGURE 12.1 *(continued)*

6. Development of the profile with critical offender characteristics.
7. Investigative suggestions predicated on the construction of the profile.

To do the profile properly, certain materials are required including complete photographs of the crime scene and a map depicting all significant locations. The profiler should be provided with the autopsy protocol in homicide cases. A medical examiner's report is important for rape and violent assault cases. The profiler must have the victim's occupation, residences, reputation at work, physical description, marital status, financial status, family background, medical history, fears, personal habits, social habits, ordinary use of alcohol and drugs, hobbies, friends and enemies, recent changes in lifestyle, and recent court actions.

In the case of sexual assault and rape victims, the profiler must conduct careful and extended interviews with the victim regarding the rapist's behavior. An analysis of that behavior is made in an attempt to ascertain the motivation underlying the assault. A profile is compiled for an individual likely to have committed the crime in the manner reported and having the assumed motivation. Interviewing the victim is the most important step in the process; it is recommended that this be done by the investigators (Hazelwood, 1983). Detailed questions are required as to the method of approach used by the offender, the way in which the offender controlled the victim, the offender's reaction to resistance where this occurred, any sexual peculiarities of the perpetrator, the verbal activity of the offender, any sudden changes in the offender's attitude during the attack, and items that the victim finds are missing after the attack.

In many ways, the process used by a profiler in developing the criminal profile is similar to that used by clinical psychologists to make a diagnosis and treatment plan. Data is collected and assessed, the situation is reconstructed, hypotheses are formulated, a profile is developed and tested, and the results are reported back. Expertise includes a lot of experience with other investigators; exchanging ideas, accumulating wisdom, and having familiarity with a large number of cases. The hypothesis should organize, explain, and make investigative sense out of information (Douglas et al., 1986).

Douglas and his group have suggested that there are stages of psychological profiling that should be followed to come to a final criminal profile that might lead to investigation and apprehension. Figure 12.2 shows diagramatically the profile process recommended by Douglas et al. (1986).

Those who are enthusiastic about the application of psychological profiling to serious criminal acts suggest that violent crimes require investigators to be diagnosticians who study the crime scene for the messages that it emits about the perpetrator's actions during the attack. From this analysis can come an understanding of the dynamics of human behavior that characterize the perpetrator. It is suggested that the fantasies of offenders give

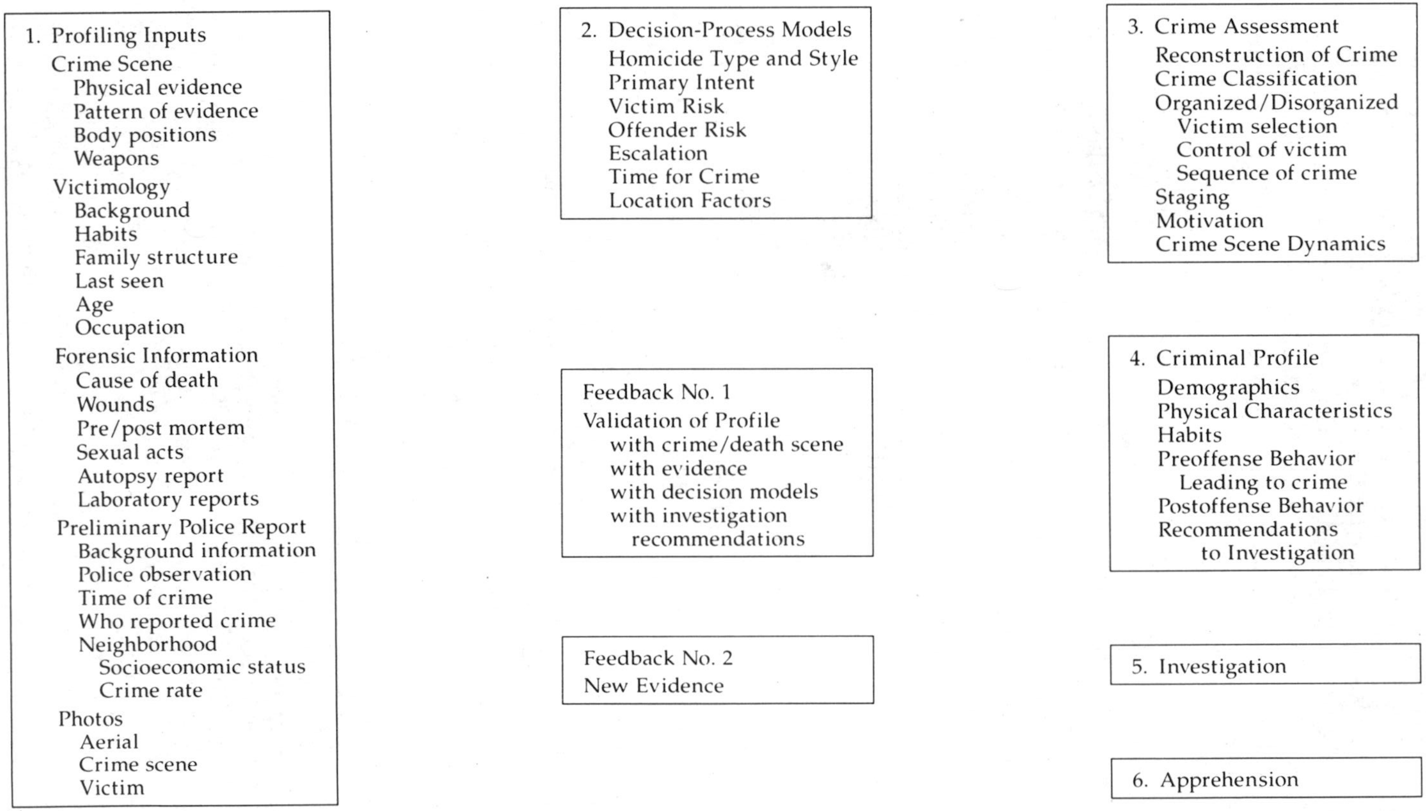

1. Profiling Inputs
   Crime Scene
   Physical evidence
   Pattern of evidence
   Body positions
   Weapons
   Victimology
   Background
   Habits
   Family structure
   Last seen
   Age
   Occupation
   Forensic Information
   Cause of death
   Wounds
   Pre/post mortem
   Sexual acts
   Autopsy report
   Laboratory reports
   Preliminary Police Report
   Background information
   Police observation
   Time of crime
   Who reported crime
   Neighborhood
        Socioeconomic status
        Crime rate
   Photos
   Aerial
   Crime scene
   Victim

2. Decision-Process Models
   Homicide Type and Style
   Primary Intent
   Victim Risk
   Offender Risk
   Escalation
   Time for Crime
   Location Factors

3. Crime Assessment
   Reconstruction of Crime
   Crime Classification
   Organized/Disorganized
   Victim selection
   Control of victim
   Sequence of crime
   Staging
   Motivation
   Crime Scene Dynamics

4. Criminal Profile
   Demographics
   Physical Characteristics
   Habits
   Preoffense Behavior
     Leading to crime
   Postoffense Behavior
   Recommendations
     to Investigation

5. Investigation

6. Apprehension

Feedback No. 1
Validation of Profile
   with crime/death scene
   with evidence
   with decision models
   with investigation
     recommendations

Feedback No. 2
New Evidence

FIGURE 12.2 A Psychological Profile-Generating Process From "Criminal Profiling from Crime Scene Analysis," by J. Douglas, R. Reisler, A. Burgess, and C. Hartman, 1986, *Behavioral Sciences and the Law, 4,* 407. Copyright by John Wiley & Sons. Reprinted with permission.

birth to violent crimes and that a *signature* aspect remains on the crime scene as an enduring part of each offender (Douglas & Munn, 1992).

Once the profile is completed, profile information can provide an investigator with the probable sex and age of the perpetrator, ethnic background, relative social status, marital status, educational level, occupational category, possible criminal background, and potential for continued criminal activities (Ault & Reese, 1980; Tetem, 1989).

If nothing else, the extensive review of all materials that is necessary to construct a psychological profile will often in itself bring to light previously overlooked investigative leads.

To demonstrate the outcome of a psychological profile, the following example on pp. 271–273 presents such a profile developed by a group of investigative officers and a psychologist

Although some of the police officers had serious doubts (as did the psychologist) about the accuracy and completeness of the profile, a number of stakeouts and surveillances were developed to anticipate the next activity of the serial rapist. Because of his activity in various apartment complexes, civilian security guards were canvassed and given brief descriptions of what they might look for, and hours during which they should be particularly vigilant.

About 4 months later, an individual was "caught in the act" as a result of the vigilance of a private security guard who called police officers and sheriff's deputies. When the interrogation of the suspect was completed, it was determined that he was responsible for most of the unsolved rapes in a three-county area. Following his trial and conviction, further interviews took place. In the end, of the 34 items on the serial rapist profile that was constructed, 23 proved to be accurate predictions or descriptions. Two were incorrect. For nine, there was no information available.

Whether this serial rapist profile was useful in apprehending the criminal or not can be debated on both sides of the question. The police themselves were very enthusiastic about the usefulness of the procedure.

EVALUATION OF PSYCHOLOGICAL PROFILING

Very few efforts have been made to validate the quality of psychological profiles and their usefulness against the criteria of success. As with computer work, the rule is "garbage in and garbage out." The quality of the crime data used is of critical importance. It is possible that psychological profiling may never advance from an art form to a science (Horn, 1988).

In a review of 193 cases where psychological profiling was done, Tetem (1989) found that 45% of the cases had been resolved. Investigators claimed that 77% of the cases studied showed that the psychological profile had been of significant assistance in the investigation. In 17% of the

PINE COUNTY SHERIFF'S OFFICE
BEHAVIORAL SCIENCE UNIT
SERIAL RAPIST PSYCHOLOGICAL PROFILE

INTRODUCTION

During January 1986, a series of reports of sexual battery received by this office began to demonstrate characteristics of the so-called serial rapist profile. Detective Jones, Sgt. Smith, and Lt. Brown brought preliminary crime data to the attention of Dr. Green, and initial meetings were scheduled to develop a *psychological profile* of the person who might be the perpetrator of this series of sexual assaults.

All crime reports, photos, witness statements, and other evidence were reviewed. Three victims were given psychological profile interviews. The first reported victim (January), a victim who was assaulted in April, and the latest victim (July 9, 1986) gave detailed responses to the psychological interview. Because a series of sexual assaults being investigated by the Anytown PD bore similarities to the Pine County Sheriff's Office cases, several Anytown Police Department officers met with the Pine County Sheriff's officers to share information. Detective White and Sgt. Black provided material and participated in several meetings.

It is not certain that all the cases evaluated were the work of one perpetrator. The preliminary analysis presented here is based on the evidence available and the emerging picture of the probable psychological style and motivation of the perpetrator, as he appears through the experience of victims and certain similarities in his behavior.

The man responsible for a number of sexual batteries since January 1986 is between 20 and 30 years of age. He is tall, between 6 ft and 6 ft 2 or 3 in. in height. His shoulders are quite broad, and his hips are narrow. His skin is smooth and relatively hairless. When and if he wears a mustache, it is thin and sparse. He tends to dress casually, preferring blue trousers or jeans, with checkered shirt or pullover sweatshirt, sometimes with a hood. He seems to prefer blue-colored clothes. He often wears soft or tennis shoes of a dark color. He is well-organized and self-assured. He speaks in a relatively calm voice of medium tone and resonance. He speaks with a vocabulary that suggests middle-class background and education. He is white. He wears no cologne or other noticeable scent. His shoe size is between 11 and 13. He may be bisexual or has had some homosexual experience. There is a probability that he has been arrested in the past, perhaps as a juvenile, for flashing or peeping. He sometimes wears sunglasses with mirror lenses and white frames. His hair may be brown or blond. He probably lives in an apartment. He probably has both a bicycle and a car.

MODUS OPERENDI

The method of operation is fairly consistent. Victims are for the most part young, single apartment dwellers. They all have automobiles. The assaulter apparently prepares his plan with some care. He surveys the apartment complex where he will operate. He goes over the surrounding area both during the day and at night. He searches for the best place to accost his victim and where to march the victim to a secluded outdoor spot to commit the sexual assault. When he enters the victim's domicile, it is usually through a sliding glass door. He seems to prefer to get to know the victim's regular habits and to capture her as she goes about some ordinary task. Whether he takes the victim from her apartment, car, or laundry room, he seems to follow the same sequence:

1. He grabs the victim securely.
2. He is wearing a hood, a towel, or shirt around his face or dark glasses to hide his identity.
3. He tells his victim she is in danger of her life and that he is carrying a knife. He cautions her to be quiet.
4. He asks for and takes the victim's money. He shows no interest in jewelry or other valuables.
5. He walks his victim away from her apartment to a semisecluded spot nearby. He clearly knows what he is doing and where he is going. He threatens his victim if she makes any noise, cries, touches him, or resists his efforts. He seldom if ever curses. He indicates that he has been watching the victim and knows something about her routine or acquaintances in the apartment complex.
6. He commits the sexual act with a ritual where he demands a kiss, asking the victim to stick out her tongue. He performs some minimal fondling and then asks the victim to fellate him. He may attempt anal intercourse. He may enter her vaginally from the rear. He is insistent but as yet, not brutal. He does not require the victim to remove all of her clothes. He does not usually remove his clothes entirely. He may withdraw and ejaculate by having the victim masturbate him. All during these proceedings he keeps his victim blind-folded with a piece of his own clothing.
7. On completion, he has the victim dress and he heads her toward her apartment complex. He may warn her not to look or impede his escape. He leaves very quietly and disappears, either on foot or by bicycle.

About half of the incidents have occurred between Friday night and early Monday morning. He has committed these batteries between 2200 and 0600 hours. As far as can be determined, he has committed none of these acts on Thursday. He operates in fairly specific clusters of apartment complexes. He moves his locus of operation between Everytown and Anytown. The degree of force he uses is escalating. He is beginning to both threaten and abuse his victims more aggressively.

Psychologically, it would appear that this perpetrator is a fairly inward person with a limited number of close friends. He probably has sexual contacts other than in the cases where he commits sexual battery. These contacts may be bisexual. He has no regular job or has a job situation where he can control his own hours. He is both obsessional and compulsive. He is given to rituals and repetitive behavior. He needs money and his motivation may become increasingly focused on burglary and robbery. Although he may not be of high measurable intelligence, he is shrewd and can be cool and unanxious.

His personality is likely to be that of a nonconforming person. He will tend to have strong and sometimes odd ideas that he holds to strongly. He is likely to be a rebellious person with poor frustration tolerance. He will tend to be impulsive even though his crimes show an ability to plan.

This culprit is willing to take risks. He particularly enjoys teasing or frustrating authority figures. He tends to believe he is capable of being very clever. If given the chance to enhance his own image, he is likely to talk about himself more than is good for him.

When the time comes to interrogate this person, it must be done very carefully. Pressure is unlikely to be helpful. Having several clearly identifiable objects from the various crime scenes in a corner of the interrogation room will help. Flattery, sympathetic listening, and general questions are more likely to elicit his response than rigid, formal or challenging approaches. He is unlikely to respond to threats. Any appeal to his vanity (skill, glib language, style, etc.) is likely to elicit conversation from him. He is unlikely to respond to Mutt & Jeff routines by the interrogators. He will probably be more talkative with male interviewers.

DISCLAIMER

This Profile is sketchy at best. It is a preliminary effort.

---

cases, the profile had actually identified the suspect. Ressler and Burgess (1985) report an inter-rater reliability in the classification of sexual homicide crime scenes from 76.7% to 92.6% measuring agreement between a trained FBI agent and a criteria evaluation by the authors.

Pinizzotto and Finkel (1990) compared the accuracy of professional psychological profilers with police detectives specially trained in personality profiling, police detectives who were untrained, clinical psychologists naive to both criminal profiling and criminal investigation, and undergraduate students. They found for both homicide and sex offense cases, profiles written by the professional profilers were richer than those written by the nonprofiler groups of detectives, psychologists, and students. The professional profilers had more correct answers to questions about the criminal, higher accuracy scores, and more correct lineup identifications for the sex offense cases than profilers, but the accuracy differences dissipated when they examined the homicide cases.

All in all, although psychological profiles are probably a potentially useful tool, spotting serial killers and serial rapists from those profiles is currently a difficult and unreliable procedure. As Monahan and Steadman (1984) point out, particular mental disorders do not correlate highly with specific crimes leading to some question about the point-to-point method of developing a picture of the perpetrator.

It is generally agreed that no profile can make up for a poor or incomplete crime scene investigation. To be useful, a profile's quality must be enhanced with sketches, photographs, accurate autopsy results, and thorough background investigations of the victim. In effect, psychological profiling of offenders carries the investigative process a step further than the usual crime scene investigation. The goal of criminal investigation and criminal profiling is the same and both depend on thoroughness of the crime scene investigator.

The procedure can be expected to provide usable data in only a modest number of highly specific types of crimes. Heilbrun (1992) reports the use of psychologists in the research section of the U.S. Secret Service. A form of profiling has been developed to identify, assess, and manage individuals who may pose a threat to those being protected by the Secret Service (the President, other executives, foreign dignitaries, etc.).

The most limiting factor about psychological profiling is the amount of training and preparation necessary to develop the skills necessary to accurately profile a crime. The profiler must possess an excellent knowledge of abnormal psychology, human behavior, crime scene investigative procedures, and forensic medicine. Much training and supervision are necessary before a psychologist or a police officer can function independently (Tetem, 1989).

CHAPTER THIRTEEN

Investigative Hypnosis

Hypnosis has been an issue of interest in jurisprudence for more than 100 years. As a phenomenon, hypnosis is an alteration in consciousness that is poorly understood. Apparently, the procedure shifts concentration so as to result in fairly intense, absorbing perceptual experiences that are always controllable and reversible. Under hypnosis, the individual experiences a relative lowering of peripheral awareness and an enhancement of focal concentration. Changes in temporal orientation allow the individual to relive the past as though it were in the present. Thus, hypnosis can be considered a shift in concentration, characterized by a parallel awareness and relative suspension of critical judgment (Spiegel & Spiegel, 1987).

LAW ENFORCEMENT APPLICATION

In law enforcement work, hypnosis is used as a tool to enhance the information available to detectives in solving crimes. In particular, the purpose is to refresh the recollection of witnesses and to better understand what a witness may have perceived (Hibler, 1988; Bowden, 1988; Reiser, 1980).

Some professionals believe that the greatest opportunity for the use of hypnosis with crime witnesses and victims is in those cases where the person was emotionally or physically traumatized by the criminal activity and may have adopted a defensive repression or denial that covers important information. In such cases, memory enhancement is the purpose of the procedure. Investigators hope to retrieve information that might be otherwise unavailable (Spiegel & Spiegel, 1987).

Some subjects are extremely hypnotizable and under duress may experience spontaneous hypnotic-like symptoms. Such subjects increase the probability of confabulation and an artificial sense of confidence in the information they provide (Orne, 1979; Diamond, 1980). The unreliability of the procedure leads many to believe that some witnesses are extremely vulnerable to manipulation and produce questionable information.

Some believe that the ideal is to have a professional psychologist or psychiatrist using hypnosis in the police setting. The Society for Clinical and Experimental Hypnosis suggests that only a trained and licensed psychologist or psychiatrist, independent of the law enforcement agency, should conduct a hypnotic interrogation. The Federal Bureau of Investigation prefers that an agent who is not otherwise involved in the investigation be present and conduct the interrogation with the hypnotized witness. It is generally agreed that hypnosis in the forensic setting should never be used as a substitute for routine investigative procedures (Spiegel & Spiegel, 1987).

PROCEDURES

To minimize the possibility of inadvertently suggesting something, the team that does the hypnosis should be essentially uninformed about the case. A prehypnotic statement should be taken from the potential witness and this should be videotaped. The subject is simply asked to tell the team what happened. The free association of the witness may be followed by specific questions to expand areas that require clarification. Special effects

---

INFORMED CONSENT
Forensic Hypnosis

I hereby give my full and complete consent to Dr. _____
to perform hypnosis with me, to ask any questions he chooses, to record the
results, and to provide these results to _____

_____.

Dr. _____ has explained the process of hypnosis, the degree to
which it requires my cooperation, the safeguards, the effects, and the uses to
which the material will be put. In addition to Dr. _____
and myself, present at the hypnosis session will be _____

_____

_____.

_____

_____
DATE

WITNESS:

_____

_____

FIGURE 13.1   A Form for Obtaining Informed Consent before Investigative Hypnosis

such as "stop action," "slow motion," and "focusing" are sometimes useful in this application of hypnosis. The interviews are likely to be quite long (Hibler, 1988). Some experts suggest that the hypnotizability of the subject should be tested using one of the standardized hypnotizability scales (Spiegel & Spiegel, 1978; Weitzenhoffer & Hilgard, 1959).

It is always important to obtain informed consent prior to subjecting any subject to investigative hypnosis. Figure 13.1 presents a form which can be used for such informed consent.

To illustrate what may be a valuable product of investigative hypnosis, the following is a statement by a police psychologist concerning a successful utilization:

> The law enforcement community is actually relatively small. People in the FBI know people in Intelligence, who know people in the Secret Service, who know people at the local level of law enforcement.
>
> I received a call from a special agent of the Secret Service in Washington asking if I would be willing to conduct hypnosis in a counterfeiting case. The facts of the case involved a woman who was tangentially associated with subjects of the Secret Service investigation. These people had disappeared, and their whereabouts were unknown. The woman in question, who had been a friend of one of the women associated with the bad guys, had received a telephone call from this woman asking for her to send some material to her. She gave her an address over the telephone. The woman mailed the material requested and then received a call from a former husband of her friend. He was threatening and abusive. He insisted that she tell him where his ex-wife was so that he could "go after her." She became frightened and tore up the slip of paper with the address.
>
> Months later, it became apparent to her that she was tangentially involved in felonious behavior. Her contact with the FBI led to interviews with the Secret Service. It became clear that she was the link to the pursuit and apprehension of these criminals. She simply could not remember anything about the address.
>
> She was introduced to the concept of hypnosis, while all of this was being videotaped. Some brief tests of hypnotizability were done and she responded fairly well. Although she was extremely nervous and tense, it was possible to induce a fairly deep trance, including arm levitation. She was regressed back to the time she received the telephone call and she was asked to describe her writing down of the address. She was able to retrieve about half of it. She was then moved forward to the time when she mailed the package, and she reexperienced the writing of the address on a manila envelope. The remainder of the address emerged.
>
> The chances that this would be successful were small, but in this case the hoped-for result happened.

Kline (1986) has suggested that the inductive phase of hypnosis is a significant part of the clinical interaction in investigative hypnosis. He suggested that hand levitation techniques and ocular fixations as well as visual imagery are the most successful methods. He further cautions that the individual conducting the hypnosis or those present must be extremely cautious not to contaminate the subject's responses during the process. Kline further suggests that valuable information is sometimes retrievable even with a very light trance.

A second illustration of an unexpected result involving a witness with significant neuropsychological deficit is of interest:

> On a Monday afternoon, in a local topless dancing establishment, a young man who had been drinking beer left with two large men. About six hours later, he was discovered with his skull fractured, suffering severe brain damage as a result of a beating with a blunt object.
>
> Because of his memory loss, the assailants were not identified. The victim was recovering slowly, with no memory for several days before the incident and for two months following the incident.
>
> The investigation continued with very few leads. There were some vague identifications at the bar about the people who were there at the time the victim left. Nothing helped the investigation.
>
> The detective in charge of the case asked whether this man might be able to remember incidents associated with the assault if he were put under hypnosis. He was assured that "brain damage is brain damage" and that the likelihood is extremely poor. It was decided, however, that this technique would be tried.
>
> At the first session, Bob was a pathetic figure. He had lost about 40 lbs. His right arm was in a flexible cast because of the brain damage eliminating his control of one side of his body. He spoke with a severe stutter and block. On interview, he could remember nothing for several days before the incident and for weeks afterward.
>
> He was introduced to hypnosis, carried through some tests, and then entered into a trance. He responded fairly well. He was regressed to the day before the incident, and indeed he was able to describe what he did at work. He was moved forward to the day of the assault and asked to wake up and "go through his day." He did so with astonishing clarity and detail. The end result was that he described his visit to the bar, being engaged in conversation by two men whom he identified and described, being invited out to their van, being assaulted and asked for his money, being robbed, and finally being beaten with a grease gun. When asked what happened at that point, he simply said "sleep." This material was turned over to the detective who then pursued apprehension of the two perpetrators.

There is little or no information on the validity and reliability of investigative hypnosis with brain-damaged subjects. This particular single incident is quite dramatic in its success.

EVALUATION OF INVESTIGATIVE HYPNOSIS

The enthusiasm by police departments for investigative hypnosis waxes and wanes. Currently, it has been dulled by some instances where the information obtained was misleading or wrong. It is well known that memory is malleable, and hypnosis has the potential to deform recollections even further. All in all, hypnosis itself cannot be expected to produce reliable information. As all law enforcement people know, witness testimony in any form is potentially unreliable, and hypnosis will frequently reflect this (Hibler, 1988). There is a consensus among scientific researchers that hypnotically-refreshed memory is inherently unreliable. In spite of this, some states continue to admit hypnotic evidence. Often the battle of the experts takes place and then the jury must make the decision as to whether the testimony is reliable and relevant. Because hypnotically refreshed memories are inherently unreliable, it does not mean that they are necessarily inaccurate. This is a knotty legal problem which is yet to be resolved (Sheflind & Shapiro, 1989).

Spontaneous material is probably more valid than that which results from direct questions. When attorneys, police officers, correctional officials, and other law enforcement individuals conduct hypnosis, it is too much to expect that their professional framework and style of questioning will not interfere with the process (Kline, 1986).

Sheehan and Tilden (1983) studied witness response under hypnosis in comparison with response under standard interrogation. They found no significant increase in either correct or incorrect material from the hypnosis but noted an increase in confidence about the material that was previously elicited.

Many investigators take the position that although investigative hypnosis is frequently unproductive, the possibility, no matter how slight, that some small detail or piece of new information may emerge makes the process worth considering. Investigators believe anything that can lead to new clues or corroborative evidence is worth pursuing (Spiegel & Spiegel, 1987).

LEGAL ASPECTS

Many consider the case of *People v. Shirley* (50 U.S.P. L.W. 2579 (1982)) as the landmark decision concerning hypnosis (Kline, 1986; Spiegel & Spiegel, 1987). In this case, the court opined:

> The principal question on this appeal is whether a witness may be allowed to testify after he has undergone hypnosis for the purpose of restoring his memory of the events in this issue. The question is new to this court but has often been litigated in our sister states and extensively studied by medical science. In accordance with recent and persuasive case law and the overwhelming consensus of expert opinion, we conclude that the testimony of such witnesses should not be admitted in the courts of California.

Because of the possibility that investigative hypnosis may contaminate a witness for future testimony, there is no longer a mass advocacy for hypnosis. Agencies familiar with these legal constraints tend to be very careful about ensuring that the conduct of the hypnosis does not "spoil" the case (Hibler, 1988).

The courts are very reluctant to admit any testimony where investigative hypnosis has been involved in any stage of the witnesses' experience. In a case considered by the U.S. Supreme Court (*Leyra v. Denno*, 347 U.S. 556 (1954)) the majority opinion held that indeed coercion was used during the hypnosis of the defendant Leyra who was accused of killing his parents. Even though tried again, Leyra was eventually freed of all charges because the courts opined that a coercive misuse of hypnosis took place that resulted in his confession.

At this moment in time, it is extremely rare for a witness who has been hypnotized to be allowed to testify in American courts. This does not, however, mean that hypnosis is not useful since the most common application today is to elicit information that can then be subject to further corroboration or exploration.

If the intent is to present a witness in court who has undergone hypnosis, or if investigative hypnosis is going to be a part of a presentation of evidence, Kline (1986) recommends six steps to maximize the acceptability of the procedure:

1. Only qualified mental health professionals should conduct the investigation.
2. The professional should be independent and not employed by law enforcement.
3. The entire examination should be electronically recorded, preferably on videotape.
4. A prehypnotic interview should elicit and record facts that the subject spontaneously recalls.
5. The prehypnotic interview and posthypnotic discussion should also be recorded.
6. Only the clinician conducting the hypnosis and the subject should be present during the hypnotic sessions.

Not all investigative hypnotists agree with this list, but it is certainly the beginning of a set of standards that can be explored and refined.

CHAPTER FOURTEEN

Psychological Autopsy

INTRODUCTION

The psychological autopsy is a concept that developed in the context of the suicide intervention movement. Farberow and Shneidman, psychologists with the Veterans Administration in California came upon a storage box in the basement of the hospital in which they worked. This box contained over 200 suicide notes of patients who had terminated their lives. The research on these notes (Farberow & Shneidman, 1961) led to other studies of suicidal behaviors (Shneidman, Farberow, & Litman, 1970) and the development of the Los Angeles Suicide Prevention Center. Working with the Los Angeles Coroner's Office and the Los Angeles Sheriff's Department, psychologists, social workers, psychiatrists, and researchers developed suicide intervention procedures that became the standard for modern suicide prevention, intervention, and postvention (Wekstein, 1979).

As their work became known, the staff of the Los Angeles Suicide Prevention Center (LASPC) was approached by a representative of the insurance industry seeking help with a complex logistical problem. In many instances, insurance companies were faced with a conflict in paying death benefits to survivors of a policyholder if there was reason to believe that the person had committed suicide. The insurance companies had many cases where the objective events leading to the death of the insured did not clearly establish whether the death was accidental, homicide, or suicide. Issues of liability and double indemnity were paramount to the insurance carriers who asked the LASPC staff to attempt to devise a method of determining whether a death was by self-termination in these cloudy cases. The result was the development of the *psychological autopsy.*

Using the results of their research and clinical experience, the staff of the LASPC developed a procedure whereby the 30 days prior to the decedent's termination a psychosocial description of the decedent's activities, interpersonal relations, attitudes, and behaviors was developed through interviews. Those interviewed included the spouse, other relatives, neighbors, supervisors, co-workers, and service personnel (barbers, mailcarriers, restaurant employees, hairdressers, physicians, gardeners, household staff, etc.).

In the original psychological autopsy, a team of psychologists and psychiatrists listened to a presentation of all the pertinent information concerning the case. Each participant filled out a summary sheet recording the psychodynamics—clues that might indicate possible suicide, or lack of suicidal behavior.

Personality elements associated with suicide in the original study included suicidal ideation, subtle communications relating to suicidal intent, reactive or psychotic depression, and schizophrenia (Farberow & Shneidman, 1961).

UTILIZATION

The original purpose for the psychological autopsy—determining whether a death was self-inflicted or not—is still one of the primary reasons for conducting such a procedure. Within the law enforcement framework, this procedure is used as an investigative tool by law enforcement agencies, prosecuting attorneys, and public defenders. When a death occurs, it is necessary for the criminal justice system to determine whether the death has been by other than natural causes. This leaves the options of homicide, suicide, or accidental death. In the psychological autopsy, behavioral scientists attempt to focus on components of the deceased person's behavior to determine whether a self-destructive motivation—conscious or unconscious—was at play. There have been psychological autopsies that helped to determine an overdose of toxic substance was not suicide, but due to poor visual discrimination between two bottles, misperceiving a toxic substance as a benign medication (Wekstein, 1979).

Before undertaking a psychological autopsy, the practitioner should ask certain questions and reach some specific agreements with the law enforcement agency. The following issues are important:

1. The psychologist must determine whether the organization or agency requesting the psychological autopsy is doing so for legitimate reasons that will in no way compromise the ethics and standards of the psychologist.
2. The psychologist must be allowed to collect sufficient data to do a professional job.
3. Sufficient time must be available to do a proper job, usually 3 months or more.
4. It must be determined whether the death has occurred recently enough so that significant persons who knew and were in contact

with the deceased before the death are likely to be able to recall things with accuracy.

5. The cost, time constraints, required access to records, and authoritative contact with witnesses must be specified to the referral source, and the psychologist must be sure that the appropriate facilities and personnel will be provided to conduct a proper psychological autopsy.

PROCEDURES

Conducting a psychological autopsy usually requires an extensive, multidisciplinary, in-depth study of the victim and the circumstances of the death. In essence it is a reconstruction of the deceased person's lifestyle. The investigation should include questions regarding depression, drug habituation, risk taking, perturbation (confusion associated with presuicidal conditions), inability to cope, and helplessness. Suicidologists refer to these areas of behavior as "signature" items (Wekstein, 1979).

The first contact for psychological autopsy is usually a telephone call from a police official, secretary, legal assistant, prosecutor, public defender, or private attorney to ask whether the psychologist can do a psychological autopsy. An affirmative answer is ordinarily followed by a brief description of the facts of the case and the questions that the attorney or law enforcement officer wishes answered. It is important for the psychologist to find out the details of the case during the initial interview and to establish the time frame involved so as to ensure sufficient time for a proper study. Arrangements should be made in writing, with a person at a relatively high level in the investigation or prosecution or defense as the case may be.

Certain psychological skills are required to conduct a psychological autopsy. After collecting the data, the psychologist will analyze this information in as objective a manner as possible and will develop conclusions that should be substantiated by elements of the case. The most important clinical skills for this work are the ability to establish rapport with a wide variety of witnesses, good clinical skills in conducting an interview, and the ability to clarify vague responses. The psychologist should have skill in encouraging disclosure. Data are collected in the context of the facts of the case as well as the psychological, sociological, environmental, situational, and epidemiological nature of suicidal behavior. The psychologist conducting a psychological autopsy should be familiar with both traditional and current research on suicidal behavior. Current literature should provide the clinician with base rates establishing the frequency of occurrence of suicide and circumstances of various suicidal behaviors by age, sex, geographic location, ethnic background, method of termination, time, location, domicile type, neighborhood, occupation, religious preference and degree of participation in religion, as well as other factors

(Ebert, 1987; Shneidman, 1981). Ebert (1987) recommends a thorough list of areas to explore as psychological autopsy guidelines.

The detailed interviews with people who have had some contact with the deceased during the 30 days prior to the subject's termination constitute the most important set of data for performing a psychological autopsy. Figure 14.1 presents a summary sheet for beginning a psychological autopsy. Figure 14.2 provides a form for taking down material that results from direct interview of witnesses. Figure 14.3 shows a summary sheet for laying out conclusions after all the material has been collected and analyzed.

The procedure probably works best as a group process, involving several psychologists and experienced investigative officers.

Date Begun _____

Date Completed _____

Subject _____ Dates Inclusive _____

Birthdate _____ Age _____ Marital Status S M D W Children _____

Religion _____ Employment _____ Living Arrangements _____

Mate _____

Parents _____

Sibs _____

Recent Events (Date of Termination _____ _____ AM)
                                                                                          PM

  1. Deaths _____

  2. Anniversaries _____

  3. Marriages _____

  4. Divorces _____

  5. Health Problems _____

  6. Other _____

Circumstances of Death

Autopsy Report

FIGURE 14.1   Psychological Autopsy—Basic Information Sheet

Responder _____ By _____ Date of Interview _____
Relation to Deceased _____
How Often in Contact with Deceased _____

Informant's Description of Deceased's Emotional State Prior to Termination

Inquiry
 1. Psychological Pain _____

 2. Frustrated Needs _____

 3. Evidence of Threats _____

 4. Evidence of Plans _____

 5. Evidence of Hopelessness/Helplessness _____

 6. Evidence of Severe Ambivalence/Depression _____

 7. Constricted Thinking _____

 8. Cry for Help _____

 9. Recent Evidence of Sudden Change in Attitude or Behavior _____

10. Use of Intoxicants _____

11. Past Attempts _____

12. Mental Health Treatment _____

FIGURE 14.2   Psychological Autopsy—Evaluation of Preterminal Month

Most Probable Scenario

Conclusions

By _____

Title _____

FIGURE 14.3   Psychological Autopsy—Summary Sheet

The following case illustrates the final product of a psychological autopsy requested by a county district attorney who had questioned the circumstances of an elderly woman's death. The issue was whether her husband or persons unknown would be suspects in a charge of murder, or whether the deceased killed herself.

PSYCHOLOGICAL AUTOPSY

NAME   Brown, Jane

REFERRAL   Jack J. Super, District Attorney of Anytown, Illiana,
            refers this case for psychological autopsy.

Mrs. Jane Brown was found in the basement of her home, dead, on April 2, 1990. She had a bullet wound in her head for which her husband, the only other resident of her home, denies complicity. At the time of her death, Mrs. Brown was 62 years of age. Her husband was 73. A number of months prior to this incident, Mrs. Brown had quit her job as a factory worker. She told her friends and family that she had been laid off, and in some cases, she said she was on compensation or medical leave. She also claimed falsely to have cancer.

Mrs. Brown handled the household finances. She had failed to make numerous payments on the mortgage of the house as well as other bills that had accrued. This took place over several years previous to her demise. The bank foreclosed on the mortgage of the house and purchased the property at a sheriff's sale toward the end of 1989. The bank then employed the services of the Anytown County Sheriff to evict the Browns from their home.

The Anytown County Area on Aging received a formal referral advising them of the eviction and indicating that Mr. Brown may not have been aware that they were about to be evicted from their home.

Ms. Eva Black, a caseworker for that agency, attempted on numerous occasions to make contact with Mr. Brown to ensure that he was aware of the problems. On each occasion, Mrs. Brown rebuffed her with one excuse or another. Finally, the agency obtained a court order and went to the home with a police officer in order to gain admittance so that the social worker could inform Mr. Brown of the impending foreclosure and eviction. Indeed, he did not know of the foreclosure proceedings. The social worker, Ms. Black, attempted on numerous occasions to provide services to the Browns to help them make arrangements to save their home, or in the alternative to provide them with shelter should they be evicted. Mrs. Brown refused such offers of assistance on each occasion. She continuously indicated that there was no real problem and that it would all work out.

On April 2, 1990, at 7:58 A.M., the Chief of Police of the Springdale Police received a telephone call from the duty dispatcher. A call had been received stating that Carl Brown's wife had shot herself in her residence. This message had been received from Tina Blue, who had been called by Betty Greene, the victim's mother, who had been called by the husband who stated that he discovered the body.

The Chief responded to the scene and arrived at 8:05 A.M. He entered the house and found Mr. Brown in the kitchen area in a very distraught state. Mr. Brown said, "Kiddo, kiddo, why did you do this to me?" The Chief asked where the wife was, and he said, "Downstairs." The officer went to the basement and observed the victim lying on the cement floor face up. She was lying with her head toward the steps. He observed a large pool of blood draining from her right side and running toward a basement drain. A closer look at the victim indicated that she was deceased. Appropriate procedures were then instituted and the crime scene secured.

A Coroner's Inquest was held with the coroner's jury ruling that the death was homicide and that Mr. Brown was responsible. Other than numerous conflicting statements given by Mr. Brown to different local and state police officers, the main evidence presented against him at the Coroner's Inquest was the expert testimony of Sam Smith, Criminologist for the State Police. This witness testified that the small blood spatters found on Mr. Brown's pajamas came, in his opinion, from a medium- to high-velocity impact. This implied that Mr. Brown was standing in the basement next to his wife when the bullet entered her head. Mr. Brown has consistently denied this.

District Attorney Super requests a psychological autopsy to determine whether there is reason to believe that Mrs. Brown committed suicide.

MATERIALS REVIEWED

Letters from District Attorney Super, outlines of the circumstances of Mrs. Brown's death, Autopsy Report, Caseworker and Case Manager Notes from the social work agency, police reports, and crime scene data.

IN-DEPTH INTERVIEWS

In-depth interviews were conducted with Reverend Taylor, Cindy Porter (deceased's daughter), Anne Bowers (daughter), Leah Adams (granddaughter), Kelly Jones (sister), Linda Lang (mother of the deceased), Pam Johnson (aunt on mother's side), Pat Hall (part-time employer), Kay Roberts (co-worker), Cathy Mills (supervisor at regular job), Eva Black (AAA case-worker), Father Rhomer, and Reverend Bell (Mrs. Brown's priests most frequently seen).

MRS. BROWN'S PSYCHOLOGICAL STATE

All who knew her generally agreed that Mrs. Brown was an energetic, hard-working, and relatively intelligent person all her life. There are indications that she always had periods of depression. Her marginal adjustment is demonstrated by having had children out of wedlock in a small town and a rigid ethnic community where such behavior was seriously frowned on.

She married a man who got much more from her than she got from him. She was clearly the leader in the marriage. As was noted by some of the relatives "Mr. Brown got a real good deal."

Most of those who knew Mrs. Brown described her as a person who was subject to extreme mood changes and regular periods of depression. She also showed a tendency to be impulsively angry.

During the last several months of her life, Mrs. Brown had significant changes in personality. Her moods became more extreme. She showed more depression. She began to act in strange ways. She developed a confabulation that she had a recurrence of cancer, insisting on this to a number of people. There was no basis in fact for this perception on her part. This may well represent a somatic delusion.

In spite of the seriousness of her confabulation about the cancer, she always reassured others that she would "beat it" in an unrealistic, overly enthusiastic manner. This kind of cryptic reassurance appeared in a number of situations.

Mrs. Brown confabulated a lot of things, particularly related to financial situations. Her relatives and friends described these as "lies" but it is possible that Mrs. Brown was experiencing serious emotional disturbance and could well have been having psychotic episodes that could account for this unrealistic thinking. There is no better demonstration than in her absolute denial of the seriousness of the foreclosure proceedings that resulted in the loss of all their security, which had been invested in the home. Her denial and evasion went beyond efforts to "lie" or to placate people. She demonstrated an adamant insistence on being in total control of the situation, and being imminently ready to resolve any conflicts that existed.

She confabulated information concerning her husband's health as well as her own. For an intelligent person, it is beyond rationality to conceive Mrs. Brown expecting people to believe in the kinds of things she said about herself and about her husband. This further supports the concept that she was experiencing a psychotic episode during the weeks previous to her death.

Mrs. Brown's mental state deteriorated severely during the 3 to 6 months previous to her death. Her uncharacteristic unreliability, her unrealistic reassurance of others, her tendency to confabulate, and the occurrence of a kleptomaniac event all speak for a serious breakdown in reality testing and mental stability.

FACTORS ASSOCIATED WITH SUICIDE

Examination of the commonly accepted factors associated with suicidal behavior indicates that Mrs. Brown was probably not using alcohol or drugs prior to her death. She did have an extensive and increasing depression. She did show signs of increasing perturbation.

Her odd behavior, particularly in reference to finances indicated that she was rapidly deteriorating in her ability to cope with realistic situations. She was becoming more and more helpless. Her life pattern was becoming more and more destructive. Although her husband was available, as the most significant other, he was of little or no use, and she had no trust in his ability to be of any help.

In the months before her death, Mrs. Brown, always an assertive person, became more hostile. She made certain remarks suggesting that life was less meaningful than it had been, and that she would welcome termination. She showed signs of a depression so extensive that it could well have been psychotic in view of the preceding notations.

During the 1 to 3 months before her death, she was confused, irrational, angry, overly optimistic about resolving very serious problems easily, demonstrated inappropriate affect, and gave treasured possessions away. The note that was found in her handbag, though idiosyncratic, would appear to be a farewell note, not particularly a cry for help, but characteristic of her lifestyle of making decisions independently and without consultation with others.

CONCLUSIONS

Analysis of the data available, and the interviews conducted suggest that to a high degree of probability, Mrs. Brown terminated her own life on April 2, 1990.

STATE v. BROWN

REVIEW OF RESEARCH

FACTORS ASSOCIATED WITH SUICIDE IN PSYCHOLOGICAL AUTOPSIES

1. Depression.	9. Hostility.
2. Drug habituation.	10. Partially dead individual.
3. Risk taking.	11. Life meaningless.
4. Perturbation.	12. Emotions crippled.
5. Inability to cope.	13. Resigned to eternal nothingness.
6. Helplessness.	14. Reactive depression.
7. Destructive life pattern.	15. Psychotic depression.
8. Role of the significant other.	16. Schizophrenia.

CURRENT USES

Very little formal evaluation of the psychological autopsy has been reported. Shneidman (1981) suggests a high level of inherent reliability and validity when the autopsy is carefully done.

In law enforcement agencies, the psychological autopsy is likely to be first viewed with skepticism by experienced investigators. In many respects, trained investigators actually do a kind of "psychological autopsy" in all homicide cases. They use their training and experience to view crime evidence, circumstances of the crime, testimony of witnesses, and information about the victim's lifestyle in deciding whether the decedent was a homicide or a suicide. Because territoriality is always a sensitive and important issue in law enforcement, the behavioral scientist must be prepared for slow acceptance and some skepticism.

An inversion of the negative reaction by police officers sometimes occurs. Where psychological autopsy has resulted in some success in resolving a case, the psychologist may become inundated with requests for psychological autopsies from the detectives who saw the value of the single instance. Detectives are always looking for an early resolution to a case and any help is greatly appreciated. The psychologist should insist that all referrals for psychological autopsy come from the chief of criminal investigation, or the chief of homicide. Once such referrals are received, psychologists should be sure that the case is appropriate for psychological autopsy and that cooperation, time, and facilities will be available.

The courts have been relatively accepting of the psychological autopsy. Moss (1988) reports that some prosecutors have become very positive about using the psychological autopsy as part of their case presentation as a result of some cases that have received much publicity. In criminal cases where motive and intent are essential, a psychological autopsy can contribute some information that could be useful during trial.

In 1981, Lichter reviewed the status of the psychological autopsy in American courts. He concluded that although the technique is relatively new as far as the courts are concerned, it has contributed to successful defenses in almost all known cases where it was admitted. He points out that there is still a danger that the evidence may be overwhelmingly prejudicial and may divert the jury's attention from other evidence and issues in the case. It is the responsibility of the trial judge to exercise discretion in determining whether to admit the testimony concerning a psychological autopsy. Lichter further points out that there are still some unresolved questions: First of all; what professional group should be administering the psychological autopsy (psychologists? psychiatrists? law enforcement officers?), and second; to what extent can an expert give an opinion under the Federal Rules of Evidence?

In a more recent case, an expert was allowed to offer testimony and opinion based on psychological autopsy. Although the case was appealed, the Appellate Court opined that such testimony is admissible (*Evans v. Provident Life and Accident Insurance Co.*, Kan. Ct. App. 64, 689, Brazil, J., 12/28/90).

A proper evaluation of the reliability and validity of the psychological autopsy will have to await the day when such procedures are more common. At the present, the psychological autopsy is still an infrequent event and thus does not lend itself to traditional research methods.

CHAPTER FIFTEEN

Management Consultation

In the business and industrial community, industrial/organizational (IO) psychologists have become well regarded consultants during the past 50 years. In the law enforcement community, psychologists have had relatively rare impact on law enforcement administration outside of supporting entry-level personnel decisions and offering psychological consultation on promotional processes or, occasionally, command decisions. The police manager has not been studied very frequently. Police managers themselves do not seem strongly interested in being studied or advised. If psychologists can help law enforcement managers to understand the value of psychological services, they may be able to help these managers reach their full organizational potential (Scrivner, 1986).

Almost all law enforcement agencies are exactly that—agencies. They are subject to the rules, regulations, opportunities, and problems of any bureaucracy. Often, the people who direct or mandate the activities of a law enforcement agency have little understanding or knowledge of the extent and the diversity of the job of law enforcement. Police managers themselves may have forgotten or blocked out their own earlier experience. They tend to operate as "bottom line" managers. Insensitivity to the psychological needs of police officers is a frequent, even usual, aspect of the style of many police executives.

The psychologist who decides to specialize in clinical work for law enforcement agencies should be prepared for the bureaucratic problems that will exist in any organization. The lack of importance many police managers attach to the psychological state of officers (and of themselves) can affect decisions throughout the agency.

Law enforcement organizations are strongly traditional, and like similar groups such as military organizations, they do not readily adapt to change. Although there is a long history of the effective use of psychological principles in enhancing management, most police managers have not readily perceived the need for management philosophies patterned after the policies of progressive businesses and corporations.

THE STRESS OF MANAGERS

Although a great deal of attention has been paid in the past few decades to the stress suffered by police officers, relatively little attention has been paid to stressors in the life of police executives. Sewell (1992) suggests that the sources of stress for police managers include the following:

1. Dependence on others who don't produce.
2. Inadequate personnel and equipment.
3. Increased community demands and pressures.
4. Increased pressures from courts, prosecutors, state and federal governments.
5. The ever-increasing political nature of the job.
6. Insufficient time for health and wellness activities because of job demands.
7. Poor training and preparation to become a manager.
8. Conflict with employee organizations.
9. Frustration in trying to accomplish lasting change.
10. A lack of trust and open dialogue between line officers and police executives.

With the increased public attention to incidents of "police brutality," police executives are under tremendous pressure from the public to stop such incidents, and from the line officers to stand by the good cops who do not participate in such behavior. Police executives on the one hand should be going out of their way to dispel the public perception that all police have a bunker mentality by addressing the issue directly with the public, especially when the use of force was justified. By the same token, police executives must have the courage to send the message that the use of excessive force is considered a failure in the police job (Bizzack, 1992).

STRESS EMANATING FROM MANAGERS

Modern police administration has been dominated by a theory of management that has emphasized central command and control. There is limited discretion by line officers. Procedures are standardized; enforcement routines are rigid; communication is from the top down and not the other way around. Efforts at reforming police management have, unfortunately, been mainly in terms of modifying political control of the agency. To operate in such a setting, police managers support role ambiguity, boredom, and role conflict, which are major stressors. These may not be inherent in police work, but they are inherent in the management style of most current police managers (Kliesmet, 1986). Kliesmet further points out that maintaining a healthy, happy force of police officers is almost impossible as long as the management style of executives continues to operate in the old system.

Although the mental health practitioner cannot serve as an industrial/ organizational psychologist for police executives, the police clinical psychologist can provide information that can help executives resolve their own stress and the stress that they create among line officers. Unfortunately, police executives tend to see mental health services as useful for "the other ranks." Glorioso (1986) has pointed out that the reluctant manager may be helped by categorizing the stressors that may occur within that particular manager's area of responsibility. Focusing the manager's attention on the occupational factors that cause stress and having the manager accept some evidence from research studies may lead to a greater acceptance of psychological services at the managerial level. Pointing out the success of stress reduction programs to police managers is sometimes a way for the psychologist to enter into a dialogue that may lead to the provision of such services to the reluctant manager.

TRADITIONAL INDUSTRIAL/ORGANIZATION SERVICES

In all probability, most police organizations could use the services of professional IO psychologists. Management training, effective listening seminars, morale surveys, development of workers' circles, two-way communication, and even such simple organizational methods as time and motion studies would help change the traditional structure of police management. These procedures would certainly help encourage police managers to deal with the ever-growing demand that such executives be more aware of society's problems and accept social responsibility to modify police activity to meet such needs.

RESEARCH

As yet, relatively little research about management of police departments has taken place. A number of studies have been started to evaluate the effectiveness of new styles of community policing that are products of modern police management and their awareness of the community's expectations. McElroy (1992) reports that in New York City, community policing is currently being studied; measurement and evaluation are planned in four broadly defined areas:

1. Internal institutional arrangements will be altered to focus on community policing.

2. Relationships between investigative and patrol personnel will be developed and studied.
3. Information will be shared across the organization and with citizens.
4. Executives will undergo problem-solving training.
5. Policies and procedures that restrict community-focused efforts will be redesigned.

The implementation of this project will be monitored and reported. This study will include a systematic assessment of how these elements are implemented. If this is an effectively designed and completed project, it will have value for all law enforcement agencies.

Getty, Elam, and Smouse (1986) attempted to delineate differences between line officers and executives through personality evaluation. They administered the MMPI and the California Psychological Inventory to a group of captains, lieutenants, and sergeants in a large metropolitan department. These profiles were compared with the profiles of a group of police cadets. The results indicated that police executives and supervisors were very much alike on most of the measures when compared with recruits. Thus, regardless of rank, police personnel in the sample seemed to be homogeneous group with respect to the personality characteristics that are measured by these instruments.

A fairly extensive effort to develop a style of consultation with management, using research data, was carried out and reported by Seymour, Boxley, and Redding (1986). They took a random sample of 725 sworn officers and surveyed them concerning their demographics and job satisfaction. They administered a burnout inventory, a stress history inventory, and a stress history. The sociodemographic questionnaire included age, sex, race, tenure, marital status, educational level, watch, rank, times married, number of children, and job status. As a result of this research, they developed six clusters that described line officers. These clusters were:

1. The mid-career crisis officer (16%).
2. The cynical but effective "John Wayne Syndrome" officer (2%).
3. The model officer—steady but stressed (36%).
4. The separators—officers with multiple and extended families (3%).
5. In between a rock and a hard place—little sense of personal accomplishment with limited growth options (24%).
6. The tenured, steady, and dependable officer (17%).

Using this data, the psychologists set up meetings with area and zone commanders to give them feedback of the results. This proved to be a positive experience for the zone commanders, and they appreciated the opportunity to discuss personnel management issues and to focus on efforts to enhance officer performance *before* it developed into a problem. Thus, the study as well as clinical data was used as a management tool to promote wellness and to promote proactive change.

STRATEGIC PLANNING

Although law enforcement is a relatively young profession, having formally being constituted only about 175 years ago, modern law enforcement, particularly in the United States, is an astonishingly efficient community service. It has, however, been traditional for law enforcement to be *reactive* rather than *proactive*. Law enforcement funding, policing styles, focus of attention, training, and responsiveness have tended to follow crises. As society becomes more complex, the demands for effective community law enforcement increase. Reactive response leaves law enforcement behind the rapid changes that have developed in society. This can result in unfortunate incidents where there is a discrepancy between community standards and their expectations for police response. Such incidents as excessive use of force, misunderstandings, racial tensions, and inadequate police response do occur. Mindful of this, police executives have been concerned about this imbalance, and have become more interested in *planning*. With the development of better management and performance evaluation techniques together with management by objectives, it has become clear that planning is the wave of the future in any successful bureaucratic venture.

Strategic planning is future planning. Kaufman and Stone (1983) express it thus:

> Its purpose is to aid in decision making relative to finding and securing a useful place for an organization in the market in society. Strategic planning is a useful tool for plotting organizational survival in the future, so that an organization's current and future operations will be compatible with that which is required in tomorrow's world. Thus, *futurity* is an essential dimension of strategic planning, as is the assumption that the world of tomorrow is not likely to be the same as the world of today. Strategic planning is more a frame of mind and a posture than it is a product. It is a process. In fact, the result of a strategic planning effort will be plans, programs, and efforts that are best expressed as middle-term or long-range plans that identify products, processes, and resources that will allow an organization to be useful in the future. For an organization to ignore strategic planning is to assume that there is a static relationship between today and tomorrow. (p. 160)

Such an assumption would be fatal for any kind of dynamic organization such as law enforcement.

Traditionally, most planning has been *microplanning*. In this procedure, management closely monitors individual and small group performance and provides consequent rewards, punishment, retraining, and reassessment of goals. In the past several decades, *macroplanning* has become a more popular way of revitalizing organizations. In this kind of planning, the organization itself is carefully evaluated in terms of its successes, its failures, its advantages and its disadvantages. Adjustments are made to increase cost-effectiveness and cost efficiency. Some police organizations have already entered into this type of management planning.

Short-term planning, which is the essence of microplanning and macroplanning, is insufficient in a society that heralds massive changes. We live in the space age, where the downfall of Communism, the end of the Cold War, new kinds of military activities, and rapid shifts in management style in large organizations have all contributed to a view of the world as a rapidly evolving dynamic organization. Such an organization requires advance thinking and advance planning. *Megaplanning* takes the widest view of an organization and what this organization can contribute to the community and society. Megaplanning focuses on the common ground in society—the people at large and organizations. The results of such planning tend to be management and organizations that are fertile, bountiful, and ethical, and that strongly contribute to a better quality of life for all. This, in essence, is future planning.

Future planning is somewhat complex and requires a fair degree of training and experience. The process should include the following:

1. The managers must identify *all* the planning partners. To omit a significant partner (worker, manager, supervisor, citizens, political individuals, geographic participants, etc.) would be to derail the effectiveness of the planning.
2. The managers must obtain the planning partner's participation.
3. The planning frame must be modified to be acceptable to all parties.
4. A needs assessment must be done to identify the needs of all partners.
5. The needs must be democratically placed in priority order, with a view to practicality.
6. Arrangements must be made to reconcile all disagreements among partners.
7. Whatever problems exist must be identified and put into priority status for resolution.
8. Interim evaluation must be conducted to obtain the agreement of partners on all processes to date.
9. Finally, methods and means to accomplish the mission must be developed and shared with all partners.

In a law enforcement setting, the most difficult early step in future planning is the identification of community needs. This can be done by conducting community polls on issues of concern. Area town meetings in different sections of the community can further elicit and identify community needs. Visits by police managers to community meetings that are scheduled for other purposes are excellent places to begin the request for community input. Mail polls can be used to randomize or stratify the samples of the community to further identify needs and opinions.

In *microplanning*, the law enforcement community has expressed its traditional management stance by monitoring individual and small group performance, with consequent rewards. Law enforcement does a modest amount of *macroplanning* through self-studies with evaluation of successes, failures, advantages, and disadvantages. *Megaplanning*, which

---

JOB SPECIFICATION TITLE   CHIEF, STRATEGIC PLANNING
EXECUTIVE BRANCH
COST CENTER   520 0000

FUNCTION

1. Megaplanning to identify existing and future needs of the community.
2. Macroplanning to establish and achieve organizational missions and objectives.
3. Development of needs assessments to define future planning and outcomes.
4. The design of research projects to validate or implement planning activities.

MAJOR WORKER CHARACTERISTICS

1. Ability to conduct gap analyses.
2. Conduct needs assessments and methods/means analyses.
3. Ability to analyze, design, and report research.
4. Versed in micro-, macro-, and megaplanning.

MINIMUM QUALIFICATIONS

1. PhD in Human Behavior.
2. Law Enforcement Academy.
3. Advanced postgraduate training in strategic planning and needs assessment.
4. Experience in strategic planning.
5. Consultation for government entities in planning.
6. Certification as a law enforcement officer.
7. Membership in American Evaluation Association.
8. Participation in the network of the Society of Police Futurists International.

WORKING CONDITIONS

Variable hours dependent on the requirements of the Sheriff, and/or the projects under way. Work may be performed in various locations including the Sheriff's Office, institutional libraries, or research centers.

FIGURE 15.1   Sheriff's Office Job Description—Chief, Strategic Planning

takes the widest view of an organization and what it can do or contribute to the community and society, currently tends to be a pretty rare phenomenon in the law enforcement community.

The law enforcement executive should develop the capacity to operate in a more successful way than in the past. Sewell (1992) points out that in the forthcoming decade, the demands on law enforcement will increase so exponentially that unless better management techniques are developed, law enforcement efficiency will suffer.

Interest in strategic planning is just beginning among police executives. The Society of Police Futurists International was first conceived in 1991, and as yet is still planning its first meeting (Canty, 1991). This organization expects to devote its energies to promoting exchange of information about future research. Part of the plan is to forge a partnership with private industry to develop the planning tools that will have significant impact on the future of policing.

At the present time, there are probably fewer than half a dozen police executives whose duties include future planning. Figure 15.1 presents the job description of a psychologist whose primary responsibility is strategic planning in a law enforcement agency.

In efforts to help police executives move toward the 21st century, psychologists will find examples in government and industry planning research that can help indoctrinate police executives into the kind of management that is likely to improve the viability of law enforcement operations as we move into the 21st century.

The extent to which psychologists can contribute to the direct operation of law enforcement is still an open question. So much depends on the interest, energy, and skill of the psychologist in being able to indoctrinate police executives into the available opportunities. The inertia of any large bureaucratic organization with a long history of methods and means in which the executives have great confidence in spite of poor results is something that psychologists ought to be able to understand, analyze, and modify.

CHAPTER SIXTEEN

Training

Law enforcement organizations are paramilitary in structure and function. Training and retraining are activities that go on at all times. Law enforcement is a vocation that can tolerate relatively few errors of fact or judgment. As a result, officers usually receive intensive initial training for their jobs and continue that training and retraining throughout their careers.

Most of the education of police officers utilizes other police officers in the role of teacher. In recent years, psychologists have been seen as useful pedagogues. This is appropriate and probably a wise choice on the part of law enforcement training officials. The doctorate is a teaching degree. Psychologists are quite articulate in most instances. They have skills to convey information. Police are being required to know more about human beings and human behavior than ever before. In the future, therefore, the law enforcement community is likely to request the teaching services of psychologists more frequently.

THE POLICE ACADEMY

Very few full-time police officers are hired without benefit of a graduation certificate from a police academy. Each state has established requirements for the number of class hours and subjects that must be covered. In addition, some states specify the level of performance the applicants must attain before they can achieve certification.

The academy may require between 300 and 700 hours of classwork, depending on the jurisdiction. The subjects taught cover the spectrum of what every line officer must know. Although the topics presented by psychologists are unquestionably important, they are generally considered "soft" areas of instruction in comparison with such topics as firearms; nomenclature, maintenance, and competence; securing a crime scene; probable cause; and arrest procedures. Nevertheless, the graduate of a modern police academy is supposed to know something about people, how to deal with them effectively, and how to represent his or her department with courtesy and efficiency.

Subjects at the Police Academy are taught in blocks of 1, 2, 4, or 8 hours. There may be sequential blocks of time. Most psychological subjects are taught in 2- and 4-hour blocks. Although the topics may deserve more thorough coverage, this must be negotiated with the director of the academy. Although psychologists are sought and accepted as teachers in the academy, their topics will seldom be assigned large blocks of time.

In some jurisdictions, psychologists may teach at the police academy without credentials other than their reputation and their professional status. In some states, the academy teacher/trainer must be certified by the state, which ordinarily requires the submission of credentials and some degree of delay. The police psychologist who intends to teach at a police academy should investigate local requirements and, where such exist, begin the certification procedure.

The following are some topics that police psychologists have most frequently taught at police academies:

1. The mentally disordered offender.
2. The nature and effects of stress.
3. Restraint and sensitivity in policing.
4. Health and wellness.
5. Community mental health services.
6. Juvenile delinquency.

A wide range of textbooks are available to psychologists for the development of such courses, including those by Russell and Beigel (1982), Yuille (1986), Irvine and Brelje (1985), and Ennis and Friedman (1986).

In preparing a presentation at the police academy, the psychologist might consider the following formalized steps:

1. Determine the extent of coverage required for the topic.
2. Prepare an outline of the plan of presentation.
3. Share the outline with supervisory and executive staff for their suggestions as to how to make the presentation more practical and understandable to police recruits.
4. Develop a final outline.
5. Time the presentation.
6. Segment the presentation to the number of hours provided by the Academy.
7. Be sure to include question-and-answer time in each segment.

Figure 16.1 is an outline proposal for a psychological training module. The module was to help police recruits understand the concept of empathy and to apply this in their everyday patrol duties.

Pursuant to the request of Major Jones, the Behavioral Science Unit has prepared a 3-hour academy training module on the nature and application of empathy in law-enforcement settings. The following outline describes the program.

I. *INTRODUCTION*—Empathy Defined
   A. *Listening with Understanding*
   B. *Experiencing in the Other Person's Shoes*
   C. *Communicating Effectively*
II. *DEFINING THE ROLE OF EMPATHY*—Where Needed
   A. *Breakdown in Communication*
      1. Message not received.
      2. Message distorted.
      3. More noise than signal.
      4. Emotion screens or filters message.
   B. *Emotionally Clouded Situations*
      1. Individual emotionally distressed.
      2. Situation emotionally charged.
      3. Previous negative interactions.
      4. Panic regarding outcomes.
III. *EMPATHY DILUTES OR NEGATES THREAT*
   A. *The Nature of Threat*
      1. Fundamentals of fear.
      2. Threats to status.
      3. Threats to survival.
      4. Threats to goals.
      5. Threats to values.
      6. Threats to balance.
   B. *Frustration Theory*
      1. Fear-frustration-aggression model.
      2. Identification with the aggressor versus empathy.
IV. *OUTCOMES OF SUCCESSFUL APPLICATION OF EMPATHY*
   A. *Confrontation Avoided*
   B. *Attention Freed for New Communications*
   C. *Negative Attitudes Diluted*
   D. *Cooperation Encouraged*
V. *WHERE TO APPLY EMPATHY*
   A. *Hostile Individuals*
   B. *Chronic Complainers*
   C. *Persons in Panic*
   D. *Suspicious Persons*
   E. *Those Who Have Strong Prejudices*

FIGURE 16.1   Outline of a Proposed Police Academy Training Module—Empathy

VI. *WHERE EMPATHY DOES NOT PROVE EFFECTIVE*
    A. *Character Disorders*
    B. *Defensive Cultural Anomalies*
    C. *Time Limitations*
VII. *EMPATHY TECHNIQUES AND MECHANICS*
    A. *Simple Acceptance*
    B. *Restatement of Content*
    C. *Reflection of Feeling*
    D. *Clarification of Feeling*
    E. *Eye Contact*
    F. *Soft Facials*
    G. *Succinct Verbalizations*
    H. *Body Language*
VIII. *TRAINING EXERCISES*
    A. *Examples*
        1. Simple acceptance.
        2. Restatement.
        3. Reflection.
        4. Clarification.
        5. Eye contact.
        6. Positive body responses.
        7. Resonant pensive gestures.
    B. *Role Playing*
        1. Hostile employee.
        2. Panic.
        3. Reluctant witness.
        4. Prejudiced colleague.
        5. Oppositional heel-dragger.
        6. Help-rejecting complainer.
        7. Nit-picking critic.
        8. Other scenarios from training group.
    C. *Feedback and review*
        1. Evaluation of training.
        2. Modifications suggested.
        3. Potential applications.

FIGURE 16.1 *(continued)*

CONTINUING EDUCATION

Even small police departments make fairly stringent efforts to develop a program of continuing education for the officers in that department. Policing is a rapidly changing profession, and with the advent of accreditation, it has become increasingly important for line officers, supervisors, and executives to maintain an awareness of changes in the field, and more effective methods of operation. Small departments may develop their own training programs or may join larger neighboring police departments in pursuing continuing education.

Many states require a specific number of continuing education credits every 2, 3, or 4 years in order for the police officer to maintain certification as a sworn officer.

With the ever-increasing group interest in human relations and growth processes within the police community, psychologists are in a unique position to provide continuing education modules for law enforcement. Some topical areas are suitable for shared presentations at the police academy, and represent updates for working officers. Psychologists have made successful continuing education presentations in the following:

1. The nature of suicide and its prevention.
2. Restraint and sensitivity training.
3. Effective listening.
4. Stress inoculation.
5. Domestic violence and its prevention.
6. Psychological profiling.
7. Techniques for interviewing children.
8. The nature of danger and its prediction.
9. Issues of insanity, competence, and criminal intent.
10. Writing effective reports describing mentally disordered offenders.

This is only a partial list. Many other topics within the field of psychology can be developed into useful training sequences for working police officers.

The construction of such training modules is similar to the development of training sequences for the police academy. There are certain steps to consider when developing continuing education courses:

1. The psychologist should understand the continuing education system of the department for which the presentation will be made.
2. Time constraints are important, and the outline should be developed within the context of the department's expectations.

3. Above all else, the presentation should offer the target audience some practical value enunciated at the beginning of the presentation.

4. In constructing the outline and the course material, the psychologist should consult with line officers, supervisors, and executives to ensure that the material relates to the real world of policing.

5. The recommendations and constraints presented in the previous section regarding Academy presentations apply to continuing education.

Figure 16.2 presents an outline for a continuing education series on restraint and sensitivity training for line officers.

The proposal was made to the appropriate staff and was accepted. The final course outline and presentation materials are presented in Appendix K. After a great deal of experimentation, the entire presentation was formed into eight 15-minute segments that were conducted during roll call before regular duty.

This particular continuing education module caused a considerable amount of interest among other departments, which requested help in establishing similar programs. As a result, an article was written to provide the information developed in this course to a wider audience (Wells, Super, Blau, & Dudley, 1992).

THE POLICE PSYCHOLOGY INTERNSHIP

Although interest and involvement in police psychology have been growing rapidly in recent years, opportunities for training and supervision have not kept pace. The usual model for the development of practical applied professional skills in psychology is to have didactic work in graduate school, followed by supervised training, followed by an internship in a real clinical setting. At the present time, very few graduate schools offer any kind of formal didactic education in police psychology. There is also a paucity of predoctoral internship training experience available.

A few agencies offer a postdoctoral internship in police psychology. The postdoctoral internship may be the most practical way of training professional psychologists to be police psychologists until graduate programs include education and training for work with law enforcement agencies. A postdoctoral internship in police clinical psychology should include certain elements:

1. The program should offer an opportunity to function as a clinical psychologist in a wide range of roles within a law enforcement agency.

RESTRAINT AND SENSITIVITY TRAINING
Presentation Outline

I. *THE ESSENTIAL ISSUES*
   A. *The Tasks of Law Enforcement*
      1. Prevent crimes.
      2. Solve crimes.
      3. Control traffic.
      4. Resolve emergencies.
   B. *Controversial Application of Function and Technique*
      1. Deadly force.
      2. Physical restraint.
      3. Communication with civilians.
      4. Response to resistance, questions, slow compliance.
      5. Affective tone and language related to race, sex, ethnic origin, nationality, intelligence, and so forth.
      6. Proper enforcement with which the civilian is unfamiliar or disagrees.

II. *CONFLICT ESCALATORS*
   A. *Ignorance of Limits of Law*
   B. *Language That Incites*
      1. Sarcasm.
      2. Vernacular.
      3. Threats.
      4. Overemotional shouting.
   C. *Behavior That Incites*
      1. Obscene gestures.
      2. Excessive threatening gestures.
      3. Inappropriate touching.
      4. Unnecessary invasion of personal space (24 inches).
      5. Unnecessary force or restraint.
   D. *Emotional Presentation That Incites*
      1. Excessive macho style.
      2. Intimidating, hostile manner.
      3. Inappropriate interruption or cutting-off.
   E. *Communication That Incites*
      1. Intradepartment.
         a. Humor on radio.
         b. Inappropriate language on reports.
      2. Extradepartment.
         a. Defensiveness to press.
         b. Arguments with civilians.
         c. Impoliteness, shortness, or criticism in responding to telephone calls.

FIGURE 16.2 An Outline Proposing Restraint and Sensitivity Training for Line Officers

III. *CAUSES OF CONFLICT ESCALATORS*
    A. *Inadequate Selection*
    B. *Inadequate Education*
    C. *Inadequate Training*
    D. *Poor Communication from Supervisors or Managers*
    E. *Poor Modeling by Supervisors, Managers, and Senior Officers*
    F. *Emotional Instability*
       1. Low self-esteem.
       2. Insecurity.
       3. Depression.
       4. Mental illness.
       5. Drug or alcohol abuse.
    G. *Character Deficiencies*
    H. *Overload*
    I. *Personal Problems*
    J. *Physical Illness*
    K. *Financial Problems*
    L. *Post-Trauma Reactions*
IV. *SOLUTIONS*
    A. *Management*
       1. Sound selection procedures.
       2. Proper training.
       3. Supplying proper equipment.
       4. Modeling.
       5. Two-way communication.
       6. Morale surveys.
    B. *Individual Law Enforcement Officer*
       1. Periodic retraining.
         a. Effective listening skills.
         b. Interpersonal skills training.
         c. Recognition of unspoken messages.
         d. Courtesy training.
       2. Traumatic incident logging, counseling, and role playing.
       3. Planning for recreational activity.
       4. Keeping physically fit.
       5. Proper diet and adequate rest.
       6. Organizing and prioritizing responsibilities.
       7. Practicing stress reduction techniques.
       8. Seek preventive help from the Behavioral Science Unit.

FIGURE 16.2   *(continued)*

2. In addition to specific focus on clinical work with police officers and their families, such an internship should ensure that the just-graduated doctoral psychologists have experience and supervision in the range of skills expected of a clinical psychologist.

3. The internship should provide the range and quality of supervision necessary for the intern to become qualified for licensure.

4. The setting should conform to the expectation that postdoctoral interns will be regarded and treated as professional psychologists.

5. There should be a formalized schedule of training, supervision, and service.

6. The intern should be given frequent formative evaluations by supervisors during the internship year.

7. The intern should have a summative evaluation at the end of the program.

8. The intern should be provided with letters of recommendation from all supervisors on completion of the program.

9. The intern should be given an opportunity for some degree of police training, ranging from familiarization interactions to attendance at the police academy and commissioning as a sworn officer.

10. Sufficient time should be provided to ensure that the intern can prepare for his or her licensing exam.

11. Supervisors should encourage the intern to participate in psychological organizations.

Figure 16.3 presents a recruitment announcement for a postdoctoral internship in police clinical psychology.

The degree of interest in this announcement was considerable. The agency received 45 applications, of which 19 were considered appropriately qualified. A selection committee made up of the Director of the Behavioral Science Unit, the two psychologists who would serve as additional supervisors, and three senior police officials reviewed all the applications and independently ranked their selections.

The announcement of the candidate's appointment was sent to all supervisors and executives in the agency and was also posted for all line officers to see (Figure 16.4).

The intern completed his year, attended the Police Academy at night, and was commissioned as a Deputy Sheriff following graduation from the Police Academy. He successfully passed the licensing examination.

Following the completion of the internship, the successful candidate requested a second year's postdoctoral internship. After discussing this with various executives in the agency, it was decided to offer a Senior Fellowship in Police Clinical Psychology as a way of evaluating how the

---

POSTDOCTORAL INTERNSHIP
In
Police Clinical Psychology

The _____ County Sheriff's Office will offer a postdoctoral opportunity to a qualified graduate of an APA-approved doctoral program in Clinical and Professional Psychology. Located in _____, the _____ County Sheriff's Office is a modern law enforcement agency employing over 500 certified officers and civilians. For the past ___ years, the _____ County Sheriff's Office has had a fully operational Behavioral Science Unit.

The candidate selected for this internship will receive supervision by three ABPP psychologists and practice in the following:

- Individual Psychotherapy
- Personality Assessment
- Crisis Counseling
- Police Selection
- Psychological Autopsy
- Fitness-for-Duty Evaluation
- Hostage Negotiation
- Wellness Programs
- Investigative Hypnosis

- Group Psychotherapy
- Neuropsychology
- Management Consultation
- Stress Management
- Psychological Profiling
- Drug and Alcohol Counseling
- Employee Assistance Counseling
- Family Counseling

The successful candidate will have an opportunity to become a certified law enforcement officer during the internship year by attending a local police academy.

STARTING DATE	September 1, 1989
COMPLETION DATE	August 15, 1990
APPLICATIONS ACCEPTED UNTIL	March 31, 1989
STIPEND	$19,000

FIGURE 16.3   A Recruitment Announcement for a Postdoctoral Internship in Police Clinical Psychology

agency could use a full-time, in-house clinical psychologist. Figure 16.5 presents the bulletin offering this Fellowship.

The requirements were such that no one but the postdoctoral intern who had been trained in this agency applied. The focus of the Senior Fellowship was to develop independent responsibility as a police clinical psychologist, and to function as the Assistant Director of the Behavioral Science Unit. This, in fact, came about and following the second postdoctoral year, the candidate was appointed Director the Behavioral Science Unit, as a full-time employee of the agency.

ANNOUNCEMENT OF APPOINTMENT
POSTDOCTORAL INTERN IN POLICE CLINICAL PSYCHOLOGY

John Super, PhD has been appointed to the Postdoctoral Internship in Police Clinical Psychology at the Manatee County Sheriff's Office. This appointment will be from 9/1/89 through 8/15/90. Duty hours shall be between 8:00 A.M. and 5:00 P.M. Monday through Friday with emergency availability whenever required.

All of Dr. Super's work will be directed and supervised by T. H. Blau, PhD, Director of the MCSO Behavioral Science Unit. Additional consulting supervision will be provided by Robert Greene, PhD (approximately 45 half-days) and Glenn Larrabee, PhD (approximately 48 days) at their clinical facilities. Dr. Super will spend approximately 28 half-days in hospital supervision under Dr. Blau at the Tampa VA Hospital.

While at the MCSO, Dr. Super will render a variety of psychological services under Dr. Blau's training and supervision including but not limited to:

- Individual Counseling
- Stress Inoculation
- Group Therapy
- Wellness Training
- Research
- Crisis Counseling
- Management Consultation
- Investigative Consultation
- Peer Counselor Training
- Stop Smoking Clinics
- Individual Stress Management
- Group Counseling

- Individual Psychotherapy
- Training Seminars
- Investigative Hypnosis
- Selection Testing and Fitness-for-Duty Evaluations
- Selection Consultation
- Critical Incident Counseling
- Test Battery Standardization
- Family Cohesiveness Training
- Family Counseling
- Relaxation Training

Requests for services may be made by calling Extension 2257.

FIGURE 16.4 Announce of Candidate's Appointment

At this early stage in the development of police clinical psychology, absolute standards for training would be premature. The material that has been presented in this chapter forms the basis of a beginning in training and education, and should be followed by the development of specialty tracks in graduate school, predoctoral internship training standards, and further development of postdoctoral opportunities for psychologists who anticipate focusing their career in the area of police clinical psychology.

THE SENIOR FELLOWSHIP IN POLICE CLINICAL PSYCHOLOGY

The _____ County Sheriff's Office will institute a Senior Fellowship in Psychology for the year 1990–1991. This position will be filled by a licensed clinical psychologist who has completed a 1-year postdoctoral fellowship in Police Clinical Psychology. The focus of the second year will be to prepare the Senior Fellow to independently operate a full-range behavioral science unit in a law enforcement agency of any size—local, state, or federal.

The following shall be the focus of training and experience during this Fellowship:

- Consulting with management on personnel, policy, procedures, and research.
- Supervising the operation and research associated with selection of law enforcement candidates.
- Supervising the selection procedures and research with correctional officers.
- Providing a full range of clinical services to sworn officers, their families, and in special instances other personnel within the department.
- Consulting with directors of all units in the MCSO.
- Providing psychological techniques and material to enhance investigative procedures.
- Conducting research.
- Presenting special training seminars for sworn personnel.
- Assuming responsibility for all forms, procedures, and reports.
- Assuming responsibility for developing and implementing new procedures and policy for the Behavioral Science Unit.
- Providing training and reference material for psychologists entering the field of police clinical psychology.
- Gaining experience as a functioning law enforcement officer with various units of the MCSO.
- Serving as associate director of the Behavioral Science Unit.
- Providing consultation and information to other law enforcement agencies with the approval of the Sheriff and Undersheriff.

FIGURE 16.5   A Recruitment Announcement for a Senior Fellowship in Police Clinical Psychology

CHAPTER SEVENTEEN

Epilogue

Is there a future for the development of a field of police clinical psychology? This question is tied to the issue of whether there is a future for policing. To examine this question, it might be instructive to look at some data that represent society's need for effective policing. A baker's dozen of statistics graphically illustrate this current status (Dodenhoff, 1993):

1. As of the beginning of 1992, there were 535,629 sworn law enforcement officers in county, city, and state police agencies throughout the United States.
2. There were 426,479 inmates in the nation's local jails by mid-1991, a 5.2% increase over 1990.
3. In 1992, 136 law enforcement officers were killed in the line of duty.
4. During 1991, 34.7 million crimes were experienced by U.S. residents 12 years or older.
5. During 1991, 14.2 million arrests were made by law enforcement agencies for all criminal offenses except traffic violations.
6. Of felony defendants who were granted pretrial release, 24% then failed to appear for scheduled court hearings during 1990.
7. As of mid-1992, 855,958 men and women were serving time in state and federal prisons.
8. During 1991, 1.1 million incidents of domestic violence were reported to police.
9. There were 1.7 million motor vehicle thefts in the United States in 1991.
10. During 1991, there were 1,965 bombings in the United States, a figure that doubled annually during the previous four years. Twenty-seven people were killed, and 246 were injured in these events.
11. There were 24,020 homicides in the United States during 1991.
12. During the first 3 months of 1992, 30,103 cocaine-related visits to hospital emergency rooms were recorded.

13. In 1990, the average time spent in prison by a person who was committed after conviction for murder was 1.8 years. In looking at all
felonies, a person who committed a serious crime during the year
1990 and was convicted of that crime could expect to spend an average of 8 days in prison.

These data indicate that American society is in desperate need of modern and effective policing. In turn, the police need all the help they can get
to properly enforce the law within the constraints and expectations of a
democratic society.

The Task Ahead

There are many opportunities for professional psychologists to serve their
community and their profession by working as police psychologists. The
psychologist may take a position as a full-time police psychologist or may
be a consultant to a police department. Psychologists may serve as teachers in a police academy, in a college-level (bachelor or associate degree)
program in Criminal Justice, or in graduate school, teaching in a police
psychology track for psychology students. Psychologists may supervise
other psychologists as well as other mental health workers in serving police needs. Finally, in some instances, psychologists may serve as police
executives, bringing behavioral science to the administration of law enforcement agencies. When that situation occurs, law enforcement will
have seen the value of behavioral science services.

STANDARDS AND ETHICS

At the present time, psychologists who work with law enforcement officers are bound by the Ethical Principles of Psychologists and Code of
Conduct of the American Psychological Association (American Psychological Association, 1992). These include a good many general principles
regarding competence, integrity, professional and scientific responsibility, respect for people's rights and dignity, and concern for the welfare
of others. In fairly general terms, these principles describe boundaries
of competence, the nature and results of psychological services, nondis-
crimination, harassment, personal problems and conflicts, misuse of the
psychologist's influence, exploitative relationships, and third-party requests for services. There are general rules for conducting evaluation
and assessment as well as intervention. Restraints, restrictions, and expectations for therapeutic intervention as well as for privacy and confidentiality are discussed and described. There is some focus on the
principles and ethics required for forensic activities (Principle 7.017.06).
This was a major revision of previous Codes of Conduct and Ethical

Standards. Many of the behaviors of police psychologists are covered and described in general.

Some specific admonitions and constraints appropriate for police psychologists are found in *Specialty Guidelines for Forensic Psychologists* (Committee on Ethical Guidelines for Forensic Psychologists, 1991). These guidelines focus on responsibility, competence, relationships, confidentiality, and privilege, as well as on methods and procedures. Neither of these documents specifically applies to the practice of police psychology. Some situations and circumstances described in this volume have yet to be tested against the formal Ethics and Standards of the psychological profession. This process will take place as psychologists gain experience in this relatively new field.

FINAL NOTES

Psychologists who have worked with police almost universally believe that their work has been worthwhile. There are great personal satisfactions in making a significant contribution to one of the most vital of community services. Psychologists who work with law enforcement promote human welfare by helping a seriously beleaguered human services profession. The opportunities for practice, teaching, and research are almost limitless. As Gilbert and Sullivan wrote over one hundred years ago, "The policeman's lot is not a happy one." With the help of psychologists, it is becoming happier, more effective, and a more useful arm of social responsibility.

The Psychological Services Offered by the Behavioral Science Unit in a Mid-Size Law Enforcement Agency

BEHAVIORAL SCIENCE UNIT

History

Psychological services to law enforcement have been used for over a hundred years. Initially explored at the end of the 19th century, this applied science did not become established until almost mid-20th century. Individual psychologists have served a variety of local, state, and federal law enforcement agencies on a consultation basis for many years. The first behavioral science unit was established in the mid-1970s by the Federal Bureau of Investigation at their Quantico, Virginia, academy. This unit has grown steadily, and is now an essential element in the FBI's forensic science services.

In local law enforcement agencies the behavioral science unit is still a rare phenomenon. Traditional law enforcement personnel tend to explore new ideas slowly, to a large extent, because of the enormous work loads that exist at all levels of law enforcement.

The Behavioral Science Unit of the Alpha Sheriff's Office (ASO) was formed in the fall of 1985. Sheriff Good saw the considerable potential for cost-effectiveness and the cost-efficiency in a range of law enforcement activities through the application of modern behavioral science methods. He invited Jane Doe, PhD, to establish and build this unit. Today, it is a full-time functioning section of the ASO, reporting directly to the Undersheriff and the Sheriff.

Services

A broad range of services is offered to the administration and the staff of the Alpha Sheriff's Office. Although the list that follows describes most

315

of these services, new applications continually arise. The psychological services which are presently offered include the following:

1. *ORGANIZATIONAL SERVICES*

   The most successful behavioral science units in various agencies have been accessible to top management. That is the style of the ASO. Included in the organizational services are:

   a. *Consultation to Management.* All managerial and supervisory ranks have access to the Behavioral Science Unit for help in organizing, reorganizing, and making the operation of the ASO more efficient.

   b. *Sworn Officer Personnel Selection.* The psychological assessment of officer candidates has been developed and put into place by the Behavioral Science Unit. Two major studies indicate that this is a cost-effective procedure. Research continually seeks to improve selection methods and procedures for all sworn personnel at the ASO.

   c. *Fitness-for-Duty Evaluations.* In accordance with Accreditation Standards, a system for psychologically evaluating those officers exposed to stress, difficult circumstances, injury, or other potentially debilitating circumstances is in place. When there is any question, for any reason, as to the psychological fitness of a sworn officer for duty, an assessment is requested by the Undersheriff, and the evaluation results are returned to him.

   d. *Special Unit Evaluation.* The Behavioral Science Unit offers psychological tests services for the annual evaluation of members of special units, as is required by the Accreditation Standards.

   e. *Hostage Negotiation Consultation.* Training, consultation, and participation are available at the request of the Hostage Negotiation Team leader.

   f. *Deadly Force Incident Evaluation.* Where an officer is involved in a deadly force situation, as a shooter, as a wounded officer, or as the partner of an officer who was wounded or killed, stress reactions can be expected. The Behavioral Science Unit offers critical incident counseling for these situations. In some instances, these procedures lead to critical incident counseling for partners, family, and other individuals who may be associated with those involved in the incident.

   g. *Police News Update.* The Behavioral Science Unit publishes a summary of nationwide news relating to law enforcement and police duties. This conglomeration of articles is put into a booklet that is distributed to all units of the ASO four times per year.

   h. *Behavioral Science Library.* The Behavioral Science Unit maintains a library of scientific articles in the field of law enforcement. Areas of interest include, but are not limited to, hostage negotiations, family violence, stress, hypnosis, polygraphy, interrogation, sex crimes, and psychological profiling.

Three times a year, the Behavioral Science Unit publishes the titles of the new articles, with a descriptive paragraph. Those members of the department who wish to read the original article, simply request the number on the descriptive bulletin and the reprint is made available to them.

2. *INVESTIGATIVE SERVICES*

In recent years, particularly with more police psychologists becoming police officers and gaining real-life experience in the field of law enforcement, psychological services are beginning to be used as aids in crime investigation. Specific behavioral science services include:

a. *Investigative Hypnosis.* Psychologists have for decades been available to use hypnosis to increase the accuracy and content of witness memory in relation to crimes. The Behavioral Science Unit of the ASO has had a fairly good record of success with this procedure and is frequently used by other agencies in helping them pursue their investigations.

b. *Serial Murder Profiling.* Procedures similar to those used at the FBI Academy to identify and describe serial murderers can be formulated by the staff of the Behavioral Science Unit.

c. *Serial Rape Profiling.* Psychological profiles of serial rapists are constructed by the Behavioral Science Unit at the request of investigating officers who believe that they are dealing with this particular kind of perpetrator.

d. *Sex Crimes Analysis.* Sex crimes may have unusual or complex psychological motivation associated with them. Psychological evaluation and analysis of crime data are available from the Behavioral Science Unit.

e. *Psychological Autopsy.* Where a question exists as to the involvement of a deceased party in a crime, a psychological autopsy can be performed to determine the motivation and involvement of the deceased individual.

f. *Cross-Agency Consultation.* As our Behavioral Science Unit has grown, its reputation has spread. We have provided consultation to the FBI, the U.S. Treasury Department (Secret Service), sheriff's offices throughout Florida, state police agencies in a variety of states, the United States Marshal's Office, and individual police agencies around the country.

3. *TRAINING*

To maintain the highest level of skill, integrity efficiency, and commitment among the Alpha Sheriff's Office personnel, training seminars are offered. All training seminars are presented upon the request of management.

During the past four years, the Behavioral Science Unit has created a variety of training functions within the ASO. Some of the specific programs include:

a. *Stress Reduction Seminars.* Stress is the foremost condition that causes law enforcement personnel to seek psychological counseling. The Behavioral Science Unit offers stress-reduction seminars that focus on the origins of stress, the effects of stress, and how to deal more effectively when coping with stressful situations.

b. *Spouse Abuse Detection, Prevention, and Intervention Training.* Spouse abuse prevention and intervention training has several basic elements. First, officers learn how spousal abuse actually occurs and the devastating effects of such abuse. Next, the nature of stress as a contributory factor to spouse abuse is addressed. Thirdly, marital factors relating to spouse abuse are reviewed. Finally, prevention and intervention techniques are taught by active role play, behavioral rehearsal, and modeling. This training includes support materials that all persons attending receive. This seminar was originally conceived by Sheriff Good to maintain the highest level of awareness and functional capacity of all sworn ASO employees in dealing with issues of family violence.

c. *Training Seminars.* A broad array of training seminars are offered by the Behavioral Science Unit on the application of the science of human behavior to practical issues in law enforcement. Included are the psychology of driving, expert witness, post-traumatic stress, credibility of the child witness, and deadly force.

d. *Public Information and Media Presentation.* The Behavioral Science Unit strives to maintain good relationships with the public and the media. This is done by way of meetings and presentations, as well as granting interviews to various media and public information systems.

e. *Peer Group Counselor Training.* Recently, police administrators have been paying increased attention to law enforcement personnel who have used deadly force in the line of duty or who have been injured in the line of duty. Such events can seriously undermine the efficiency and effectiveness of involved officers and their colleagues. The Behavioral Science Unit provides counselor training for individuals who may have experienced personal injury or who may have used deadly force in the line of duty. These peer counselors can be more useful in critical incident counseling than many professional mental health workers.

4. *PERSONAL SERVICES*

Traditional and nontraditional psychological services for sworn members of the ASO and their families have been offered during the past four years. These mental health services include:

a. *Individual Psychological Counseling.* The Behavioral Science Unit offers psychological counseling to Alpha Sheriff's Office employees. The individual counseling offered is usually short term, ranging between one and six sessions. Should Behavioral Science Unit personnel decide the presenting problem requires long-term care, a referral will be made to a community agency. A referral resource directory of agencies and professionals who offer both quality services and affordable costs is being developed.

b. *Group Psychological Counseling.* It is not uncommon for situations to arise where persons face similar conflicts or similar trauma. During such times, it is often most efficient and/or expedient to utilize group psychological counseling.

c. *Family Counseling.* Law enforcement personnel are faced with many stressful situations on a daily basis. Functional coping mechanisms used on the job are frequently taken home no matter how inappropriate they may be in a family setting. This can result in many law enforcement officers experiencing problems within the family. Family counseling is available on a limited basis to help reduce conflict.

d. *Critical Incident Counseling.* Critical incident counseling involves support and conflict resolution with individuals who have been involved in a deadly force incident, have been injured, or have witnessed a trauma to a partner or associate. Because critical incident counseling is most effective when conducted very soon after the experienced trauma, this is considered a high-priority service.

e. *Stress Reduction Counseling.* Stress reduction counseling is offered by the Behavioral Science Unit. Persons employed in law enforcement organizations often experience considerable stress. When severe or prolonged, stress has a depressing effect on functional capacity. In the field of law enforcement, deceased functional level can have life and death ramifications.

   In addition to stress reduction counseling, a stress reduction kit has been developed by the Behavioral Science Unit. The kit includes a cassette player with headphones, several tapes to help with stress reduction and related problems, a colorimeter stress reduction card, and instructions for all the material. The stress reduction kit or any part thereof will be loaned to Alpha County personnel on request.

f. *Family Consultation and Evaluation.* The Behavioral Science Unit offers limited child and adolescent psychological evaluation. In addition, the Behavioral Science Unit offers marital counseling on a limited basis. Psychological evaluations are limited to screening evaluations for the purpose of making initial recommendations. Where long-term marital counseling is indicated, referral will be made.

g. *Employee Assistance Referrals.* Should individuals require counseling of more than six sessions, referral services will be provided. At present, the Behavioral Science Unit is developing a referral service network. All providers of mental health care in Alpha County are being surveyed. The results of this project will provide an efficient referral network for members of the ASO.

h. *Health and Wellness Programs.* There is a growing awareness in law enforcement agencies of the importance of wellness and health. Increasing attention is being paid to the interaction of the mind and body, both influencing one another. Health and wellness programs, including environmental management plans, are available from the Behavioral Science Unit.

i. *Stop Smoking Programs.* Smoking has been shown to be related to various physical abnormalities, ranging from heart and respiratory conditions to cancer. Most physicians believe that smoking can compound any physical abnormalities a person may sustain. The Behavioral Science Unit offers stop-smoking programs in the form of counseling, literature, and tapes to all Alpha County Sheriff's Office personnel.

j. *Drug and Alcohol Counseling.* Drug and alcohol abuse usually have devastating effects on the family as well as the work situation. The Behavioral Science Unit offers brief counseling for persons who may face such problems. The Behavioral Science Unit staff can make referrals, where necessary, to inpatient programs.

5. *RESEARCH*

The Behavioral Science Unit has conducted a number of research studies and has other studies ongoing. Two of these studies have been published in *The Police Chief.* Currently, the following research efforts under way:

a. *Effectiveness of Psychological Tests in Selection of Employees.* At present, many organizations include psychological tests in screening procedures for potential employees. Due to the complexities of law enforcement, many screening tests that can be used in other organizations are not as effective with law enforcement personnel.

Thus far, we have been relatively successful in providing the Personnel Service with test procedures to predict the likelihood that patrol officers will function adequately on duty. At present, the Behavioral Science Unit is conducting research to assess the effectiveness of psychological tests in the selection of correctional employees.

b. *Family Homicide Prediction.* As indicated by Sheriff Good, the Behavioral Science Unit has identified indicators associated with family homicide. The Behavioral Science Unit consults with law enforcement officers and with community social agencies in identifying, predicting, preventing, and intervening in situations that may lead to family homicide.

c. *Understanding Crack (Cocaine) Usage.* At the request of Sheriff Good, the Behavioral Science Unit, with the cooperation of the Public Defender's Office, has studied the social and psychological conditions leading to the use of crack (cocaine) and the legal consequences of this. As the data gleaned from the in-depth evaluation of 37 convicted crack felons are analyzed, results will be used to develop treatment.

d. *Evaluation of Effectiveness of Family Violence Training.* The Behavioral Science Unit has analyzed the data collected during the family violence prevention and intervention training of all sworn officers in the ASO. Training program modifications will be made to increase the effectiveness of the training system.

6. *ASSESSMENT OF EFFECTIVENESS*

It is difficult to assess the effectiveness of behavioral science services. A study by the Behavioral Science Unit is under way to determine the cost-effectiveness of the sworn officer selection program that has been in place at the ASO for over three years. Preliminary results indicate that considerable sums of money have been saved as a result of the selection battery. Further studies as to the efficiency of sworn officers who are selected with the aid of psychological tests versus those who have not been so selected are under way.

Morale surveys and functional efficiency studies are possible in the future, depending on the funding available for such projects. Perhaps the most telling answers to questions of whether the Behavioral Science Unit has been effective are the escalating requests for service over the past four years. At this point in time, demands for service are such that a waiting period is necessary before all but emergency situations.

7. *DIRECTING REQUESTS FOR SERVICE*

a. *Nonconfidential Services.* Requests for any of the nonpersonal services rendered by the Behavioral Science Unit should come to the Director of the Behavioral Science Unit, through the Sheriff and/or the Undersheriff. These requests will be dealt with on a priority basis, either in terms of the emergency nature of such request, or in terms of the backlog of requests that exist at that time.

None of the services rendered in this area are to be considered confidential. In those instances where the referral is for a fitness-for-duty evaluation, the report will be directed to the Undersheriff and the Sheriff. Furthermore, the disposal of that information will be at the discretion of management. The actual test materials, however, will be kept confidential.

b. *Confidential Services.* A great many mental health services provided by the Behavioral Science Unit involve individuals, their families, and their personal problems. It is understood and agreed between the Behavioral Science Unit and the Sheriff that such contacts are privileged and confidential. All materials will be kept in a locked file by the Behavioral Science Unit staff. All such materials, even participation of members of the ASO in any kind of a treatment setting, are confidential.

Within the framework of this privilege and confidentiality, the staff of the Behavioral Science Unit are duty bound to abide by the principles and ethics of the American Psychological Association, and the ethical constraints of the Illiana Board of Examiners of Psychology. Certain exclusions to the confidentiality and privilege rule, such as Duty to Warn, will be explained to anyone seeking mental health services with the Behavioral Science Unit. When a referral is made from the Behavioral Science Unit to a professional in the community, records will only be transferred at the specific written request of the individual with whom the Behavioral Science Unit has worked.

8. *LIMITATION OF SERVICES*

In some instances, the Behavioral Science Unit cannot and should not offer mental health services. Those areas include:

a. Contacts that require more than 6 to 12 sessions. Referral will be made to an appropriate mental health provider within the community.

b. Requests for services that are outside of the expertise or availability of the staff members of the Behavioral Science Unit.

c. At present, services are limited to sworn, full-time personnel, unless directly referred by the Sheriff or Undersheriff.

9. *LOCATION*

The Behavioral Science Unit is presently located on the fourth floor of the Alpha County Sheriff's Office District No. 1. There is a second office located at 123 Elm Street. Appointments for initial interviews should be made by dialing Extension 2273 or 2257.

The Behavioral Science Unit office at 123 Elm Street will be open at a variety of times. Those who wish to receive services there should ask the Behavioral Science Unit staff member at the time an appointment is requested.

Proposed Standards

TO   Council of Police Psychological Services (COPPS)

FROM   Academy of Police Psychologists (APP)

RE   Annual Report (Bartlett, 1991)

The annual meeting for 1990 was held in Tampa, Florida, on March 29–30. The APP was formed to develop standards for Police Psychological Services. The designated areas were:

1. Preemployment Selection.
2. Fitness-for-Duty Evaluation and Standards.
3. Special Duty Evaluation.
4. Confidentiality.
5. Quality Assurance for Referral Sources.
6. Critical Incident Stress Debriefing.
7. Hostage Negotiation.
8. Education and Training.
9. Stress Management.
10. Psychological Profiling.
11. Hypnosis.

The Academy has received information for the first 7 of 11 categories. The other sections have COPPS members assigned. However, they have not been developed sufficiently to be submitted.

PREEMPLOYMENT SELECTION

The following standards are proposed as guidelines for professional practice in the area of preemployment psychological testing of law enforcement officer candidates. They do not represent mandatory standards, but are presented as a useful framework for agencies and individuals who are charged with the responsibility of conducting defensible psychological screening programs.

The proposed guidelines were taken from two sources. One source questioned twenty-seven (27) police psychologists from sixteen (16) different states. The average number of psychological evaluations completed each year by the 27 respondents was two hundred seventy one (271) screenings (Inwald, 1990b). The second source is the IACP Police Psychology Section's "Guidelines for Providers of Pre-Employment Psychological Evaluation Services to Law Enforcement Agencies," adopted at their 1986 annual meeting.

Overview

1. The preemployment psychological assessment should be used as one component of the overall selection process. The psychological recommendations should not be used as the sole criterion for a "hire/no hire" decision. Candidates denied employment based, even in part, on the psychological evaluations should be allowed an opportunity to appeal the decision to the hiring authority.

Developments

2. Before conducting their own clinical assessments of candidates, practitioners should be familiar with the research literature available on psychological testing for law enforcement officers.
3. Only licensed or certified psychologists, trained and experienced in psychological testing, interpretation, and law enforcement psychological assessment techniques, should conduct psychological screening for law enforcement agencies.
4. Data on psychological attributes considered most important for effective officer behavior should be obtained from job analysis, interviews, surveys, or other appropriate data-gathering techniques to aid in the development of hiring standards.
5. If possible, baseline data on critical criteria measures (such as rates of serious incidents, negative reports, etc.) should be collected for future comparisons before a psychological testing program is implemented.
6. Efforts should be made to provide administrators with information regarding the benefits and limitations of psychological assessment procedures so that realistic goals may be set.
7. Provisions should be made for the security of all testing materials.

Testing

8. The comprehensive psychological test battery including objective, broad-based validated personality instruments should be administered to applicants. Test results should be available to the evaluator before follow-up interviews are conducted.

9. Written psychological tests should be validated and interpreted to aid in the selection of applicants.

10. If mail order or computerized tests are employed, a licensed or certified psychologist must interpret and verify individual results. This psychologist shall be readily available for on-site consultation and follow-up with administrators and candidates. Mail order or computer tests results should not be provided to administrators as an assessment of ability. This function requires a face-to-face interview to assess emotional stability.

Interview

11. It is strongly recommended that individual face-to-face interviews for candidates be conducted before a final evaluation psychological report is made.

12. A standard interview format should be employed with all psychological material including available background data and test results evaluated by interviewers in advance.

13. Core questions in the interview, also allowing for open-ended follow-up questions, should be periodically reviewed and possibly edited so that practitioners can increase their probability of collecting the most relevant information in a limited period of time.

Evaluation

14. Administrators directly involved in making hiring decisions should be provided with written or oral reports. These reports should evaluate the suitability of the applicant for the job based on analysis of all psychological material including available data, test, and interview results. If oral reports are submitted, the psychologist should maintain documentation of findings supporting the oral recommendations. The final report should include any reservations that the psychologist might have regarding the validity or reliability of the results.

15. While a clinical assessment of overall psychological suitability may be made, clinical diagnoses or psychiatric "labeling" of candidates should be avoided when the goal is to identify those individuals whose psychological difficulties may adversely affect specific job performance.

16. Specific cutoff scores should be avoided unless there is clear evidence that such scores are valid and have been cross-validated in research studies in the agency where they will be used.

17. Clear disclaimers should be made so that reports evaluating current emotional stability or suitability for a job in law enforcement will not be deemed valid after a specific period of time.

Follow-Up

18. Preemployment test results should not be used for purposes other than making preemployment hiring decisions and doing follow-up research where individual officer identities are protected.
19. Continuing efforts should be made to validate final "suitability" ratings using behavioral criteria measures.
20. Each agency should maintain adverse impact analysis by sex and ethnicity.
21. Providers of psychological testing services should be prepared to defend their procedures, conclusions and recommendations if a decision based, even in part, of psychological results is challenged.

STANDARDS FOR FITNESS-FOR-DUTY EVALUATIONS

The purpose of the law enforcement psychological fitness-for-duty evaluation is to determine whether, due to mental limitation, character disorder, or emotional illness, a law enforcement officer is significantly impaired in the performance of his/her duties. The evaluation is a two-stage process. Stage one is the assessment for the presence or absence of psychological disorder. Stage two is an assessment of the impairment of work-related functioning. The result of the two-stage process should be a report with a final recommendation to the agency regarding fitness for duty. Often treatment recommendations, duty limitations, and other conditions are offered as part of the fitness-for-duty assessment.

Standard I

Evaluations of psychological fitness-for-duty should be performed by licensed psychologists or certified psychiatrists who have substantial familiarity with law enforcement duties and responsibilities and who are also familiar with the clinical issues involved in the case. Where specified issues (e.g., substance abuse, neuropsychological dysfunction) are beyond the scope of expertise of an otherwise qualified evaluator, a consultation with a specialist is appropriate; however, final assessment regarding fitness for duty must be determined by a law enforcement mental health professional.

Standard II

Evaluations must be performed in conformity with American Psychological Association/American Psychiatric Association ethical principles.

Standard III

Waiver forms must be provided to officer candidates prior to the examination and must specify in clear language:

a. For whom the examiner is conducting the examination (usually the appointing authority).
b. The purpose of the examination.
c. The scope of the individual's authority to whom results may be reported.

Standard IV

Where no psychological dysfunction is evident, a finding of fit for duty (from a psychological viewpoint) necessarily follows.

Standard V

Examiners must avail themselves of a wide range of sources of information in examining each case, including evidence from supervisors, spouses, personnel documents, medical sources. Reliance simply on a mental status examination is often misleading and thus insufficient in most cases.

Standard VI

A fitness-for-duty evaluation is not and should not be used as a substitute for disciplinary or legal action.

Standard VII

It is desirable that an appeal process be incorporated into procedures.

Standard VIII

Psychological assessment results should be communicated to referral sources in a clear understandable language by an individual capable of interpreting professional language and concepts. This would ordinarily be a licensed psychologist or certified psychiatrist.

Standard IX

The results of the examination should be presented to the appointing authority in a timely manner in the form of a clear report. The report must include a diagnosis and a statement of which (if any) work-related functions are compromised as a result of the psychological disorder. The report should also stipulate the status of the officer's fitness for duty. The alternatives include:

a. Fully fit.
b. Fit for light/restricted duty.
c. Conditionally fit for duty (fit so long as employee follows prescribed activity, e.g., alcoholism treatment).
d. Unfit pending intervention (e.g., completion of an alcohol treatment program).
e. Unfit for duty.
f. Combination of above.

Thus, the diagnosis should bear directly on the work-related limitations. In turn, treatment recommendations should follow from work-related limitations.

Standard X

Where treatment or other intervention is recommended as a result of the examination, the evaluator must then avoid a dual relationship with the employee (i.e., the mental health professional should not provide treatment and simultaneously continue to formally monitor the employee's fitness for duty).

SPECIAL DUTY EVALUATION

Increasing numbers of departments are requesting psychological evaluations of individuals who apply for or who are assigned to such special units as SWAT, Hostage Negotiations, and undercover teams. This selection/evaluation system is relatively new. Psychologists who participate in this should be aware that there are no base rates available, and that any decision-making process is bound to be subjective and possibly biased. The implication in these evaluations is "the avoidance of psychopathology." It should be borne in mind that what some may consider "psychopathological" others may consider a necessary skill or characteristic for successful activity in the work being considered.

Standard I

Those who receive the reports should always be given the disclaimer that these results are tentative and experimental. It should be indicated that these results are clinical psychological estimates, and are not based on research material.

Standard II

In the course of functioning as an evaluator for special duty, it is the responsibility of the police psychologists to begin building a database. Conducting in-house research should be a part of the duties of the psychologist and administrative managers should know that this is not only desirable, but necessary. Internal consistency would be a first step, followed by prospective studies.

Standard III

The psychologist should make every effort to do a careful task analysis for the various duties involved. Every effort should be made to ensure construct and face validity from the very beginning.

Standard IV

Any system of evaluation that does not have a firm database should include options for reevaluation where questions as to competency or adequacy emerge. If negative findings are presented, the psychologist should be prepared to defend them on a rationale/theoretical basis, as well as to offer a reevaluation to ensure the reliability of the findings.

Standard V

Because individuals change and are subject to constant stress in the law enforcement business, especially in special duty situations, regular monitoring (on an annual basis, at least) should be strongly recommended to administrative managers.

CONFIDENTIALITY

Confidentiality refers to the keeping of secrets. It is essentially an "anti-gossip" construct. It is a long-standing tradition, dating back to the Hippocratic oath of physicians that information passing between the doctor and the patient shall not be discussed in any situation which might be embarrassing or deleterious to the patient. This does not bar clinical discussions with colleagues, but does forbid casual discussion of the information.

By contrast, "privilege" is a legal construct which, in many instances, mandates that information concerning a patient may not be provided under penalty of law.

The American Psychological Association (APA) states, "Psychologists have a primary obligation to respect the confidentiality of information obtained from persons in the course of their work as psychologists. They reveal such information to others only with the consent of the person or the person's legal representative, except in those unusual circumstances in which not to do so would result in clear danger to the person or to others. Where appropriate, psychologists inform their clients of the legal limits of confidentiality."

Confidential Information in Police Work

1. Psychological testing that is part of the selection procedures.
2. Psychological testing in fitness-for-duty referrals.
3. Psychological information derived from the assessment of special teams or units.
4. Information that is generated in the course of a counseling or therapeutic relationship.
5. Psychological information that emerges from investigative psychological work, such as forensic hypnosis.

In order to transfer the information derived from the preceding sources to any party requesting such information, the psychologists must be certain that the individual from whom the information has been derived is aware of how the information will be used, and has given informed consent (must be in writing) for the transfer of the information. Inherent in this informed consent is the individual's awareness of who will receive the information, how it will be used, and how it will be stored.

Release of Confidential Information in Police Work

1. The individual signs a specific release information form.
2. A "Duty to Warn" situation occurs where the individual may act in a manner dangerous to self or others.
3. The individual is accused of capital crime, and the individual's defense attorney requires access to the information in the pursuit of a defense of his/her client.
4. The psychologist is a defendant in a legal matter, criminal or civil, where the services rendered and the results of such services are at issue (such as in a malpractice suit).

The psychological work done in a police department is complex, and there is a propensity for police personnel to seek as much information as possible. This can result in role conflicts.

GENERAL RULES OF CONFIDENTIALITY IN POLICE WORK

Standard I

In all matters undertaken by the police psychologists, informed consent should be obtained. This means that the services should be thoroughly described, the limits of confidentiality discussed, and the client's awareness of these factors made a matter of record in a signed form.

Standard II

Where the services are clearly being done for the department (i.e., selection, fitness for duty, monitoring of psychological condition of members of special units), it should be made clear before any sort of psychological services are rendered that the individual is not the client and that the information will be forwarded to specific parties.

Standard III

It is vital that written arrangements be made with the head of the agency which states specifically how various psychological materials and information will be used, who will have access to such information, where such information will be stored, and realistic limits on the availability of this information to unauthorized personnel.

Standard IV

On all documents which forward psychological information to others, there should be a disclaimer stamped at the end of every report which states: "The results of psychological tests and other procedures are informational. They are to be available only to authorized personnel as mandated by the regulations of this department. They are considered confidential to all others. Psychological test data and psychological information are never to be used for hiring, firing, or promotions. They are advisory only."

QUALITY ASSURANCE FOR REFERRAL RESOURCES

One of the most important jobs that the psychologists can do in a law enforcement agency is to refer individuals for professional help outside of the agency where such help is requested or required. In functioning as a referring agent, the police psychologists should follow certain restraints and expectations.

Standard I

No referral should ever be made to an individual or organization with whom the referring psychologist has any kind of financial arrangement or involvement.

Standard II

The police psychologist should understand the training and background of those to whom he/she refers. The referring psychologist should be certain that the services that are required are within the scope of competence of the individual or the organization to whom the officer or the officer's family is referred.

Standard III

The police psychologist should have sufficient communication with the professionals to whom he/she refers so that it is fairly certain that these individuals:

a. Understand the nature of the police officer's profession and the special stresses under which law enforcement personnel operate.

b. That the individual to whom the department is referred is willing to maintain contact with the referring psychologist without revealing confidential information.

c. It is the responsibility of the referral agent to know what kinds of fees are charged to the individuals who are being rendered the services and to be able to convey this and other pertinent information to the department member or the family member who is being referred.

d. The psychologist who makes the referral should follow up at 3- and 6-month intervals, asking the individual referred to fill out a rating scale as to quality and satisfaction of service. This should not identify the individual filling out the form, but should identify the practitioner who rendered services. The psychologist who makes the referral should make every effort to keep these records and develop an awareness of the level of satisfaction that is attained by department members referred to various professionals.

CRITICAL INCIDENT STRESS DEBRIEFING

A critical incident is any accident, traumatic experience, or any incident involving the use of deadly force by a sworn officer in which the officer is directly or indirectly involved. Critical incidents certainly include any incident in which the individual officer's own life is placed in immediate jeopardy. It may also include attendance at crime scenes which are particularly gruesome and/or unexpected, as well as mass killings. Departments should have a clear policy and procedure statement which includes the use of a psychologist in debriefing the individual officer after a critical incident.

Standard I

Referral to the psychologist after a critical incident should be automatic.

Standard II

Referral to the psychologist after the critical incident should occur within 72 hours of the incident.

Standard III

The Critical Incident Stress Debriefing should be a privileged and confidential communication between the officer and the psychologist. The only communication back to the department should be that the individual attended the session.

Standard IV

Minimally, the following subjects should be addressed in the Critical Incident Stress Debriefing (CISD):

  a. It should be communicated to the individual officer that the CISD is a privileged and confidential communication and the individual officer should be encouraged to relate the event knowing that the context is nonjudgmental.
  b. Common post-traumatic signs and symptoms should be identified for the individual officer. These include initial sleep disturbance, appetite disturbance, involuntary recollections, gastrointestinal disturbances, as well as other common acute difficulties.
  c. The individual officer should be apprised of more long-term "red flags," such as social isolation, signs of depression, nightmares, intense distress at exposure to events that symbolize the traumatic event, startle responses, etc.
  d. The individual officer should be able to clearly recognize the difference between immediate and acute symptoms and those that are chronic and more pathological.
  e. The individual officer, if relevant, should be made aware that his/her immediate family is also at risk.

f. The individual officer should be made aware of potential medical, psychiatric, and counseling referral sources should symptoms persist.

In summary, a Critical Incident Stress Debriefing is meant to be primarily educational in focus. It is not judgmental, and usually does not require treatment. However, the individual officer should leave the stress debriefing with a clear notion of how to seek further treatment if specific symptoms persist or develop.

PSYCHOLOGIST'S INVOLVEMENT IN HOSTAGE NEGOTIATIONS

The role of psychologists in hostage negotiations has been that of consultant to the negotiating team about the emotional status of the hostage taker. Strategies in dealing with the hostage taker are recommended. Adequate data have been collected that hostage negotiation significantly reduces the injuries or death in direct confrontations between police and others. Also, an increasing number of police departments have recognized the factor of vicarious liability when negotiators and their departments have been vulnerable to suits for negligence. Increasingly, psychologists are recognized for their special knowledge of personality dynamics that not only can assist the police officers in charge, but can add to the training of negotiators and the resolution of hostage incidents.

Training

Standard I.   Psychologists should receive appropriate graduate training in psychology from accredited institutions.

Standard II.   Psychologists should receive formal training in police hostage negotiations.

Standard III.   Psychologists should have familiarity with usage and psychological literature in the appropriate areas such as personality, psychopathology, prediction of violence, bargaining power, terrorism, vicarious liability, victimology, crisis intervention, stress management, etc.

Standard IV.   Psychologists should gain experience or familiarity with types of offenders.

Standard V.   Psychologists have a responsibility to maintain current knowledge through ongoing training and continuing education.

Consultation

Standard I. Psychologists should establish an ongoing relationship with the negotiating team and command personnel that they service.

Standard II. Roles and expectations should be clarified with the team, supervisors, and command personnel.

Standard III. Psychologists should actively participate in the ongoing training of the hostage negotiation teams.

Standard IV. Psychologists should provide a system for evaluating their effectiveness as a consultant. This instrument should include feedback from the negotiating team, the tactical response team, command-level personnel and, if possible, the hostage taker after the incident is resolved.

Operations

Standard I. Psychologists should function as a member of the negotiation team, and should not typically serve as the primary negotiator. Maintaining an observer stance will enhance objectivity.

Standard II. Psychologists should bear in mind that the consultation is provided within the framework of a law enforcement response, and that the department has the ultimate responsibility for decisions about the management of the hostage situation.

Standard III. If qualified, psychologists should be involved in debriefing of the released hostages, and of the departmental personnel involved in the incident.

Standard IV. Psychologists should clear all media contact with the on-scene commanding officer, with careful consideration given to the issues of professionalism and confidentiality.

Standard V. Psychologists should review and solicit any available intelligence data on persons involved in the situation and responsibly consider the weight and credibility of the source and information.

Ethics and Responsibility

Standard I. Psychologists should adhere to the ethical standards of the American Psychological Association.

Standard II. Psychologists should be cautious to limit opinions for guidance only to his/her areas of confidence.

Standard III. Psychologists should balance responsibilities of the department, hostages, and hostage taker.

Personal Factors

Standard I. Psychologists should be committed to the negotiation response.

Standard II. Psychologists should especially consider his/her own beliefs, values, and attitudes in areas that may affect his/her actions in a hostage situation (e.g., use of force, power, and authority, etc.).

RESOURCE

McMains, Michael J. 1988. *Psychologist's Role in Hostage Negotiations in Police Psychology: Operational Assistance.* James T. Reese and James M. Horn, (Eds.). Washington, DC: U.S. Government Printing Office.

A Sample of Request for Proposal (RFP) for Psychological Services

DATE   FISCAL DIVISION

SUBJECT   Request for Proposal Number 57-91

PROPOSAL TITLE   Psychological Services

OPENING DATE AND TIME

PLACE   Sheriff's Operation Center
                    Fiscal Division

Proposals will be received until the time and date shown and will be read aloud immediately thereafter at the "Place" indicated above.

Proposal Conference   (Date and Time) at the "Place" indicated above

Note: For your convenience a self-addressed mailing label is provided with this proposal package. PLEASE USE THIS LABEL WHEN RETURNING PROPOSALS.

REQUEST FOR PROPOSAL
PSYCHOLOGICAL SERVICE

REQUEST FOR PROPOSAL

1.0 Purpose

The intent of this Request for Proposal and resulting contract is to obtain the services of a licensed Psychologist to administer preemployment screening, specialty teams screening, fitness-for-duty evaluations and provide other consultations as needed by the XXXX Sheriff's Office for law enforcement as well as detention personnel as described in this specification.

2.0 Background

During the period of June 1990, the XXXX Sheriff's Office contracted for 578 interviews, 426 test batteries (145 for Detention and 281 for Road Deputies) and 209 hours, more-or-less, or hourly services in an effort to employ/retrain psychologically and emotionally stable individuals, capable of dealing with the stresses and responsibilities incumbent upon Sheriff's Office personnel, the Sheriff's Office desires to enter into an agreement with a proposer that will assist in accomplishing this goal.

3.0 Scope of Services

The Awardee shall provide service as an independent contractor and not as an agent or representative of the Sheriff; all assignments of work will be handled through the Sheriff's Office Staff Psychologist and all responses to assignments will be returned to same. When test batteries are required, they will be provided to the Sheriff's Office to administer and return for evaluation by the Awardee.

Services should be provided for each area as outlined below using materials as specified. In the event new improved methods of evaluation are developed and introduced as "tested and approved" for use in the law enforcement environment, the Sheriff's Office would expect to be appraised of such and would at that time consider revising the current evaluation program. This may or may not affect cost of service, and this would be negotiated at the time of such change.

3.1 Preemployment Screening. The highly stressful nature of law enforcement and its impact on Sheriff's Deputies/Detention Deputies and Communications Dispatchers, and their families, have been increasingly recognized as acute issues by criminal justice administrators. Emotional stability within this environment is a prime requirement for effective law enforcement work. This aspect of a comprehensive psychological screening and evaluation program is to eliminate candidates with personality disorders or active emotional disturbances.

Screening will consist of the below listed test batteries and their evaluation:

Battery 1—Road Deputy, Tactical, Civilian Firearms Instructor

a. Minnesota Multiphasic Personality Inventory.
b. Inwald Personality Inventory.
c. Trait Anger Scale.
d. Incomplete Sentences Blank.
e. Psychological History.

Battery 2—Detention/Bailiff Deputy, Communications Dispatcher

a. Minnesota Multiphasic Personality Inventory.
b. California Personality Inventory.
c. Fundamental Interpersonal Relations Orientation-Behavior.
d. Incomplete Sentences Blank.
e. Psychological History.

Screening shall further consist of a clinical interview, to include an explanation of the applicant's demonstrated strengths and weaknesses by the evaluating psychologist during the interview.

Upon completion of the applicant's screening, the evaluating psychologist shall provide the XXXX Sheriff's Office with a recommendation as to the applicant's acceptability for employment. The evaluating psychologist shall establish a *BASE LINE* performance standard. Applicants whose overall performance falls below the established *BASE LINE* shall be deemed *UNACCEPTABLE* and it shall be recommended by the evaluating psychologist that they *NOT BE HIRED*. The evaluating psychologist must further design a scale which demonstrates positive performance from the *BASE LINE* to the Optimum or Ideal with an indication of the applicant's position on the scale accompanied by a recommendation *TO HIRE*.

3.2 Specialty Team Screening. Will consist of Battery 1 tests from Paragraph 3.1, evaluation of tests, clinical interview and any other method of evaluation the Awardee deems necessary to provide a recommendation as to the applicant's acceptability for duty on the respective team. Tests for this process may be administered by Awardee or Sheriff's Office Staff Psychologist.

3.3 Fitness-for-Duty Evaluation. Will consist of either Battery 1 or Battery 2 tests from Paragraph 3.1, evaluation of tests, clinical interview, and any other method of evaluation the Awardee deems necessary to provide a recommendation as to the employee's acceptability for regular duty. Tests for this process may be administered by Awardee or the Sheriff's Office Staff Psychologist.

In the event an individual is found unfit for duty, a recommendation will be required as to what nature of treatment or counseling may be required.

3.4   Other Services.   Will be on an as needed basis and will be of the following nature:

a. *Management Consultation.* To provide information essential for managing overall program, serve as consultant on special cases requiring special attention, attend Command Staff meetings when requested.
b. *Traumatic Incident Consultation and Consultation on Use of Deadly Force.* To determine if further counseling and of what nature may be required for each individual.
c. *Timely Reports.* In the event an individual is found unfit for duty or traumatic incident/use of deadly force consultation has occurred, a comprehensive follow-up psychological evaluation will be conducted to determine fitness for duty as soon as practical.

   The Sheriff's Staff Psychologist will require a written comprehensive report of the individual fitness or lack of fitness for duty as soon as practical.
d. *Specialized Training.* As required for Sheriff's Office Personnel and on an as-requested basis.
e. *Expert Testimony.* Awardee shall be prepared to analyze the predictive validity of its ratings and the impact on particular population groups, as it relates to statistical data collected on behalf of the Sheriff's Office.

   Awardee shall be responsible for defending its procedures against legal or administration challenges. Further, in the event of an applicant's appeal of negative recommendation, Awardee shall be available for appearance as an expert witness on behalf of the Sheriff.

3.5   Qualifications.   It is preferred that the psychologist assigned to this contract have a clinical background, although, an industrial background will be considered. The Psychologist shall be licensed to practice in the State and shall maintain a place of business in the County. Proof of license and business location will be required of awardee. *A background in law enforcement/detention psychological assessments is preferred.* Proposers are cautioned to provide as much detail as possible pertaining to their capabilities, experience, and approach to the tasks outlined in this proposal.

3.6   Maintenance of Records.   Awardee shall maintain records accumulated under the terms of the contract, as deemed necessary by the Sheriff's Office and Awardee. Records and supporting documentation shall be retained for a minimum period of seven (7) years, at which time the Sheriff's Office shall be given the option to continue retention. Awardee shall comply with Chapter 119 and Chapter 267 of the Statutes.

3.7   Reports.   The Awardee will provide the Sheriff's Office with an ongoing analysis of the program's effectiveness. The Sheriff's Office will be provided quarterly reports that will include the number of individuals utilizing the program (e.g., preemployment psychological screening, psychological screening for specialized units, traumatic incident counseling, and fitness-for-duty referrals). The reports will review all activities for the quarter with suggestions for program reinforcement.

4.0   General Contract Terms and Conditions

4.1   Proposals must be presented in a SEALED envelope/container addressed to:

SHERIFF
ATTN: Fiscal Division

To prevent inadvertent opening, the self-addressed mailing label provided with this proposal package must be on the outside of the envelope/container.

If our specifications, when included in our Request for Proposal, are not returned with your proposal, and no specific reference is made to them in your proposal, it will be assumed that all specifications will be met. When material, descriptive literature, or Proposer's specifications which accompany the proposal, contain information that can be construed or is intended to be a deviation from our specifications, such deviation must be specifically referenced in your proposal response.

4.2   Responsibility.   The responsibility for getting the proposal to the Sheriff's Office on or before the stated time and date will be solely and strictly the responsibility of the Proposer. The Sheriff will in no way be responsible for delays caused by the United States Postal Service or a delay caused by any other occurrence, or any other method of delivery. The Proposer shall be responsible for reading very carefully and understanding completely the requirements in the specifications. Proposals will not be accepted after the time specified for receipt. Such proposals shall be returned to the Proposer unopened with the notation, "This Proposal Was Received after the Time Designated for the Receipt and Opening of Proposals."

4.3   Time for Consideration.   Proposers warrant by virtue of proposing that the price quoted in his proposal will be good for an evaluation period of thirty (30) calendar days from the date of proposal opening unless otherwise stated. *Proposers will not be allowed to withdraw or modify their proposals after the opening time and date.*

4.4   Prices.   All proposals submitted must show the *net proposal price* after any and all discounts allowable have been deducted. State sales tax and federal excise taxes shall not be included as the Sheriff's office is tax exempt. The Sheriff will issue exemption certificates to the successful Proposer when requested.

4.5   Proposal Errors.   When errors are found in the extension of the proposal prices, the unit price will govern. Proposals having erasures or corrections must be initialed in ink by the Proposer.

4.6   When to Make Delivery.   Deliveries resulting from this proposal are to be made during the normal working hours of the Sheriff's Office. It is the Proposer's responsibility to obtain this information.

4.7   Proposal Submittal Costs.   Submittal of a proposal is solely at the cost of the Proposer, and the Sheriff's Office in no way is liable or obligates itself for any cost accrued to the Proposer in coming up with the Proposal Submittal.

4.8   No Proposal.   *If the receipt of this request for proposal is not acknowledged, the Proposer's name may be removed from the Proposer Mailing List.*

4.9   Acceptance and Rejection.   Sheriff's Office reserves the right to reject any and all proposals received by reason of this request, or to negotiate separately in any manner necessary to serve the best interests of the Sheriff's Office. Consultants or Proposers whose proposals are not accepted will be notified in writing.

5.0   Special Contract Terms and Conditions

5.1   Procedures.   The extent and character of the services to be performed by the psychologist shall be subject to the general control and approval of the Director of Fiscal Division and the Administration Division Commander or their authorized representative(s). The Psychologist shall not comply with requests and/or orders issued by other than the Director of Fiscal or the Administration Division Commander or their representative(s) acting within their authority for the Sheriff's Office.

5.2   Contract Period.   The contract shall be effective for one (1) year from the date of award. By written mutual consent between the Sheriff's

Office and the awardee, the contract may be extended on an annual basis for up to two (2) additional years.

5.3   Termination.   Subject to the following provisions, the contract may be terminated by either party upon thirty (30) days advance written notice to the other party; however, if any work or services hereunder is in progress, but not completed as of the date of termination, then this contract may be extended upon written approval by the Sheriff's Office until said work or services are completed and accepted.

  a. *Termination for Convenience.* In the event that this contract is terminated or canceled upon request and for the convenience of the Sheriff's Office without the required thirty (30) days advance written notice, then the Sheriff's Office shall negotiate reasonable termination costs, if applicable.

  b. *Termination for Cause.* Termination by the Sheriff's Office for cause, default, or negligence on the part of the Psychologist shall be excluded from the foregoing provision; termination costs, if any, shall not apply. The thirty (30) days advance notice requirement is waived in the event of Termination for Cause.

  c. *Termination Due to Unavailability of Funds in Succeeding Fiscal Years.* When funds are not appropriate or otherwise made available to support continuation of performance in a subsequent fiscal year, the contract(s) shall be canceled and the contractor shall be reimbursed for the reasonable value of any nonrecurring costs incurred but not amortized in the price of the supplies or services delivered under the contract.

5.4   Inconsistencies in Conditions.   In the event there are inconsistencies between the General Contract Terms and Conditions; the Special Contract Terms and Conditions; and other schedules contained herein, the latter shall take precedence.

5.5   Nonassignability.   The resulting contract may not be assigned without the prior written consent of the Sheriff's Fiscal Director.

5.6   Modification and Amendment.   The resulting contract may not be modified or amended without prior written consent of the Sheriff's Fiscal Director.

5.7   Invoicing and Payments.   Contractor may invoice the Sheriff's office in duplicate for services on a monthly basis.

The invoice shall show: Subject Name; Services Performed; Cost.

Always show purchase order number on invoices.

Timely payment of invoices is incumbent upon the _____ County Sheriff's Office and in no case shall payment of a properly approved invoice exceed thirty (30) calendar days from date of receipt.

Invoices should be mailed to: Sheriff
                                Attention Fiscal Division

A properly executed invoice, with supporting documents, must be approved by the County Sheriff's appointed Administrative Division personnel and forwarded to the Fiscal Division.

6.0   Evaluation of Proposals (Selection Factors)

The General Contract Terms and Conditions set forth certain criteria that will be used in the receipt of proposals and selection of the successful Proposer. In addition, the criteria set forth below will be considered.

A Proposal Analysis Group (consisting of Sheriff's Office staff members) will independently read, review, and evaluate each proposal and a recommendation will be made to the Sheriff on the basis of the following criteria and as depicted on the Proposal Evaluation Matrix contained herein. The Proposers submitting proposals shall include with that proposal statements on the following:

a. Qualifications of doctor assigned to the contract.
b. Comparable experience in psychological screening, testing, and evaluating law enforcement and detention applicants.
c. References (i.e., satisfaction of former and current clients) along with names and addresses of all parties for whom comparable work has been performed.
d. Cost of Services (i.e., price proposal).
e. A certified financial statement or other documentation to permit the Sheriff's Office to determine financial responsibility.
f. History of malpractice claims in which payment was made in excess of $5,000, including all pending litigation.

Once each member of the Proposal Analysis Group has independently read and rated each proposal and completed a Proposal Evaluation Matrix, a composite evaluation will be developed that indicates the group's collective ranking of the highest rated proposals in a descending order. At this point, the Proposal Analysis Group will conduct interviews with *only* the top ranked Proposers (usually the top three, depending on the number of proposals received). The Proposal Analysis Group will conduct all subsequent negotiations. This group will make the appropriate recommendation for the resulting contract award.

PSYCHOLOGICAL SERVICES
PROPOSAL EVALUATION MATRIX

PROPOSER'S NAME _____

	Maximum Points	Score
1. Qualifications of Doctor assigned to our contract	30	_____
2. References (satisfaction of former clients)	20	_____
3. Comparable experience	20	_____
4. Cost of Services	30	_____
TOTAL	100	_____

WHAT ARE THE THREE PRIMARY REASONS YOU HAVE FOR RECOMMENDING THIS PROPOSER?

_____

_____

_____

WHAT ARE THE THREE PRIMARY REASONS FOR REJECTING THIS PROPOSER?

_____

_____

_____

GENERAL COMMENTS/CLARIFICATIONS/QUESTIONS _____

_____

_____

_____

_____

NAME OF EVALUATOR _____ DATE _____

7.0 Instructions for Submitting Proposals

7.1 Addendum and Supplement to Request. If it becomes necessary to revise any part of this request or if additional data is necessary to enable an exact interpretation of provisions of this request, revisions will be provided to all Proposers who receive or request this RFP.

7.2 Questions and Inquiries. Questions and inquiries must be submitted in writing, and will be accepted from any and all Proposers. Questions will be answered in writing and both questions and answers will be distributed to all Proposers who received the RFP provided, however, that all questions are received at least ten (10) calendar days in advance of the proposal opening date.

7.3   Preparation and Submittal of Proposals

a. All proposals shall be signed in ink by the individual or authorized principal of the Proposer.

b. All portions of the request for proposals requiring executing by the Proposer are to be returned with the proposals.

c. *Each Proposer shall submit five (5) copies of their proposal (including price proposal) to the Sheriff's Office Fiscal Division* as indicated on the cover sheet of this Request for Proposal.

7.4   Withdrawal of Proposals

a. All proposals submitted shall be valid for a minimum evaluation period of thirty (30) calendar days following the date established for opening to allow time for consideration.

b. Proposals may be withdrawn on written request from the proposer at the address shown in the solicitation *prior to* the Proposal Opening Time.

c. Negligence on the part of the proposer in preparing the proposal confers no right of withdrawal after the time fixed for the opening of the proposals.

7.5   Miscellaneous Requirements

a. All proposals shall provide a straight forward, concise delineation of the Proposer's capabilities to satisfy the requirements of this request. Emphasis should be on completeness and clarity of content.

b. Proposers who submit a proposal in response to this RFP may be required to make an oral presentation of their proposal.

c. The contents of the proposal submitted by the successful Proposer and this RFP will become a part of any contract award as a result of this solicitation. The successful Proposer will be expected to sign a contract with the Sheriff's Office. See Attachment A for a copy of the Standard Agreement.

d. The Proposer is prohibited from assigning, transferring, conveying, subletting, or otherwise disposing of this agreement or its rights, title, or interest therein or its power to execute such agreement to any other person, company, or corporation without the previous consent and approval in writing by the Sheriff's Office.

8.0   Form of Proposals/Proposal Content

8.1   Detail.   Interested Proposers are cautioned to provide in their proposal as much detail as possible pertaining to their capabilities, experience, and approach to the services outlined in this proposal.

8.2   At a minimum, each proposal must address each of the following items:

    a. A description of how you propose to accomplish the required services outlined under *Scope of Services*. In addition, please specify the approach or methodology you intend to utilize, if applicable. Provide this information in the form of a cover letter.

    b. A statement of the experience and professional capability for each person who would be assigned to accomplish these services (i.e., resumes of key personnel to be assigned).

    c. Names of clients for whom similar services have been performed (i.e., applicable experience in performing specified services).

    d. Schedule of proposed charges (price proposal).

9.0   Insurance

Awardee shall procure and maintain at its own expense, during the life of this Agreement, professional liability insurance in the amount of Five Hundred Thousand ($500,000.00) Dollars combined single limit. The policy shall:

    a. Show insured.

       Sheriff as additional named

    b. Include the severability of interest provisions.

    c. Provide that all liability coverages required under this Agreement are primary to any liability insurance carried or any self-insurance programs of the Sheriff.

Prior to commencing work under a resultant contract, the Awardee shall furnish the Sheriff's Office with the Certificate of Insurance. Sixty (60) calendar days' notice of cancellation, nonrenewal, or change in the insurance coverages is a requirement.

10.0   Indemnification

Awardee shall, defend, hold harmless, and indemnify the Sheriff from and against any and all liability, loss, claims, damages, costs, attorneys' fees, and expenses of whatever kind or nature, which the Sheriff may sustain, suffer, or incur or be required to pay by reason of his negligent performance under this Agreement. The indemnity hereunder shall continue until the services provided under this Agreement have been fully performed or the Agreement has been terminated by passage of time or otherwise canceled, as hereinabove provided but shall remain in full force and effect with respect to any performance during the period of the Agreement.

SHERIFF

BY: _____

/Director

Fiscal Division

REQUEST FOR PROPOSAL FOR PSYCHOLOGICAL SERVICES
SHERIFF   PROPOSAL NO. 57-91

LETTER OF INTENT

The undersigned acknowledges the General Terms and Provisions of this Request for Proposal and intends to respond to the RFP for Psychological Services for the County Sheriff's Office. We understand that any changes, clarification, and addenda to the RFP will be promptly communicated to the individual authorized below to receive this information.

_____

NAME

_____

COMPANY NAME

_____

ADDRESS

_____

_____

_____

TELEPHONE NUMBER

I _____ will
I _____ will not
be attending the Proposal Conference.
Indicate who, if anyone, will accompany you.

_____

11.0 Proposal Forms, Schedules, and Other Miscellaneous Forms to be Executed

11.1 Persons Associated with the Project. Provide the name and qualifications of the principal member of your firm and all persons who will be directly associated with the contract. State the duties of each person as relates to this contract.

11.2   References.   Offerors shall provide business references on this form. References shall be current or previous clients for whom similar service has been performed.

A. Firm Name   _____
   Contact   _____
   Title   _____
   Mailing Address _____
   Phone   _____

B. Firm Name   _____
   Contact   _____
   Title   _____
   Mailing Address _____
   Phone   _____

C. Firm Name   _____
   Contact   _____
   Title   _____
   Mailing Address _____
   Phone   _____

11.3   Proposal Form

PROPOSAL TITLE: Psychological Service   PROPOSAL NO. 57-91

By signing this proposal, the undersigned affirms that said proposal is made without any understanding, agreement, or connection with any other person, Proposer, or corporation providing a proposal for the same purpose and that this proposal is in all respects fair and without collusion or fraud. The undersigned understands that this proposal must be signed in ink and that an unsigned proposal will be considered incomplete and subject to rejection by the Sheriff's Office.

THE UNDERSIGNED, BY THE SIGNATURE EVIDENCED, REPRESENTS THAT THE PROPOSER ACCEPTS THE TERMS, CONDITIONS, MANDATES, AND OTHER PROVISIONS OF THE FOREGOING INSTRUCTIONS TO PROPOSERS AND THE SPECIFICATIONS, SAID DOCUMENTS BEING THE STRICT BASIS ON WHICH THE SAID PROPOSER MAKES THIS PROPOSAL. ALSO, THE UNDERSIGNED (PROPOSER), BY THE SIGNATURE EVIDENCED, AGREES TO INDEMNIFY AND HOLD HARMLESS THE SHERIFF AND ANYONE DIRECTLY OR INDIRECTLY EMPLOYED BY HIM FROM AND AGAINST ALL

CLAIMS, DAMAGES, LOSSES, AND EXPENSES (INCLUDING COURT COSTS AND ATTORNEY'S FEES) RESULTING OUT OF ANY ALLEGED INFRINGEMENT OF PATENT RIGHTS OR COPYRIGHTS HELD BY OTHERS AS ARISES OUT OF THE PROPOSER'S PERFORMANCE OF ANY CONTRACT AWARDED BY THE SHERIFF PURSUANT TO THIS PROPOSAL.

A. Preemployment Screening
   Test Battery 1 (Road Deputy;
   Civilian Firearms Instructor) $_____/battery
   Clinical Interview $_____/interview
   Test Battery 2 (Detention/Bailiff
   Deputy; Communications Dispatcher) $_____/battery
   Clinical Interview $_____/interview

B. Specialty Team Screening
   Test Battery 1 $_____/battery
   Clinical Interview $_____/interview

C. Fitness-for-Duty Evaluation
   Test Battery 1 $_____/battery
   Test Battery 2 $_____/battery
   Clinical Interview $_____/interview

D. Other Services
   1. Management Consultation $_____/hr
   2. Traumatic Consultation $_____/hr
   3. Use of Deadly Force Consultation $_____/hr
   4. Specialized Training $_____/hr
   5. Expert Testimony $_____/hr

E. Other additional charges _____
_____
_____

This Proposal is hereby signed as of the date indicated by an official authorized by the Proposer.

PROPOSER:

By: PLEASE PRINT   Name _____
                     Title _____
                     Date _____
                     Phone _____
                     Signature _____ (SEAL)

A Proposal Submitted in Response to the RFP Presented in Appendix C

POLICE SERVICES INSTITUTE IS A SUBSIDIARY OF PSYCHOLOGICAL SEMINARS, INC.

Sheriff
Fiscal Division

RE: RFP 57-91
Psychological Services

Gentlemen:

We are pleased to provide the following proposal, in response to your RFP #57-91, PSYCHOLOGICAL SERVICES.

SCOPE OF SERVICES

As experienced evaluators of Law Enforcement Personnel, PSI is fully cognizant of the psychological factors that indicate and contraindicate selection. The screening test batteries (Batteries 1 & 2) which the Department has selected are acceptable as a minimum, and in order to enhance the services as well as to respond more adequately to legal and administrative challenges, we would add the Wonderlic Personnel Test. We would add to Battery 2 the Correctional Officer's Interest Battery, which has been found to be predictive of success in the detention officer's job.

Psychometric testing will be conducted by the Sheriff's Office and returned to PSI for evaluation. Clinical interviews will be conducted in our XXXX office, most convenient to the XXSO.

Services in which PSI has extended experience and is prepared to offer, in accordance with this proposal, include:

- Preemployment Screening.
  - —Road Duty, Tactical, Civilian Firearms Instructor.
  - —Detention/Bailiff Deputy, Communications Dispatcher.
- Speciality Team Screening.
- Fitness-for-Duty Evaluation.
- Management Consultation.
- Traumatic Incident Consultation.
- Consultation on Use of Deadly Force.
- Specialized Training.
- Expert Testimony.

Attachment A provides a summary of additional services available on request. Examples of psychological screenings as well as Fitness-for-Duty Evaluation can be found in Attachment B.

Records will be maintained in accordance with the conditions of the contract, the Florida statutes, and the standards of the American Psychological Association.

PROFESSIONAL EXPERIENCE

Drs. Alberts and Blau will be the primary evaluators and consultants. Both Drs. Alberts and Blau have extensive experience in law enforcement. Dr. Blau is a certified law enforcement officer in the State of Florida. His extensive experience in working with law enforcement can be found in the Curriculum Vitae appended to this document (Attachment C).

Dr. Alberts maintains a primarily assessment-oriented practice and conducted evaluations for the Temple Terrace Police Department for several years. Additional details of Dr. Alberts' background can be found in his Curriculum Vitae (Attachment C).

Additional staff, under Drs. Alberts' and Blau's direction, may be required, depending on the flow of consultations.

REFERENCES

A. Name: Manatee County Sheriff's Office
   Contact: Sheriff Charles Wells or Dr. Super
   Title: Sheriff, Manatee County
   Address: 515 11th Street West, Bradenton, FL 33505-7727
   Tel: (813) 747-3011

B. Name: Plant City Police Department
   Contact: Sgt. Bill McDaniels
   Title: Training Director
   Address: 611 South Collins Street, Plant City, FL 33556
   Tel: (813) 752-3131

C. Name: Temple Terrace Police Department
   Contact: Tom Matthews
   Title: Chief
   Address: North 56th Street, Temple Terrace, FL 33617
   Tel: (813) 989-7110

SCHEDULE OF PROPOSED CHARGES

Attachment D contains the schedule of proposed charges for the various services requested in RFP #57-91.

INSURANCE

Insurance will be maintained in accordance with the agreement. PSI, its principals, and staff have no history of malpractice claims in which payment was made in excess of $5,000, and none has pending litigation.

FINANCIAL STATEMENT

A year-end financial statement is appended.

ADDITIONAL DOCUMENTATION

Sworn Statement is enclosed.

    We would be pleased to have the opportunity to meet with the Proposal Analysis Group to answer questions or to assist in any way your selection of a suitable contractor.

    We look forward to an opportunity to be of service to the XXSO.

Very truly yours,

Theodore H. Blau, PhD   Fred L. Alberts, Jr., PhD

THB:FLA:dmh

Attachment A

POLICE SERVICES INSTITUTE
213 East Davis Boulevard
Tampa, Florida 33606
(813) 253-3587

PSYCHOLOGICAL SERVICES FOR LAW ENFORCEMENT

The Police Services Institute is a broad service psychological organization providing services for law enforcement organizations at the local, state, and national levels. The staff and consultants of the Police Services Institute include psychologists, law enforcement officers, and psychologists who are also sworn law enforcement officers.

The goal of the Police Services Institute is to provide the highest level of professional psychological services to meet the recruitment, training, management, and operational needs of law enforcement agencies.

Cost-effective services are provided to help curtail long-range expenses for the organization. Rapidly escalating costs of lawsuits, dropouts, disability pensions, and other low cost-benefit occurrences, require preventive psychological services to reverse this growing trend.

SERVICES

The Policy Services Institute can provide the following services to qualified law enforcement agencies:

RECRUIT PSYCHOLOGICAL SCREENING

Accreditation Standards now require that all law enforcement agencies that expect to be accredited will use a psychological screening battery for the selection of recruits for training, or for the selection of officers for placement. The Policy Services Institute has a variety of screening batteries that can be utilized for these purposes, depending on the requirements of the department. These selection batteries can be given at the agency, or at the offices of the Police Services Institute.

FITNESS-FOR-DUTY EVALUATIONS

When an officer has been involved in a critical incident situation, the question of the officer's fitness to return to duty is often an issue that faces police managers. The Policy Services Institute is prepared to offer psychological evaluation for such officers, with recommendations for both treatment and/or return to duty.

In special instances, some officers may have received a medical disability or partial disability pension as a result of job-related occurrences or job-related stress. Periodic reevaluations may be necessary to determine whether such pension recipients are in continuing need of support or whether they may return to full or partial duty. The Police Services Institute is equipped to do psychological evaluation of such situations.

SPECIAL TEAM EVALUATION

Psychological evaluation is available to ensure that members of special teams (SWAT, Narcotics, Undercover, Delta Force, Internal Affairs, and so forth) are psychologically fit to tolerate stressful jobs that will be expected of them. Accreditation standards also recommend that members of such teams be screened psychologically each year to ensure that they have not developed pathological psychological traits that would interfere with their effective functioning. The Police Services Institute can provide this type of screening.

TRAINING

Modern law enforcement agencies are aware that training is a cost-beneficial preventive measure. The Police Services Institute has a variety of training materials and live presentations that are available to law enforcement agencies. Subjects include:

- Stress Inoculation.
- Stress Reduction.
- Identifying Potential Family Violence.
- Dealing with the Mentally-Disordered Offender.
- Hostage Negotiation.
- Preparing to Be an Expert Witness at Court.
- Preventing Personal Problems at Home.
- Effective Listening.
- Empathy Training.
- Using Psychological Services in Criminal Investigation.

RESEARCH

The staff of Police Services Institute are prepared to conduct research studies that may be required by a qualified law enforcement agency. During litigation against an agency involving selection methods, the availability of local norms for both recruit selection and fitness-for-duty evaluations is often an issue. The Police Services Institute can prepare local norm projects for departments that desire such research. Research studies on a variety of subjects have been done by the Police Services Institute. Publication reprints are available describing some of this work.

COUNSELING

Police Services Institute offers a full range of counseling services for law enforcement. These include:

- Critical Incident Counseling.
- Postshooting Trauma Counseling.
- Deadly Force Survivors Counseling.
- Personal Counseling.
- Stress Reduction Counseling.
- Retirement Counseling.

MANAGEMENT CONSULTATION

Police management is one of the most difficult administrative tasks in any organization today. Modern police managers know the value of morale surveys, effective training and selection methods, objective personnel procedures, and promotional policies. The psychologists of the Police Services Institute are trained and experienced in consultation with top managers and are available on an incident or contractual basis.

INVESTIGATIVE CONSULTATION

Modern criminal investigation utilizes a broad range of psychological techniques which include:

- Investigative Hypnosis.
- Psychological Profiling.
- Psychological Autopsy.
- Interview Techniques with Child Witnesses.

The experienced police psychologist working with the investigator, provides information that may be useful in analyzing crime data or working with difficult or unproductive witnesses.

INITIAL CONSULTATION

If a department believes that it may have some use for the services of the Police Services Institute, initial contact can be made by telephone. Contact should be made by the chief executive officer (chief or sheriff) or by the CEO's immediate assistant (deputy chief, undersheriff, first deputy, assistant chief).

To discuss your requirements or ask specific information, call:

Dr. T. H. Blau (813) 253-3587

Attachment B

EXAMPLES OF TESTING REPORTS PREVIOUSLY DONE BY PSI

POLICE SCREENING INSTITUTE
213 East Davis Boulevard
Davis Islands
Tampa, Florida 33606
(813) 253-3587

APPLICANT PSYCHOLOGICAL SCREENING

NAME OF APPLICANT
DEPARTMENT   Police Department
REFERRED BY   and Chief
DATE OF SCREENING   April 11, 1990

SCREENING PROCEDURES

Minnesota Multiphasic Personality Inventory (MMPI)
Wonderlic Personnel Test, Form IV
Writing Sample
Interview

RESULTS

Ms.   presents herself in a neat, straightforward manner. She communicates in a brief, clear, and articulate style. Her social skills include good eye contact, modest presentation of self, and straightforward language. She appears to be a person of high energy, intelligent and responsive.

Intellectual Factors

In comparison with adults of all ages and all educational levels, Ms.   falls at about the 70th percentile. This means that she can use her intellect and reasoning skills equal to or better than 70 out of 100 in the general population. This would place her in the High Average range of intellectual capacity.

Personality Factors

No unusual personality characteristics were found in Ms.   . She does have a tendency to deny any kind of problems; however, this is characteristic of successful police officers.

FINAL SUMMARY EVALUATION

Personality

+ .... + ... + ... X+ .... +

Very Poor   Average   Outstanding

Writing

+ .... + ... + ... + .X. .... +

Very Poor   Average   Outstanding

Interview

+ .... + ... + ... X .... +

Very Poor   Average   Outstanding

Intelligence

+ .... + ... + ... X .... +

Very Poor   Average   Outstanding

RECOMMENDATION

Psychological test results are advisory and should never be used as the sole basis of hiring or firing decisions.

X. .... + ... + ... + ... +

No significant   Borderline   Serious
psychological problems.   psychological
                                            problems.
                                            Retest if
                                            candidacy to
                                            be continued.

Ms.   appears to be an excellent candidate for law enforcement.

Theodore H. Blau, PhD
Licensed Psychologist (FL PY 00002060)

POLICE SCREENING INSTITUTE
213 East Davis Boulevard
Davis Islands
Tampa, Florida 33606
(813) 253-3587

APPLICANT PSYCHOLOGICAL SCREENING

NAME OF APPLICANT

DEPARTMENT   Police Department

REFERRED BY   Sergeant   and Chief

DATE OF SCREENING   June 26, 1991

SCREENING PROCEDURES

Minnesota Multiphasic Personality Inventory (MMPI)
Wonderlic Personnel Test
Writing Sample
Interview

Intellectual Factors

Mr.   level of intellectual functioning exceeds 54 percent of the individuals in the norm group and is described as Average. This level of performance is slightly above the median score found among police patrol officers.

Personality Factors

Mr.   responses to the validity items of the MMPI revealed a psychological profile that is rather doubtful. This rarely occurs, but can occur among psychologically naive and unsophisticated individuals who are feigning the absence of psychopathology and wish to present themselves beyond moral or social reproach. While it is not at all uncommon to have personality profiles of applicants, particularly police applicants, that are rather defensive, the current profile is suggestive of an individual who has a pervasive denial of difficulties; the evaluation should be broadened if he is to continue to be considered a competitive applicant.

FINAL SUMMARY EVALUATION

Personality
```
                            *
  + .......... + .......X. +............ +...........+
 Very Poor              Average              Outstanding
```

Writing

+ . . . . + ... X . . . . . + ... + ... +

Very Poor   Average   Outstanding

Interview

+ . . . . + ... +X . . . . + ... +

Very Poor   Average   Outstanding

Intelligence

+ . . . . + ... +X . . . . + ... +

Very Poor   Average   Outstanding

RECOMMENDATION

Psychological test results are advisory and should never be used as the sole basis of hiring or firing decisions.

+ . . . . + ... +X . . . . + ... +

No significant   Borderline   Serious
psychological problems.   psychological
                                            problems.
                                            Retest if
                                            candidacy to
                                            be continued.

*Results of the personality inventory
yielded a large number of L items & the
validity of the profile is doubtful.

Fred L. Alberts, Jr., PhD
Licensed Psychologist (FL PY 3346)

FLAjr:goh

Attachment C

RESUMES OF DR. BLAU & DR. ALBERTS
(sent under separate cover)

<u>Attachment D</u>

Dr. Theodore Blau
213 E. Davis Blvd.
Tampa, FA 33606

11.3 PROPOSAL FORM

PROPOSAL TITLE: Psychological Service   PROPOSAL NO. 57-91

By signing this proposal, the undersigned affirms that said proposal is made without any understanding, agreement or connection with any other person, Proposer or corporation providing a proposal for the same purpose and that this proposal is in all respects fair and without collusion or fraud. The undersigned understands that this proposal must be signed in ink and that an unsigned proposal will be considered incomplete and subject to rejection by the _____ County Sheriff's Office.

The undersigned, by the signature evidenced, represents that the proposer accepts the terms, conditions, mandates and other provisions of the foregoing instructions to proposers and the specifications, said documents being the strict basis upon which the said proposer makes this proposal. Also, the undersigned (proposer), by the signature evidenced, agrees to indemnify and hold harmless the sheriff and anyone directly or indirectly employed by him from and against all claims, damages, losses and expenses (including court costs and attorney's fees) resulting out of any alleged infringement of patent rights or copyrights held by others as arises out of the proposer's performance of any contract awarded by the sheriff pursuant to this proposal.

A. Pre-Employment Screening
    Test Battery 1 (Road Deputy;
    Civilian Firearms Instructor) $ __100.00__ /battery
    Clinical Interview $ __50.00__ /interview
    Test Battery 2 (Detention/Bailiff
    Deputy; Communications Dispatcher) $ __125.00__ /battery
    Clinical Interview $ __50.00__ /interview
B. Specialty Team Screening
    Test Battery 1 $ __100.00__ /battery
    Clinical Interview $ __50.00__ /interview
C. Fitness for Duty Evaluation
    Test Battery 1 $ __100-$350__ /battery

Test Battery 2 $__100-$350__/battery

Clinical Interview $__100__/interview

D. Other Services

   1) Management Consultation $__150__/hr

   2) Traumatic Consultation $__150__/hr

   3) Use of Deadly Force Consultation $__150__/hr

   4) Specialized Training $__200__/hr

   5) Expert Testimony $__200__/hr

E. Other additional charges __Should extensive additional testing such__ __as neuropsychological evaluation be required, this will be discussed__ __with the SO Fiscal Department before such special testing would__ __be done.__

This Proposal is hereby signed as of the date indicated by an official authorized by the Proposer.

PROPOSER:

By: PLEASE PRINT   Name __Theodore H. Blau, Ph.D.__

                      Title __Co-Director, Police Services Institute (PSI)__

                      Date __September 16, 1991__

                      Phone __(813) 253-3587__

                      Signature _____ (SEAL)

Glossary: Police Argot

APB: All Points Bulletin. Older term for BOLO.

BIMBO: A female, usually quite young, of questionable moral character. Often one considered to have extremely loose sexual morals.

BOLO: An acronym for "be on the lookout." A special kind of bulletin exchanged among police departments giving the picture of a suspect and pertinent material. It is a more localized form of the FBI "wanted" poster.

BOBBY: A British police officer. Named after Robert "Bobby" Peel, founder of the British Metropolitan Police Force during the 19th century.

BUY-BUST: A narcotics squad operation wherein undercover agents arrange to make a buy of narcotics with the dealer, and during the ensuing negotiations arrest or "bust" the dealer.

BULL: In both England and the United States, a patrol officer. A derivation of the "Bull Street Runners." The original station house of the Metropolitan Police Force in London was on Bull Street, and the officers were called "runners."

CAPER: A singular illegal activity, such as a kidnapping, a burglary, a bank robbery.

CATCHING: The job of a police detective who is responsible for answering all new calls at that particular time. As in, Who is catching today?

CI: Confidential Informant. Also referred to as a "snitch."

COLLAR: A term used to designate an arrest. Where the offense is large, the offender is dangerous, or the officer ensures a good chain of evidence for the prosecutor, it is often referred to as a "good collar." Probably a long-used term associated with a 19th-century style of arresting culprits whereby the officer would grab the offender's collar, twist it, and control the person's movements in that way.

COOPING: A police term for sleeping on the job. Generally used in larger jurisdictions. Officers on routine patrol will find a place where the patrol car can be hidden and they can take a nap, or sometimes may use the living quarters of people on their own patrol route to "catch up on their sleep." Strictly forbidden, and cause for severe reprimand or dismissal.

COP A PLEA: When a criminal is faced with arrest and/or almost certain conviction, he or she may offer to be cooperative and admit to a lesser offense. Court officers will allow this when they believe that their case is not strong, and that the resolution of the crime and the sentencing can be done expeditiously if the individual confesses to an offense lesser than the original charge (i.e., charged with first-degree murder, a criminal who "cops a plea" to manslaughter.)

DIRT BAG: Known criminal. Tenderloin figure with a past record or a high potential for committing felonious acts.

DMV: Department of Motor Vehicles.

DOA: Dead on Arrival. Used on the reports of a homicide where on arrival at the hospital, receiving facility, or emergency room, a physician pronounces the individual dead.

DUI: Driving under the influence (of alcohol or drugs).

FI: Field Investigation. An officer, when seeing a person that he/she considers suspicious, may stop the individual and ask them their name, address, ordinary business, and their reason for being in the neighborhood (unless there is a reasonable cause, the officer cannot enforce the request or make a search). Most citizens will be happy to show identification and identify themselves. If the individual attempts to escape, or acts in a suspicious manner, the officer may proceed further.

The Field Investigation is usually recorded on a 3 × 5 card. This card has a place for name, address, identification, occupation, physical description, scars, street name or nickname, and any other circumstances under which the person was found by the officer. If a crime is reported in that neighborhood at a later date, the field investigation card, filed with headquarters, may be a starting point for identifying and interrogating suspects who are in the neighborhood at the time. These cards are turned in to the office when the police officer completes his or her tour of duty and are filed by date and by name.

FLUTE: A cola bottle filled with whiskey that is used by alcoholic officers to maintain their habit while apparently drinking a "soft drink."

HEADQUARTERS LOG: A book into which a chronological record is entered of all personnel, equipment, and assignments at the scene of a crime; it will later be brought back to headquarters and integrated with the crime report. A log of all persons and activities at the scene of the crime.

HEELED: Both police and underworld argot for carrying a firearm. It usually means concealed.

HINKY: Crazy. Tending to act peculiar. An unreliable individual. Unpredictable.

HOOKER: Prostitute.

IN THE JOB: One policeman telling another that he is in police work.

KA: Known Associates. A term used by police to designate the people with whom a known or suspected criminal tends to associate. Will often appear in crime reports or case summaries. Useful to detectives when attempting to apprehend a known or suspected felon who has taken flight to avoid prosecution.

MAG LIGHT: A flashlight made of metal, ranging from 8 to 18 inches in length, with shatterproof glass and a hooded lens. Used by police officers as an alternative to a baton or night stick. Banned in some departments as a dangerous weapon.

ME: Medical Examiner.

MUG: Argot for "to photograph." When a prisoner is brought into a police station, after the arrest report is made out, he is usually "mugged and printed" meaning photographed and fingerprinted.

NCIC: National Crime Information Center. An information center accessed by a computer that can give all kinds of information about automobiles, people, records, and so forth.

OD: Overdose (usually illicit drugs, sometimes prescribed drugs).

ON PATROL: Superficially meaning that a police officer is going about his or her duties outside the police station or the precinct. Sometimes a special reference to a police officer going to a favorite restaurant or bar for a period of time.

ON THE JOB: Currently on duty, working as a police officer in the jurisdiction being discussed.

PATCH: Alternate term for "turf." The area that an officer patrols and refers to as "my patch" or "my turf." In American policing, a proprietary term meaning that the officer is responsible for this area, and also that the officer has considerable power in that particular patrol district.

PATROL GUIDE: The book of directions, instructions, and procedures that form the basis of all police activity in a particular jurisdiction.

PERP: Short for "perpetrator." The assumed committer of a crime. Used when the identity of the criminal is unknown.

PHYSICAL EVIDENCE: Anything at a crime scene that one can pick up, photograph, put into an envelope, or identify as connected with the crime.

PIECE: Argot for "gun." Specifically refers to a handgun, usually concealed.

PIMP: An individual, almost always a male, who directs the activities of one or more professional prostitutes. This individual feeds, clothes, supervises, disciplines, and takes most of the earnings of the women (and sometimes men) on his "string."

PIMPMOBILE: A luxury automobile (usually a Lincoln or a Cadillac) that is decorated in gaudy colors and accessories, with a garish interior. The personal and business vehicle of a pimp, usually in large cities.

RAP SHEET: Official record of a criminal's past activities. Lists arrests, convictions, and sentences served.

SKELL: Mostly used in large-city police departments by police officers to designate a chronic felon or a professional criminal. Not to be confused with "dirt bag" which designates any undesirable character who appears to have a high potential to be a lawbreaker.

SLIM JIM: A long, thin metal rod carried by many police officers to allow them to assist motorists who have locked themselves out of their cars. The device allows the officer to slip the metal between the window and the rubber molding on the outside of the car door and unlatch the driver's side door lock.

SNITCH: In police terms, this refers to an individual with criminal background or criminal connections who, for personal gain, favors, or mitigation of a charge will give the police information about other criminals or crimes. When the individual does this on a regular basis they are considered to be a confidential informant (CI).

SNUFF: To kill.

SPLASH PAD: A domicile, apartment, or room that is maintained by a police officer aside from his usual residence. This may be a place where he keeps special materials or entertains in a clandestine manner.

STAND-UP GUY: A police officer who is known to be reliable, and who would be willing to participate in a "cover up" to protect a fellow police officer.

SHOO FLY: A member of the Internal Affairs Division of any police department. These officers investigate other officers.

TAIL: An individual who conducts surveillance on another individual. Can also refer to a vehicle conducting surveillance on another vehicle by following it.

TEN-CODES: These are numerical codes used by dispatcher, and law enforcement officers to communicate. Partly, the codes are used to save time, be explicit, and standardize communication; another reason is to code transmissions so they will be less likely to be understood by those who are trying to monitor police signals. Some common codes:

10-4   Message Received

10-24   Send Help Immediately—Trouble

10-46   Urgent

10-71   Send Ambulance

THROWAWAY: A knife or gun carried by a police officer who intends, should he or she be involved in a deadly force situation, to have a weapon to place at the scene of the crime to exculpate himself or herself. Usually a cheap gun or a switchblade knife. Strictly illegal.

T/P/O: Time and place of occurrence. This is part of a police report where the first responder (first officer to the scene of the crime) indicates the best estimate as to the time and the place that an event (crime) occurred.

VIG: This word is short for "vigorish." This is a specific argot used by loan sharks. The word represents the percentage of interest per week that is charged for a loan. The phrasing might be "I loaned him five large ones with three points vig." This would mean that the loan shark loaned the individual $5,000, at an interest rate of 3% ($150) per week.

Sources for Psychological Tests Frequently Used in Police Recruit Selection

Bender-Visual Motor Gestalt
Western Psychological Services
12031 Wilshire Boulevard
Los Angeles, CA 90025
(800) 648-8857
(213) 478-2061

Psychological Corporation
Harcourt Brace Jovanovich, Inc.
555 Academic Court
San Antonio, TX 78204-2498
(800) 228-0752

**California Personality
 Inventory**
Consulting Psychologists
 Press, Inc.
3803 East Bayshore Road
P.O. Box 10096
Palo Alto, CA 94303
(800) 624-1765
(415) 969-8901

**Clinical Analysis Questionnaire
 (CAQ)**
Institute for Personality and
 Ability Testing, Inc.
P.O. Box 188
Champaign, IL 61824-0188
(800) 225-4728
(217) 352-4739

**Edwards Personal Preference
 Schedule**
Psychological Corporation
Harcourt Brace Jovanovich, Inc.
555 Academic Court
San Antonio, TX 78204-2498
(800) 228-0752

FIRO-B
Consulting Psychologists Press, Inc.
3803 East Bayshore Road
P.O. Box 10096
Palo Alto, CA 94303
(800) 624-1765
(415) 969-8901

Hilson Personnel Profile
Hilson Research, Inc.
82-28 Abingdon Road
Kew Gardens, NY 11415
(718) 805-0063

Holmes-Rey Stress Scale (SRE)
University of Washington Press
P.O. Box 85569
Seattle, WA 98145

Inwald Personality Inventory
Hilson Research, Inc.
82-28 Abingdon Road
Kew Gardens, NY 11415
(718) 805-0063

*Law Enforcement and
    Development Report (LEADR)*
Institute for Personality and
    Ability Testing
P.O. Box 188
Champaign, IL 61824-0188
(800) 225-4728
(217) 352-4739

*Law Enforcement Personal History
    Questionnaire*
Hilson Research, Inc.
82-28 Abingdon Road
Kew Gardens, NY 11415
(718) 805-0063

Metropolitan Achievement Test
Psychological Corporation
Harcourt Brace Jovanovich, Inc.
555 Academic Court
San Antonio, TX 78204-2498
(800) 228-0752

*Millon Multiaxial Personality
    Inventory*
National Computer Systems, Inc.
P.O. Box 1416
Minneapolis, MN 55440
(800) NCS-7271
(612) 933-2800

*Minnesota Multiphasic Personality
    Inventory (Standard form and
    MMPI-2)*
National Computer Systems, Inc.
P.O. Box 1416
Minneapolis, MN 55440
(800) NCS-7271
(612) 933-2800

Myers-Briggs Test
Consulting Psychologists Press, Inc.
3803 East Bayshore Road
P.O. Box 10096
Palo Alto, CA 94303
(800) 624-1765
(415) 969-8901

Nelson-Denny Reading Tests
Riverside Publishing Co.
8420 Bryn Mawr Avenue
Chicago, IL 60631
(800) 323-9540

*Personality Assessment
    Inventory*
Psychological Resources, Inc.
P.O. Box 998
Odessa, FL 33556
(800) 331-TEST

16-PF
Institute for Personality and
    Ability Testing, Inc.
P.O. Box 188
Champaign, IL 61824-0188
(800) 225-4728
(217) 352-4739

*Strong-Campbell Interest
    Inventory*
Psychological Corporation
Harcourt Brace Jovanovich, Inc.
555 Academic Court
San Antonio, TX 78204-2498
(800) 228-0752

Consulting Psychologists Press
3803 East Bayshore Road
P.O. Box 10096
Palo Alto, CA 94303
(800) 624-1765
(415) 969-8901

Thematic Apperception Test
Psychological Corporation
Harcourt Brace Jovanovich, Inc.
555 Academic Court
San Antonio, TX 78204-2498
(800) 228-0752

*Wechsler Adult Intelligence
   Scale-Revised*
Psychological Corporation
Harcourt Brace Jovanovich, Inc.
555 Academic Court
San Antonio, TX 78204-2498
(800) 228-0752

Wonderlic Personnel Test
E. F. Wonderlic Personnel
820 Frontage Road
Northfield, IL 60093-8007
(800) 323-3742

Fitness-for-Duty Questionnaire

LAW ENFORCEMENT FITNESS-FOR-DUTY QUESTIONNAIRE*

I. IDENTIFICATION

Name of Employee _____

Department and Division _____

Date of Examination _____ Date of Report _____

Examiner _____

    Diagnosis

        Axis I _____

               _____

               _____

        Axis II _____

               _____

               _____

II. WORK-RELATED LIMITATIONS

Examiners: Please comment on the impact of the mental limitation(s) diagnosed above on work-related activities below using the following code:

1. NONE   No impairment in work-related function.

2. SLIGHT   (. . . or occasional) Adequate performance is slightly or occasionally compromised but not to such an extent that deviations automatically come to the attention of supervisors, create serious danger, or are life threatening.

3. MODERATE   Adequate performance is so compromised that deviations are likely to come to the attention of supervisors and close colleagues. The individual's deficits in this area may create a dangerous situation.

4. MARKED   Performance on this dimension is so compromised that it will be apparent to supervisors, peers, and citizens. Deficits in this area

*Permission given to reproduce this questionnaire by Anthony V. Stone, PhD, MPH. For further information, Dr. Stone can be contacted at: Ridgeview Institute, 4015 South Cobb Drive, Smyrna, GA 30080.

are such that, if the deficit is in a critical area, continuing to permit the employee to perform his job would be imminently dangerous to the employee, colleagues, and/or citizens.

N/A   Not assessed on this dimension.

Rating

1. Ability to understand, remember, and execute complex instructions. _____

2. Ability to maintain attention and concentration. _____

3. Ability to work at a steady pace and to complete work assignments within an appropriate schedule. _____

4. Ability to maintain regular attendance and be punctual. _____

5. Ability to work without substantial supervision. _____

6. Ability to maintain a high level of alertness. _____

7. Ability to exercise flexibility in decision making. _____

8. Ability to exercise good judgment in unpressured situations. _____

9. Ability to exercise good judgment in pressured situations. _____

10. Ability to interact effectively and appropriately with:

     The public. _____

     Supervisors. _____

     Work peers. _____

11. Ability to maintain socially appropriate behavior. _____

12. Ability to adhere to agency standards of neatness and cleanliness. _____

13. Ability to take charge, evoke, and authoritative posture, and command respect. _____

14. Ability to be aware of hazards and take appropriate precautions. _____

15. Ability to set realistic goals. _____

16. Ability to drive a vehicle in a safe manner. _____

17. Ability to drive an emergency vehicle in a safe manner. _____

18. (If a supervisor) Ability to appropriately supervise others. _____

19. Ability to make life-and-death decisions involving self and others. _____

20. (If alcohol or substance abuse) Ability to maintain abstinence from substances at work. _____

21. (If alcohol or substance abuse) Ability to maintain control over all use of substances. _____

22. Ability to effectively coordinate sensory experiences and motor activity. _____

23. Ability to tolerate verbal abuse from others. _____

24. Ability to use adequate judgment involving deadly force. _____

25. Ability to conform to the law in the handling of personal matters. _____

26. Ability to use restraint and otherwise avoid the use of force or threatened force in the handling of domestic matters. _____

III. CONCLUSION

A. Overall, I find that the above-captioned individual is (check one):

_____ fit for duty unconditionally.

_____ unfit for duty.

_____ fit for duty with the following contingencies:

_____

_____

_____

B. If the above-captioned individual is unfit for duty, I find that it is (check one, if appropriate):

_____ likely

_____ unlikely

that he/she will regain full fitness for duty in the foreseeable future.

C. If the above individual is unfit for duty and is likely to regain fitness for duty in the foreseeable future, the following intervention(s) and/or conditions should be met:

_____

_____

_____

_____

D. Additional comments:

_____

_____

_____

_____

IV. SIGNATURE

_____

Name of Licensed Professional   License Number

_____

Signature of Licensed Professional   Date

Post-Traumatic Stress Syndrome Interview

A. *Event Reexperienced*

1. Distressing, recurrent, intrusive recollection

_____

_____

_____

_____

_____

2. Recurrent, distressing dreams of events

_____

_____

_____

_____

_____

3. Sudden reliving of the event (flashback)

_____

_____

_____

_____

_____

4. Intense distress at exposure to events symbolizing event

_____

_____

_____

_____

_____

B. *Avoidance of Stimuli Associated with the Trauma or Numbing*
  1. Avoids thoughts or feelings associated with the event

  _____

  _____

  2. Avoids activities or situations that arouse recollections of the trauma

  _____

  _____

  3. Inability to recall relevant aspects of the trauma

  _____

  _____

  _____

  4. Markedly diminished interest in significant activities

  _____

  _____

  5. Feelings of detachment or estrangement from other people

  _____

  _____

  6. Restricted range of emotion

  _____

  _____

  7. Sense of foreshortened future and expectations

  _____

  _____

  _____

C. *Increased Arousal*
  1. Difficulty falling or staying asleep

  _____

  _____

  _____

  2. Irritability or outbursts of anger

  _____

  _____

  3. Difficulty concentrating

  _____

  _____

  _____

4. Hypervigilance

_____

_____

_____

_____

5. Startle response

_____

_____

_____

_____

6. Physiological reactivity when at a place or event symbolizing or resembling the trauma

_____

_____

_____

_____

Peer Counselor Training Outline

TRAUMATIC INCIDENT INTERVENTION: PEER COUNSELING TRAINING

Introduction

A. The concept of the traumatic incident defined. Sudden threat.
B. The victims of trauma.
    1. Critical incident.
    2. Killed in the line of duty—partners and family.
    3. Assaulted and attacked in the line of duty.
    4. Survivors of suicides.
    5. Other traumas.
C. The effects of post-trauma events.
D. The intervenors.

The Critical Incident Counselor

A. Current status in the field.
B. Personal traits required.
C. Motivation.
D. Educational background.
E. The special place of experience.

The Nature of Stress

Intervention Points

Intervention Skills

A. Professional identification.
B. Commitment.

C. Objectivity.

D. Tolerance.

E. Support.

F. Confidentiality.

G. Availability.

H. Patience.

I. Knowledge of legal and interpersonal requirements.

The Counselor's Tasks

A. Getting the facts.

B. Establishing identity in roles.

C. Creating a sanctuary.

D. Establishing the alliance.

E. Effective listening.

F. Reassurance.

G. Support.

H. Availability.

I. Follow-up.

Counseling Techniques

A. Supportive and nonintrusive techniques.

B. Intrusive techniques.

Problems, Pitfalls, and Opportunities

A. Dealing with other intervenors.

B. The press.

C. Administrative problems and barriers.

D. Well-wishers and do-gooders.

E. Long-range effects and flashbacks.

F. Overload for the counselor.

G. Burnout and the counselor.

H. Overload prevention.

I. Role playing.

J. Professional consultation.

CRITICAL INCIDENT PROCEDURES

Critical Incident refers to traumatic events that may be experienced by law enforcement personnel or their families. The essential element of such events is the threat to the survival or the continued functioning of the individual.

A traumatic event is one of such intensity that it is likely to produce symptoms or reactions in the average law enforcement officer. Such traumatic events have certain common characteristics:

1. The event is likely to be sudden and unexpected.
2. The event is a threat to the officer's existence or well-being.
3. The event may include an element of loss (a partner, physical ability, position).
4. The event may result in an abrupt change in the officer's values, confidence, or ideals.

Some of the more frequent critical incidents faced by law enforcement officers include:

1. Line-of-duty death of an officer.
2. Wounding or injury of an officer in line of duty.
3. Involvement in a hostage situation.
4. An officer's use of deadly force.
5. An officer's suicide.

Other unexpected events that occur less frequently than the above can result in reactions common to traumatic or critical incidents.

Effects

The effects of a critical or traumatic incident on the officer or those closely associated with the officer may vary considerably. Any of the immediate and longer-range effects will depend on the personality and previous experience of the officer. In general, three phases of reaction can be expected following a traumatic event:

I. *The Initial Phase.* This period, which immediately follows the traumatic event, is sometimes referred to as the *impact phase.* This phase can be described by the following:
   A. Begins with the traumatic event and continues until the stressor no longer has a direct effect.
   B. May last a few minutes or several days.
   C. The officer's focus of attention is on the present and on the traumatic event. This phase seems to last longest in instances of an officer's death or in cases of deadly force. The officer or surviving partners are involved with repetitions of the event during investigations and

other discussions. Senior officers, the media, and lawyers may require that officers continue to focus on the traumatic event for days or even weeks.

D. Reactions by the traumatized officer may include:

1. Feeling or acting stunned or bewildered.
2. Narrowing of attention.
3. Isolation of emotions.
4. Behavior is automatic, with bland emotions. The more the events following the traumatic event continue to stress the officer, the longer and more intense this phase is likely to be.

II. *The Recoil Phase.* This phase begins with the end of the impact phase and lasts until the officer is able to settle back into his or her usual routine of everyday duty and living. This phase can last from several days to several weeks. This phase is characterized by the need to retell the story. This is a way of attempting to master the traumatic event. This phase may be characterized by:

A. A tendency to be overreactive to ordinary events.
B. A need to share and receive support from other officers.
C. Depression, impotent rage, withdrawal, anxiety, bad dreams, sleep disturbance, somatization, and other acute emotional reactions.

III. *The Post-Traumatic Period.* This third phase usually begins when the officer returns to a regular routine. Stability seems to have returned but the long-range effects of a traumatic critical incident may appear in this phase. The officer may experience:

A. Periodic episodes of depression or hopelessness.
B. Insomnia and/or disturbing dreams.
C. Continuation or reexperiencing of reactions from the earlier phases.

Intervenors

There are two significant characteristics of those who can be of greatest help to the victims an survivors of traumatic or tragic critical incidents: acceptance by the victims/survivors and the skill and experience to be of service. The most effective intervenors may have either or both significant characteristics. The most commonly available intervenors are:

1. *Fellow Officers.* Generally highest in acceptance by victims and survivors, fellow officers may range from low to high in counseling skill and/or experience. Potential to help is high, whereas potential to worsen the situation is quite low except in the case of insensitive or destructive personalities.
2. *Immediate Supervisors.* The same potentials as fellow officers with the added potential to arrange smooth transitions and necessary administrative details.

3. *Unit Commanders.* As an authority figure of considerable significance in the lives of all concerned, the commander of the unit in which the traumatic incident occurred is in a position to counsel, give general support, and set a standard and model for helpful behavior. The unit commander can also ensure that the immediate supervisor takes care of all administrative matters and gives the supervisor support and guidance during all three phases of the traumatic incident process.

4. *Peer Counselors.* The police officer who has been designated and trained as a peer counselor can be the first line of professional assistance in a traumatic critical incident. The peer counselor is also valuable in providing continuing support, monitoring, or follow-up intervention where effects of trauma are long term or chronic.

5. *The Chaplain.* In most law enforcement departments, the chaplain is seen as the most neutral and the most available source of understanding and support. Spiritual counsel is especially helpful when the trauma involves a death.

6. *The Mental Health Professional.* Psychologists, psychiatrists, and other professionally trained mental health workers may be helpful or not in traumatic critical incident situations involving law enforcement officers and their families. Unless the mental health professional has worked frequently and intensively with law enforcement personnel, he or she may be unaware or insensitive to the embarrassment, shame, distrust, or emotional distance that most highly functional and practical people like police officers feel in respect to "shrinks." A mental health professional who has also been a law enforcement officer can be especially effective.

7. *Other Officers' Family Members.* Mates and other family members of officers can be particularly helpful in lending support to the families of slain officers or of officers who are victims of other traumatic incidents. Almost every law enforcement agency has an informal network of officers' spouses who are ready and able to help out in emergencies.

8. *The Media.* There is probably no more universal influence in any community than the media. Newspapers and television reporters, editors, and producers can have powerful effects—positive and negative—following a traumatic incident. The journalist must weigh many factors in deciding how to treat any newsworthy event. Traumatic events involving law enforcement personnel are almost always considered of major interest to readers and viewers. Whether such reporting is sympathetic and supportive, or as in some instances distressing or even destructive to victims and survivors depends on a complex variety of motivations, bureaucratic requirements, and personalities of news gatherers, directors, and presenters.

9. *The Citizenry*. In the United States, perhaps more than in any other country in the world, citizens contact law enforcement personnel directly with opinions, evaluations, and commentary. This is as it should be in a democracy. Following a critical incident, the communications received by a law enforcement officer or family member from concerned, interested, or opinionated citizens can have a significant positive or negative effect.

Intervention Points

Help should be available and rendered appropriately at all significant times following a traumatic critical incident. The range of possible intervention times is from immediately following the event to as long as a year later. In general, the earlier the appropriate intervention, the more effective it is likely to be.

1. *At the Scene.* Conflict control, stabilization, and support immediately following the critical incident can make the difference between an acute or a long-lasting chronic post-traumatic stress. The most effective intervenors—positive and negative—at the scene are fellow officers, immediate supervisors, unit commanders, the media, and civilians present at the scene.

2. *The Investigation.* Regardless of the persons or emotional trauma that may be involved, the regulations and procedures mandated to be followed with respect to a critical incident must be accomplished. The traumatized individual, partners, other officers, or even family members may be required to give testimony. The immediate supervisor and unit commander would be the most significant intervenors in this phase.

3. *The First 24 Hours.* During the impact phase, and as the officer enters the recoil phase, the peer counselor, the immediate supervisor, and the mental health professional are most likely to provide the most positive intervention.

4. *Week One.* As the officer-stress victim moves from the recoil phase to the post-traumatic period, the immediate supervisor, the peer counselor, and the mental health professional continue to be the first-line intervenors. The unit commander can sometimes be of supportive assistance.

5. *Weeks 2–4.* As the officer returns to duty and becomes involved in familiar routines, partners, fellow officers, and the immediate supervisor are in the best position to monitor and intervene if stress reactions continue or develop. Where necessary and appropriate, the peer counselor or mental health professional may continue with crisis consultation or support.

6. *Months 1–6.* Where stress reactions, job-related problems, or family-related problems continue or appear in this time period following the traumatic event, professional help is indicated. Although the peer counselor and supervisors may be supportive and encourage further help, it is likely that stress reactions extending for this period of time have deeper roots that must be explored in a professional mental health setting.

Intervention Techniques

Some intervention techniques can be used effectively by almost any intervenor, whereas other techniques require special training or qualifications. The inappropriate use of some intervention techniques can be in some cases dangerous (clinical exploration, interpretation). The effectiveness of any intervention technique to help relieve post-traumatic stress will be governed to a large extent by the timeliness, tone, style, and intent with which the intervention is conducted. Some of the more commonly favored techniques for the relief of post-traumatic stress include:

1. *Attentive Listening.* This technique can be used by any intervenor. The willing ear is usually somewhat helpful in any stress-relief effort. Good eye contact, an occasional nod, and genuine interest without comment are the essential mechanics of this technique.

2. *Being There with Empathy.* Simply "being there" and indicating availability, concern, and an awareness of the turbulent emotions of the stressed individual add reassurance and hope.

3. *Reassurance.* This technique is valuable only if the reassurance is reality oriented. Reassuring the victim that routine matters will be handled, premises and property will be secured, family will be protected, and the victim's responsibilities will be taken over by others can provide helpful support.

4. *Supportive Counseling.* This technique requires formal training. Using counseling procedures such as "effective listening," restatement of content, clarification of feeling, reassurance, community referral, and networking, the victim can be helped to reintegrate himself or herself into a return to less stressful circumstances. Peer counselors are particularly skilled in these techniques.

5. *Group Grief Sharing.* Applicable to death-of-an-officer incidents, meetings of family, partners, associated law enforcement personnel and others closely associated with the dead officer can provide significant opportunities to prevent or relieve excessive stress responses. The more emotional these meetings become, the better.

6. *Interpretive Counseling.* This intervention technique can be used by peer counselors or professional mental health workers to stimulate the victim to search for and discover the underlying emotional

stresses that tend to intensify a naturally stressful traumatic event. This procedure should only be used when the victim's emotional reaction is significantly greater than the circumstances of the critical incident warrant. Interpretive counseling may reveal emotional difficulties that require more extensive professional help than that which can be provided in the context of crisis consultation.

7. *Clinical Exploration.* The victim of a traumatic critical incident may develop a series of stress reactions that do not abate with the preceding crisis procedures. When this happens, the victim may suffer a *chronic post-traumatic stress disorder.* This condition can be severely debilitating and requires help from an experienced mental health professional. Extended post-traumatic stress requires referral for clinical exploration of the condition. Psychologists, social workers, psychiatrists, and other mental health professionals who have experience and training in working with law enforcement personnel are in the best position to help.

Conditions of Intervention

Intervention techniques and skills must be applied in appropriate ways following a traumatic critical incident. The following are some of the most important conditions:

1. *Immediacy.* The hours immediately following a critical incident constitute the time frame of critical entry. All techniques other than interpretive counseling and clinical exploration tend to be most effective in the 12 to 24 hours following the trauma.

2. *Briefness.* All previously described techniques are best with a minimum of verbiage, repetition, or long-windedness. Language should be concise and communication brief.

3. *Privacy.* Except for the Group Grief Sharing, all of the other intervention techniques are best provided to the victim as privately as possible.

4. *Respect.* The traumatized victim of a critical incident may respond in unusual or unexpected ways. The intervenor who expects to render effective help must be prepared to tolerate unusual behavior and continue to respond with acceptance and respect. It is destructive for an intervenor to become distressed by a victim's behavior and criticize or attempt to control the victim's responses by being authoritarian or demanding that the victim "shape up."

5. *Support.* At all times, the intervenor in a traumatic critical incident situation must be supportive. Whether in earlier or later stages, intervention is more likely to be successful if the victim sees the intervenor as fully supportive, on the victim's side, and willing to do anything within reason to make the burden of being a victim as painless as possible.

Making Critical Incident Procedures Operational

Each law enforcement department must develop its own standardized procedures for response to traumatic events. Written regulations and procedures tend to be rigid. In the case of procedures developed and specified for dealing with traumatic events, the application of the required actions should be subject to the judgment and availability of the intervenors. Larger departments should have trained peer counselors and mental health staff or consultants. Smaller law enforcement units should develop close ties with larger departments so that trained and experienced intervenors can be "borrowed" when an emergency situation arises.

In general, critical incident response procedures can be codified in departmental regulations or orders under headings similar to the following:

1. *Activation.* Regulations dealing with official response to traumatic incidents should begin with clear-cut descriptions of the event that would require a critical incident response from the department.
2. *Crisis Team Manager.* Department procedure manuals should designate the individual(s) who are to be contacted as soon as a critical incident occurs. These individuals should be senior staff who are trained and experienced in responding and managing rapidly and efficiently.
3. *Crisis Team Members.* Specific members of the department should be designated on an ongoing duty roster as crisis team cadre. The crisis manager should choose those members for the response and management team who are most experienced as well as newer team members who would profit from the experience of serving with more seasoned crisis intervenors.
4. *Press Liaison.* Some departments have a permanent public information officer. Other departments have no formal press contact personnel. Reporters and other newspersons can be significant intervenors— helpful or unhelpful—in a critical incident situation. One member of the crisis management team should be prepared to meet with the press and to provide accredited press representatives with:
   a. All the facts consistent with the law, department policy, and the best interests of the ongoing investigation.
   b. A briefing as to the concerns about victims and survivors and how the press may be most helpful as intervenors.
   c. Around-the-clock availability to answer questions and provide a single-source liaison between the press and the crisis manager.
5. *Initial Assignments.* Department procedural manuals or regulations should provide specific information as to assignments for the crisis manager and crisis team members for the various kinds of critical incidents likely to occur.

6. *Meetings and Reports.* The department procedural manual should specify the times when the crisis management team should meet in respect to the different kinds of crises likely to be encountered. The types of formal and informal reports to department management should be specified in detail.

Line-of-Duty Death

The death of an officer in the line of duty affects all members of the department as well as the fallen officer's family and friends. The entire community is likely to feel the loss. When the partner or the supervisor of a fallen officer becomes aware of or is notified of a line-of-duty death, the following procedures are to be followed:

1. The chief of the department, the sheriff, or the director of public safety is to be notified forthwith.
2. The designated crisis team manager is to be notified and dispatched immediately to the scene.
3. The crisis manager is to report his or her presence to the supervisor at the scene.
4. The crisis manager will designate a crisis team member as staff leader at headquarters to establish communications with the crisis manager at the scene and to assemble the crisis team members designated by the crisis manager. The staff leader will be directed by the crisis manager to contact the fallen officer's partner, best friend, the chaplain, and where appropriate, the fallen officer's former training officer. These should be apprised of the details of the situation and placed on alert.
5. When the crisis manager has established the relevant details of the incident, he or she should formulate an action plan to accomplish the following:
   a. Notification and support of family survivors.
   b. Continuing communication with senior staff.
   c. Press liaison.
   d. A 24-hour plan for utilization of the crisis team.
6. This preliminary plan should be cleared immediately with the senior officer at the scene and with the sheriff, chief, director of public safety or other chief executive of the agency.
7. Once cleared, the plan should be implemented. The crisis manager should assign a crisis team member to the scene and immediately return to headquarters to supervise the crisis plan implementation.

The details with which each procedure is described will depend to some extent on the size and resources of any specific department. Standards will develop as techniques of intervention are developed, tested, and modified. Much of the effectiveness of these procedures will depend on the skill, experience, and sensitivity of the department's leadership and the officers selected to act as crisis team members and managers.

DEADLY FORCE PEER COUNSELING
PROCESS CHECKLIST

DATE _____ TIME _____ CALL FROM _____ DEPT _____

OFFICER _____ SCENE _____

INCIDENT _____

_____ Approval to help by _____   _____ Media statement to

_____ ID to senior officer at scene/   senior officer

structure   _____ Offer to meet with

_____ ID to officer/victim   other officers in group

_____ Precounseling statement   _____ Follow-up at officer's

_____ Catharsis session   home

_____ Support and reassurance   _____ 2-day contact

_____ Officer to contact family/   _____ 3-day contact

partners   _____ 1-week contact

_____ Accepted _____ Rejected   _____ 4-week contact

NARRATIVE SUMMARY AND RECOMMENDATIONS _____

_____
_____
_____
_____
_____
_____

Counseling Completed _____ BY _____

A Four-Hour Stress Inoculation Program

STRESS AND STRESS REDUCTION TRAINING

Instructor's Outline

I. *The Nature of Stress*
   A. Stress is created by *change*, particularly unexpected change. It can be very distressing for individuals to find that change for the *better* sometimes leads to stress.
   B. Originally, stress was coined as an engineering term meaning external force directed at some physical object.
   C. Stress was scientifically studied by Hans Selye in 1956.
   D. Stress of sudden wealth, University of Michigan, Irish Sweepstakes Study. Read *Plain Talk About Stress* (Public Affairs Pamphlet). Questions?
   E. All emotions not just fight or flight. Stress can be best described as a process, not a thing. Stress on a neurological level.
      1. Automic nervous system.
      2. Sympathetic nervous system.
      3. Parasympathetic nervous system.
      4. General Adaptation Response.
         a. Three stages: Alarm, Resistance, and Exhaustion.
      5. Physiological Response. One man's passion is another man's poison.
      6. How feeling is interpreted determines whether distress is experienced, but stress is common physiological component.

7. Keeping with James-Lange Theory of Emotion. Emotional feeling results from familiar patterns of feedback from bodily organ changes. So we feel something emotionally, but we may interpret what we feel from the environment.

F. From a homeostatic perspective, stress causes disequilibrium, which in turn causes strain. The strain then triggers changes in the system aimed at restoring balance or equilibrium. This means that change, quantitative or qualitative, for better or worse, produces stress.

1. *A Physiological Response.* The mind then attempts to balance or normalize the body.

G. *Some Stress Is Good.* It results in anxiety and motivates us. How much stress is good? We do not know, but there is a relationship between anxiety and performance. Yerkes and Dodson animal research.

H. *Stress Is Cumulative.* It can be "put away" only for a short period of time.

I. *Overload and Burnout.*

1. Freudenburger paper (1989) coined term "burnout."

a. *Symptoms*—callous, fatigued, critical.

J. *Environmental Factors.* These can be very important leading to stress.

K. *Health Factors.* These can determine the degree of stress that the individual can tolerate. Influence each other: flu, mumps.

1. Stress decreases body's natural warriors (killer cells, *T* cells, and macrophanges, which make up the core of the body's defense against invading germs, viruses, etc.).

L. Circadian rhythms (day/night, light/dark) are the balancing mechanisms for timing life. Disruptions of these rhythms make the individual more prone to stress, because they represent significant change. Shift work.

M. Many cultural factors either help or hinder an individual deal with stress. Since change leads to stress, the more rigidity a cultural background requires of individuals, the more prone they are to stress when there is any change.

N. Family factors are very important in the creation of stress. Most people have relatively rigid expectations for what should be involved in a family relationship. These may be unrealistic. When things occur that are "different" from expectation, stress will increase.

O. Fill out the Holmes Schedule of Recent Events scale.

P. *Stress-related disorders.* These include ulcers, heart attack, arthritis, asthma, allergies, sexual dysfunction, immunological suppression, hypertension.

II. *Stress and Violence*

  A. If persons experienced less stress, the frequency of domestic violence would drastically decrease.

    1. *Warning signs* that indicate stress.

      a. Avoidance of work.
      b. Criticalness.
      c. Depression.
      d. Physical body changes.
      e. Withdrawal from social contacts.
      f. Nervousness.
      g. Compulsive work habits.
      h. More and more time uptight.
      i. Stress Symptom Scale—fill out.
      j. Stress Prevention Scale—fill out.

    2. *Questions.*

Break

    3. *Preventing Stress.* Too often people wait until they suffer ill effects.

      a. Physical Activities.

        (i) What if I told you that engaging in physical activity can decrease the chances of having stomach ulcers, heart attacks, strokes, and hypertension and lessen the discomfort of arthritis and allergies, and is associated with increased self-esteem, positive self-concept, and achievement motivation?

STUDY

A-DISABLED PERSONS			B-ABLED PERSONS		
1 Physically Active	2 Socially Active	3 In- Active	1 Physically Active	2 Socially Active	3 In- Active

        Results: Physical activity, more so than social activity was associated with positive self-concept, increased self-esteem, and increased achievement motivation, whether abled or disabled.

      b. *Personal and Social Interactions.* School, joking, talking.
      c. *Accomplishing Work Overload Successfully.* List—helping gain control and command.

    d. *Breaks, Recreation, and Vacations.*

       (i)   Recreation.

       (ii) Four 3-day weekends annually.

       (iii) Two-week vacation.

    e. *Proper Food.*

       (i)   Four food groups.

       (ii) Staff survey—how many had a good breakfast?

    f. Increasing Durability to Stress. Controlling illness through the body's own chemistry.

       (i)   Persons can fail to perform up to ability if (1) there are too few essential nutrients, or (2) some substance is present that prevents nutrients from being properly utilized.

       (ii) Improper diet can lead to neuroglycopenia (low blood sugar). This deprives the brain of its primary source of energy (glucose), which can result in tension, dizziness, headaches, fatigue, decreased sex drive, weak spells, and nervousness.

           Whole grain is the best source of nourishment to maintain proper glycogen, which stores in the liver. Why do many companies continue to use bleached enriched white flour for baking?

           (1) It does not turn rancid like whole-grain flour because it's missing the germ, which contains many healthy nutrients.

           (2) It does not attract insects as readily as whole-grain flour. Insects probably know they cannot survive on it.

           Rats Study. Fed commercial enriched white bread. Did not thrive as those on a whole-grain bread diet. "After about 90 days, $2/3$ of them were dead of malnutrition and the others were severely stunted."

4. *Stress Awareness.*

    a. *Colorimeter.* Everybody try. If black and tense, or blue and relaxed.

    b. *Review* possible sources of personal stress (Holmes Stress Scale). See if there is anything you would want to change.

    c. *The Role of relaxation and biofeedback.* Self-monitoring.

       (i)   Biofeedback.

       (ii) Relaxation.

(iii) Stress Reduction Kit.

  d. Exercise and relaxation.

5. *The Family Counsel.*

  a. Purpose and implementation.

  b. Role-playing (5 minutes).

6. *The Peer-Counseling Support Group.*

  a. Description.

  b. How to form a support group.

7. *Crisis Consultation.*

  a. Referring people.

8. *Kinds of Professional Help Available.*

  a. Mental health professionals.

9. *Personal Prevention Directions.*

  a. *Personal exercise program.* Simple formula on how to exercise properly.

    (i) $220 - \text{Age} \times 4/5 =$ maximum heart rate tolerable. Example—Age 50: $220 - 50 \times 4/5 = 136$ beats per minute.

    (ii) That is the pulse rate you should achieve three times per week for 20 minutes.

    (iii) *Measuring Pulse:* Pulse rate = pulse beats for 10 seconds $\times 6$.

  b. *Healthful eating.*

    (i) There are presently hundreds of diet fads. Although a few look promising, the best way we know to take off weight and keep it off is by creating a negative energy balance. That is; consume less calories than you spend or burn off. For best weight reduction program, exercise and decrease calories consumed.

    (ii) System to assess caloric intake to lose weight.

      (1) 10 calories per day $\times$ body weight equals number of calories to maintain present weight.

      (2) With exercise, 11 calories $\times$ body weight for maintenance.

      (3) With heavy exercise, 12 calories $\times$ body weight for maintenance.

  c. Appropriate recreation and hobbies.

  d. Create effective personal relationships.

Restraint and Sensitivity Training Program

RESTRAINT AND SENSITIVITY TRAINING

Contents

Presentation Outline

IV. SOLUTIONS
  A. Community.
  B. Management.
  C. Individual Law Enforcement Officer on the Job.
  D. Individual Law Enforcement Officer at Home.
  E. Proviso.
  Resources

RESTRAINT AND SENSITIVITY TRAINING

Presentation Outline

I. THE ESSENTIAL ISSUES
  A. The Tasks of Law Enforcement.
  B. Controversial Application of Functions and Techniques.
    1. Deadly force.
      a. Hand-to-hand combat.
      b. Shoot to wound.
      c. Racial bias.
    2. Physical restraint.
      a. Removal of perpetrator from a house.
      b. Handcuffing behind the back.
      c. Use of intermediate-level weapons.
    3. Communication with civilians.
    4. Response to resistance, questions, or slow compliance.
    5. Affective tone and language.
      a. Race.
      b. Sex.
      c. Ethnic origin.
      d. Affective tone.
    6. Proper enforcement that is unfamiliar to the civilian.
II. CONFLICT ESCALATORS
  A. Ignorance of the Limits of the Law.
  B. Language That Incites.
    1. Sarcasm.
    2. Use of vernacular.
    3. Threats.
    4. Overemotional shouting.

C. Behavior That Incites.
  1. Obscene gestures.
  2. Excessively threatening gestures.
  3. Inappropriate touching.
  4. Unnecessary invasion of personal space.
  5. Unnecessary force or restraint.
D. Emotional Presentation That Incites.
  1. Excessively "macho" style.
  2. Intimidating, hostile mannerisms.
  3. Inappropriate interruption or cutting off.
E. Communication That Incites.
  1. Intradepartment.
    a. The use of humor on the radio.
    b. The use of inappropriate language on reports.
  2. Extradepartment.
    a. Defensiveness to the press.
    b. Arguments with civilians.
    c. Telephone call response.
III. CAUSES OF CONFLICT ESCALATORS
  A. Inadequate Selection.
  B. Inadequate Education.
  C. Inadequate Training.
  D. Poor Communication from Senior Officers.
  E. Poor Modeling by Senior Officers.
  F. Emotional Instability.
    1. Low self-esteem.
    2. Personal insecurity.
    3. Depression.
    4. Mental illness.
    5. Drug or alcohol abuse.
  G. Character Deficiencies.
  H. Overload.
  I. Personal Problems.
  J. Physical Illness.
  K. Financial Problems.
  L. Post-Trauma Reactions.
IV. SOLUTIONS
  A. Community.

B. Management.
   1. Sound selection procedures.
   2. Proper training.
   3. Supplying proper equipment.
   4. Modeling.
   5. Two-way communication.
   6. Morale surveys.
   7. Traumatic incident follow-up.
C. Individual Law Enforcement Officer on the Job.
   1. Courtesy.
      a. Introductions.
      b. Voice tone and volume.
      c. Address.
      d. Body language.
      e. Personal opinions.
      f. Profanity and demeaning remarks.
      g. Response to citizen provocation.
      h. Explain what you do.
      i. Listening.
   2. Citizen satisfaction and the law.
D. Individual Law Enforcement Officer at Home.
   1. Planning for recreational activities.
   2. Keeping physically fit.
   3. Maintaining proper diet and adequate rest periods.
   4. Organizing and prioritizing responsibilities.
   5. Practicing stress reduction techniques.
   6. Preventive\Interventive mental health assistance.
E. Proviso.

I. THE ESSENTIAL ISSUES

A. The Tasks of Law Enforcement

Most police officers and managers understand the tasks of law enforcement. In broad concepts, law enforcement has been developed first to
maintain the peace. When this fails, it has become the role of law enforcement to solve crimes. Modern times have added the aspect of traffic control to the responsibilities of law enforcement. With the advent of "911,"
law enforcement has been tasked with the responsibility of resolving a
wide range of emergencies.

Whether explicitly stated or tacitly understood, most law enforcement officers and managers believe that the tasks imposed on them by society and their own particular communities are impossible to fully achieve. The reasons law enforcement personnel believe that societal expectations are impossible to ever fully obtain are as follows:

1. The number of people who engage in crime has increased exponentially in the past few years.

2. Even when caught, the culprit returns to society much more quickly than ever before.

3. While in jail or prison, the culprit learns more advanced and more sophisticated ways of breaking the law.

4. While in jail, the culprit establishes communication with other members of the crime community so that future activity becomes more coordinated and more efficient.

5. The pay scale for law enforcement officers and the budgets that are made available limit the effectiveness of selection, education, and training procedures.

6. The number of crimes that take place are so extensive, depending on the environment, that insufficient numbers of detectives can be assigned to solve crimes. As a result, only a small percentage of crimes are ever solved. Considering the lack of resources and the legal and professional limitations placed on law enforcement officers, the number of crimes that are solved is astonishing.

7. The largest task of most law enforcement agencies is the control of traffic. Since 1990 the number of vehicles on American roads has escalated making the task nearly impossible. The larger the city, the more complex the highways and access routes. Since virtually every accident must be investigated and reported, the assets and resources of the agency are always taxed. During heavy periods of utilization (early morning, evening rush hour, weekends, and holidays) the task is an impossible one in terms of society's expectations.

8. Since the advent of "911," the already seriously taxed resources of law enforcement agencies have been diluted even further. Because of the minor nature of many "911" calls (cat in tree, neighbor parking on property), it is impossible to meet the expectations of society in the response to "911." This results in law enforcement being criticized as being unresponsive and inadequate.

Most municipalities of size have developed a triage system whereby the most serious "911" calls are given priority. This results in a somewhat more efficient utilization of the system, but it also results in more citizens' complaints that the police are "unresponsive."

B. Controversial Application of Functions and Techniques

Because the task given to law enforcement is so varied and involves so many crisis and danger situations, there is bound to be a high degree of controversy when people look at law enforcement activities from different perspectives. Most of citizens' complaints center around one of the following six areas:

1. *Deadly Force.* The rules and regulations concerning how, when, why, and where law enforcement officers may use their power of deadly force are clearly outlined. In real-life situations, the law enforcement officers has seconds, or in some cases, a portion of a second, to decide whether to use the power of deadly force. These human decisions cannot always be "correct." Some of the common complaints and the comparable realities are as follows:

   a. *Hand-to-Hand Combat: The officer should have used some hand-to-hand combat techniques, rather than shooting the assailant.* This concept, engendered by the motion pictures, is an impossible one. Most hand-to-hand combat moves are more for the movies and television than for real life. To attempt to use such techniques with an angry, deranged, frightened assailant in possession of a deadly weapon ensures injury or death to the police officer.

   b. *Shoot to Wound: You should have aimed to wound the assailant and not to kill him.* The same applies here as in the preceding example. Law enforcement officers are taught to shoot for the "center mass" of the body. This is the technique that is most likely to stop a dangerous assailant. Even hitting such an assailant does not guarantee he/she will not continue to attack and inflict injury or death on the officer or other citizens who the officer is entrusted to protect. This has happened frequently, and every law enforcement officer is familiar with this possibility.

   The ability to place a bullet from any weapon in a specific area is, again, mostly a myth. Even though an officer can be trained to a very high level of accuracy on the police range, in emergency situations it is very unlikely that appropriate stance, planning, aiming, and slow, smooth firing can be accomplished. For example, should a knife-wielding assailant attack an officer directly, it would be necessary for the officer, as quickly as possible, to draw and fire his/her weapon when the assailant is at least 20 feet away. If the officer initiates these moves when the assailant is closer, it is likely that the officer will be mortally wounded or killed.

   c. *Racial Bias: Cops shoot more small ethnic group members than whites.* Whatever the statistics may demonstrate in any particular part of the country, these numbers are artifacts. The police officer will shoot when he/she feels in danger of loss of life or serious bodily injury to the self, a fellow officer, or a civilian. Deadly force is frequently governed by the environment in which the incident occurs, the degree of danger in the neighborhood where the incident occurs, and the stance and attitude of the individual who poses the threat. When these circumstances result in statistics showing greater use of deadly force with nonwhite perpetrators, it is generally a result of the preceding factors, rather than any kind of racial bias. In an emergency, there simply is not enough time to cognate racial bias. The officer recognizes and responds to perceived danger.

2. *Physical Restraint.* A great many complaints are lodged against law enforcement officers for "police brutality." This almost always refers to something witnessed by a civilian or experienced by a civilian during an arrest procedure. The law enforcement officer is trained to place potential perpetrators in a position where they can be handcuffed. Then, the officer can conduct a frisk for concealed weapons. In making an arrest, the officer is in considerable danger between the initiation of the arrest and the actual securing of handcuffs on the suspect. Should the individual have a concealed weapon, while the officer is busily engaged in trying to bring the perpetrator's two hands together and engage the handcuffs, the individual may free one hand, draw a weapon, and injure or kill the officer or others at the scene. It is at this point that an officer is likely to use some form of aggressive physical action to distract the perpetrator's attentions from any possible plan to attack the officer. Thus, before grasping the subject's hands, the officer may kick the subject's calf or foot, demand in a raised voice that the subject spread the legs further, or place a hand in the back and push vigorously against the subject. By momentarily distracting the person, handcuffs can be more safely applied.

If the officer is instructed not to do this, injury and death will increase significantly. The research shows that the most dangerous individuals are those intent on escaping from the officer. They will use weapons at their disposal to further this goal. Because individuals perceive the handcuffing process as the "last chance" to escape, this is when they will most likely attack the officer in an attempt to flee. Although complaints of physical restraint are most common at this point, there are others:

a. *Removal of Perpetrator from a House.* When an officer makes an arrest on a warrant or because of an ongoing felony, it may be necessary to remove the perpetrator from his or her residence. Sometimes, family members will try to interfere, either because of spontaneous emotional feelings or their disbelief that the family member has committed a crime and is under arrest. When circumstances in the environment during an arrest occur that threaten police officers, they cannot stand by idly, but must take action to command and control the situation. This may mean "body checking" an attacking family member, hustling the person to be arrested out of the house so that the danger of interference is decelerated, or in some cases threatening the interfering family member with arrest for interference. If the person attempting to interfere with the arrest becomes agitated and threatening, a police officer may try to "counsel" the individual. If the disturbance persists, however, the officer has no choice but to do whatever is necessary in the area of applying force or restraint to keep the interaction from escalating. In some cases, it may be necessary to arrest the agitators. This leads to claims of police brutality, excessive use of force, and increased disrespect by the members of the neighborhood toward law enforcement.

b. *Handcuffing behind the Back.* Complaints are received that police officers are "too rough" when handcuffing persons behind the back. Without training and repeated experience, civilians don't realize that with handcuffs in the front, the individual can still attack the officer or others quite efficiently, even using the handcuffs as a weapon. Civilians seeing someone's arms put behind the back, sometimes with an accompanying exclamation of pain or cursing, assume that the officer is purposely inflicting pain on the assailant. The fact that many of those being arrested curse, swear, and complain to officers for no reason other than they are angry at being caught does not enter the minds of the observers.

c. *Use of Intermediate-Level Weapons.* Police officers, at one time, carried nightsticks, slap gloves, and blackjacks. Most departments forbid the use of the latter two instruments because their use can result in excessive use of restraining force.

Officers are trained in the proper use of a nightstick or baton and more recently the ASP (collapsible baton). There are situations in which officers simply cannot use their hands to control agitated persons during dangerous situations. The situation may be such that the officer does not wish to use deadly force. The baton is thus an important element in the police officer's defense system as an intermediate response.

Officers are forbidden to draw their weapons to threaten others. If they draw their firearms, they do so seriously with intent to protect the life and physical health of themselves or others. Officers are trained not to bluff with their weapons, but to use them when necessary to protect life and physical safety. Police agencies hope that, over the course of events, officers convey this serious and unequivocal message: "If I, as a law enforcement officer, am forced to unholster my weapon, I will not hesitate to shoot you to protect the life and physical health of others. Therefore cease behaving in a threatening manner."

If an officer uses a baton or similar device as an offensive weapon, it is quite likely that he or she will be under serious charges by the department. The situations under which such intermediate forces are applied are limited.

3. *Communication with Civilians.* Many civilians take offense when they are addressed by a police officer. Sometimes, the police officer is gruff and direct. Sometimes, in emergency situations, the officer may shout. Most complaints against police officers by civilians occur when the officer, in a seemingly angry and aggressive manner, tells people to move, leave the scene, go home, or get out of the way. It is difficult for civilians to understand that the officer would probably not be making the request unless some emergency or dangerous situation was occurring. Time is of the essence in such situations, and officers simply do not have the opportunity to explain to each individual why they are making the request or why their demeanor is abrupt or hostile. No one likes to be shouted at or ordered about. In the interest of safety, however, this may be necessary.

4. *Response to Resistance, Questions, or Slow Compliance.* When police officers communicate with civilians they expect compliance with orders. Civilians are bound by law to do so. Police officers know that people who resist direction will increase the danger being addressed at the time. If a civilian says "Why should I move?" in the midst of an emergency, the officer is likely to respond with considerable force, "Move it, now!" Sometimes, when civilians complain about this kind of behavior, they are asked, "Did the officer first ask you in a quieter voice to move?" A common answer is "Yes, but I didn't realize he meant right then." When civilians fail to react to an order, there is not much an officer can do other than to use a forceful expression. It does, however, often result in complaints.

When a police officer gives an order to a civilian, it generally means there is an emergency situation and rapid compliance is necessary. The civilian may respond slowly because of age and infirmity or as a means of expressing aggressiveness. In either case, the officer has only a fraction of a second to decide whether to speed up the process. There is no question that sometimes an officer may try to speed up a civilian who is not capable of moving faster. For many civilians, however, this is a quiet way of saying, "I'm not going to do what you want me to do." Such defiance poses a danger of interference in the police officer's job and must be dealt with sternly. Nevertheless, this is a source of civilian complaints.

5. *Affective Tone and Language.* It is often said, "It's not what you say, but the way you say it." There is no question that this is true. Many complaints against police officers relate not only to what the officer says, but the way in which it is said. Some of the most common complaints relate to the following:

a. *Race.* When referring to an Asian-American, police officers should use that general, generic descriptor. There is no excuse for calling such a citizen a "Chink." Officers who have grown up in families where such words are used commonly may make this error when under stress. An officer may not even mean anything critical by the use of such terms. Their use may be understandable in an emergency situation, but it is not excusable. A lot of discredit falls on police officers when anyone in law enforcement uses racial slurs.

b. *Sex.* Insensitive police officers may denigrate women, gays, lesbians, or transsexuals. There is no doubt that this goes on. This is not lawful and is therefore against departmental policy. Because police officers are human beings, the development of prejudices is understandable. Everyone has some sort of prejudice. As with many aspects of their work, law enforcement officers are expected to be "cleaner than a whistle." They must do everything they can to modify, change, and when necessary suppress natural prejudices that they may have. Whenever a sexual slur is expressed by a police officer, as with racial slurs, it reflects badly on all members of the department.

c. *Ethnic Origin.* There are many incidents where law enforcement officers, in the course of their duties, may identify an individual's ethnic origin by using offensive slang. This, as with other slurs, is unacceptable and forbidden. The use of terms such as "kike," "Paddy," and "dago," are often regionally meaningful. Frequently, people of these national origins may use the terms affectionately among themselves but resent them being used by someone who does not belong to that ethnic group or that nationality. It is mandatory that police officers do not use this kind of prejudiced language in addressing civilians.

d. *Affective Tone.* The tone of voice in which the officer addresses people makes a lot of difference, depending on whether it is a tone of respect or a tone of contempt and disgust. Combining a negative emotional tone to some designation of race, sex, ethnic origin, or nationality is unacceptable. Certainly, police officers were prone to do this much more in the past than in recent years, largely because they were poorly educated and had little acculturation. Today's law enforcement officer is better educated and knows much more about what is expected of a police officer in the real world. Tone of voice is, however, a source of many civilian complaints and an area that should be constantly an issue of concern to every law enforcement officer.

6. *Proper Enforcement That Is Unfamiliar to the Civilian.* A fair number of citizen complaints occur when the officer enforces a law or a regulation that is unknown to the civilian. For instance, there may be rules about how many people may gather in public to make protests. An individual may cross the line between expressing an opinion and committing assault with threats. It is not uncommon for civilians arrested for threatening a police officer to claim that their rights of free speech have been denied. The civilian simply is unaware that a verbal threat with the potential of being carried out is considered an assault. They are also usually unaware that an assault on a police officer carries a higher penalty than an assault on a civilian.

This places an unreasonable, but real, burden on each law enforcement officer. The enforcement of a law that is unknown or unfathomable to a civilian might reasonably require the officer to explain the infraction to the civilian. In most cases, when the officer invokes the law, the situation has reached the point of tumult that the civilian is not listening and may be making dangerous threats or taking unacceptable actions against the police officer. This is a frequent source of civilian complaints against officers and must be investigated and resolved.

II. CONFLICT ESCALATORS

A. Ignorance of the Limits of the Law

Various jurisdictions require various degrees of knowledge on the part of police officers as to the strict limits of the law. Many jurisdictions spend a great deal of time, not only during academy training, but also with continuing education, instructing law enforcement officers as to the constitutional rights of citizens, the limits involving probable cause, and other issues related to the correct application of the powers of arrest and the powers of law enforcement officers to maintain the peace.

Where an officer is ignorant of the limits of the law, and a civilian attempts to remind the officer of this (in some cases it may be attorneys or civil rights activists), conflict can escalate. The officer may become threatened and increase efforts to maintain control of the situation.

B. Language That Incites

The way things are said can incite civilians to respond in kind and thus increase the probability of conflict between the law enforcement officer and the civilian. Social psychology research tells us that a hostile response significantly increases the probabilities of a hostile rejoinder. A gentler response often results in a gentler rejoinder. Language that incites includes the following:

1. *Sarcasm.* In response to a civilian's attempts to explain a situation to an officer, the officer may interrupt with "Yeh, and I suppose your mother is in the hospital and you're rushing to be at her deathbed?"

2. *Use of Vernacular.* Addressing a civilian as "you scum bag," or referring to a civilian ethnically as "kike," "nigger," "spic," "chink," or other common designators that offend and denigrate.

3. *Threats.* Threats were a traditional way that police officers in the "old days" maintained control in difficult situations. Unfortunately, the propensity for police officers to use threats has been escalated by the many movie and television dramas that depict police officers as threatening figures. They are setting unfortunate models for younger police officers. Language such as "Put your hands on your head, or I'll blow your head off!" or "Move it—now! Or you're dead meat!" are seldom appropriate in modern law enforcement.

4. *Overemotional Shouting.* Connected with the preceding notion and usually associated with a threat, but not necessarily so, the police officer who shouts wildly, gesticulates, or in other ways loses control is likely to incite a negative response and/or a complaint from civilians. The potential for escalating the conflict becomes greater when the officer resorts to such behavior.

   In certain situations (drug busts), emotional shouting and threatening directives are a part of gaining the attention of dangerous subjects. It conveys a message to the felons that there is no hope, reason, or potential for them to act in a dangerous manner. Aside from these very special situations, shouting is more a personal choice than a valuable tool when dealing with civilians.

C. Behavior That Incites

Some actions of law enforcement officers can escalate conflict. Sometimes described as "body language," this behavior is really much more complex. It certainly does not have to do solely with the way in which the officer uses his or her body. The following are the most common inciting behaviors:

1. *Obscene Gestures.* Obscene gestures such as "giving the finger" are more common today than every before. They represent an infantile, uncontrolled effort to express frustration and powerlessness. There is no place for such expressions in the professional law enforcement officer's style or manner. Law enforcement officers who use such

gestures can expect to be chastised and can expect an escalation in conflict.

2. *Excessively Threatening Gestures.* The officer who "reaches" for his or her weapon, draws the weapon in a threatening manner, or who slaps the baton against the opposite palm in a threatening manner is likely to be escalating conflict. To draw a weapon in situations that do not call for deadly force is to expose the officer to an Internal Investigations charge. Threatening gestures incite civilians.

3. *Inappropriate Touching.* The only time an officer should place hands on a subject is in preparation for making an arrest or for a stop and frisk. Pushing with the hand to move someone along and poking with the fingers are usually inappropriate behaviors and are bound to escalate conflict.

4. *Unnecessary Invasion of Personal Space.* Research on personal threat indicates that individuals have a heightened awareness and sensitivity when another person comes within 48 inches of them, and become extremely threatened when the distance diminishes to less than 24 inches. Law enforcement officers should be aware of the distance they place between themselves and a civilian during communication. When personal space is invaded at a distance closer than 24 inches, threat becomes extreme, and this will likely accelerate the conflict.

5. *Unnecessary Force or Restraint.* The use of special techniques such as the "choke hold," or the "chicken," which inflict unnecessary pain, are behaviors that will incite the civilian, create an escalation of potential danger to the officer, and certainly lead to civilian complaints against officer. It is a delicate line between what force is necessary to control an individual being arrested and what may be categorized as "unnecessary force."

D. Emotional Presentation That Incites

The way a person says things, and the presentation of self are involved in communication. It is well known that people who are happy in their work extend that attitude to those they serve. Conversely, people who are miserable in their work also extend negative feelings to those they serve.

The following presentations of self are most likely to lead to an escalation of conflict and complaints against law enforcement officers:

1. *Excessively "Macho" Style.* The so-called John Wayne syndrome includes presenting the self as a tough, stoic, dangerous individual. Again, television and motion picture dramas tend to depict police officers this way. Such portrayals sensitize the civilian population and present unfortunate models for young officers.

2. *Intimidating, Hostile Mannerisms.* Although associated with the macho style, it is not the same. The distinguishing feature is that a problem exists that the officer angrily asserts was caused by the civilian's actions or lack thereof. The officer who chooses an intimidating, hostile manner as opposed to a polite, clear, controlled presentation is encouraging negative attitudes toward himself and fellow officers.

3. *Inappropriate Interruption or Cutting Off.* Conflict is escalated in any situation where an individual is deprived of the right to respond, or to finish what he or she is saying. The officer who uses this technique to maintain control or to express his or her own anger is guilty of an emotional presentation that is likely to incite conflict.

E. Communication That Incites

With the amount of recording, eavesdropping, and electronic surveillance that goes on today, it is likely that much of what used to be communication between and among officers is now available to the public. All "911" calls are recorded. Much radio traffic among law enforcement officers is recorded. Although the intention of an officer may be simply to be humorous or to pass the time, the results can escalate conflict and cause civilian complaints. Most commonly complaints include:

1. *Intradepartment*
   a. *The Use of Humor on the Radio.* The system of using code numbers to convey messages has saved a great deal of time and trouble. Where officers communicate with each other in conventional language, the opportunity to use inappropriate or humorous language increases. There have been incidents where newspapers have obtained transcripts of police officers talking to each other or to the dispatcher, to the detriment of all.
   b. *The Use of Inappropriate Language on Reports.* Police officers' reports, in many circumstances, are available to the press. The officer who goes beyond reporting requirements to express an opinion for which there is no reasonable or substantial logic is likely to get into trouble that sometimes involves the whole department.
2. *Extradepartment.* Police officers are under society's magnifying glass. Although police officers should have the right of free speech, people in general give more credence to what police officers say than to the average individual. Some of the common areas in which police officers get into trouble, raise conflict, and bring criticism on themselves and their department include the following:
   a. *Defensiveness to the Press.* When approached by the press, police officers should pleasantly but firmly decline to comment on almost

all issues. This may be unfair in terms of considering the police officer as a civilian on off-duty hours. On or off duty, however, the individual will most likely be quoted as a law enforcement officer.

If a police officer decides to talk to the press, he or she should understand that their information may be edited, and in some cases distorted.

b. *Arguments with Civilians.* Police officers are sometimes the object of intense questioning, criticism, or even ridicule by civilians. It is unwise for any police officer to enter into an argument, particularly in a public place, with a civilian who is attempting to incite conflict. These admonitions for police officers to be very careful in what they say may be viewed as being unfair. Nevertheless, every police officer represents all other police officers as well as the department.

c. *Telephone Call Response.* Whenever a police officer responds by telephone, there is an opportunity to escalate conflict if this officer is short, impolite, or critical. Large numbers of civilian complaints occur when dispatchers or police officers respond curtly. Again, television and the movies encourage this behavior by suggesting that a tough, critical, sardonic attitude represents appropriate police response. Nothing could be further from the truth.

III. CAUSES OF CONFLICT ESCALATORS

A. Inadequate Selection

With the management selection tools that are available today, it should be possible to select candidates for law enforcement training who are physically fit, have a good work record, have made a good adjustment to the community, and show few if any signs of psychological disturbance or pathology. Although selection cannot predict perfectly, in most instances, it can certainly eliminate the extreme misfits.

B. Inadequate Education

Poorly trained and prepared officers stem from an inadequate educational system. The curricula of police academies should include training on the identification of conflict situations and on resolution of conflicts with citizens in the earliest phases of interaction.

C. Inadequate Training

Much of training begins when the officer has graduated from an academy. Field training is a critical time for new officers to learn the practicalities of policing as well as the special nature of their community. Training systems should include sensitivity training, role playing, awareness of conflict-escalating situations, and conflict-reducing techniques.

D. Poor Communication from Senior Officers

Unless managers are explicit about what they expect of line officers, errors, misunderstandings, and problems are sure to arise. It behooves the good supervisor or manager to continually express to the troops in measurable behavioral terms expectations concerning courtesy, sensitivity, and conflict avoidance.

E. Poor Modeling by Senior Officers

It is almost impossible to expect a specialized bureaucracy such as law enforcement to follow the rule to "Do as I say, not as I do" rule. If the senior officers and the supervisors in the agency model appropriate sensitivity and conflict-avoidance, the troops under them will be likely to behave similarly when interacting with civilians.

F. Emotional Instability

A number of causes of emotional instability can be identified by close observation of the law enforcement officer. Some of the more specific sources of instability include:

1. *Low Self-Esteem.* The individual has some question about his or her ability, skills, worth, or training. These should be identified and corrected as early as possible.
2. *Personal Insecurity.* Those officers who are easily threatened, and who misread the environment, taking things personally and defensively are more likely to cause conflict than those who feel personally secure.
3. *Depression.* When a law enforcement officer has internalized conflict to the point where they feel helpless, hopeless, and perturbed, they are not going to be in a position to be sensitive to conflict situations and to avoid them.
4. *Mental Illness.* Approximately 12% of all adults in the United States will suffer some form of severe mental illness. Police officers are people and are subject to the stresses and pressures that may result in emotional disorder. Opportunities to identify the presence of such situations and to offer remedial help are vital in an effective law enforcement agency.

5. *Drug or Alcohol Abuse.* Alcohol is the most severely abused drug in our country. The abuse of alcohol as well as other drugs represents some deep emotional disturbance and a kind of "giving up." Opportunities to identify this and resolve such problems must be built into every law enforcement agency if conflict escalation is to be avoided. Under the influence of drugs or alcohol, officers are more likely to manifest insensitive attitudes and physical abuse.

G.   Character Deficiencies

A certain number of people in our society strongly believe that they are not their brother's keeper and that they have no real responsibility. Such people are dangerous in society and are especially dangerous when employed as law enforcement officers. A person without sufficient character to understand his or her responsibilities to society is likely to cause serious conflict. Such people should be screened out before they become officers.

H.   Overload

Overload is the preliminary condition to burnout. It consists of stress related to job demands and requirements including such things as unusual occurrences on the job, demands above and beyond the call of duty, shift work, bureaucratic annoyances and a whole range of difficulties to which there is usually no solution. When an individual is overloaded, they tend to lose control of situations that they would ordinarily handle well.

I.   Personal Problems

Again, police officers are also human beings. They have mates who are not always helpful and supportive. Their children have problems. They have all the difficulties and frustrations that everyone has, but often are too busy or too tired to resolve even the simplest difficulties. It becomes circular—the family does not receive support from the officer because of lack of time, and without support, the family causes more personal problems for the officer.

J.   Physical Illness

Physical illness affects judgment and dulls the individual's sensitivity making for conflict situations. Officers with a physical ailment may not give the situation at hand their complete attention. Police officers commonly go to work even though they are feeling unwell, a policy that holds risks for everyone.

K. Financial Problems

Financial concerns and debts can preoccupy a law enforcement officer. Being distracted by any topic outside the scope of the situation at hand may cause the law enforcement officer to seem callous and uncaring.

L. Post-Trauma Reactions

When an officer has been traumatized, or is part of a team where a member has been traumatized, injured, or killed, there will be a period of time when the officer is particularly prone to overexcitability, loss of control, and participation in conflict escalation.

IV. SOLUTIONS

The sensitivity and restraint practiced by the vast majority of law enforcement officers are among the highest of any profession. The responsibilities of being a law enforcement officer can be intense. The many roles that law enforcement officers must fulfill, including law enforcer, maintainer of the peace, and public servant (some citizens act as if they should also be psychologists, attorneys, bouncers, and in some cases psychics), make it evident that the successful law enforcement officer practices a considerable restraint and sensitivity.

The amount of restraint and sensitivity that law enforcement officers exhibit is reciprocally determined by the community, the law enforcement agency, and the individual officer.

A. Community

Greater commitment is now being seen to increase the working relationship between the law enforcement officer and the citizens of the community they serve. Community-oriented policing is, perhaps, the best way to enlist the community's help in combating crime, maintaining the peace, and bettering law enforcement-community relations. By involving the community in policing, many citizens, for the first time, begin to feel that law enforcement agencies are working with them and not against them.

Security is a basic psychological need of human beings. There is no better way to decrease conflict between groups (law enforcement personnel and citizens) than by having them combine forces in a structured, organized manner to achieve a commonly desired superordinate goal. In community-oriented policing, a central goal is the security and well-being of both law enforcement officers and the community to which they belong. Hence, a powerful human need can be satisfied by practicing a community-oriented style of policing.

Within the law enforcement agency, two primary areas essentially contribute to the amount of sensitivity and restraint mustered by law enforcement officers in the field. They are (1) management policy and (2) the individual style and practices of law enforcement officers.

B. Management

1. *Sound Selection Procedures.* Due to the litigious nature of today's society and public demands for honesty and integrity among law enforcement officers, selection procedures are more stringent now than ever before. The selection procedures for many agencies, particularly accredited agencies, consist of several steps. These steps include physical fitness assessment, in-depth personal history assessment, complete background investigation, polygraph examination, medical examination, illegal substance use and abuse testing, visual acuity screening, and psychological screening. In many agencies, the successful completion of a law enforcement academy program is preliminary to selection procedures.

   Tests and standards are much more stringent than they were just 10 years ago. Of all the applicants who apply for law enforcement positions, approximately 1 in 10 is hired. This means that law enforcement officers are the cream of the crop.

2. *Proper Training.* Continuing education and proper training is the benchmark of all professionals. It is vitally important to keep abreast with changing laws, regulations, and tactics. Hence, it is required that all law enforcement officers receive continuing training to maintain certification.

   It behooves the management to ensure that deputies attend training sessions on a variety of topics. It also behooves the management to help defray the costs so deputies can afford to maintain skills and knowledge on the cutting edge in the science of law enforcement.

3. *Supplying Proper Equipment.* Beyond the deputies' request for upgraded or replacement equipment, this issue is left to the sole discretion of management. If deputies request unconventional equipment, management should organize pilot studies whereby small numbers of deputies can test the equipment to determine its effectiveness within the agency's structure.

4. *Modeling.* "As goes the head, there goes the body." We know from families, governmental organizations, private industry, and social clubs that members model and aspire to be like those in charge. Hence, the "do as I say, not as I do" attitude is ineffective.

If upper-level management advocates a "kick butt and ask questions later" philosophy, so will the street-level law enforcement officers. Conversely, if the upper-level management presents as a model of restraint and sensitivity while maintaining a prudent respect for the law, the law enforcement officer in the understructure will most likely behave accordingly.

5. *Two-Way Communication.* All successful agencies practice two-way communication. This framework encourages advancements in the way the law enforcement profession is practiced. Front-line officers, better than anyone else, are in touch with evolving societal needs and demands. Hence, they, better than anyone else, are able to convey changes that may need to be effected to maintain the highest levels of efficiency. Two-way communication involves more than chain of command.

If upward communication falls on deaf ears, future communications will probably not be as readily forthcoming. Hence, the upper-level management will not be as in touch with the happenings and needs of the law enforcement officer on the street.

Although street deputies are most in tune with the changing needs and demands of the citizenry, upper-level management personnel are most likely able to effect the changes necessary to keep up with the demands. Without two-way communication, the intrastructure and the agency as a whole are rendered less effective.

6. *Morale Surveys.* Anonymous morale surveys are innocuous, yet they are a relatively efficient means to assess general levels of morale, conduct, and the efficiency of current practices or changes within agencies. Ongoing morale surveys are pertinent to the agency's mission and should be administered at least annually. With each succeeding morale survey, feedback should be solicited for changes or current practices that have been implemented in the previous year. Morale surveys present a method whereby upper-level management can demonstrate their concern and interest in the opinions, attitudes, and functioning of the street-level officer and the community.

7. *Traumatic Incident Follow-up.* It is recommended that any officer who has been involved in a traumatic incident be required to log the incident and receive at least one counseling/evaluation session. Additionally, supervisors should receive ongoing training in the recognition of symptoms associated with exposure to traumatic incidents. With greater knowledge, supervisors will be better able to counsel line officers and recommend that they receive traumatic event stress debriefing. This can aid in keeping the effects of exposure to traumatic events in check. The officer will be less likely to come under the influence of stressors and engage in behaviors that

are damaging to themself, the agency, and the community. Through this procedure, officers will not be stigmatized or singled out as weak, as everyone who is exposed to a traumatic incident will receive at least one mandatory debriefing session.

C. Individual Law Enforcement Officer on the Job

This section deals directly with those things the officer can do to demonstrate sensitivity and restraint to community members. Perhaps the most effective allegiance for the prevention of crime is that between the citizens of the community and the law enforcement officers. It is vitally important to foster good relationships between them. Community members must not view the law enforcement agency's interest in them as something contrived superficially, but instead must see it as an ongoing relationship. Although this concept includes the community, citizens are not the base component. That is, they are free to choose whether they become involved in community policing. The officer, however, can be required to comply. One way to demonstrate concern about police–community relations is through periodic retraining. Through this channel, the importance of police–citizen relationships with a common goal of crime prevention can be reinforced. All professionals—whether medical, legal, or mental health—require refresher courses or retraining. Hence, periodic retraining does not indicate ignorance, but rather demonstrates a sensitivity and a knowledge of human limitations. How often have you made a mistake and yet knew the correct way to do something? This happens to all of us occasionally. Hence, we can all benefit from periodic refresher courses. To be reminded of the correct way to do things or to learn improved methods for the prevention of crime is beneficial to both the community and the police agency. Good interpersonal skills are often taken for granted, on the incorrect assumption that people who choose to serve the public as a career automatically practice such skills.

Interpersonal skills training is an effective means to teach sensitivity and restraint, which indirectly fosters better community–police agency relationships. In essence, interpersonal skills training teaches or reinforces the ability to get along with others. Interpersonal skills are not necessarily a natural talent. Whereas some officers just seem to get along with most people, other officers have to work at developing interpersonal skills. One of the underpinnings of interpersonal skills particularly for law enforcement officers is courtesy.

1. *Courtesy.* Courtesy is important in law enforcement. In fact, the word *courtesy* is given credence in most law enforcement agencies' directive manuals. Courtesy is a concept that is often discussed but is seldom taught. Through courteous interactions with the

citizenry of the community, police officers can foster better relationships and decrease the probability of negative law enforcement–community interactions.

Thomas Lange, chairman of the advisory board for the Pinellas Police Academy, has outlined several different guidelines for practicing courteous behavior. These guidelines are adapted from the January 1989 issue of the *Police Chief*.

a. *Introductions*. First impressions are extremely important. It is a good practice to introduce yourself at stops or other contacts whenever practical or possible. Initial greetings are perhaps the best way to set the tone of the remainder of the interaction. Many officers take pride in being able to issue a citation to an individual and afterwards have the individual thank them as a result of the interaction. This type of interaction can be initiated by a positive initial contact.

b. *Voice Tone and Volume*. Tone of voice is of particular importance. The tone of voice will convey more of a message than what is actually said. It is important to be cognizant not to express anger, contempt, or ridicule unintentionally. This is not to say that you should approach all situations with a robotic monotone voice. It is to say, however, that you be careful not to unintentionally provoke a citizen to anger or scorn as a result of tone of voice. For example, how many ways can you interpret the phrase, "What were you thinking when you did that?"

There are times that a loud commanding voice will be necessary. In fact, an officer should not be meek in most situations. It is sometimes imperative that officers shout loud commanding statements to individuals to maintain public safety. Officers should, however, be careful that their voice volume does not increase in volume out of frustration, fear, or excitement. This may escalate the negative tone of a law enforcement/citizen contact to a point where violence may occur. A quiet, level voice is heeded more often in normal contacts than is a loud voice. A loud voice will ofttimes represent an authority figure in an individual's past; hence, he or she may become belligerent and not comply as readily with officers' request at that point and in the future.

c. *Address*. The first name of the citizen should not be used in most situations. It is better to use the last name of the individual, with Mister or Miss. Nicknames should not be used. An individual with "Sonny" tattooed on an arm should not be referred to as "Sonny." If the last name is not known, sir or ma'am will suffice.

d. *Body Language*. It has been estimated that 30% of what we hear and believe from a person results from speech; 70% is the result of expression, voice inflection, and body language. It is vitally important that officers protect themselves. On the other hand, it is important for a law enforcement officer to attempt to identify situations that may escalate into negative interactions if the officer approaches the individual with overly aggressive body language. This may be in the form of resting the hand on the butt of a holstered weapon or gesturing with a nightstick, a flashlight, or even a finger. These things can be done without forethought. Watch yourself. The community is watching you.

When talking with an irate citizen, you know that it may seem as if a person's pointing finger is 16 inches long and is resting squarely beneath the nose when you're being lectured. It is quite uncomfortable and may result in an aggressive interaction. Crowding an individual is another indicator of discourtesy. There will definitely be situations such as handcuffing or doing a stop-and-frisk where it will be critically important to get into the individual's 24-inch buffer zone of personal space. It is vital, however, to not enter this buffer zone, unless the officer believes the individual is dangerous or refuses to comply with the law. It is quite intimidating for the individual when this zone is breached. Most individuals disdain people coming into their 24-inch buffer zone.

e. *Personal Opinions.* It is important that an officer never express personal opinions about the unimportance of a complaint, such as a cat being stuck in a tree or the neighbor's kid riding a bike on the lawn. Although some complaints are not as serious as others, you should treat all complainants professionally. This will increase community respect for yourself and your agency.

f. *Profanity and Demeaning Remarks.* Profanity and demeaning remarks should never be used. Anything that will ridicule a citizen may provoke the person to act defensively. Sometimes, it may feel good to do so, but there is a good chance that demeaning a citizen will catch up to you through supervisors, internal affairs, or the press.

g. *Response to Citizen Provocation.* Few jobs require more self-control than that of being a law enforcement officer. Restraint is something that an officer must practice. When confronted by an outraged citizen, the officer must concentrate on the matter at hand and respond to the complaint, as opposed to responding to the emotional expression of the complaint. During these contacts, citizens may obnoxiously direct anger and frustration against law enforcement employees. At these times, there is a temptation for the officer to respond back with equal or greater provocation. This is especially the case when the citizens' inappropriate actions cause a worsening of the situation. It is crucial for an officer not to give in to the temptation to one-up a citizen. One way to avoid this is to concentrate on the initial complaint. Do not respond to the underlying message or insult that a citizen may have leveled against you. The best way to handle such an insult is to simply ignore the emotionally charged content and to respond to it by paraphrasing the surface content. If the officer chooses, he or she may attempt to look at it from the viewpoint of the citizen in an attempt to understand the individual's feelings. If the unacceptable behavior continues to escalate, there may be instances when the officer must give appropriate warnings to curb the behavior. These warnings should be given in a calm, cool, and collected format. Any sarcasm, finger pointing, or anger at this point will serve only to infuriate the complainant. This will increase the probability that problems will arise later. It is much easier for an officer to explain his or her actions to citizens than it is for a supervisor to explain for the officer.

h. *Explain What You Do.* Providing explanations for what we do is important. Law enforcement personnel may think that citizens know what infraction they have committed. Never take this for granted. As law enforcement officers, you know how difficult it is to keep up with the evolving laws, general orders, and so forth. There is a lot of ignorance about the law among most of the public. That is, the public who are not chronic offenders.

i. *Listening.* A complaint that is commonly received by supervisors and internal investigators is that the officer would not listen to the citizen. This often comes in the form of "the officer was hard, he was cold, he didn't take the time, he interrupted me when I was trying to answer a question." Effective listening is very important. When interacting with the citizenry, a little bit more time allocated to the interaction initially may pay large dividends. Listening is not the same as hearing.

Listening involves concentrating on what the speaker says, interpreting the speaker's words, evaluating the meaning, and responding. You can listen to complainants without being swayed from your stance. Listening is a common courtesy that can create an atmosphere where the complainants feel they are being heard and a wrong is being corrected.

When listening, it is important to convey that you understand what the speaker has to say. This can be done by making frequent eye contact, by leaning slightly forward, and by making neutral comments such as "go ahead," "I see," and the like. Additionally, research has shown that most speakers verbalize at the rate of 200 words per minute. It is estimated that the mind can process about 400 words per minute. So, when an individual is speaking to you, it is important to think about underlying messages. It is also important to wait your turn and not interrupt the individual. Sometimes spending more time listening creates much more positive interactions than when you spend time talking—be patient.

To listen effectively, it is not important for the officer to necessarily respond by agreeing or disagreeing. Often, it is just as effective to serve as a mirror. It is also important not to give advice which is outside the realm of law enforcement. Such advice giving can backfire and come back later to haunt the law enforcement officer and his or her agency.

2. *Citizen Satisfaction and the Law.* Research indicates that experienced law enforcement officers believe that courtesy is one of the five most important attributes of any law enforcement officer. Courtesy involves restraint and sensitivity. Research has also shown that some specific elements determine whether citizens report being satisfied or dissatisfied after interactions with law enforcement officers. An officer who is perceived to be an effective communicator and who can listen well is more likely to leave citizens satisfied than an officer who is seen as an ineffective communicator. Being a good listener is at least as important as being a good speaker.

Law enforcement officers who are effective listeners have several factors in common: A friendly style as well as general goodwill toward others. Precision, being nonargumentative, and flexibility are also considered to be important characteristics of a law enforcement officer with good communication skills. A precise communicator tries to be accurate and unambiguous and will stick to the facts. A flexible communicator does not interrupt others when they are speaking and is capable of relaying messages in a variety of ways. A nonargumentative communicator is not quick to challenge others, does not respond unthinkingly, and has little difficulty in dropping disagreements and not going back to them.

The previous items have indicated what the officer can do to demonstrate restraint, sensitivity, and courtesy. Now, we'll look at what officers can do in their personal lives to relieve stressors and pressures that may make them more prone to reacting in an insensitive manner.

D. Individual Law Enforcement Officer at Home

1. *Planning for Recreational Activity.* Many law enforcement officers begin to view themselves as beings who live to work rather than work to live. Planning for recreational activity is vitally important. Recreation, if taken apart, literally says *re-creation.* This should enable officers to recharge their batteries.

2. *Keeping Physically Fit.* Keeping physically fit has many benefits. Working out in the weight room, running, or engaging in aerobic

activities can aid in bleeding off stress and tension. In addition, a physically fit person has a higher probability of surviving altercations with minimal injuries.

Many agencies have incentive programs for their law enforcement officers to maintain certain levels of physical fitness. A few benefits of physical fitness training include more efficient physical functioning, higher self-esteem, increased stress tolerance, and greater energy levels.

3. *Maintaining Proper Diet and Adequate Rest Periods.* The importance of proper diet and adequate rest cannot be overestimated. Essentially, people can get out of themselves only what they put into themselves. Without maintaining a proper diet and the necessary sleep, officers are going to be more likely to lose their temper and to make mistakes in the field. A proper diet and adequate rest can be looked at as a precursor to practicing restraint and sensitivity.

4. *Organizing and Prioritizing Responsibilities.* In today's fast-paced world, everyone experiences his or her share of problems. What is important is that we recognize the difference between those problems we face and the problems of others. Many individuals experience more personal difficulties when they begin to take responsibility for other people's actions and problems. It is imperative that we draw a clear line between our problems and the problems of others. It is important that we organize and prioritize our problems as well as our responsibilities. This allows us to prepare an efficient attack and resolution as our difficulties are clear.

5. *Practicing Stress Reduction Techniques.* The practice of stress reduction techniques is essential. Although 85% of police work is community service and maintaining the peace, there is no way of knowing when the 15% that involves law enforcement will occur. Law enforcement by its very nature is quite ambiguous and, therefore, stress provoking. Further, law enforcement is the only nonmilitary profession where an individual must literally be prepared to engage in physical battle, perhaps to the death, on a daily basis in defense of self and others. Practicing stress reduction techniques need not take long. If you don't already have a technique, brief stress reduction tapes are marketed. Stress reduction can be practiced whenever an individual has 15 minutes of free time.

Officers who keep stress in check are more likely to practice adequate restraint and sensitivity. They will not be "on edge." These law enforcement officers will be more relaxed and comfortable with themselves and will convey this to the citizens with whom they have contact.

6. *Preventive/Interventive Mental Health Assistance.* If officers experience problems that are stress or job related, it is important for them to

seek proper assistance. Services provided by private mental health practitioners and mental health agencies can be an asset. Approximately one in three of all people will at some point in life require the assistance of a mental health professional. Due to the ambiguous, stressful nature of law enforcement, it is estimated that at least as many law enforcement personnel will seek mental health counseling. It is important that the recognition of the need for assistance be acted on as early as possible, so preventive measures, as opposed to interventive measures, can be applied. If the officer is experiencing serious emotional difficulties, interventive mental health assistance is indicated.

E. Proviso

Following all the guidelines and solutions presented here will not make an officer perfect. The perfect officer would probably be a social worker, an attorney, a bouncer, and a priest, but not necessarily in that order. The order would change, depending on the dictates of the situation. You are the best we have to offer. All of you have been carefully selected. Following the aforestated guidelines does not guarantee that you will never have a dispute with a citizen or a supervisor, or be involved in an internal affairs investigation. Following as many of these guidelines as possible, however, will lessen the probability that any such problems will occur. We ask that you try some of the recommendations put forth to you. Finally, we ask that you continue to strive for positive community relations by continuing and increasing your practice of restraint, sensitivity, and courtesy.

RESOURCES

Brooks, D., Shoemaker, T., & Winsor, J. (1979). A transactional approach to viewing policing styles. *Journal of Police Science and Administration, 7*(3), 292–299.

Channing Bete Co. (1989). *What everyone should know about alcohol.* South Deerfield, MA: Author. (Originally published 1973)

Channing Bete Co. (1989). *What everyone should know about stress.* South Deerfield, MA: Author. (Originally published 1975)

Channing Bete Co. (1989). *About stress management.* South Deerfield, MA: Author. (Originally published 1984)

Channing Bete Co. (1991). *About improving your interpersonal skills.* South Deerfield, MA: Author. (Originally published 1984)

Channing Bete Co. (1990). *How to improve your listening skills.* South Deerfield, MA: Author. (Originally published 1987)

Deangelis, T. (1991, July). Police stress takes its toll on family life. *APA Monitor,* p. 38.

Delattre, E. (1991). *Against brutality and corruption: Integrity, wisdom, and professionalism.* Tallahassee, FL: Florida Criminal Justice Executive Institute.

Dugan, J., & Breda, D. (1991). Complaints about police officers: A comparison among types and agencies. *Journal of Criminal Justice, 19,* 165–171.

Glauser, M., & Tullar, W. (1985). Communicator style of police officers and citizen satisfaction with officer/citizen telephone conversations. *Journal of Police Science and Administration, 13*(1), 70–77.

Hendricks, J. (1977). Transactional Analysis and the Police: Family Disputes. *Journal of Police Science and Administration, 5*(4), 416–420.

Lange, T. (1989, January). Cultivating the practice of courtesy. *Police Chief,* 35–36.

Nicolletti, T. (1990, July). Training for de-escalation of force. *Police Chief,* 37–38.

Pennebaker, J. (1985). Traumatic experience and psychosomatic disease: Exploring the roles of behavioral inhibition, obsession, and confiding. *Canadian Psychology, 26*(2), 82–94.

Pugh, G. (1986). The good police officer: Qualities, roles, and concepts. *Journal of Police Science and Administration, 14*(1), 1–5.

Scanlon, R. (1990 April). Police Enemy #1: Stress. *Law Enforcement Technology, 17*(4), 18–21.

References

Abram, H. (1970). *Psychological aspects of stress.* Springfield, IL: Thomas Publishers.

Adler, T. (1989). Integrity test popularity prompts close scrutiny. *APA Monitor, 20*(12), 7.

Akerstedt, T. (1988). Sleepiness as a consequence of shift work. *Sleep, 11*(1), 17–34.

Allen, S. (1986). Suicide and indirect self-destructive behavior among police. In J. Reese & H. Goldstein (Eds.), *Psychological services for law enforcement.* Washington, DC: U.S. Government Printing Office.

Alpert, G., & Dunham, R. (1986). Community policing. *Journal of Police Science and Administration, 14*(3), 212–222.

American Psychiatric Association. (1981). *Diagnostic and statistical manual.* Washington, DC: Author.

American Psychiatric Association. (1987). *Diagnostic and statistical manual of mental disorders* (3d ed., rev.). Washington, DC: American Psychiatric Association.

American Psychological Association. (1992). Ethical principles of psychologists and code of conduct. *American Psychologist, 47*(12), 1597–1628.

American Psychological Association, American Educational Research Association, and National Council In Measurement of Education. (1985). *Standards for educational psychological testing.* Washington, DC: American Psychological Association.

Archibald, E. (1986). Confidentiality when the police psychologist is evaluator and caregiving practitioner. In J. Reese & H. Goldstein (Eds.), *Psychological services for law enforcement.* Washington, DC: U.S. Government Printing Office.

Ashton, D., Wiesen, J., Applebaum, D., Fine, H., Gore, P., Jefferson, K., Gilmore, M., Garrity, N., & Reynolds, J. (1984). Documentation of the development of the November 14th, 1981 entry-level police services examination of the Commonwealth of Massachusetts. *Psychological Documents, 14*(2), 32. (Document #2667)

Ault, R., Jr., & Reese, J. (1980, March). A psychological assessment of crime profiling. *FBI Law Enforcement Bulletin, 49.*

Ayres, R. (1990). *Preventing law enforcement stress: The organization's role.* Alexandria, VA: The National Sheriff's Association.

Baehr, M., Furcon, J., & Froemel, E. (1968). *Psychological assessment of patrolmen qualifications in relation to field performance* (LEAA Project No. 046). Washington, DC: U.S. Government Printing Office, Superintendent of Documents.

Bailey, E. (Ed.). (1989). *The encyclopedia of police science.* New York: Garland Publishing.

Baker, T. (1992). Crime scene analysis: A behavioral science approach. *The Chief of Police, 7*(4), 29–38.

Bales, J. (1988). Integrity tests: Honest results? *APA Monitor, 19*(8), 1–4.

Bandura, B. (1977). Self-efficacy: Toward a unifying theory of change. *Psychological Review, 84,* 191–215.

Bard, M. (1970). *Training police as specialists in family crisis intervention.* Washington, DC: U.S. Government Printing Office, U.S. Department of Justice.

Barefoot, J. (1975). *Undercover investigation.* Springfield, IL: Thomas Publishers.

Barth, A. (1961). *Law enforcement versus the law.* New York: Collier Books.

Bartlett, E. (1991). *Annual report of the Academy of Police Psychologists.* Unpublished report of the Academy of Police Psychologists to the Council of Police Psychological Services.

Baruth, C. (1986). Pre-critical incident involvement by psychologists. In J. Reese & H. Goldstein, (Eds.), *Psychological services for law enforcement.* Washington, DC: U.S. Government Printing Office, Superintendent of Documents.

Baruth, C. (1988). Routine mental health checkups and activities for law enforcement personnel in dealing with hostage and terrorist incidents by psychologist trainer/consultant. In J. Reese & H. Goldstein (Eds.), *Police psychology: Operational assistance.* Washington, DC: U.S. Department of Justice, FBI, Superintendent of Documents.

Bell, D. J. (1982). Police women: Myths and reality. *Journal of Police Science and Administration, 10*(1), 112–120.

Bell, L. (1988, June). The unfair family affair. *Police.* 29–31.

Bennett, M., & Hess, J. (1991). Cognitive interviewing. *FBI Law Enforcement Bulletin, 60*(3), 8–12.

Berberich, J. (1986). Managing the directed referral. In J. Reese & H. Goldstein (Eds.), *Psychological services for law enforcement.* Washington, DC: U.S. Government Printing Office.

Bernstein, J. (1989). Assessment center preparation. *The National FOP Journal, 18*(1), 26–29.

Beutler, L., Storm, A., Krikish, P., Scogin, F., & Gaines, J. (1985). Parameters in the prediction of police officer performance. *Professional Psychology, 16*(2), 324–335.

Bittner, E. (1970). *The functions of the police in modern society* (DHEW Publication #(ADM) 75-260). Washington, DC: U.S. Government Printing Office.

Bittner, E., (1990). *Aspects of police work.* Boston, MA: Northeastern University Press.

Bizzack, J. (1992). Police leadership and curb-side justice. *Law Enforcement News, 18*(354), 1–11.

Blak, R. (1986). A department's psychologist's response to traumatic incident. In J. Reese & H. Goldstein (Eds.), *Psychological services for law enforcement.* Washington, DC: U.S. Government Printing Office, Superintendent of Documents.

Blanch, N. (1977). Psychology for law enforcement—service and survival. *Police Chief, 44*(8), 66–68.

Blau, T. (1986). Deadly force: Psychological factors and objective evaluation—a preliminary effort. In J. Reese & H. Goldstein (Eds.), *Psychological services for law enforcement.* Washington, DC: U.S. Government Printing Office.

Blau, T. (1988). *Psychotherapy tradecraft.* New York: Brunner/Mazel.

Blau, T. (1989). The policeman's lot is not a happy one. (Review of J. Yuille (Ed.), Police selection and training: The role of psychology.) *Contemporary Psychology, 34*(3).

Blau, T. (1991a). *Adolescent psychotherapy.* Training tape by Psychological Seminars, Inc., 205 E. Davis Blvd., Tampa, FL 33606.

Blau, T. (1991b). The psychological examination of the child. New York: Wiley.

Blau, T., & Blau, R. (1988). The competency and credibility of children as witnesses. In J. Reese & J. Horn (Eds.), *Police psychology: Operational assistance.* Washington, DC: U.S. Government Printing Office, U.S. Department of Justice, FBI.

Blau, T., Super, J., & Brady, L. (1993). The MMPI good cop/bad cop profile in identifying dysfunctional law enforcement personnel. *Journal of Police and Criminal Psychology, 9*(1).

Blum, R. (Ed.). (1964). *Police selection.* Springfield, IL: Thomas Publishers.

Blumenthal, R. (1993). Gay officers find acceptance on New York's police force. *The New York Times, 142* (249), 1.

Borum, W. (1988). A comparative study of negotiator effectiveness with 'mentally disturbed hostage-taker' scenarios. *Journal of Police and Criminal Psychology, 4,* 17–20.

Borum, R., & Philpot, C. (1993). Therapy with law enforcement couples: Clinical management of the "high-risk" lifestyle. *American Journal of Family Therapy* (In press).

Bouza, A. (1978). *Police administration.* New York: Pergamon Press.

Bouza, A. (1990). *The police mystique.* New York & London: Plenum Press.

Bowden, J. (1988). Employing forensic hypnosis. *The National Sheriff, 40*(5), 49–52.

Bratz, L. (1989). Stress. In W. Bailey (Ed.), *The encyclopedia of police science.* New York: Garland Publishing.

Bray, D., Campbell, R., & Grant, D. (1984). The assessment center and the measurement of potential business management. *Psychological Monographs, 80*(17) (#625).

Breckenridge, A. (1949). The constitutional basis for cooperative crime control. *Journal of Criminal Law, Criminology, and Police Science, 39,* 565–583.

Burnett, R., Johns, E., & Krug, S. (1981). Law enforcement and development report (LEADR). Champaign, IL: Institute for Personality & Ability Testing, Inc.

Butcher, J. N. (1979b). Use of the MMPI in personnel selection. In J. N. Butcher (Ed.), *New developments in the use of the MMPI.* Minneapolis, MN: University of Minnesota Press.

Butcher, J. (1992). MMPI-2; A step in the right direction. *The National Psychologist, 1*(3), 12–13.

Butcher, J., Dahlstrom, W., Graham, J., Tellegen, A., & Kaemmer, B. (1989). *Manual for the Restandardized Minnesota Multiphasic Personality Inventory: MMPI-2.* Minneapolis, MN: University of Minnesota Press.

Butler, L., Meredith, K., & Nussbaum, P. (1988). Changing personality patterns of police officers. *Professional Psychology, 19*(5), 503–507.

Canty, W. (1991). Two views of the future. *Law Enforcement News, 17*(356).

Cattell, R. (1991). *Sixteen Personality Factor Questionnaire.* Savoy, IL: Institute for Personality and Ability Testing, Inc.

Cattell, R., Eber, H., & Tatsuoka, M. (1970). *Handbook for the 16 Personality Factor Questionnaire (16PF).* Champaign, IL: Institute for Personality and Ability Testing, Inc.

Chandler, J. (1990). *Modern police psychology for law enforcement and human behavior professionals*. Springfield, IL: Thomas Publishers.

Charles, M. (1982). Women in policing: The physical aspect. *Journal of Police Science and Administration, 10*(2), 194–205.

Charles, M. (1986). *Policing the streets*. Springfield, IL: Thomas Publishers.

Chapman, S., & Johnston, T. (1962). *The police heritage in England and America*. East Lansing, MI: Michigan State University.

Childers, J. (1991). Plateauing in law enforcement. *FBI Law Enforcement Bulletin, 60*(6), 16–18.

Clark, J. (1991). Minnesota plans for its first single-purpose college. *Law Enforcement News, 17*, 340–341.

Cobb, S., & Kasl, S. (1977). *Termination: The consequences of job stress*. Washington, DC: U.S. Department of HEW, Public Health Service, Center for Disease Control. National Institute for Occupational Safety and Health. (NIOSH Publication #77-224)

Cohen, S., Smith, A., & Tyrrell, D. (1993). Negative life events, perceived stress, negative affect, and susceptibility to the common cold. *Journal of Personality and Social Psychology, 64*(1), 131–140.

Commission on Accreditation for Law Enforcement Agencies. (1989). *Standards for law enforcement agencies*. The standards manual of the law enforcement agency accreditation program. Fairfax, VA: Commission on Accreditation for Law Enforcement Agencies.

Committee on Ethical Guidelines for Forensic Psychologists. (1991). Specialty guidelines for forensic psychologists. *Law and Human Behavior, 15*(6), 655–665.

Conroy, R. (1990). Critical incidents stress debriefing. *FBI Law Enforcement Bulletin 15*(2), 20–22.

Cooper, C., & Payne, R. (Eds.). (1978). *Stress at work*. New York: Wiley.

Cordner, G. (1989). Administration. In W. Bailey (Ed.), *The encyclopedia of police science* (pp. 1–7). New York: Garland Publishing.

Cramer, J. (1964). *The World's Police*. London: Cassell & Company, Ltd.

Crank, J., & Jackson, B. P. S. (1993). The relationship between police belief systems and attitudes toward police practices. *Criminal Justice and Behavior, 20*(2), 199–221.

D'Agostino, C. (1986). Police psychological services: Ethical issues. In J. Reese & H. Goldstein (Eds.), *Psychological services for law enforcement*. Washington, DC: U.S. Government Printing Office.

Dahlstrom, W. (1992). Comparability of two-point high-point code patterns from original MMPI norms to MMPI-2 norms for the restandardization sample. *Journal of Personality Assessment, 59*(1), 153–164.

Dahlstrom, W., & Welsh, G. (1960). *An MMPI handbook: A guide to the use in clinical practice and research*. Minneapolis, MN: University of Minnesota Press.

Danto, B. (1978). Police suicide. *Police Stress, 1*(11), 32–36.

DeAngelis, T. (1993). Workplace stress battles fought all over the world. *APA Monitor, 24*(1), 22.

DeAngelis, T. (1991a). Honesty tests weigh in with improved ratings. *APA Monitor, 22*(6), 7–8.

DeAngelis, T. (1991b). Police stress takes its toll on family life. *APA Monitor, 22*(7), 38.

deCarufel, A., & Schann, J. L. (1990). The impact of compressed work weeks on police job involvement. *Canadian Police College Journal, 14*(2), 81–97.

Deitz, R., & Reese, J. (1986). The perils of police psychology: Minimizing the role conflicts. *Behavioral Sciences and the Law, 4*(4), 385–400.

Delprino, R., & Bahn, C. (1988). National survey of the extent and nature of psychological services in police departments. *Professional Psychology, 19*(4) 421–425.

Denton, L. (1993). APA/National Institute of Occupational Safety and Health Conference. *APA Monitor, 24*(1), 22–24.

Diamond, B. (1980). Inherent problems in the use of pretrial hypnosis on a prospective witness. *California Law Review, 68*, 313–349.

Dodenhoff, P. (1993). Justice by the numbers. *Law Enforcement News, 19*(373), 27.

Dodrill, D. (1981). An economical method for the evaluation of general intelligence in adults. *Journal of Consulting and Clinical Psychology, 49*(5), 668–673.

Dohrenwend, B. S., Dohrenwend, B. P., Dodson, M., & Shrout, P. (1984). Symptoms, hassles, social supports and life events: The problem of confounded measures. *Journal of Abnormal Psychology, 39*, 222–230.

Douglas, J., & Munn, C. (1992). Violent crime scene analysis—*modus operandi*, signature and staging. *FBI Law Enforcement Bulletin, 61*(2), 1–10.

Douglas, J., Ressler, R., Burgess, A., & Hartman, C. (1986). Criminal profiling from crime scene analysis. *Behavioral Sciences and the Law, 4*(4), 401–421.

Doyle, A. (1987). *The return of Sherlock Holmes*. New York: The Mysterious Press.

DuBois, P., & Watson, R. (1950). The selection of patrolmen. *Journal of Applied Psychology, 34*, 90–95.

Dunham, R., Pierce, J., & Castaneda, M. (1987). Alternative work schedules: Two field quasi-experiments. *Personnel Psychology, 40*(2), 215–242.

Dunnette, N., & Motowidlo, S. (1976). *Police selection and career assessment*. Washington, DC: U.S. Department of Justice.

Ebert, B. (1987). Guide to conducting a psychological autopsy. *Professional Psychology: Research and Practice, 18*(1), 52–56.

Ebert, B. (1986). The mental health response team: An expanding role for psychologists. *Professional Psychology: Research and Practice, 17*(1), 580–585.

Eisenberg, T., Kent, D., & Wall, C. (1973). *Police personnel practices in state and local governments*. Washington, DC: The Police Foundation.

Ellison, K. (1986). Development of a comprehensive selection procedure for a medium-size police department. In J. Reese & H. Goldstein (Eds.), *Psychological services for law enforcement*. U.S. Government Printing Office.

Ennis, B., & Friedman, P. (1986). *Legal rights of the mentally handicapped—Vol. II*. Washington, DC: Practicing Institute—The Mental Health Law Project (Handbook series #58).

Farberow, N., & Shneidman, E. (Eds.). (1961). *The cry for help*. New York: McGraw-Hill.

Farkas, G. (1986). Stress in undercover policing. In J. Reese & H. Goldstein (Eds.), *Psychological services for law enforcement*. Washington, DC: U.S. Government Printing Office.

Fisher, D. (1990). High-school suicide crisis intervention. *FBI Law Enforcement Bulletin, 59*(5), 5–8.

Fitzhugh, W. P. (1984). New roles in consultation with police. In L. Ritt (Ed.), *Innovations in clinical practice: A sourcebook*. Sarasota, FL: Professional Resource Exchange.

Fitzsimmons, E. (1986). N.Y.P.D. psychological screening of police candidates: The screening process, issues, and criteria in rejection. In J. Reese & H. Goldstein

(Eds.), *Psychological services for law enforcement.* Washington, DC: U.S. Government Printing Office.

Flanagan, C. (1986). Legal issues between psychology and law enforcement. *Behavioral Science and the Law, 4*(4), 371–384.

Flanagan, C. (1991). The ADA and police psychology. *Police Chief, 58*(12), 14–16.

Fletcher, C. (1991). *What cops know.* New York: Villard Books.

Franzese, P. F. (1987). The sworn officer versus civilian as police psychologist. *Public Service Psychology,* Division of Public Service, APA, *12*(1), 19.

Freudenberger, H. (1984). Substance abuse in the workplace. *Contemporary Drug Problems, 11*(2).

Freudenberger, H. (1989). *Burnout: Past, present, & future concerns.* New York: Hayworth Press.

Friendly, H. (1965). The Bill of Rights as a code of criminal procedure. *California Law Review, 53,* 929–979.

Fuselier, G., VanZandt, C., & Lanceley, F. (1991). Hostage/barricade incidents. *FBI Law Enforcement Bulletin, 60*(1), 7–12.

Fyfe, J. (1980, November). Always prepared: Police off-duty guns. *Annals of the American Academy of Political and Social Science,* 452–481.

Fyfe, J. (1982). *Readings on police use of deadly force.* Washington, DC: The Police Foundation.

Fyfe, J. (1988). Defining the good cop. *Contemporary Psychology, 33*(7), 615–616.

Fyfe, J. (1989). Deadly force. In W. Bailey (Ed.), *The encyclopedia of police science.* New York: Garland Publishing.

Gallagher, R., & Bemsberg, C. (1978). *Hostage negotiation for police.* Schiller Park, IL: Motorola Teleprograms.

Garforth, J. (1974). *A day in the life of a Victorian policeman.* London, England: George Allen & Unwin, Ltd.

Geller, W. (1982). Deadly force: What we know. *Journal of Police Science Administration, 10*(2), 151–177.

Geller, W. (1993). Put friendly-fire shooting in perspective. *Law Enforcement News, 18*(37), 9.

Gennaro, A., Nora, A., Nora, J., Stander, R., & Weiss, L. (1979). *Blakiston's pocket medical dictionary, 4th ed.* New York: McGraw-Hill.

Getty, V., & Elam, J. (1988). Identifying characteristics of hostage negotiators and using personality data to develop a selection model. In J. Reese & J. Horn (Eds.), *Police psychology: Operational assistance.* Washington, DC: U.S. Department of Justice, FBI, Superintendent of Documents.

Getty, V., Elam, J., & Smouse, A. (1986). Mean MMPI and CPI profiles of supervisors and command personnel in a municipal police agency. In J. Reese & H. Goldstein (Eds.), *Psychology services for law enforcement.* Washington, DC: U.S. Government Printing Office.

Girodo, M. (1991a). Symptomatic reactions to undercover work. *The Journal of Nervous and Mental Disease, 179*(10), 626–630.

Girodo, M. (1991b). Drug corruptions in undercover agents: Measuring the risk. *Behavioral Science and the Law, 9,* 361–370.

Girodo, M. (1991c). Personality, job stress, and mental health in undercover agents. *Journal of Social Behavior and Personality, 6*(7), 375–390.

Glass, D. (1977). *Behavior patterns, stress and coronary disease.* Hillsdale, NJ: Erlbaum.

Glorioso, J. (1986). Understanding the reluctant police manager. In J. Reese & H. Goldstein (Eds.), *Psychological services for law enforcement.* Washington, DC: U.S. Government Printing Office.

Goldberg, L., Grenier, J., Gunion, R., Seachrest, L., & Wing, H. (1991). *Questionnaires used in the prediction of trustworthiness in pre-employment selection decisions: An APA task force.* Washington, DC: American Psychological Association.

Golden, C. (1987). *Screening test for the Luria-Nebraska Neuropsychological battery.* Los Angeles, CA: Western Psychological Services.

Goldstein, A., Hoyer, W., & Monti, P. (1979). *Police and the elderly.* New York: Pergamon Press.

Goldstein, A., Monti, P., Sardino, T., & Green, D. (1979). *Police crisis intervention.* New York: Pergamon Press.

Goldstein, J. (1960). Police discretion not to invoke the criminal process: Low visibility decisions in the administration of justice. *Yale Law Journal, 69,* 543–594.

Goleman, D. (1992). New light on how stress erodes health. *New York Times— Science Times,* December p. B5.

Golembiwski, R., & Kim, B. (1990). Burnout in police work: Stressors, strain, and phase model. *Police Studies, 13*(2), 74–80.

Gordon, J. (1969). *Perspectives on law enforcement.* Princeton, NJ: Educational Testing Services.

Gough, H. (1984). A managerial potential scale for the California Psychological Inventory. *Journal of Applied Psychology, 69,* 223–240.

Gough, H. (1991). *California psychological inventory administrator's guide.* Palo Alto, CA: Consulting Psychologists Press.

Graf, F. (1986). The relationship between social support and occupational stress among police officers. *Journal of Police Science and Administration, 14,* 178–186.

Grant, D. (1984). Personnel selection. In R. Corsini (Ed.), *Encyclopedia of Psychology, 3,* 29–32.

Grennan, S. (1987). Findings on the role of officer gender in violent encounters with citizens. *Journal of Police Science and Administration, 15*(1), 78–85.

Grossman, L., Haywood, T., Kavanaugh, W., Ostrov, E., & Wasyliw, O. (1990). Sensitivity of MMPI validity scales to motivational factors in psychological evaluations of police officers. *Journal of Personality Assessment, 55*(3 & 4), 549–561.

Hagaman, J., Wells, G., Blau, T., & Wells, C. (1987). Psychological profile of a family homicide. *The Police Chief, 54*(12), 19–23.

Hargrave, G., & Hiatt, D. (1989). Use of the California Psychological Inventory in law enforcement officer selection. *Journal of Personality Assessment, 53*(2), 267–277.

Hargrave, G., Hiatt, D., Ogard, E., & Karr, C. (1993). *Comparison of the MMPI and the MMPI-2 for a sample of peace officers.* Manuscript submitted for publication.

Hays, J. R., Roberts, T. K., & Solway, K. S. (Eds.). (1981). *Violence and the violent individual.* New York: S. P. Medical and Scientific Books.

Hazelwood, R. (1983 September). The behavior-oriented interview of rape victims: The key to profiling. *FBI Law Enforcement Bulletin, 52.*

Hazelwood, R., & Warren, J. (1989). The serial rapist: His characteristics and victims. *FBI Law Enforcement Bulletin, 58*(2), 18–25.

Hazelwood, R., & Warren, J. (1990). The criminal behavior of the serial rapist. *FBI Law Enforcement Bulletin, 59*(2), 11–15.

Heilbrun, K. (1992). Careers. *Psychology Law Society News, 12*(3), 5.

Hiatt, D., & Hargrave, G. (1994). *Psychological assessment of gay and lesbian law enforcement applicants.* Manuscript submitted for publication.

Hibler, N. (1988). Managing a forensic hypnosis program. In J. Reese & J. Horn (Eds.), *Police psychology: Operational assistance* (pp. 199–208). Washington, DC: U.S. Government Printing Office, Federal Bureau of Investigation.

Higginbotham, J. (1991). The Americans with Disabilities Act. *FBI Law Enforcement Bulletin, 60*(8), 24–32.

Holmes, T., Amundson, M., & Hart, C. (1986). *Manual for the Schedule of Recent Experience (SRE),* Seattle, WA: University of Washington Press.

Holmes, T., & Rahe, R. (1967). The social readjustment rating scale. *Journal of Psychosomatic Research, 11,* 213–218.

Hoover, L. (1989). Psychological services units. In W. G. Bailey (Ed.), *The encyclopedia of police science.* New York: Garland Publishing.

Horn, J. (1988). Criminal personality profiling. In J. Reese & J. Horn (Eds.), *Police psychology: Operational assistance* (pp. 211–224). Washington, DC: U.S. Government Printing Office, Federal Bureau of Investigation.

Humm, D., & Humm, K. (1950). Humm-Wadsworth Temperament Scale appraisals compared with criteria of job success in the Los Angeles Police Department. *Journal of Police Psychology, 30,* 63–75.

Hurrell, J. (1986). Some organizational stressors in police work and means for their amelioration. In J. Reese & H. Goldstein (Eds.), *Psychological services for law enforcement.* Washington, DC: U.S. Government Printing Office.

Hurrell, J., Pate, A., & Kliesmet, R. (1984). *Stress among police officers.* Cincinnati, OH: Public Health Service Centers for Disease Control. National Institute for Occupational Safety and Health (Publication #84-108).

Hyatt, D., & Hargrave, G. (1988). MMPI profiles of problem police officers. *Journal of Personality Assessment, 52*(4), 722–731.

Hymowitz, K. (1991, August 19 & 26). Babar the racist. *The New Republic.*

International Association of Chiefs of Police. (1977). *The Patrol Operation.* Baltimore, MD: International Association of Chiefs of Police, Bureau of Operations and Research.

Inwald, R. (1988). A five-year follow-up study of departmental terminations as predicted by 16-pre-employment psychological indicators. *Journal of Applied Psychology, 73*(4), 703–710.

Inwald, R. (1990a). The Hilson Research Model for screening public safety applicants. In P. Keller & S. Heyman (Eds.), *Innovations and clinical practice: A sourcebook* (p. 9). Sarasota, FL: Professional Resource Exchange, Inc.

Inwald, R. (1990b). *Fitness-for-duty evaluation guidelines: A survey for police/public safety administrators and mental health professionals.* 1990 APA Meetings, Boston, MA.

Irvine, L., & Brelje, T. (Eds.). (1985). *Law, psychiatry, and the mentally disordered offender—Vol. II.* Springfield, IL: Thomas Publishers.

Jamieson, J., & Flanagan, T. (Eds.). (1989). *Source book of criminal justice statistics.* Washington, DC: U.S. Government Printing Office, U.S. Department of Justice, Office of Justice Programs, Bureau of Justice Statistics (NCJ-118318).

Jones, G. (1992). Health and fitness programs. *FBI Law Enforcement Bulletin, 61*(7), 6–11.

Kanatz, H., & Inwald, R. (1983). A process for screening out law enforcement candidates who might break under stress. *Criminal Justice Journal, 2*(4), 1–4.

Karson, S., & O'Dell, J. (1976). *A guide to the clinical use of the 16-PF.* Champaign, IL: Institute for Personality and Ability Testing, Inc.

Kaslow, F. (1986). An intense training experience: A six-day post-graduate institute model. *Journal of Psychotherapy and the Family, 1*(4), 73–82.

Kassin, S., & McNall, K. (1991). Police interrogations and confessions. *Law and Human Behavior, 15*(3), 233–251.

Kaufman, R. (1991). *Strategic planning plus.* Glenview, IL: Foresman.

Kaufman, R., & Stone, B. (1983). *Planning for organizational success.* New York: Wiley.

Kay, G. (unpublished personal communication from author). *Personality assessment inventory in screening law enforcement applicants.* Police in public safety section, mini-convention, *Police psychology in the nineties.* 100th Anniversary Convention, American Psychological Association, August 1992, Washington, DC.

Kelling, G. (1974). *The Kansas City Preventative Control experiment: A summary report.* Washington, DC: The Police Foundation.

Kennedy, D., & Homant, R. (1981). Non-traditional role assumption and the personality of the police women. *Journal of the Police Science and Administration, 9*(3), 346–355.

Klein, R. (1989). Police peer counseling: Officers helping officers. *FBI Law Enforcement Bulletin, 58*(10), 1–4.

Kliesmet, R. (1986). Labor/management stress relievement. In J. Reese & H. Goldstein (Eds.), *Psychological services for law enforcement.* Washington, DC: U.S. Government Printing Office.

Kline, M. (1986). Hypnosis in police work. In W. Bailey (Ed.), *The encyclopedia of police science.* New York: Garland Publishing.

Klockars, C. (1985). *The idea of police.* Beverly Hills, CA: Sage.

Klyver, N. (1986). L.A.P.D.'s peer-counseling program after three years. In J. Reese & H. Goldstein (Eds.), *Psychological services for law enforcement.* Washington, DC: U.S. Government Printing Office.

Kolman, J. (1982). *A guide to the development of special weapons and tactics teams.* Springfield, IL: Thomas Publishers.

Lachar, D. (1974). *The MMPI: Clinical assessment and automated interpretation.* Los Angeles, CA: Western Psychological Services.

Lazarus, R. (1976). *Psychological stress and the coping process.* New York: McGraw-Hill.

Lazarus, R., DeLongis, A., Folkman, S., & Gruen, R. (1985). Stress and adaptational outcomes—the problem of confounded measures. *American Psychologist, 40*(7), 770–778.

Lefkowitz, J. (1977). Industrial-organizational psychology and the police. *American Psychologist, 32*(5), 346–364.

Lester, D. (1986). Attitudes of police officers to rotating shifts. *Psychological Reports, 59*(3), 1090.

Lester, D., Gronau, A., & Wondrack, J. (1982). The personality and attitude of female police officers: Needs, androgyny, and attitudes toward rape. *Journal of Police Science and Administration, 10*(3), 357–360.

Levitt, E., Browning, J., & Freeland, L. (1992). The effects of MMPI-2 on the scoring of special skills derived from MMPI-1. *Journal of Personality Assessment, 59*(1), 22–31.

Levitt, E., & Webb, J. (1992). The MMPI is still preferred over the MMPI-2. *The National Psychologist, 1*(2).

Levy, R. (1966). *Proceedings of Conference for Police Professions*. Lansing, MI: Michigan State University Press.

Lichter, D. (1981). Diagnosing the dead: The admissability of the psychiatric autopsy. *American Criminal Law Review, 18*, 617–635.

Linden, J., & Klein, R. (1986). Critical issues and police peer counseling. In J. Reese & H. Goldstein (Eds.), *Psychological services for law enforcement*. Washington, DC: U.S. Government Printing Office.

Litchford, J. (1991). The Americans with Disabilities Act. *Police Chief, 58*(1), 11–13.

Lohman, J., & Misler, G. (1966). *The Police and the community*. A report prepared for the President's Commission on Law Enforcement and Administration of Justice. Washington, DC: U.S. Government Printing Office.

Loo, R. (1986). Police psychology: The emergence of a new field. *The Police Chief, 53*(2), 26–29.

Loo, R., & Meredith, C. (1986). Recruit selection in the Royal Mounted Police. In J. C. Yuille (Ed.), *Police selection and training*. Netherlands: Martinus Nijhoff Publishers.

Lord, L. (1989). Policewomen. In W. P. Bailey (Ed.), *The encyclopedia of police science* (pp. 491–502). New York: Garland Publishing.

Lundstrom, R., & Mullan, C. (1987). The use of force: One department's experience. *FBI Law Enforcement Bulletin, 56*(1), 6–9.

Lyman, J. (1964). The Metropolitan Police Act of 1829. *Journal of Criminal Law, Criminology and Police Science, 55*, 141–154.

McCord, R., & Wicker, E. (1990). Tomorrow's America—law enforcement's coming challenge. *FBI Law Enforcement Bulletin, 59*(1), 28–32.

McCormick, A. (1984). Good cop/bad cop: The use of the MMPI in the selection of law enforcement personnel. Presented at the 19th Annual Symposium *Recent Developments in the Use of the MMPI*. Tampa, Florida.

McCreedy, K. (1974). Selection practices and the police role. *Police Chief, 41*(7), 41–43.

McElroy, J. (1992). Judging community policing: Focus on implementation. *Law Enforcement News, 18*(350), 1.

McEuen, O. L. (1981). *Assessment of some personality traits that help to predict potential for success or failure as a police officer*. Ph.D. Dissertation, The Fielding Institute, Los Angeles, California.

McMains, M. (1986). Post-shooting trauma: Demographics professional support. In J. Reese & H. Goldstein (Eds.), *Psychological services for law enforcement*. Washington, DC: U.S. Government Printing Office, Superintendent of Documents.

McMains, M. (1988). Psychologists' roles in hostage negotiations. In J. Reese & J. Horn (Eds.), *Police psychology: Operational assistance* (pp. 281–317). Washington, DC: U.S. Government Printing Office, Federal Bureau of Investigation.

MacDonald, J., & Michaud, D. (1987). *The confession—interrogation and criminal profiles for police officers*. Denver, CO: Apache Press.

Machell, D. F. (1989). The recovering alcoholic police officer and the danger of professional emotional suppression. *Alcoholism Treatment Quarterly, 6*(2), 85–89.

Madamba, H. (1986). The relationship between stress and marital relationships of police officers. In J. Reese & H. Goldstein (Eds.), *Psychological services for law enforcement*. Washington, DC: Superintendent of Documents.

Maher, G. (1986). Hostage negotiations. In W. Bailey (Ed.), *The encyclopedia of police science*. New York: Garland Publishing.

Major, V. (1991). Law enforcement officers killed from 1980–1989. *FBI Law Enforcement Bulletin, 60*(5), 2–5.

Manolias, M., & Hyatt-Williams, A. (1986). Study of post-shooting experience in firearms officers. *Report of the joint working party on organizational health & welfare.* London, England: New Scotland Yard.

Margiolis, B., Kroes, W., & Quinn, R. (1974). Job stress: An unlisted occupational hazard. *Journal of Occupational Medicine, 16*(10), 654–661.

Martin, S. (1980). *Breaking and entering.* Berkeley, CA: University of California Press.

Megargee, E. (1972). *The California psychological inventory handbook.* San Francisco, CA: Jossey-Bass.

Meredith, N. (1984). Attacking the roots of police violence. *Psychology Today,* May 1984.

Meyer, E. (1986). *Ambush-related assaults on police: Violence at the street level.* Springfield, IL: Thomas Publishers.

Miller, W. (1958). Lower-class culture as a generating milieu of gang delinquency. *Journal of Social Issues, 14,* 5–19.

Mitton, M. (1985). *The policeman's lot.* London, England: Quiller Press.

Monahan, J., & Steadman, H. (1984, September). Crime and mental disorder. *Research in brief.* U.S. Department of Justice, National Institute of Justice.

Morey, L. (1991). *The personality assessment inventory: Professional manual.* Odessa, FL: Psychological Assessment Resources, Inc.

Moss, D. (1988, February). Psychological autopsy touted. *American Bar Association Journal,* 34.

Mosse, G. (1975). *Police forces in history.* London, England: Sage.

Muir, W. (1977). *Police: Street corner politicians.* Chicago, IL: University of Chicago Press.

Muller, B., & Bruno, L. (1988). *Ethnic differences in personality assessment or police candidates.* Paper presented at the 23rd annual symposium on recent developments in the use of the MMPI, March 1988, St. Petersburg, FL.

Myron, N., & Goldstein, A. (1979). *Hostage.* New York: Pergamon Press.

Neal, B. (1986). The K Sale (MMPI) and job performance. In J. Reese & H. Goldstein (Eds.), *Psychological services for law enforcement.* Washington, DC: U.S. Government Printing Office.

Nislow, J. (1988). How to find psychologically sound recruits. *Law Enforcement News, 14,* 1–7.

Noesner, G., & Dolan, J. (1992). First responder negotiation training. *FBI Law Enforcement Bulletin, 61*(8), 1–4.

Norton, J. J. (1986, February). Police psychological services. *Police Chief,* (entire issue).

O'Neil, P. (1986). Shift work. In J. Reese & H. Goldstein (Eds.), *Psychological services for law enforcement.* Washington, DC: Superintendent of Documents.

Orne, N. (1979). The use and misuse of hypnosis in court. *International Journal of Clinical and Experimental Hypnosis, 27,* 311–341.

Orth-Gomer, K. (1981). Intervention on coronary risk factors by changing work conditions of the Swedish policemen. *Reports from the Laboratory for Clinical Stress Research, 127,* 29.

Ostrov, E. (1986a). Police/law enforcement and psychology. *Behavioral Sciences and the Law, 4,* 353–370.

Ostrov, E. (1986b). Use of multiple sources of information when doing mandatory psychological evaluations of police officers. In J. Reese & H. Goldstein (Eds.), *Psychological services for law enforcement.* Washington, DC: U.S. Government Printing Office.

Ostrov, E. (1987). Mandatory police evaluations: The Chicago model. *The Police Chief, 54*(2), 30–35.

Ottmann, W., Karvonen, M., Schmidt, K., Knauth, P., & Rutenfranz, J. (1989). Subjective health status of day and shift-working policemen. *Ergonomics, 32*(7), 847–854.

Pape, J. (1990). Employee development programs. *FBI Law Enforcement Bulletin, 59*(9), 20–25.

Peacock, B., Glub, R., Miller, M., & Klune, P. (1983). Police officer's responses to 8- and 12-hour shift schedules. *Ergonomics, 26*(5), 479–493.

Pendergrass, V., & Ostrov, N. (1986). Correlates of alcohol use by police personnel. In J. Reese & H. Goldstein (Eds.), *Psychological services for law enforcement*. Washington, DC: Superintendent of Documents.

Petrich, J., & Holmes, T. (1977). Life change and onset of illness. *Medical Clinics of North America, 61*(4), 825–837.

Pinizzotto, A., & Finkel, N. (1990). Criminal personality profiling—an outcome and process study. *Law and Human Behavior, 14*(3), 215–233.

The President's Commission on Law Enforcement and Administration of Justice. (1973). *Task force report: The police*. Washington, DC: U.S. Government Printing Office.

Price, B., & Gavin, S. (1982). A century of women in policing. In B. Price & N. Skoloff, (Eds.) *The Criminal Justice System and Women*. New York: Clark Boardman Co.

Prochaska, J., DiClemente, C., & Norcross, J. (1992). In search of how people change—applications to addictive behavior. *American Psychologist, 47*(9), 1102–1114.

Psychological Seminars. (1992). *Progressive relaxation tape*. Psychological Seminars, Inc., 205 E. Davis Boulevard, Tampa, FL 33606.

Public Law 101-336. (1990). The Americans with Disabilities Act. Washington, DC, 101st Congress.

Pynes, J., & Bernardin, H. (1989). Predictive validity of an entry-level police officer assessment center. *Journal of Applied Psychology, 74*(5), 831–833.

Reed, B. (1986). Post-concussional syndrome: A disability factor in law enforcement personnel. In J. Reese & H. Goldstein (Eds.), *Psychological services for law enforcement*. Washington, DC: U.S. Government Printing Office, Superintendent of Documents.

Reese, J. (1979, August). Obsessive-compulsive behavior: The nuisance offender. *FBI Law Enforcement Bulletin, 48*.

Reese, J. (1987). *A History of Police Psychological Services*. Washington, DC: U.S. Government Printing Office.

Reese, J., & Goldstein, H. (Eds.). (1986). *Psychological services for law enforcement*. Washington, DC: U.S. Government Printing Office, Superintendent of Documents.

Reese, J., & Horn, J. (Eds.). (1988). *Police psychology: Operational assistance*. Washington, DC: U.S. Department of Justice, Federal Bureau of Investigation.

Reese, J., Horn, J., & Dunning, C. (Eds.) (1992). *Critical Incidents in Policing—Revised*. Washington, DC: U.S. Government Printing Office.

Reiser, M. (1972). *The police department psychologist*. Springfield, IL: Thomas Publishers.

Reiser, M. (1980). *Handbook of investigative hypnosis*. Los Angeles, CA: LEHI Publishing.

Reiser, M. (1982a). *Police psychology: Collected papers.* Los Angeles, CA: LEHI Publishing.

Reiser, M. (1982b). Selection and promotion of policemen. In M. Reiser (Ed.), *Police psychology: Collected papers.* Los Angeles, CA: LEHI Publishing.

Reiser, M. (1982c, March). Crime-specific psychological consultation. *The police chief.*

Reiser, M., & Klyver, N. (1987). Consulting with police. In I. Weiner & A. Hess (Eds.), *Handbook of forensic psychology.* New York: Wiley.

Reitan, R. (1984). *Aphasia and sensoriperceptual deficits in adults.* Tucson, AZ: Reitan Neuropsychology Laboratories, Inc.

Reith, C. (1956). *A new study of police history.* Edinburgh: Oliver & Boyd.

Remington, F. J. (1965). The role of the police in a democratic society. *Journal of law, criminology and police science, 45,* 361–365.

Ressler, R., & Burgess, A. (1985). The men who murder. *FBI Law Enforcement Bulletin, 54*(8), 2–6.

Rider, A. (1980, June, July, & August). Firesetter: A psychological profile. *FBI Law Enforcement Bulletin, 49.*

Robinson, C. (1975). The mayor and the police—the political role of the police in society. In G. Mosse (Ed.), *Police forces in history.* London, England: Sage.

Rodgers, D. (1992). The MMPI-2: Improvement or marketing ploy? *The National Psychologist, 1*(3), 14–15.

Rokeach, M., Miller, M., & Snyder, J. (1971). The value gap between police and policed. *Journal of Social Issues, 27*(2), 155–171.

Rose, R., & Levine, M. (Eds.). (1979). The crisis in stress research: A critical reappraisal of the role of stress in hypertension, gastrointestinal illness and female reproductive function. *Journal of Human Stress, 5*(2), 1–48.

Russell, H., & Beigel, A. (1989). *Understanding human behavior for effective police work* (2d ed.). New York: Basic Books.

Sawyer, S. (1989). The aftermath of line-of-duty death. *FBI Law Enforcement Bulletin, 58*(5), 13–16.

Saxe-Clifford, S. (1986). The Fitness-for-Duty evaluation: Establishing policy. *Police Chief, 53*(2), 38–39.

Scharf, P., & Binder, A. (1983). *The badge and the bullet: Police use of deadly force.* New York: Praeger.

Scrivner, E. (1986). Utilizing psychological techniques to develop police management skills. In J. Reese & H. Goldstein (Eds.), *Psychological services for law enforcement.* Washington, DC: U.S. Government Printing Office.

Scuro, J. E. (1985, February). Psychological impact of criminal and civil litigation on officers. *Law and Order.*

Scuro, J. E. (1982, August). Police shooting to the grand jury: An abrogation of executive purgatives by police administration. *Law and Order.*

Scuro, J. (1992, March). The Americans with Disabilities Act. *Law and Order,* 59–63.

Seafield 911. (1991). Signs of developing alcoholism. *Supervisor's training manual.* Seafield 911: 5151 S.W. 61st Ave., Davie, FL.

Selye, H. (1956). *The stress of life.* New York: McGraw-Hill.

Sewell, J. (1983). The development of a critical life event scale for law enforcement. *Journal of Police Science and Administration, 11*(1), 109–116.

Sewell, J. (1992). The law enforcement executive: A formula for success. *FBI Law Enforcement Bulletin, 61*(4), 22–26.

Seymour, G., Boxley, R., & Redding, M. (1986). Consultation as management education: Using data to promote change. In J. Reese & H. Goldstein (Eds.), *Psychological services for law enforcement*. Washington, DC: U.S. Government Printing Office.

Shaw, J. (1986). MMPI selection procedures. In J. Reese & H. Goldstein (Eds.), *Psychological services for law enforcement*. Washington, DC: U.S. Government Printing Office.

Sheehan, P., & Tilden, J. (1983). The effects of suggestability in hypnosis on accurate and distorted retrieval from memory. *Journal of Experimental Psychology: Learning, Memory, Cognition, 9,* 283–293.

Sheflind, A., & Shapiro, J. (1989). *Trance on Trial*. New York: Guilford Press.

Shneidman, E. (1976). (Ed.). *Suicideology: Contemporary developments*. New York: Grune & Stratton.

Shneidman, E. (1981). The psychological autopsy. *Suicide and Life Threatening Behavior, 11,* 325–340.

Shneidman, R., Farberow, N., & Litman, R. (1970). *The psychology of suicide* (pp. 485–518). New York: Science House.

Shusman, E., & Inwald, R. (1991). A longitudinal validation study of correctional officer job performance as predicted by the IPI and the MMPI. *Journal of Criminal Justice, 19*(4) 173–180.

Simon, B. (1990). Impact of shift work on individuals and families. *Families in Society, 71*(6), 342–348.

Simons, Y., & Barone, D. (1991). Stress and social support in road patrol deputies. Presented at the 99th Annual Meeting of the American Psychological Association, San Francisco, CA (David Barone, Center for Psychological Studies, 3301 College Ave., Ft. Lauderdale, FL 33314).

Skogan, W. (1990). *Crime and the spirit of decay in American neighborhoods*. New York: Free Press.

Skolnick, J. (1967). *Justice without trial: Law enforcement in a democratic society*. New York: Wiley.

Smith, B. (1960). *Police systems in the United States* (2d ed.). New York: Harper & Row.

Soloman, R., & Horn, J. (1986). Post-shooting traumatic reactions: A pilot study. In J. Reese & H. Goldstein (Eds.), *Psychological services for law enforcement*. Washington, DC: U.S. Government Printing Office, Superintendent of Documents.

Sorenson, R., Gorsuch, R., & Mintz, J. (1985). Moving targets: Patient's changing complaints during psychotherapy. *Journal of Consulting and Clinical Psychology, 53*(1), 49–54.

Southworth, R. (1990). Taking the job home. *FBI Law Enforcement Bulletin, 59*(11), 19–25.

Sparrow, N., Moore, M., & Kennedy, D. (1990). *Beyond 911: A new era for policing*. New York: Basic Books.

Spielberg, C., Spaulding, H., Jolley, M., & Ward, J. (1979). Selection of effective law enforcement officers. The Florida Police Standards Research Project. In C. Spielberg (Ed.), *Police selection and evaluation*. New York: Praeger.

Spielberg, C., Ward, J., & Spaulding, H. (1979). A model for the selection of law enforcement officers. In C. Spielberg (Ed.), *Police selection and evaluation*. New York: Praeger.

Spiegel, D., & Fink, R. (1979). Hysterical psychoses and hypnotizability. *American Journal of Psychiatry, 136,* 777–781.

Spiegel, H., & Spiegel, D. (1978). *Trance and treatment: Clinical uses of hypnosis.* New York: Basic Books.

Spiegel, D., & Spiegel, H. (1987). Forensic uses of hypnosis. In I. Weiner & A. Hess (Eds.), *Handbook of forensic psychology.* New York: Wiley.

Stone, A. (1990). Psychological Fitness-for-Duty evaluation. *Police Chief, 57*(2), 39–53.

Storms, L., Penn, N., & Tenzell, J. (1988). Policemen's perception of real and ideal policemen. Presented at the 17th Annual Meeting of the Society of Police and Criminal Psychology. San Antonio, Texas, October 18, 1988.

Strawbridge, P., & Strawbridge, D. (1990). *A networking guide to recruitment, selection, and probationary training of police officers in major police departments in the United States of America.* New York: John J. College of Criminal Justice.

Strentz, T. (1988). A terrorist psychological profile. *FBI Law Enforcement Bulletin, 57*(4), 13–19.

Stuart, R. (1980). *Helping couples change.* New York: Guilford Press.

Tafoya, W. (1990). The future of policing. *FBI Law Enforcement Bulletin, 59*(1), 13–17.

Tepas, D. (1990). Do eating and drinking habits interact with work schedule variables? *Work and Stress, 4*(3), 202–211.

Terry, C. (1981). Police stress: The empirical evidence. *Journal of Police Science and Administration, 9*(3), 61–74.

Tetem, H. (1989). Offender profiling. In W. Bailey (Ed.), *The encyclopedia of police science.* New York: Garland Publishing.

Thomas, D. (1991). *Henry Fielding.* New York: St. Martin's Press.

Toffler, A. (1990). The future of law enforcement—dangerous and different. *FBI Law Enforcement Bulletin, 59*(2), 2–5.

Trojanowicz, R., & Carter, D. (1990). The changing face of America. *FBI Law Enforcement Bulletin, 59*(1), 6–11.

Trotter, R. (1987, November). Psychologists with a badge. *Psychology Today.*

U.S. Bureau of the Census. (1990). *Statistical abstract of the United States: (Law enforcement, courts, & prisons).* Washington, DC: U.S. Government Printing Office.

U.S. Department of Health and Human Services. (1988). *The health consequences of smoking: Nicotine addiction.* A report of the Surgeon General. Washington, DC: U.S. Government Printing Office.

U.S. Department of Labor. (1992). *Occupational Outlook Handbook, 1992–1993.* Bulletin 2400, Bureau of Labor Statistics. Washington, DC: U.S. Government Printing Office.

U.S. Office of Strategic Services. (1948). *Assessment of men.* New York: Rinehart.

Violanti, J. (1988). Operationalizing police stress management: A model. In J. Reese & H. Goldstein (Eds.), *Police psychology: Operational assistance.* Washington, DC: U.S. Department of Justice, Federal Bureau of Investigation.

Violanti, J. (1990). Police retirement—the impact of change. *FBI Law Enforcement Bulletin, 59*(3), 12–15.

vonMayrhauser, R. (1992). The mental testing community and validity—a prehistory. *American Psychologist, 47*(2), 244–263.

Wasyliw, O., Grossman, L., Heywood, T., Ostrov, E., & Cavanaugh, J. (1988). *Efficacy for MMPI validity scales in mandatory Fitness-For-Duty police evaluations.* Presented at the 96th annual Convention of the American Psychological Association, August 12, 1988. Atlanta, GA.

Weiner, B. (1986). Confidentiality and the legal issues raised by the psychological evaluations of law enforcement officers. In J. Reese & H. Goldstein (Eds.),

Psychological services for law enforcement. Washington, DC: U.S. Government Printing Office.

Weiss, J. (1989). Deadly confrontations. *The Police Marksman, 14*(2).

Weitzenhoffer, A., & Hilgard, E. (1959). *Stanford Hypnotic Suggestibility Scale.* Palo Alto, CA: Consulting Psychologists' Press.

Wekstein, L. (1979). *Handbook of suicideology.* New York: Brunner/Mazel.

Wells, C., Getman, R., & Blau, T. (1988). Critical incident procedures: The crisis management of traumatic incidents. *The Police Chief,* October, *55*(1), 70–74.

Wells, C., Super, J., Blau, T., & Dudley, T. (1992). Avoiding excessive use of force through conflict prevention and de-escalation. *Sheriff, 44*(2), 17–20.

Whisenand, P. (1989). Personnel selection. In William G. Bailey (Ed.), *The encyclopedia of police science.* New York: Garland Publishing.

White, J. (1987). Results of a police mental health survey. *Private correspondence* (John H. White, Ph.D., Sergeant of Police, 16619 Deer Park Drive, Dallas, TX 75248-2206).

Wilkinson, R. (1984). *American tough.* West Port, CT: Greenwood Press.

Wilson, J. (1963). The police and their problems: A theory. In C. J. Friendrich & S. Harris (Eds.), *Public Policy, 12,* 189–216.

Wilson, J. Q. (1967). Police morale, reform and citizen respect: The Chicago case. In D. J. Bordua (Ed.), *The police: Six sociological essays.* New York: Wiley.

Wonderlic, E. (1983). *Wonderlic personnel test manual.* Northfield, IL: Wonderlic & Associates.

Yuille, J. (1986). *Police selection and training—the role of psychology.* Dordrecht/Boston/Lancaster: Martinus Nighoff Publishers. (Published in cooperation with NATO Scientific Affairs Division)

Zelig, M. (1988). Ethical dilemmas in police psychology. *Professional Psychology, 19*(3), 336–338.

Author Index

Subject Index

DATE DUE

MAY 28 '0?			
JE 18 '01			
GAYLORD			PRINTED IN U.S.A